T0115869

THE
DARK
SACRAMENT

THE
DARK
SACRAMENT

TRUE STORIES OF MODERN-DAY
DEMON POSSESSION AND EXORCISM

David M. Kiely and
Christina McKenna

HarperOne
An Imprint of HarperCollinsPublishers

HarperOne

PHOTOGRAPHY CREDITS

Page vi: St. Michael: British Library, London; Photo: HIP/Art Resource, NY.
Page xxxiv: Canon Lendrum: Photo by the *Belfast Telegraph*—used with gracious permission.
Page 154: Father McCarthy's effects: Background by James Miller, foreground by David Kiely.

THE DARK SACRAMENT: *True Stories of Modern-Day Demon Possession and Exorcism.* Copyright © 2007 by David M. Kiely and Christina McKenna. All rights reserved. Printed in the United States of America. No part of this book may be used or reproduced in any manner whatsoever without written permission except in the case of brief quotations embodied in critical articles and reviews. For information, address HarperCollins Publishers, 195 Broadway, New York, NY 10007.

HarperCollins books may be purchased for educational, business, or sales promotional use. For information, please e-mail the Special Markets Department at SPsales@harpercollins.com.

HarperCollins Web site: http://www.harpercollins.com

HarperCollins®, 📖®, and HarperOne™ are trademarks of HarperCollins Publishers.

FIRST HARPERCOLLINS PAPERBACK EDITION PUBLISHED IN 2008

Library of Congress Cataloging-in-Publication Data is available upon request.

ISBN 978–0–06–123817–8

HB 12.12.2022

Darkness cannot put out the light.
It can only make God brighter.

—ANONYMOUS

"St. Michael the Archangel Slaying a Demon,"
from the Hours of Joanna of Castille, c. 1475–1500.

CONTENTS

IMPORTANT NOTE

◈

You are about to read ten true-life accounts of exorcism in present-day Ireland. When preparing *The Dark Sacrament* we conducted interviews with a great many people on the island. The principals in the ten cases we chose for inclusion are all very much alive, with but one exception. In this case we relied on the excellent accounts supplied by the key participants.

The names in this book are fictitious, apart from that of Reverend William H. Lendrum, an exorcist who already enjoys prominence in Ireland and agreed to be identified. From the outset we assured those interviewed that they would remain anonymous—if they so wished. All but Canon Lendrum chose anonymity.

Among them are those who requested that we go even further, that we change important details, such as settings and minor participants, so that the originals could no longer be identified. Those individuals feared reprisals of one kind or another.

For these reasons the reader should note that we have, where possible, disguised the family circumstances of those concerned, e.g., the number of persons in a particular household, the gender of the offspring, and so on. Similarly, settings have been changed. While we may look at events that actually occurred in, say, a market town in the midlands, the real name of that town is never used. We will have translated the events to a locality in another part of the island of Ireland, in order to safeguard the privacy of our contributors, be they lay or cleric. The alternative to "naming names" was a text overburdened with the like of "John W— lived in the town of T—." This would have been less than satisfactory. Moreover, in all cases we have placed the clergymen concerned in parishes other than their own.

We have also reconstructed certain scenes and conversations for the benefit of the narrative, while at the same time ensuring that such reconstruction remains faithful to the essence of the testimony given.

We approached our subject in a spirit of unbiased investigation. We were careful not to draw our own conclusions when examining the accounts of paranormal manifestation related by both victim and deliverer. To be sure, no one—including the witnesses themselves—can ever be certain that any single account is objective, and this fact we took into careful consideration when compiling this collection.

In the final analysis, it was a combination of faith and reason that prompted us to reject the one case history and embrace the other. It soon became apparent whose testimony was dependable, when set against those one could dismiss as fantasy. The ten cases we present are, to the best of our knowledge, reliable.

We cannot express strongly enough our gratitude and appreciation to the two groups of people who made this book possible.

First, they are the exorcists: those men of God who gladly granted us the benefit of their knowledge and experience.

Second, they are the victims: those individuals who endured great hardship—in some cases over several years—when pursued by the paranormal. They gave freely and willingly of their time to speak to us, often for many hours and in the course of many sessions. They did this for the most altruistic and selfless reasons; their prime concern was to share with others their traumatic experiences. They did so in the understanding that others, being thus alerted to possible danger, would not have to suffer as they did.

We salute their courage.

DAVID M. KIELY AND
CHRISTINA McKENNA
ROSTREVOR, 2007

WHY THIS BOOK?

❖

I can only remember that December morning in mono-
chrome. Me at the parlor window, my chin resting on the
sill, staring out at the mist-veiled mountains, the dew-beaded
grass, a crow perched still and deathlike on a fence post. All
quiet, shrouded, hidden, as if the world held a finger to its
lips in a warning hush.

And then suddenly through the mist in the lane, two
dark figures advancing on the house: the exorcist and his
assistant.

—CHRISTINA McKENNA
My Mother Wore a Yellow Dress, 2004

When I turned eleven, I made two inalienable discoveries, the one
creative, the other spiritual. The two discoveries would be linked
and, over time, would fuse, to give me a heightened understanding
of this journey we call life. Through a box of oil colors my mother
bought me and an easel my father made for me, I taught myself to
paint. On the very day I finished my first picture, a door suddenly
opened into another world. It was a far darker world than the one I
had so lovingly represented on the canvas.

In the early hours of one October morning, a strange "visitor"
entered our home and remained for six long and terrifying weeks.
It came quietly in the beginning, stealing into my young brother's

bedroom, tapping its way from beneath the big oak wardrobe, and settling under the bed.

Over the days, the tapping grew to a scratching sound, as though something were clawing the underside of the mattress; it grew louder still, in time becoming a hammering on walls and doors. We were all frightened and distraught. Wherever my little brother went, it pursued him. My parents took him to the Marian shrine at Knock in County Mayo, but it followed in the car, started up under his hotel bed, and then followed him all the way home again. He could not go to school. He could not sleep and, as a consequence, neither could any of us: his three brothers and five sisters.

In retrospect, I see that this entity conformed to that which is known in psychical circles as a poltergeist, or "noisy spirit." It introduced itself by knocking, then grew louder and more truculent, overturning furniture, displacing objects, tipping us out of bed. It used a child as its focus and was more active during the hours of darkness. And, although it did not seem especially evil in intent, there was the feeling that the longer it continued unchecked, and the more our fears increased, the more likely it was to turn malevolent.

I remember the frantic search my mother embarked upon to find a priest who could banish our visitor. I remember also my knees aching on the cold floor of my brother's bedroom, where we as a family would kneel, reciting rosary upon rosary. And the number of Masses that were offered in that room. And the succession of clergymen who came and went. All to no avail.

Until, that is, there came a very special kind of clergyman, one versed in "such matters," whose humility and holiness conferred on him the extraordinary and rare status of exorcist.

I retain an image of this unique man. He is tall, exudes a venerable air, and is dressed entirely in black. When he enters our home, he pats us children on the head, speaks briefly with my parents in a gentle voice, then retires to the afflicted room and quietly shuts the door.

More important than the memory of his physical appearance is the tremendous effect he left in his wake. All the fear and chaos of the previous weeks were swept away, and a great peace descended. He had performed what I regarded as a miracle. We were free.

Our phantom visitor would never come calling again.

Since that episode, all those years ago, I have often wondered about the nature of the spectral universe, and how the exorcist can wield such power in that universe. What manner of entities live there, in that other world? Why do they sometimes intrude upon this one? What exactly does the exorcist do? Why are some individuals a target of paranormal phenomena and others not? Is it all part of God's plan, or do we draw such things to us through our goodness, our wickedness, our ignorance, or the unresolved issues of our ancestral past?

This book attempts to explore some of these questions, and so dispel a little of the ignorance that surrounds this disturbing, yet fascinating, subject.

Socrates asserted that there was only one good—knowledge—and only one evil—ignorance. We hope that, by the time you have finished reading *The Dark Sacrament*, you may be inclined to concur with those wise words.

CHRISTINA McKENNA
ROSTREVOR, 2007

EXORCISM IN OUR TIME

❖

My dear brothers, never forget, when you hear the progress
of enlightenment vaunted, that the most exquisite of the
Devil's wiles was persuading us that he doesn't exist.

—CHARLES BAUDELAIRE
"The Generous Gambler," 1864

This is a dark book. It is also a book of enlightenment in a specific
sense, because it attempts to throw a little light into the more ob-
scure and secret areas of human experience. In doing so, it will challenge the reader's notions of this life, the afterlife, and—for want
of a better expression—dimensions that lie beyond the physical.
Broadly speaking, it deals with the paranormal.

It treats of the concept of Satan, also known as the Devil, and
examines the possibility that he might, after all, be a real and un-
fabled entity.

Such a hypothesis will astonish the rationally minded; others
will doubtless find it disturbing. Still others will consider it high
time that the gloves came off and the "great dragon" of Revelation
was confronted head on.

There is one serious drawback in all this: very little is known
about this elusive enemy. At one time, in another century, the Devil
was as well defined as any adversary of flesh and blood. "High on a

throne of royal state," John Milton wrote, "Satan exalted sat ... and princely counsel in his face yet shone, majestic, though in ruin."

The words appear early on in *Paradise Lost,* the great epic in which the poet recounts events that followed the angel Lucifer's expulsion from heaven. The descriptions of hell sound strange to our ears, yet in Milton's own time—he published the poem in 1667—his imagery would have been the accepted one. There are burning lakes and caverns, teeming with vast hosts of demon armies, all under the command of a rigid hierarchy of generals, chief among whom is Satan himself.

Few Christians living in the seventeenth century doubted the existence of hell and its rulers. There were many reminders in ecclesiastical art: paintings, sculpture, stained glass, the admonishments of the bestiary. Even the fearsome gargoyles set atop cathedrals were modeled on a fairly precise and generally prevailing picture of how demons *actually* looked; in the seventeenth century, all art was representational art. It was generally agreed that the Devil himself was a horned creature with a forked tail, who might sometimes appear as a serpent.

BEFORE THE ENLIGHTENMENT

In our time, we regard all this as superstition, the infantile fantasies of a primitive society. We are to a certain degree justified in thinking this; the seventeenth century seems impossibly distant. Although William Harvey had established the circulation of the blood in 1628, his contemporaries still clung to antiquated nostrums. For example, most physicians held that a variety of ailments were attributable to "humors," and that leeches—to "let" blood—could assist in a multitude of cures. Sorcerers were feared. Across Europe, in Germany in particular, an unknown number of victims, perhaps tens of thousands, were tortured and put to death on suspicion of their being witches.

The so-called Great Hunt for witches in Britain and mainland Europe spanned two centuries, petering out around 1650. By then there were no more witches, real or imaginary, to burn.

In America, the hysteria took a little longer to run its course—four more decades, in fact. In the little community of Salem, Massachusetts, in March 1692, nine-year-old Betty Parris began acting strangely. She would go into a trance, flap her arms as if trying to take flight, and emit animal noises. The doctors were baffled, even more when Betty's "illness" began to infect her friends. The Salem witches affair had begun.

In all, the tragic events that ensued led to the deaths of no fewer than twenty-two men and women, all accused of witchcraft. Nineteen were hanged, others tortured to death; many others went insane in prison. All were accused of having made pacts with the Devil; no case was ever proven.

It should be remembered that until the Enlightenment, it was universally accepted that all illnesses—plague in particular—were punishments from God, and not a consequence of poor hygiene, as many surely were. And if the sicknesses were not the wrath of God, they were the work of the Devil, his demons, and his earthbound disciples.

In such a world of belief and unbelief, it is not surprising that evil entities were held responsible for mental disorders. Not until the late eighteenth century would it be thought otherwise, and the years leading up to the twentieth century saw the coming of age of the scientific approach to our place in the universe. It was a cosmology that no longer had any room for Lucifer and his nefarious associates. While the concept of heaven—or in any event an afterlife of some description—remained an article of Christian belief, the notion of hellfire and eternal damnation, with all the attendant medieval imagery, was no longer considered respectable. We felt we had outgrown such primitive thinking.

THE AGE OF SCIENCE

With the closure of the gates of hell came the opening of entire branches of medical science: disciplines that could at last explain, in natural terms, what traditionally had been attributed to demonic influence. Even before the twentieth century, when men were attaching imposing labels to complexes of illnesses, it was decided that possession and oppression were nothing of the sort, but were symptomatic of "schizophrenia" and other forms of psychosis. It was found that many such afflictions could be cured—and if not cured, then at least held in check—by confinement to institutions, electroshock therapy, counseling, and, in recent times, an elaborate complex of medications.

There is nothing wrong with all of this; indeed, it would be foolish to make light of such extraordinary achievements in the treatment of a diversity of mental disorders. But there is a difficulty. In the rush to embrace the new "science" of psychiatry, the medical men were eager to jettison belief in evil forces, demonic oppression and affliction, and to ascribe natural causes to *all* mental diseases of unknown etiology. It could be argued that they were, in effect, playing into the hands of the very Devil they wished to sideline.

In recent years, however, there has been a grudging reassessment of this position. While most psychiatrists are content with diagnosing mental illness in terms of abnormal brain function, chemical imbalances, and personality disorders brought about by nature or nurture, there are those who acknowledge that a small percentage of cases appear to challenge medical science. In short, they defy explanation—and indeed fall outside the known pathology of mental illness. Interesting in this regard is that many of these exceptional cases exhibit symptoms that have been traditionally associated with demonic influence.

MILLENNIUM FEVER AND THE DEVIL

In our time, the subject of demonic possession lay dormant until comparatively recently. To many it appeared that this "sudden" interest in the occult had sprung from nowhere. They can point out that, before the 1960s, the Devil had no place in mainstream society. That was to change when, in 1966, Howard Stanton Levey gave himself out as Anton Szandor LaVey, and established the Church of Satan in San Francisco.

It is likely that LaVey, who died in 1997, was little more than a self-publicist who did not take his devil-worship seriously. Yet he began his "movement" at a time when Timothy Leary, a Harvard lecturer in psychology, was experimenting with LSD and other "mind-expanding" drugs. LaVey had little difficulty in attracting a following. With the founding of the Church of Satan, the Devil had left the shadows and gone aboveground.

Perhaps the defining moment of this narco-satanism came in the summer of 1969 with the frenzied slaughter of Sharon Tate and others. The perpetrators were the Manson "family," and evidently the crime was satanically motivated. The Devil had arrived in America.

THE EXORCIST: SATAN ON CELLULOID

In 1971, William Peter Blatty's novel *The Exorcist* appeared, to be followed by a motion picture of the same name.

The effects of that single Hollywood production were seismic. Until 1973, the release date, exorcism was seldom spoken of in lay circles, much less experienced. That was to change, as long lines formed outside movie theaters, and people emerged white-faced, having seen director William Friedkin's stunning and altogether alarming dramatization of Blatty's book. The film was to spawn many imitators and introduce an incredulous public to a subject that the churches had for centuries kept from all but a few.

It is a curious fact that from the moment the movie was shown in Ireland, Britain, and mainland Europe, there was a veritable epidemic of "possession" symptoms presented by psychiatric patients, many consistent with those shown in *The Exorcist*. The simple explanation is, of course, that fakery was at work, and that those patients for whom attention seeking was always an intrinsic part of their illness were doing no more than ratcheting up the pressure on their therapists. In other words, the "demonic possession" was a cry for help.

The principle of Occam's razor, that the simplest explanation is usually the correct one, could certainly be applied with profit in most such cases. Yet a handful seem to fall outside the ambit of rationality, defying, as they do, reductionism. That of Anneliese Michel is perhaps the most celebrated, and one of the more recent "possession" motion pictures, *The Exorcism of Emily Rose,* was based loosely on her tragic circumstances.

A native of Würzburg, Germany, Anneliese began experiencing epileptic fits and "demonic" attacks when she was eighteen. The bishop, Dr. Josef Stangel, ordered the case to be investigated by an authority on such matters, who diagnosed possession. The bishop gave permission for an exorcism, to be performed by a Salvatorian priest with the assistance of a local pastor.

It was found that ten months of weekly exorcism could not banish the entities that had "occupied" the young woman's body. They allegedly included Lucifer, Adolf Hitler, Emperor Nero, and Cain. Such was the ordeal that Anneliese endured during the protracted exorcisms that she eventually died. Too little attention had been given to Anneliese's anorexia, and possible anorexia nervosa, which may have hastened her end: at the last, she was refusing all food and drink. A jury would find both the officiating clergymen and the girl's parents guilty of "negligent homicide"; all four had, it was decided, allowed Anneliese to starve herself to death. Each was given a six-month custodial sentence, but this was mercifully suspended for three years.

That same year—1976—saw the publication of a groundbreaking book on exorcism. Entitled *Hostage to the Devil: The Possession and Exorcism of Five Contemporary Americans,* it was written by Malachi Martin, a "laicized" Catholic priest. By laicization is understood that the priest, usually voluntarily, has clerical character, control, or status withdrawn. Father Martin was a former Jesuit and a native of Ballylongford, County Kerry, Ireland.

He died in 1999 at the age of seventy-eight, and left a legacy of controversy. His detractors claimed that *Hostage* was a tissue of lies. Even the greatly respected psychiatrist and author M. Scott Peck declares in his final book, *Glimpses of the Devil*, that Malachi Martin "was perhaps the most bald-faced liar I have ever known." It is a curious statement, given that Dr. Peck was a great admirer and confidant of Father Martin; he actually dedicated the book in question to the exorcist. Yet he went on to aver, "In everything that deeply mattered to me and my quest for the Devil, I knew him to speak only God's truth."

Whatever the truth about his personal life and unorthodox activities, Malachi Martin's book had a profound effect on both Church and laity. Never before had the subject of exorcism been examined in public, and in such detail, by a professional exorcist, and one, moreover, who wrote with such verve and élan. *Hostage to the Devil* became a best seller.

By this time, possession and exorcism were being openly debated around the world. This renewed interest had given rise to a frenzy of demon hunting, especially among the more extreme evangelical movements. By the start of the 1980s, at prayer meetings across America, demons were being expelled from the "possessed" as routinely as the collection plate was passed. The meetings were awe-inspiring, if not to say frightening, events, with hysterical people dropping to the floor, roaring and foaming at the mouth. Such "deliverance ministries" had America in thrall. Before long, the rest of the world would follow suit. At the time of this writing, the Ellel Ministries, a born-again group offering deliverance from "unclean" spirits, is expanding rapidly. Begun in Lancaster in 1986, Ellel has a presence on four continents—Britain alone has four training centers. There is even a "Pastors' School" in Siberia; ten years ago such a venture would have scarcely been conceivable.

The Church of England bishops have, of late, become increasingly concerned by the proliferation of such maverick exorcists and fundamentalist groups. Whether this reflects a jealous fear that others are encroaching on their turf or a concern based on careful evaluation of such ministries remains to be seen. The difference between the established churches and the newcomers is, inter alia, the length and comprehensiveness of training. Whereas the Anglicans require many years, Ellel training is accomplished in a matter of weeks. The courses are packaged slickly, and the language used owes less to the theology lecture hall and more to the business seminar. "Satan's strategies and tactics" are examined with the enthusiasm of an advertising executive evaluating a competitor's latest campaign, and the training shows "how demonic footholds can be established in a person's life and presents key principles by which the captives may be set free."

It will hardly come as a surprise that clerics of the old school are expressing their disquiet. Dr. M. Scott Peck once asked Father Martin his opinion of the exorcisms—or, more properly, the deliverances—performed with such aplomb by the charismatic "healers."

"They're generally just casting out their own fantasies," he replied. "But very occasionally, usually by accident, they do catch a real fish."

THE RESTLESS DEAD AND EVIL SPIRITS

Ghosts are sometimes known as the "restless dead." It is important to establish that such entities are considered to be the "souls" or "spirits" of human beings. This is to distinguish them from non-human entities that have never drawn breath, those which are often referred to as demons. It is such a broad area of investigation that it would be impossible to do more than touch upon it here. We do so in order to clear up a misconception: namely, that all paranormal activity is somehow of demonic origin.

The exorcist will be at pains to point out that, while demonic oppression *may* accompany paranormal activity, there are many instances where it plainly does not. In such cases the exorcist must allow for the presence of an earthbound spirit, or spirits.

Such entities, also referred to as the "unquiet dead," have been the subject of some interesting studies. In the mid-1800s, it was proposed that there are three categories of spirit, and each was assigned its own rung on the ladder of spiritual evolution. There were the "low spirits," those trapped in the world of the living; "second-degree spirits," who desire only to promote goodness on earth; and "perfect spirits," those who have reached the pinnacle of their evolution. The three categories are, by and large, still accepted by modern psychic investigators.

The "low spirits" are of particular interest to the exorcist. It is believed that, during their lifetimes, such entities were wedded to materiality and so failed to develop spiritually. For this reason they are unable to "move on," choosing instead to oppress or disturb the living. At their most malign, they can be considered to be evil spirits; at their least harmful, they are classified as poltergeists.

These theories were given currency in recent times by the notable British psychiatrist Dr. Kenneth McAll (1910–2001). He became interested in the powers of "possession" while working in China as a missionary-surgeon. During the turbulent war years, he was confronted by phenomena that led him to an exploration of possession. He went on to dedicate his life to treating mental illness with reference to extraphysical causation.

Dr. McAll's revolutionary thesis, introduced in his seminal work, *Healing the Family Tree*, was that many supposedly "incurable" patients were the victims of ancestral control. By drawing up a family tree, he claimed to be able to identify the ancestor who was adversely affecting his patient. He would then sever the bond between the ancestor and the patient by having a clergyman celebrate a service of Holy Communion. The ancestor would be delivered back to God, and the transgenerational hold consequently broken.

It was, in effect, a most unorthodox form of exorcism, or deliverance. It is an important area, insofar as it examines what one might call "indirect" possession. Dr. McAll concluded that the dead may become pawns in the struggle for the souls of the living, that souls in transition, or "dislocated" souls, may become possessed by evil, so that they in their turn can possess the living, and so drive the living into despair, or worse.

"Evil symptoms and their inevitable fruit of despair, which leads to suicide," he believed, "bear the marks of the evil one battling with those who are sensitive to the uncommitted dead."

EXORCISM: SOME DEFINITIONS

Before going further, it may be useful to examine our definitions. In the way of words, *exorcise* has undergone a shift in meaning since earlier times. Its roots are in Greek: *exorkizein* literally means "to out an oath." To exorcise, then, is to place a demon on oath, and so command it by the power of God to depart and not trouble the afflicted again. In our time, it is also acceptable to speak of the exorcism of places and inanimate objects, when obviously an oath is neither demanded nor sworn. Such exorcisms are common practice; for instance, a priest will exorcise all sacred vessels and paraphernalia before their employment in divine service.

The Catholic Church recognizes two distinct forms of exorcism: the solemn and the unofficial. Before performing a solemn exorcism, a priest is obliged to obtain the permission of a bishop. There are sound reasons for this. In the first place, the rite must be enacted in the name of the Church, and it is used for the expulsion of evil spirits. This is dangerous territory, whether or not one holds with the existence of such entities. Done incorrectly, or by an individual not properly qualified or equipped to perform the rite, a solemn exorcism can end in disaster, for victim and exorcist alike. Malachi Martin recounts the case of a priest he called Michael Strong, who failed to exorcise a possessed man in wartime Nanking, China. Father Martin met him shortly before his death some years later and was dismayed at the other priest's physical decline, a "general appearance of delicate survival, of a hair's-breadth balance in him, between life and the disappearance from life." Evidently the entity had taken its toll of both exorcee and exorcist.

Simply put, [Father Strong said] evil has power over us, some
power. And even when defeated and put to flight, it scrapes you
in passing by. If you don't defeat it, evil exacts a price of more
terrible agony. It rips a gash in the spirit.

The solemn exorcism is undertaken only rarely. It requires that
the priest *converse* with the entity. It is principally in this regard that
the solemn exorcism differs from the informal.

An unofficial exorcism may be applied to a number of situations
and circumstances. Moreover, it can be performed by religious and
layperson alike. No permission is required and the exorcist does not
act in the name of the Church, be it Roman Catholic or Protestant.
Hence a Protestant minister can be said to perform an exorcism
when delivering a place or an individual who is beset by the so-
called restless dead—the soul of a deceased person.

This is an important distinction. *In short, exorcism is used to expel
both malignant and bothersome entities.*

Lastly, the term *deliverance* is used today in a broad sense. Generally speaking, it applies both to Catholic and Protestant exorcism,
and is the term of choice for most Protestant denominations, in
particular those of the Reformed communions. The word, which
appears frequently in these pages, is sometimes interchangeable
with exorcism, especially when applied to the cleansing of a place.
Within the Christian framework, it is generally accepted that
whereas both Protestant and Roman Catholic priests engage in a
deliverance ministry, exorcism is largely a Catholic rite.

THE PARANORMAL AND THE DEMONIC

We have established that paranormal activity need not necessarily signal the presence of the preternatural. (By preternatural is meant that
which is higher than the physical yet subordinate to the supernatural
or divine; the word derives from the Latin *præter naturam,* "beyond
nature.") One case examined in this book has no relation to evil: that

of little "Lucy" (pp. 131–153), who saw a succession of apparitions. It is difficult to interpret the disturbances the family experienced as an attempt by the Devil or other demons to influence the household.

That said, it will be seen that other cases began with ostensibly innocent occurrences, such as the case of the "child Sarah" (pp. 98–130), only to progressively develop into something sinister. This appears to be a relatively common phenomenon, when so-called poltergeist activity makes way for malevolence. In his impressive study entitled *But Deliver Us from Evil,* Reverend John Richards goes some way toward explaining the phenomenon. At one point, he refers to the haunting known as the Epworth Poltergeist, which began in Doncaster, England, in the parental home of John Wesley, founder of the Methodist movement. It was 1716 and John was thirteen at the time.

It is difficult to say if there was anything demonic in the affair. Everyone, except the dog, seems to have become accustomed to the situation, which suggests that the early fear of the children was largely the fear of the unknown rather than the fear of evil. But it must be remembered that the Curé d'Ars was haunted by what A. R. G. Owen calls, "a strong resemblance to poltergeist activity." These incidences are usually taken to have a predominantly spiritual significance because of the Curé's stature as a man of God and as an evangelist. When similar happenings occur in the home of John and [his younger brother] Charles Wesley it may not be without spiritual significance either. Even if no demon were involved, the Enemy would have been pleased if the intervention of the unknown had opened the door to fear which might distort and undermine the spiritual lives of the young boys; the greatest danger—then as now.

Richards's closing observation is an important one. Both John Wesley and his brother Charles went on to become Christian ministers, following in their father's footsteps. Although there is little in the accounts of the haunting to suggest the presence at Epworth of a demon—much less one that required exorcising—there is likewise no evidence that would *preclude* a preternatural agency. At this long remove in time, nearly three hundred years after the events, it is of course impossible to determine the precise nature of the haunting. Nevertheless, the circumstances bring to mind words spoken by a Catholic priest we interviewed: "Old Nick won't waste his time going for the sheep. He'll go for the shepherd instead. By weakening the shepherd he can get at the flock."

What better focus of attack for any aspiring demon than the home of three ministers, one already practicing, two to come?

SOME CAUTIONARY TALES

"I don't understand why journalists are making such a fuss about this," Father Daniel Corogeanu told the press in June 2005. "Exorcism is a common practice in the Orthodox Church. Other priests use my methods."

His "methods" included crucifixion: the chaining of a young nun to a cross after binding her and stuffing a rag into her mouth to prevent her from crying out as she was made to suffer a slow and agonizing death. She died of thirst, compounded by shock and asphyxiation.

The scene of the botched exorcism was a convent in northwestern Romania, the victim a twenty-three-old nun, Maricica Irina Cornici. Her death was the culmination of a short, unfortunate life that began in an orphanage, where the girl was systematically abused. Three months before she died, she had visited the convent, found solace there, and decided to join the community.

She began to hear voices—external locution—and to display further symptoms one associates with schizophrenia. Yet no physician was summoned; instead, the young woman was "diagnosed" as a demoniac. Father Corogeanu, the spiritual head of the convent, undertook the task of exorcising her.

Two salient facts emerged during the subsequent murder trial. The convent in question, the Holy Trinity, was built in 2001 by an attorney and had not been sanctified by the Orthodox Church. Nor was Corogeanu a qualified priest; he had never completed his studies. He had his heart set on becoming a professional footballer or a lawyer, but chose the religious life when denied a place at university.

For nine days, four nuns helped the "exorcist" to restrain Maricica; this included chaining her to a cross while Father Corogeanu said prayers over her.

When asked why he had not summoned medical help as a preliminary, the priest replied: "You cannot cast out the Devil with pills. You banish devils with fasting and prayer."

In the wake of the tragedy, the bishop shut down the convent and had the community transferred elsewhere. Father Corogeanu was sentenced to fifteen years in prison for the murder, and the four nuns who helped him were also given lengthy custodial sentences. To prevent further abuses, the Orthodox Church in Romania has vowed to introduce psychological tests for men entering the monastic life.

The case must serve as a warning to those unqualified "exorcists" who meddle in spiritual matters, and to those who allow them to. Rogue preachers—some properly ordained, many not—find demonic influences at work in hitherto unsuspected places. If we are to believe their sometimes outrageous claims, demons are at the root of every human foible. Derek Prince, a Pentecostal minister who died in 2003, identified the demons of caffeine, compromise, cosmetics, criticism, fantasy, gossip, infidelity, masturbation, nicotine, and sleepiness, while maintaining that the Devil is also behind Tourette's syndrome.

Frank and Ida Mae Hammond warn against not only the "demons" of non-Christian religions but also the vile spirit of vegetarianism. (A cynic might point out that this west Texas couple operate out of the biggest meat-producing state in America.)

The Hammonds speak of "demon groupings," each embracing a number of specific "spirits." The groupings include "Bitterness," which embraces the demons of resentment, hatred, unforgiveness, violence, temper, anger, retaliation, and murder. There is also—most worryingly—the grouping termed "Mental Illness." It includes insanity, madness, mania, retardation, senility, schizophrenia, paranoia, and hallucinations. Oddly enough, Frank and Ida Mae do not seem to share Derek Prince's "demonization" of Tourette's syndrome.

Medical practitioners are understandably concerned by this trend, this willingness to see demons everywhere. It is even more alarming when self-styled clergymen perform "exorcisms" and people die at their hands.

PROFILE OF A TRUE EXORCIST

According to the *Catholic Encyclopedia,* an exorcist is "in general, anyone who exorcises or professes to exorcise demons, in particular, one ordained by a bishop for this office, ordination to which is the second of the four minor orders of the Western Church." All ordained priests are uniquely predisposed to effect deliverance.

In practice, however, very few men have what it takes to be a *successful* exorcist. Exorcists are special. One might even say that they are a unique body of men. In the course of our research we were privileged to meet a small number of them. Without exception we came away from such meetings with the sense of having shared the company of an extraordinary individual. Perhaps Emerson had such a man in mind when he wrote that "the best effect of fine persons is felt after we have left their presence."

The successful exorcists have one attribute in common: humility. They never brag about "their" prowess or achievements, never seek to impress. Each is at pains to establish that he is no more than a conduit, that he himself possesses no special "gifts," be they of a spiritual or intellectual nature.

It is not hard to see a certain symmetry in this, once we accept the possibility of an evil force at work in the world, one intent on influencing the susceptible. To combat evil, then, there must be a proportionately vigorous application of good. Such virtue is hard earned, not given.

The Rubrics of the Catholic Church prescribe that an exorcist "be properly distinguished for his piety, prudence, and integrity of life." In his comprehensive study of evil, *Demons! The Devil, Possession and Exorcism,* Dr. Anthony Finlay sets out the qualifications necessary for a "suitable" exorcist. "In the face of often extraordinary situations," he writes, "rare attributes are required in an exorcist, strong and unwavering qualities which will strengthen the chances of success in the fearsome battle against so great an evil."

Preparation is of crucial importance. Spiritual fortification through prayer would seem an obvious prerequisite, but Finlay also stresses the need to fast before attempting the ritual. He is careful, though, to differentiate between the scriptural idea of fasting and our modern equivalent. "Fasting in the biblical sense," he points out, "is not necessarily synonymous with the complete abstinence from food and drink, which itself would render the exorcist physically inadequate to the task." Yet he goes on to assert that Christ's disciples—the fishermen and the others of modest means—were better candidates than most churchmen of our day, largely because the apostles, and those who came after them, turned their backs on excess. In our time, it is increasingly difficult to find clergymen who have not drifted far from these first principles.

We [priests] have become used to the comforts of society, and we find it difficult to give them up, even in such a cause as freeing someone from evil influences. How many of us throw away our worldly goods and follow Him, as Christ said was necessary?... Simplicity in behavior, frugality in manner, lack of ostentation and of any kind of excess was His rule. His disciples manifested these qualities and in this respect were much more suited to confront evil in possession of Man than we are today. How many of us can claim to live up to the rule or vow, at least in the

Roman Catholic Church, of voluntary poverty and scrupulous adherence to absolute obedience? It is precisely in these areas that many clergy of today are lacking. Days of prayer and fasting are regarded as too onerous and as a result lip service only is often given to the solemn occasion. We are not sufficiently prepared, with our desirable houses, cars, housekeepers, secretaries, money in the bank or schemes for making money, ambitions or whatever, for the enormous task of casting out the Devil.

Finlay ends on a cautionary—and utterly chilling—note. He reminds us that the Devil can see through the exorcist who is unprepared, be it spiritually, mentally, or physically.

He [Satan] knows that underneath the show of bravado there is a soft underbelly, a weakness, a vulnerability which he can exploit. As a result he knows he it is who will emerge the victor. The unfortunate sufferer remains unchanged in all this—if he is lucky. Often he is left worse off than before.

THE BATTLE FOR HEARTS AND MINDS

It was inevitable that a respected critic would emerge to debunk the whole charade of the unqualified exorcist. In 2001, Michael Cuneo, a Fordham University professor, published *American Exorcism* (with the wry subtitle *Expelling Demons in the Land of Plenty*). It exposed the dubious practices of charismatic and evangelical preachers and their "deliverance ministries." In a devastating broadside, he turned his attention to one such typically American organization, the Faith Movement. He identifies it as belonging to the same culture as "the tabloid television business, with its mock seriousness, its weepy sensationalism, its celebrity fawning—soul food for the bloated and the brokenhearted." Or to the shopping mall: the "community without contact, community contrived precisely to avoid contact."

It is all too good to be true, he asserts, this fake American dream. It is "living, strutting, pulsating caricature: One almost expects it at any moment to break into a Bugs Bunny cartoon."

> The Faith Movement is … a collage of American clichés. The preacher as snake oil salesman or used car salesman; the preacher as Vegas showman. Miracle-workers in pink Cadillacs and pinkie rings, soul-savers in three-piece glitter suits and sixty-dollar haircuts. This is the world of the Faith Movement. Gushing emotionalism, grasping materialism, tears on demand, hustles blessed with a thousand "Amens." The product of old-fashioned hucksterism, New Thought optimism, and Southern-fried born-againism, the Faith Movement is one of the fastest-growing enterprises on the American religious scene today—and also one of the most wildly controversial.

Cuneo reports that he was present at a great many deliverances of the sort, and was not impressed. He reports that, in many cases, the participants witnessed what they claimed to be paranormal manifestations, but that at no time did he himself share their experiences. He concludes that most—if not all—such banishments were either fraudulent or can more easily be explained in terms of psychiatric disturbance.

Cuneo had succeeded in polarizing the entire debate, leaving the general reader to ponder the question: Whom are we to believe? To many, the answer seems to lie midway between science and superstition. The aforementioned Dr. M. Scott Peck, who died in 2005, was perhaps the most notable among those who chose the middle ground.

In one of his early books, *People of the Lie,* the Harvard-educated psychiatrist alludes briefly to two cases from his medical files that forced him to reconsider his position on the preternatural. He recounts a particularly harrowing experience, during which a patient presented undeniable—for Peck at least—evidence of demonic possession. The disturbed young woman seemed to physically change before his very eyes. He recalls her face as wearing an expression "that could be described only as Satanic. It was an incredibly contemptuous grin of utter hostile malevolence." Later Peck tried to emulate that grin in his bathroom mirror and found it impossible.

The change did not confine itself to the woman's face. Her entire body suddenly became serpentine. She writhed on the floor like a huge, vicious snake and actually attempted to bite the members of his team. "The eyes were hooded with lazy reptilian torpor," he recalls, "except when the reptile darted out in attack, at which moment the eyes would open wide with blazing hatred."

In the face of such a monstrous metamorphosis, the psychiatrist was forced to concede the existence of an external entity present in his patient. "I now know that Satan is real," Dr. Peck concluded in his book. "I have met him." He confessed also that, of the hundreds of cases he treated in the course of his professional life, a full 5 percent of symptoms presented by patients could not be explained in terms of present-day medical science.

In the conclusion to his final book, *Glimpses of the Devil*, Peck summed up his convictions, arrived at in the course of treating a young woman he called Jersey. Her case alone had effected his conversion from skeptical psychiatrist to believer in an entity that was the very personification of evil. His newfound belief went beyond faith; Peck knew with certainty that such an entity existed and furthermore had minor demons under his control. He wrote:

By the Devil, I mean a spirit that is powerful (it may be many places at the same time and manifest itself in a variety of distinctly paranormal ways), thoroughly malevolent (its only motivation seemed to be the destruction of human beings or the entire human race), deceitful and vain, capable of taking up a kind of residence within the mind, brain, soul, or body of susceptible and willing human beings—a spirit that had various names (among them Lucifer and Satan), that was real and did exist.

Reverend William H. Lendrum

PART ONE

THE CANON: REVEREND WILLIAM H. LENDRUM

Canon Lendrum is quick to point out that his background, accomplishments, and ministry in the Church are in the category of the ordinary and commonplace. He makes no claim to any special favors or unusual gifts.

He was born in 1924 in Belfast of a working-class family. He describes his parents as "good people," who were ambitious for their children but "not overly religious."

At school, he applied himself diligently to his work and enjoyed sports. His realization that he must follow a spiritual path came soon after he entered university in 1943.

"I was studying commercial science at Queen's in Belfast, when I realized that I wanted to become a minister," he recalls. "It was nothing earth-shattering, or anything like that. I simply understood the path I must follow in life." He dropped out of the course and transferred to Trinity College Dublin. After six years' study, he was ordained an Anglican priest in 1951.

Two years later he married Leah. They have five daughters and thirteen grandchildren.

Since his ordination, Canon Lendrum has served in four parishes in Belfast, was a chaplain in four hospitals and chairman of the

Church's Ministry of Healing committee for many years. He began his deliverance and exorcism ministry in the early 1970s.

"I have to admit that there was a time in my life when I might have agreed with removing the Devil from the official teaching of the Church," he explains. "I'd been brought up with a scientific worldview. I had never found it easy to grasp the concept of a being whom we call Satan, Beelzebub, or the Devil, whose purpose and aim was to lead people away from God and into sin and rebellion. Just as difficult for me to accept was the New Testament teaching which tells us that, under this being, there is an army of lesser beings called demons whose job is to control, influence, or destroy lives.

"I have no doubt that there are men within the Christian ministry, including bishops, who hold the same view. I cannot criticize them or impute blame, for that was my own vague notion for some years after my ordination."

However, in 1974, when the minister turned fifty, he met a young woman who relieved him of all doubt that Satan was real.

"It was while I was carrying out my duties as chaplain in a Belfast hospital that I met Alice. She was in her twenties and had deep emotional problems. I prayed with her regularly, and she made the decision to repent of her sins and put her trust in God.

"She was discharged from hospital, and my wife and I helped out as best we could. Then one evening, I got a call from a parishioner whom Alice was staying with. The lady asked me to come over because Alice was being very difficult."

Reverend Lendrum arrived and was shocked to find a very different Alice from the one he thought he knew. She was "scowling and ugly" and ranting loudly, hardly making any sense at all. Then he noticed something very odd about her speech. She was talking about herself in the third person, using *she* and *her* instead of *I* and *me*. It was the first indication that a demon, and not Alice, was doing the talking.

During that first exorcism, the minister was taunted continually by the demon. It would say: "You can't get rid of *me*, little man! You're making a fool of yourself. She belongs to *me*. I knew her before you came along," and so forth.

At one point, Alice fainted. When she came around, she asked why the minister was in the room. It was obvious that since his arrival, Alice had been shut out and the demon had taken her over, body and soul.

Canon Lendrum made inquiries into her background. He discovered that when she was younger, Alice had been initiated into a satanic cult. She had made vows to obey and serve Satan.

He decided that a major exorcism was called for. He gathered a small group of people, including a medical doctor, to assist him and succeeded in casting out several demons. But not all. Halfway through the ritual, Alice ran into a corner of the room.

"They're trying to take me away from you but they will not succeed," she was heard to say. "I'm going to stay with you."

"I knew then it was hopeless," the canon says. "After that, she passed out of my influence. I'd see her occasionally, prostituting herself in the red-light district of Belfast, looking haggard and worn-out by a life destroyed by the demonic. She died in her forties—was found lying in a doorway. Oh, you can't imagine the melancholy horror and sadness I felt when I heard that!"

During the past forty years, Canon Lendrum has seen a huge increase in interest in the supernatural. He believes that the more materialistic a society becomes, the more people turn to other philosophies to find meaning. He points to the New Age movement as an example of this alternative "soul searching," and notes that the occult is more popular today than ever before.

"If people do not find what they need in the Church, they will look for it elsewhere. This is a serious indictment of today's Church because it means that we have failed to get our message across that Jesus is 'the Light of the world,' and that those who follow Him 'have the light of life.' We have failed to convince people that He is 'the bread of life,' who satisfies the deepest longings of the human heart."

In his experience, demonic oppression is far more common than possession. At the same time, he concedes that those who are severely demonized or possessed would be very unlikely to seek the help of the Church.

"I have no doubt that spirits can and do impinge on human life. They can play some part in causing (or more likely worsening) the things that trouble and depress humankind, but great care has to be taken not to give people the impression that they are 'occupied' or 'indwelt' or 'possessed.' They may not be! It is one thing to be taken over or controlled by evil spirits who dwell within. It is another to be influenced or oppressed, from time to time, by spirits that are without. Indeed, it may be true to say that all of us have gone through the experience of being attacked from 'without' at times and we have not realized it. The sudden argument that blew up on the way to church. An unexpected difficulty as we do something important for the Kingdom of God. A temptation that overwhelms us just when we thought we had conquered it! Malevolent spirits are always around to take advantage of our weaknesses.

"Spirits seem to have a channel to those who frequently suffer such attacks. The task of the exorcist is to rebuke the spirit and command it to depart, forbid its return, and seal up the channel it has established in the victim's life."

Canon Lendrum is very clear on what qualifies an individual to carry out the work of deliverance and exorcism. Obviously, faith, courage, leadership, and authority are essential attributes, but "reluctance and a willingness to obey" he sees as necessary safeguards against a man getting involved for the wrong reasons.

"It is a mistake to believe that evil spirits and demons do not exist at all, and equally so to see demons under every bed. Both attitudes are as damaging to the witness of the Church and its healing ministry. It is the skeptic who believes only in what he can touch and see."

He concurs with the wise words of C. S. Lewis in *The Screwtape Letters*:

There are two equal and opposite errors into which one race can fall about the devils. One is to disbelieve in their existence. The *other is to believe and feel an excessive and unhealthy interest in them. They themselves are equally pleased by both errors and hail a materialist or a magician with the same delight.*

Canon William Lendrum is a unique individual. Well past retirement age, he is energetic and fearless. It seems that to the few clergymen courageous enough to assume the awesome mantle of exorcist, there is no such thing as resting on one's laurels. There is always that "one last case" to tackle.

The five cases that follow represent some of the canon's most harrowing brushes with evil.

HEATHER: A CASE OF ANCESTRAL EVIL

———— ✠ ————

"There is a demon in the room," Canon Lendrum announced calmly.

The calmness was a mask. Inwardly, he was dismayed. He had not expected this. The canon had come to rid the house of an earth-bound spirit, and to his mind, all had gone according to plan. He had already removed his surplice and was busy stowing the Communion vessels in his case. That was when he heard the low, menacing growl coming from the couch behind him.

He turned. Minutes before, the demure young woman had partaken of the Eucharist. Now she was hideously transformed. Her neck had become impossibly elongated, the facial skin had tightened, and the lips were drawn back into a mocking smirk. The eyes that fixed him with blazing hatred were no longer those of Heather Mitchelson.

It was 1992. Canon William H. Lendrum, then age sixty-eight, had been battling the preternatural for more than two decades. Now, fifteen years later, he remembers that incident with trepidation, for it differed greatly from the work his ministry usually requires. That day, the canon tells us, he came face-to-face with great evil; it was a case of demonic possession that would require a major exorcism.

The Anglican Church—much like the Catholic Church—has a strict protocol governing exorcism. A minister is obliged to alert his bishop before proceeding. This is largely a matter of courtesy, but in the case of a major exorcism, it is the minister's bounden duty.

That day, however, there was neither time nor opportunity to notify the bishop. For Canon Lendrum, the danger was clear and present in Heather Mitchelson. He would have to act at once.

"There is a demon in the room," he said again.

His two assistants did not share his calm. They occupied chairs to the left and right of Heather. They had followed closely every stage of the Eucharist. Both were experienced participants in the sacred rite of exorcism; both were schooled in the ways of extra-physical entities. For all that, they were shocked, taken unawares. They, too, had imagined it was all over.

Now Heather was lunging at her partner, Joe. He looked terrified. With two quick, curt gestures, Canon Lendrum motioned to him to remove himself from harm's way. Joe retreated to the back of the room.

There was no time for the canon to retrieve his sacred instruments, but he did not truly need them; prayer would be enough. He advanced on Heather.

"You foul and evil spirit, in the name of Jesus Christ—"

"You'll never get rid of me!" The woman slithered off the couch, cackling and taunting. "She's mine, *mine, mine, mine.*"

The voice was that of a very old woman. It seemed to issue, by turns, from the young woman's mouth and from various points in the room. She was writhing on the floor, her body coiling and un-coiling itself, her tongue lolling obscenely.

The exorcist was left in no doubt: these were the words and ac-tions of the demoniac, the possessed. Not too long before this, he had confronted a young man who had likewise hissed and wriggled in much the same manner when he prayed over him. On that occa-sion, he had been unsuccessful. The demon had won the battle. The canon recalls the chilling words that issued from the young man's mouth, the voice greatly distorted.

"He belongs to *me*. I am *not* going." And with that the young man fled from the house.

This time, the canon was determined not to be thwarted. He mustered the words of power, which unclean entities go in dread of.

"In accordance with the authority that he has given to his Church," he intoned, "I bind you, and I forbid you to speak or interfere with this woman."

He placed a hand on Heather Mitchelson's head. She recoiled from his touch. Within moments, she was on her feet, snarling. He backed away. He was no longer calm.

He could not believe that she could summon such energy. She was barely five feet tall and weighed perhaps ninety pounds, but her arms and fists seemed to belong to a strongly built man. She caught him in a body lock. His two assistants sprang to the canon's defense and tried to pull her off, but she shrugged the men away with the ease of a freestyle wrestler, knocking them to the floor.

The exorcist was faltering. Another blow to the jaw nearly felled him. He struggled to retain his balance as the assistants tried again to restrain her.

"In the name of Jesus—stop!" the canon shouted.

His words had an astonishing effect. Heather fell to the floor as if struck by a heavy object. She lay still as a stone, eyes wide and staring, all strength seemingly drained from her. The canon, recovered somewhat but still a little groggy from the blows he had sustained, bent over her.

"In the name of Jesus Christ, I command you to release your name!"

On hearing the words "Jesus Christ," Heather went into a violent spasm. The canon's assistants grasped her arms and legs. At that moment, she was as much a danger to herself as to others; she was flailing about, out of control. But by and by the fit subsided. The assistants relaxed their grip and allowed Heather to sit up, very slowly. The canon retrieved his cross and prayer book.

Heather seemed to slump down into herself; her posture became that of an old, decrepit being. The shoulders grew hunched; her chin sank low onto her chest. She began cackling. Joe, still in his position of safety, was aghast. He was recalling other cackling, other incidents. That which he feared was returning.

"She's *mine*. She's always been *mine*." It was the voice of the old woman again. "You can't have her. Never, *never, never!*"

"I command you, in the name of Jesus, give me your name."

"Damn you!" came the curse from Heather's lips.

"I command you, in the name of Jesus Christ, give me your name."

He noted that the holy name was finding its mark, wearing the demon down.

"Damn you, damn you, damn you." She spat into the canon's face. "She never belonged to *him*. She's ours. We serve the Master. Before the sperm met the egg she was ours."

The voice began to jabber, the words pouring out in a demented meter of their own, like a travesty of a children's play song.

"Before the filth met the filth she was ours! In the darkness of the womb she was ours. In the depths of the garden she was ours. Always ours, always ours...*ours!*" The final word was drawn out in a harsh, rasping hiss.

The demon was playing for time. The canon recognized the gibberish for the desperate delaying tactic it was. Soon, the pleading would start.

"In the name of Jesus Christ, I command you, give me your name."

Heather's body was contorting again. She curled herself into the fetal position and lay back down.

"Sal...Sala...Salac...Salaci...Salacia!" She drummed out the name in a childlike, staccato rhythm.

At a signal from Canon Lendrum, his assistants went to lift her back onto the couch. It should have been simple. It was not: they found her to be as immovable as granite. They could not budge her; it was as if an unseen force was pinning her to the floor. It was yet another sign—as if further evidence were needed—that Heather was demonically possessed. The canon strode to her and raised a hand.

"I command you, vile spirit, in the name of Jesus Christ, leave this woman now!"

Heather's body seemed to relax. She uncurled herself and lay flat on her back, eyes staring at the ceiling. The assistants held her arms and legs as the canon continued to pray over her.

"You vile spirit, I am speaking to you now in the name and with the authority of Jesus Christ. At my command, you will depart from this woman whom you have tormented for many days and nights, and you will go to your own place—"

Suddenly Heather shot upright. It was as if an invisible hand had yanked her by the hair. The sardonic expression was back. She began moving her head from side to side in a weaving motion, smiling and drooling.

Another demon was making its presence felt; the canon was certain of it. There was a marked difference in Heather's features. This time, her face seemed to flatten; the mouth drooped.

"In the name of Jesus Christ I command you—"

"We will *never* leave her." The deafening roar cut across the canon's words. The new voice was quite unlike that of the old woman; it seemed to emerge from the floor itself. "We'll *kill* her first!"

Then the voice took on the cadence of a schoolyard bully's— malicious, singsong, mocking.

"We tried her before with her blades and pills, blades and pills, blades-and-pills—"

"I *command* you in the name of *Jesus Christ*, release your name!"

The face took on a haughty look. The sneer was back again, but there was another personality, another consciousness, behind it.

"I am Uncle Seth," a masculine voice announced. "Lover of the little ones. Robber of the little souls. Killer of the Innocents."

The words had a robotic timbre, slowed and slurred, like an old gramophone winding down. On the last syllable, the young woman's hands flew to her throat. They began to squeeze. She was choking; her face was turning blue. The canon's assistants rushed to break the grip of those hands—and found they could not.

Heather Mitchelson was throttling herself to death.

"Please," Joe cried, "can't somebody *do* something?"

But the canon stilled him with a gesture. He had cautioned Joe not to speak unless spoken to. In the meantime, the assistants were winning. It was not the first time they had had to contend with a display of unnatural strength by the possessed. After a struggle, they pried Heather's hands away and pinioned her arms behind her back. She would do no more mischief—not to herself, not to anybody.

"I *command* you in the name of *Jesus* to depart from this woman," the canon urged in a mighty voice. It surprised Joe with its volume and intensity. "I have bound you and stripped you of your power to resist—"

Heather's head began to weave from side to side again.

"We take them in the dark...always in the dark...in the depths of the dark. We walk for the Master in the dark."

The voice was faltering under the authority of the canon's. The demoniac's neck slackened and her head fell to one side. As was the case from the beginning, the eyes remained wide open and unblinking.

"You will go quietly, and you will hurt no one as you leave!" the canon ordered.

"No! Please, don't send us to *him*." The voice was that of a pleading child. "We cannot go to him.... Please, not to the cold place. We need the warm...the bodies of the warm...to live in the blood of the bodies of the warm."

The voice began to chant with a breathless urgency: "...of the warm, of the warm...to do for the Master in the bodies of the blood of the warm—"

"Go now to that place that the Lord Jesus Christ has appointed for you!"

"...to kill with the hands of the bodies of the warm...to rage in the sweat in the blood in the warm—"

"There you will remain until he releases you!" the canon thundered.

"... to see through the eyes of the bodies of the warm...to live in the dark in the blood of bodies...warm ..."

The voice was becoming weak and hesitant. The canon was certain that the final expulsion was near. He spoke with renewed vigor and authority.

"In the name of Jesus Christ, go *now* to that place that the Lord has appointed for you. In the name of Jesus Christ I command you!"

"Warm...please, we need the warm. Please!"

The assistants relaxed their grip. Heather fell back onto the floor with closed eyes. She had fainted.

The canon's voice continued to rise in volume as the demon's grip weakened. "Go *now* to that place that the *Lord Jesus Christ* has appointed for you and there *you will remain* until *he* releases you!"

Something extraordinary happened at that moment. A dramatic change occurred, but it was invisible to all in that room. Joe reports a "lifting." A presence had departed.

The young woman opened her eyes and looked about her, plainly disoriented.

"What am I doing on the floor?" she asked, in all innocence. She turned to the young man near the window. "Joe? What's going on?"

In common with most victims of possession, Heather had no recollection of what had just taken place. For the best part of two hours, her entire being had been invaded by an alien force. Now there was only Heather Mitchelson.

The ordeal was at an end. The ghosts of family evil had been laid to rest.

In the winter of 1992, twenty-four-year-old Heather Mitchelson and her partner, Joe Kilmartin, were living in a rented home on the outskirts of Balbriggan. It is a small town in County Louth and lies a little to the north of Dublin City. Joe drove a truck for a living and Heather worked in a dry cleaners in the town. To the outsider, they were the average young couple, outwardly no different from their friends and neighbors.

But outward appearances can be deceptive. Inside, Heather carried the scars of years of abuse. She had had the great misfortune to be born into a family that was far from ordinary.

Her mother, Bernadette Rafters, was just seventeen when she gave birth to her daughter. Her marriage to Dessie Mitchelson, then twenty-seven, was a disaster in the making. Dessie was a drunk, a failure, who moreover had a violent streak. It was a volatile mixture. Dessie was bad with relationships, was forever getting into arguments with his buddies—and would generally take it out on his young wife. He beat her often, for no reason. When Bernadette became pregnant with Heather, it seemed to be the spur he needed to beat her even more.

It did not end there. The arrival of the baby had an even worse effect on Dessie. He was jealous of the affection lavished on it. The beatings started again. Before long, he was even hurting the infant.

Bernadette should have read the danger signs but evidently did not. She became pregnant twice more by Dessie; two boys were to join Heather in the unhappy family. Dessie abused them as well.

His alcoholism grew steadily worse; home life grew correspondingly unbearable for Heather and her siblings. They found themselves having to flee the home frequently—often in the middle of the night—and finding sanctuary with a succession of relatives. By all accounts, the relatives were not much better than the children's parents. Bernadette, as a result of her husband's abuse, simply could not cope and spent lengthy periods in mental institutions. From time to time the children were given over to foster care.

When Heather turned five, an event occurred that, tragic though it was, ensured that the children found a more permanent "home." Dessie died in a car accident. Bernadette, freed at last from her husband's tyranny, left the children in her mother's safekeeping and went to England to find work. In this she was successful. She sent "Nan Sal" regular payments from her salary, on the understanding that she would return by and by.

We do not know if the children fared any better under the eye of Nan Sal. The grandmother's home was a dilapidated cottage outside of town. Given the family background and the horrors they had endured from the beginning, one can assume that their day-to-day reality continued to be one of bleak dejection and fear.

What we *do* know is that a strong bond developed between Heather and Nan Sal. It was not, however, the healthy, loving bond one might expect, but something altogether more sinister. In the years she lived with her grandmother, the child would become initiated into a world of evil—an evil that was to pursue her for the remainder of her life.

In all, the children spent five years with their grandmother; Nan Sal died in 1978. Bernadette returned to her children, took up with another man, and the family became a stable unit. Or so one might hope. But evil has the uncanny knack of seeking out the weak and the vulnerable. The "stepfather" turned out to be far worse than Dessie Mitchelson. According to Heather, he was a serial child abuser. To complete the picture of depravity, he seemed to have her mother's tacit approval to do whatever he pleased with the children.

Given such circumstances, Heather and her brothers stood little chance of ever leading normal, well-adjusted lives. The boys emerged into adulthood as aggressive and violent as their father. Like Dessie, they abused alcohol—and drugs—and were frequently in trouble with the law. Heather, for her part, withdrew into herself; she developed an eating disorder, tried to kill herself twice, and, like her mother, suffered prolonged periods of depression that required hospitalization.

It was while she was undergoing treatment, having survived her second suicide attempt, that she had the good fortune to meet Joe Kilmartin. He was visiting his sister, who shared Heather's hospital room. When Heather was well again, Joe looked her up. Romance followed. They set up a home together. Heather, for the first time in her life, felt settled and happy. Having endured an abusive father, deviant relatives, and a pedophile stepfather, she had found a "normal" man.

Her happiness was to last a little short of two years. In 1992, she had her first experience of the preternatural.

The encounter took place after dark. Joe was not at home; he often worked nights. Heather was roused from sleep.

Her bedside clock told her that it was close to three in the morning; it was still dark, and would be dark for hours yet, this being late February.

Standing at the foot of the bed was the figure of an elderly woman, clearly visible by the light given off by a street lamp close by Heather's window. The figure was stooped, the lined face set in a smile.

Heather was alarmed, and with good reason. She was looking at the woman whom she had not seen since the age of ten. Nan Sal had been dead all of fourteen years.

The grandmother was wearing what could have been a pale blue nightgown but might equally well have been a ball gown; it was a long, flowing garment with a frilled neckline and cuffs. Heather wanted to scream but was too frightened to do even that. She shrank back against the headboard.

"Nan Sal," she ventured, surprised that she could even find her voice, "what do you want?"

She hoped that, by speaking, she might cause the vision to disappear and prove it was nothing but a dream. The last thing she expected was for her dead relative to answer her. Like most people, Heather had grown up with the notion of ghosts being no more than moving images, phantoms that do not as a rule interact with the real world of the living. Now the phantom was proving her wrong, and the words her dead grandmother uttered filled her with abject terror.

"Heather," the vision said, "soon you'll be with me."

As if that were not frightening enough, the ghost of Nan Sal went further. It raised its hands to its throat and made strangling motions.

There were no more words spoken. As the hands were lowered, Heather saw a ring glinting on the old lady's middle finger. She remembered that her grandmother used to wear a ring of striking appearance, but in her agitation did not consider if it was the same one. The apparition was disappearing slowly, fading away to nothing—as ghosts sometimes do. Heather was shaking with fear. For there could be no interpretation of the words other than that Heather was soon to join her grandmother in the afterlife.

She stumbled out of bed, desperately calling out for Joe. But her voice rang through the dark, vacant house, making her feel even more frantic and helpless. He would not be returning before noon that day. She had to face this alone.

Sleep was out of the question. She ran from the bedroom, pulling the door shut. Whom could she call? It was after three. They'd have me locked up, she mused grimly, recalling her mother's record of committal to institutions and her own suicide attempts. She vowed to spend the rest of the night on the couch. She would keep calm, watch some television, drink tea—a lot of calming tea.

At eight o'clock, she called in sick. She had to tell somebody about her frightening experience. She tried Joe's sister, but could not reach her. She knew her friends would ridicule her. As a last resort, she called the person who had been closest of all to Nan Sal: her mother, Bernadette.

"Ah, you were only dreaming, daughter." There was, as expected, a lack of concern in the voice. "I wouldn't worry about it."

"No, I was *not* dreaming, Mommy. I was wide awake and she was standing right beside the bed." Heather was annoyed at her mother's unsympathetic tone. "She was wearing a blue gown of some sort and I saw that ring she always wore. You know the one—with the big garnet or whatever it was."

There was a prolonged silence at the other end of the line.

"Mommy, are you still there? Mom?"

"I might as well be honest," Bernadette said at last. "Your granny was buried in a blue nightgown, and the ring went with her, too."

"Oh, my God, I'm going to die!" Heather cried. She broke into sobs. "I don't want to die now. I never want to leave Joe. I'm so happy with Joe. What'll Joe do?"

She waited to hear some consoling words but knew in her heart that they would not be forthcoming. She dried her tears.

"Mommy, are you still there?"

"Don't be such a bloody idiot," the mother said and hung up.

It was the last straw. Heather's nerves, raw after her sleepless night, got the better of her. She broke down, slumped to the floor, and wept uncontrollably.

She had been here before. Twice. Heather felt the old fears returning, the ones that had driven her to the edge of despair on two occasions, that had been responsible for her choosing the ultimate escape route. Twice she had attempted to cut short her life; twice there had been somebody on hand to save her from herself. Now she was alone.

She heard something. It was something Heather had not heard in two years, and she had hoped never to hear it again. But there it was.

The voice—the man's voice.

It only ever spoke to her when she felt hopeless and despairing. In the past she would hear it sometimes inside her head, at other times outside. It was coming from somewhere down the hall.

"*The blades are in the bathroom, Heather.*" The words were delivered in a calm, authoritative tone. "*Go and do it now. You know it makes sense.*"

Heather looked down the hall, rigid with fright. There was no one to be seen. The voice came again, this time more rapid and urgent than before, beating out the words in a lilting meter.

"*The blades are in the bathroom, Heather. Go and do it now. The blades are in the bathroom, Heather. Go and do it now—*"

"No!" she screamed, clamping her hands over her ears. But now the voice was inside her head and getting louder.

"*… do it now, do it now. The blades are in the bathroom, Heather. Go and do it now. Now, now, now—*"

"Stop it, stop it, stop it!" she wailed, burying her face in her hands and curling up into herself.

All at once, just as suddenly as it had started, the voice stopped. She lowered her hands, slowly, unsteadily. Was she safe now?

"*You know it makes sense!*"

She jumped. The voice was close, next her ear, whispering in her ear. "*You know it makes sense!*" There was a strong smell of nicotine. Heather screamed.

Uncle Seth, her mother's boyfriend, had always said that, and usually after having perpetrated some vile act on her. "Shut up!" he would say as she howled in pain. "Keep quiet about this, Heather. No one else is to hear about it. You know it makes sense."

But Seth had drowned himself six years past. How could it be him?

She struggled to her feet—and surprised herself when she discovered that the act of getting up made her immediately feel better. A calm was enveloping her whole body. She was no longer afraid. She knew what she had to do.

"*Do it now. Do it now.*" The voice continued to whisper in her ear. It was no longer strident, but slow and soothing. "*You know it makes sense. The blades are in the bathroom, Heather. Do it now. You know it makes sense.*"

"Yes…yes," Heather heard herself say. She felt tired; lack of sleep was taking its toll. She moved to the bottom of the stairs, with the voice in her ear—the languid and soothing voice.

She placed her foot on the first tread, listening to the hypnotic voice. She was still in her nightgown and barefoot.

"*The blades are in the bathroom, Heather. Do it now. You know it makes sense.*"

She started to climb the stairs. The hypnotic voice seemed to keep time with her steps.

"*Do it now. Do it now. Do it now!*"

She kept her eyes fixed on the open bathroom door. There, in the bathroom, she knew, lay blessed release. Death seemed so natural. All her anxiety had drained away. The words were so very reassuring.

She was almost there. The bathroom door stood open, beckoning. Heather looked down at her wrists. Each bore a double ring of raised, hard skin, like the cicatrices she had seen once on a *National Geographic* show. The people of some primitive island or other did that to themselves; they cut themselves, watched the blood flow. They did it in the cause of "beauty." It was the most natural thing in the world. Heather had done it to herself; twice before. She could do it again.

"*Do it now,*" the voice whispered again. "*Now. Do it now. Now. Do it now. Do it now.*"

She stood inside the bathroom door, staring at the cabinet.

"*Do it now. You just know . . . you just know it makes sense.*" The voice—Uncle Seth's voice—was coming in waves, washing over her, pulling her closer and closer toward the "beauty" of oblivion.

She reached for the cabinet handle with the same yearning the alcoholic feels when reaching for the first drink of the day.

"*Do it now!*" the voice cajoled. "*Now—*"

"Heather!"

She stopped, pulled up sharp. It was another voice, cutting in on Seth's.

"Heather, are you up there?"

She went out to the landing. There was a man standing at the bottom of the stairs. A stranger in her home.

"Heather, it's me. What's the matter with you?"

She stared down at him. Who was this guy? What was he doing in her house?

"*He wants to kill you, Heather.*"

The voice was in her head again, clamorous, insistent.

"*Don't go down to him. Don't go near him!*"

"Heather?" The man came slowly up the stairs. "Heather, are you all right? It's me, honey. Joe."

"*That's not Joe!*" The voice was urgent now. "*He only looks like Joe. He wants to kill you.*"

"Heather?" She heard the stranger speaking to her, as if over a great distance. "What is it? What's wrong?"

"*You must kill him first, Heather. You must!*"

"Jesus, Heather, what's the matter?" Joe was to confess later that he was scared. He had never seen his partner like this before. Her eyes were wide and staring. She seemed in some kind of trance.

He put a hand on her arm. At his touch she flinched. She looked at him as if seeing him for the first time.

"Joe, what are you doing here?"

"*F*** you!*" said the voice. "*F*** you, Heather! If you tell him about us, we'll really make you suffer. Really suffer!*"

"Help me!" she cried and collapsed into Joe's arms.

He made them coffee. Heather could at last tell somebody about the apparition, somebody who would listen with a sympathetic ear. She told Joe about the grandmother and what she had said. She dared not tell him about the voice. She was too afraid. That dreadful, whispered warning still echoed in her head.

Joe Kilmartin is a down-to-earth, skeptical man. On hearing Heather's account, he was naturally incredulous. He dismissed the whole thing as a bad dream. He had never in his life seen a ghost and consequently did not believe in them. He had often upbraided his partner for reading horoscopes and visiting fortune-tellers. As far as Joe was concerned, if she believed in "all that rubbish," she was quite capable of "seeing things," too.

They went out for a drink that evening and ran into some friends. The company helped Heather to unwind. Over the next few nights, with Joe by her side and no more visions at the bedside, Heather was prepared to admit that the experience could well have been an illusion, brought on by stress or too many late nights.

Come the weekend—and especially on Friday nights—the couple had a routine. Too weary to go out socializing after a busy week, they would buy a six-pack of beer, rent a video, and treat themselves to a quiet evening at home.

That Friday, they had just settled down and were about to start the VCR when there came a commotion from upstairs. Their bedroom was directly above the living room. More noises came; it was as though something, or somebody, was moving about up there. But who?

Heather began to tremble with alarm.

"Oh, my God!" she cried. "It's *her*. She's come back!"

"What, your granny?"

He had been looking forward to *Terminator 2*. It came highly recommended and he was not going to let a figment of Heather's imagination spoil it for him.

"It's only Rip," he said. Rip was their young German shepherd. The dog was known to wander about the house.

"No, it can't be." Heather was panic-stricken. "I put him outside earlier on."

At that moment, as if on cue, Rip barked outside in the yard. Joe would have to come up with another explanation. Heather was ready to scream.

"All right, honey," he said, "all right. I'll go and take a look."

As he expected, there was no one in the bedroom. But he did notice what he describes as "a foul kind of a smell, like drains, or stale pee." He wondered what it could be. He opened the window to air the room, shut the door behind him, and returned downstairs.

Halfway through the movie, it happened again. The second disturbance convinced Joe that it was not Heather's imagination. From directly overhead, he heard a series of thuds; it was if someone was jumping from one part of the room to another. The thuds were loud, so heavy that the light fixture trembled. Joe paused the video. "I'll check it out."

"Take Rip with you, will you?" Heather pleaded.

Grown nervous himself, Joe brought the dog in and set out to investigate. But Rip was having none of it; he would not venture up the stairs. He stood with his front paws on the bottom step, barking up at something unseen.

Heather was frantic by then. She could not remain in the house a moment longer. Breda, one of Joe's aunts, lived a few miles away. They would spend the night with her. They had to pack an overnight bag, but Heather refused to go upstairs. Joe steeled himself for the task. He went up and pounded loudly on the bedroom door.

"You better get the f*** out of there before I come in!" he warned, fear lending him a bravado that he knew would be short-lived.

He flung the door wide and flipped the light switch. Nothing happened. He cursed. The bulb was blown. He would have to pack the bag by the light from the hallway.

Without giving it much thought, he grabbed anything at hand and shoved it into the bag. He noted the same unpleasant stench, even though the window was open. He said nothing of this to Heather.

They were ready to leave. Rip would ride in the back with the overnight bags. Joe went to Heather's side and offered words of reassurance. He took one last look at the house.

"My blood ran cold," he says. "I happened to glance up at the bedroom window. We slept at the front of the house. I remember distinctly that I had just opened the window. But *somebody* had shut it."

That was not all. As Joe watched, he saw what looked like a figure standing just beyond the opened drapes. He could swear that he saw the drapes move. That was enough for him. He climbed into the car and they sped off.

He said nothing to Heather about the shape at the window. She was upset enough.

The couple spent three nights with Aunt Breda. Her home was small: big enough for one, cramped for three people and a dog. On balance, it was inconvenient for everyone involved. Breda was afraid of dogs; Joe disliked his aunt's disapproval of his cohabiting with his girlfriend; Heather felt that she was intruding in another woman's house. But they managed.

They left when Heather felt up to returning home. Breda, a deeply religious woman, gave her nephew a small crucifix, together with a novena, and promised to pray for them. She assured them that, as far as she knew, a ghost never harmed anyone. Joe wholeheartedly agreed. It was with such assurances, coupled with Joe's promise to adjust his work timetable to exclude night shifts, that Heather agreed to return home.

They went back in daylight and found things much as they had left them. Joe went first to the bedroom and was relieved to find that the strange odor had gone. But the window was shut, and that fact disturbed him.

He had bought spare lightbulbs, but they proved unnecessary. Inexplicably, the light in the bedroom was working normally. Loose wiring, he thought, and made a mental note to check it.

That night, Joe fell asleep without difficulty. With Heather it was otherwise; she lay awake for a long while, listening to his breathing, until she, too, finally nodded off.

Something roused her in the early hours. She had the distinct impression that somebody had just run fingers through her hair. She could still feel her scalp tingling from the touch.

She raised herself on an elbow. She thought it likely that Joe had done it in his sleep; but Joe lay with his back toward her, sleeping soundly. She lay back down again and pulled the comforter over her head.

Heather was fully awake when it happened a second time. The fingers of a spectral hand pressed themselves deep into the nape of her neck and raked swiftly through her hair, right to the crown of her head. All she would remember later was her uncontrollable screaming and seeing Joe's startled face, his arms reaching out to console her.

The following day, Heather insisted that they move out again. Joe refused, despite her pleading. He thought she was going crazy—which was understandable, given her history. He advised her to see the doctor. Heather rejected the suggestion out of hand. She was not sick, she told him. She had not taken medication for two whole years and did not feel depressed. Scared, yes, but not depressed. For the first time in her life she had stability: a partner who loved her, a home, and a steady job. She was determined that nothing would jeopardize this hard-won security.

They reached a compromise. Joe pledged that they would only move out again if *he* saw, or sensed, the ghost. Heather had little choice but to agree.

Joe still said nothing about the night they left to move in with his aunt. But he had his reasons. "I wasn't at all sure what I saw that night," he admits. "I mean, it was dark; we were both upset. I thought: could be I *did* shut that window. Could be I only saw a shadow or the reflection of a cloud or something."

A week passed without any further manifestations. Heather's nights remained undisturbed.

Joe had other concerns about his partner, though. They were concerns that he could not voice to anyone, not even to his aunt. He was worried about a change that had come over Heather.

He traced the beginning of the change to the day he had come back early from work, the morning she was in the bathroom. Her trancelike demeanor had puzzled him. His first thought was that she was on drugs, but she assured him later that she did not take any, not even prescription drugs.

From that day on, Heather was not the same person. Even her posture was different somehow. She seemed to slouch more, and sometimes, when seated, she would cross her legs at the ankles, much in the way an old woman would. The unpleasant odor he had first detected in the bedroom seemed to follow her around. It resembled stale urine; Heather had always prided herself on her personal hygiene. She liked to smell nice.

These physical anomalies were not, in themselves, as troubling as Heather's deteriorating relationship with the dog. Rip refused to go near her. This was very unusual. Heather and the dog had been inseparable. Now Rip seemed unwilling to share the same room with her and would only settle when Joe appeared.

There were times during their conversations when Joe had the distinct impression that Heather was listening not to him but to someone else. She would cock her head to one side and chuckle. One night, he caught her talking to herself in the bathroom. The language was unintelligible, like nothing he had ever heard before.

He challenged her about it. "Who were you talking to in there, honey?"

She looked at him as if *he* were the crazy one. "You were hearing things," she said simply. "I wasn't talking to anyone. I was brushing my teeth."

Still, Joe was prepared to put up with these things. So long as the grandmother did not appear to Heather again, life was tolerable. He had concluded that his sighting of the figure at the bedroom window that day had, most likely, been an illusion.

Aunt Breda's crucifix, which he had placed in the bedroom, was obviously doing its work.

His optimism was short-lived; Nan Sal was to return. This time, she did not wait until the house was dark and silent before making her presence known. Nor did she choose the bedroom.

Joe was adamant that the first apparition had been a figment of Heather's imagination. He was still skeptical.

"I'll believe it when I see it myself," he had told her.

It was Friday, March 6. The couple were on the couch watching television. They might never have known about the presence of their "visitor" had Rip not alerted them. The dog was dozing on the hearthrug when, without warning, he leaped to his feet. He began barking furiously.

Joe and Heather turned. In the corner, partially lit by the standard lamp, stood the figure of an old woman. Nan Sal. Heather saw that she was wearing the same blue gown. Her hands were extended in a beckoning gesture and she wore the same fixed grin as before.

The grin was not a mirthful one; it seemed utterly malevolent. Heather was terrified. Joe was speechless, his skepticism melting away like snow in a skillet. But he recovered quickly. He stood up.

"Get out of here!" he shouted at the apparition. "Get out! We don't want you here!" They were the first words that came into his head.

But nothing happened. The old woman still stood grinning balefully. Heather was howling with terror. Joe tried again. "For Christ's sake, get out!" he cried.

At that, the visitant raised its hands to its throat and made the throttling gesture that had so frightened Heather. As before, it slowly disappeared.

Joe switched on the light. Rip was whining, ears back, his tail between his legs. He seemed to be staring at the place where the apparition had been. Joe found himself staring, too, trying to come to terms with what he had just seen.

He heard a gurgling noise. Heather was still on the couch; she had her back to him, and her shoulders were shaking. She seemed to be having some kind of fit.

"Heather?"

She did not respond. The gurgling grew louder. Joe came around to the front of the couch. He could not believe what he was seeing: it was the most macabre sight he had ever witnessed. Heather's eyes were bulging; in the light from the standing lamp he could see that her face was discolored. She was choking. Joe saw the cause. There, "as clear as day," was a hand, fastened about her throat. But it was not Heather's. It was an aged, wizened hand where Heather's should have been, and it was trying to choke the life out of her. The hand ended at the wrist in a frilled blue cuff and wore a brass ring on the middle finger.

Joe was petrified. He was witnessing the inconceivable. His rational mind told him it was nonsense, that such things did not happen. Yet he could not doubt the evidence of his eyes. Heather was under attack. Her face had turned purple under the hand's murderous grip and her eyes had swiveled in her head, so that only the whites were visible. She was gasping for breath. He had to act.

Overcoming his revulsion, he seized the grisly hand. It was cold to the touch and seemed immensely strong, the tendons and muscles feeling like nylon ropes. As he tried to free her, Heather grasped his shoulder with her "other" hand, the normal one. He heard her attempting to call out his name.

He was frantic. But even as he struggled, he was registering yet another impossibility.

"It was that other hand," he says. "I knew Heather was trying to help me. She'd gripped my shoulder and was squeezing. But it wasn't her hand. It was like someone with long fingernails. It felt like eagle talons digging into my flesh. But I knew that Heather's nails were bitten to the quick. Always had been. She was one of these nervous people who are forever biting their nails."

Using both hands, and all the strength he could muster, he managed at last to break the hold. As he did so, he felt "a warm sensation" beneath his grip, as the phantom hand relaxed. "When I looked again," Joe says, "it was Heather's hand I was holding on to. Her *real* hand."

Heather was free. She collapsed onto the rug, choking and coughing, and gasping for air. Later she would confess that she never felt closer to death than she did that evening.

"Are you all right, honey?" Joe asked, bending over her.

She could only nod.

"We're leaving," he said. "Right now! We're getting out of here."

But Nan Sal had not finished with them. At that moment they heard footsteps overhead, followed by their bedroom door opening.

It was enough. They picked up a few belongings, found a bag in the kitchen, and hurried to the front door. Joe fetched Rip's leash and kept him by his side. They would spend the night with Aunt Breda again. Heather went to the front door.

The door would not open.

The knob refused to turn. It was jammed. She thought perhaps the safety was on. It was not. Inexplicably, the lock was stuck. They could not leave.

"Let *me!*" Joe yelled.

It refused to budge. It was as though it was welded shut.

"Oh, Christ!" he screamed. "What the f*** is going on?"

From upstairs came the sound of mocking laughter. They turned, terror-stricken. At the top of the stairs stood the grand-mother, dressed as before. She was grinning. Then she began to cackle. It was loud, and utterly chilling.

If the door would not open, they would find another way out, Joe decided. Taking Heather by the hand, he rushed back into the living room. Rip was growling and yelping by turns, terrified. Joe struggled with the window. It had not been opened fully in years.

"Oh, Jesus, hurry!" Heather pleaded.

The window yielded at last. Joe forced it up. Rip needed no prompting; he leaped through to freedom. Heather followed. Once out, Joe allowed the frame to drop with a crash. He heard glass shat-ter; he did not care. They reached the safety of the car.

On the journey to his aunt's house, Joe struggled to regain his composure. He was jabbering and swearing and trembling, his mind in turmoil. He could not come to terms with the terrible events. Rip, in the back seat, lay whimpering.

But Heather was eerily calm. She sat quietly, staring straight ahead. He could not understand it. Was she in shock? They had both experienced unimaginably terrifying events. She had almost died. How, he asked himself, could she be so calm?

"Heather, are you okay?"

She did not answer, seemed unaware that he had even spoken. "Heather? Honey?"

She said nothing. Instead, her hands shot out, and latched onto the steering wheel. She was forcing the car toward the wrong side of the road.

"Heather, what the f*** are you doing?"

Joe wrestled for control of the wheel—and found he was no match for her strength. Her hands were locked in position, forcing the car on a collision course. The road was treacherous; it had rained heavily for most of the day. Their fighting for control of the wheel was sending the car into a skid.

Up ahead in the distance, Joe could see the lights of a truck approaching.

"Heather, let go!"

He had to stop the car. He knew that if he tried to brake, the car might end up on its roof—or worse. The headlights of the truck were drawing closer.

"Jesus Christ, Heather, stop it!" he yelled.

As if by magic, she released her grip on the steering wheel.

They were in the path of the oncoming truck. The gap was closing rapidly. Joe heard the blaring of twin air horns; six banks of high-intensity headlights flashed, flooding the car with light, half-blinding him. He heard Rip's frantic barking. And, through all the sound and the fury, he heard something he would never forget. It was the same mocking laughter that had driven them out of their home just minutes before.

There were four of them in the car now.

He flung the wheel wildly, sending the car out of the truck's path, missing it by inches. He saw a tree coming up to meet them. But they avoided it. The car ended up with the front wheels in a ditch. The truck drove on.

Joe collapsed over the wheel, sweating and shaking. He was unable to speak. Rip was moaning and scratching at the rear window, desperate to get out. The derisive laughter continued. He looked across at Heather—and froze. She sat with her head thrown back. The cackling was emerging from her throat.

Joe found his voice. "What…what the f*** are you doing?" he screamed into her face. "You nearly got us killed!"

She stopped laughing abruptly and turned to look at him for the first time. "Thought we'd have some fun," she said in a flat voice.

Joe was horrified.

"I figured she was in shock," he explains. "I thought she might be having a seizure or a fit of some kind. All I know is that she wasn't herself. I didn't like to do it, but I slapped her hard across the face. Thought that would make her snap out of it."

But Heather did not flinch. She was smiling.

"Fun!" he cried.

"Yes, fun. Breda's not at home. She's in the f***ing church praying her useless prayers. So we'd have been sitting outside her house, twiddling our f***ing thumbs, waiting on the bitch."

"What?" Joe had never heard her talk about his aunt that way. "How could you know what Aunt Breda was doing? We didn't have time to call her."

"I know everything. They show me." She cocked her head to one side in an unnerving way. "She dropped her f***ing rosary beads on the bus, so she'll be in a bloody flap when we get there."

"Oh, my God. What's got into you?"

"Exciting, isn't it? They're telling me now when you're going to die." She said it with a smile—a wide, ugly grin. Yet the rest of the face remained immobile; the forehead and cheeks were drawn taut, the eyes wide open and staring.

"Wouldn't you like to know?" she continued. The voice was challenging. It did not belong to Heather.

Joe was stunned. He tried to speak, but the words would not come.

"Shall I tell you?" she said tauntingly. The mouth twisted into a contemptuous smirk. "When you're going to die?"

Still he could not speak. His jaw seemed paralyzed.

Jesus, help me! The phrase rose out of nowhere in his consciousness. *Jesus, help me.* He struggled to free his voice. He succeeded.

"Jesus, *help me!*" he cried, pressing his temples and shutting his eyes tight against the nightmare that was not a nightmare.

It was as though a spell had been broken. Rip stopped whining. There was a deathly silence. Joe opened his eyes. He was afraid—afraid to clap eyes on who it might be in the passenger seat.

"Heather," he ventured, hoping that the sound of her name might bring about her "return." Slowly, carefully he allowed himself to look her way.

She was sitting bolt upright, staring through the windshield at the dark, wet hedge.

"The bitch is back now," she said, half to herself, "so we can go."

With that, she left the car. Joe heard a heavy thud at the rear and felt the vehicle lurch. He buried his face in his hands and began to weep. Wild thoughts were assailing him.

"I think I believed at that moment that Heather was going to kill me," Joe recalls. "She'd just told me that she knew when I was going to die. If someone was going to kill you, wouldn't they know that—the moment of your death?"

He desperately wanted to flee from the car, but sheer terror had drained him of all energy. He could not move. There was no escape. He could only wait and pray.

"Jesus, help me!" he sobbed over and over. "Jesus, help me!"

He heard the passenger door open.

Someone was climbing in beside him. A hand shook his shoulder. "What happened? Joe, why have we stopped?"

He looked into Heather's concerned face. The *real* Heather had returned. The car was no longer wedged in the ditch. Miraculously, it had righted itself and was now on the grass shoulder, facing in the right direction.

"What happened?" Heather asked again, growing anxious.

Joe stared at her in disbelief. She seemed totally unaware of the havoc she had just caused.

"Joe, you're scaring me." She started to cry. "What on earth happened?"

"I—I don't know," he managed to say. "I think…we…skidded." His mouth was dry. His head ached. He was drenched in sweat.

"I must have blacked out. Did I?" Heather asked. "I don't remember a thing."

"Yes…yes, you did."

He got the engine running. He had barely the strength to maneuver the car back onto the road again.

They drove the rest of the way in silence. When, at last, they arrived at his aunt's house, Joe prayed that he would find her at home, watching television or something. He wanted so desperately for her to be there. Don't let me hear you took the bus, he thought, over and over; anything but the bus.

He rang the doorbell. Breda answered; she was wearing her hat and overcoat. Joe's heart sank.

"Gosh, you're in luck," she said. "I've just come in from Mass."

He knew that her parish church was a ten-minute walk away. No bus needed.

Joe wondered if they might stay with her again for a few days. She seemed to take it in stride. She made them coffee. She could see how upset her nephew was. She made small talk.

"Would you believe it?" she said with a rueful smile. "I lost my rosary on the bus. Isn't that just like me?"

Joe felt as though he were losing his mind. He stared in disbelief at Heather, but Heather was nodding sympathetically.

"The bus driver was very good," Breda was saying. "He took my phone number and said he'd ring me if he found them. They were from Lourdes, you see, so God willing someone finds them and turns them in."

"God willing," Heather repeated kindly. "Don't worry, Breda, I'm sure they'll turn up. Won't they, Joe?" She looked to him for confirmation.

"Well, you...You'd bloody well know, Heather, wouldn't you?" He was dazed by the unreality of the moment. "You would bloody know!"

They stared at him in astonishment. Aunt Breda put a hand to her heart.

"Joe! What's got into you?"

"Maybe you should ask her that!" He pointed a trembling finger at Heather. "I know what I need: a bloody drink, and to get as far away from *her* as possible!"

He left the house. He needed to be alone with his thoughts. Heather needed help; they both did.

The next day, at Joe's insistence, Heather went to see her doctor. After speaking to her at length, he took Joe aside. The man confessed his bafflement; what he heard from Heather made no sense.

Joe told him everything he knew. He thought that the doctor would laugh, accuse him and Heather of wasting his time with superstitious nonsense. He did not. He advised something few medical practitioners would even consider in the circumstances. He recommended that Heather go and see a Christian minister.

There was a good man he knew—the best man in the "profession" of deliverance. They would have to travel, though: Canon William H. Lendrum lived eighty miles away, in Belfast.

An appointment was made and, on a spring evening in 1992, Heather Mitchelson and Joe Kilmartin presented themselves at the home of the canon. He introduced them to his two assistants, and the exorcism began. The canon expected it would be no more arduous than celebrating a Eucharist....

We are sitting in the living room of Canon William Lendrum's Belfast home as he relates the details of Heather Mitchelson's case.

At age eighty-two, he can look back over an astonishing four decades of battling demons and other paranormal entities. During those decades, he tells us, he came upon few cases of actual possession. Heather's was the exception rather than the rule.

Yet he has witnessed an ever-increasing call on his ministry in recent years, and expresses a wish that the church hierarchy would take a more robust approach to exorcism.

"People are a little afraid of this subject," he says. "They don't wish to be reminded of the ugly side of life, the more frightening side. They believe that by bringing such things into the open they leave themselves vulnerable. They don't seem to realize that not confronting these things gives the Devil free rein to do as he chooses."

He recalls Heather Mitchelson with fondness. He was gratified that he could—if only for a time, as events would show—liberate a young woman who had fallen foul of so much evil, yet had battled through.

"When Heather came round after the exorcism, she remembered nothing," he says. "This is a common occurrence. The demon can take over the entire consciousness, you see. I knew I wasn't speaking to Heather throughout it all. Afterwards, she said she felt 'beautiful and clean' within, but 'empty' as well, as if something had been taken away from inside of her. The change in her was extraordinary; her whole demeanor, even her voice, was different. I prayed over her and she rededicated her life to Jesus."

We wonder if Heather was possessed by her dead relatives or by evil spirits. The canon has firm opinions on this. "I'm inclined to believe that the dead don't come back for any good reason, but that evil spirits can masquerade as the dead," he says. "Roman Catholicism holds that souls in purgatory might return to ask for prayers, and that's another view. There is the distinct possibility, in Heather's case, that the uncle and grandmother were both demonized in their lifetimes. I think that it was highly likely. There was no emphasis on a prayer life as far as I'm aware, and therefore no defense against evil. That is not a judgment, but simply a statement of fact."

Canon Lendrum is quick to point out that an exorcism will be effective only as long as the person who receives it keeps his or her part of the bargain. That is how he sees it: as a bargain. When people are exorcised, they make a pact with God, as it were, that they will remain "on the straight and narrow."

"You know, the most difficult part for me is not the exorcism itself," he says. "The most difficult part is encouraging a person who has never been religious to return to the Lord after their deliverance. Heather was one such person.

"She'd never been taught about God, you see. I was very much reminded in this case of the warning in Exodus, the one about the sins of the father being visited upon the children, unto the third and fourth generations.

"A child who doesn't learn about God's love and compassion from the parents is an easy target. The father in this case was very violent and abusive—as was the stepfather. Having to cope with this, day after day, week after week, year after year, has a terrible effect on children. They suffer tremendous 'psychic stress.'

"It is easy to see how evil can be promulgated over generations, if the individuals concerned have neither the fortitude nor the resources necessary to put an end to it. Oh, you can be sure," he says with a sigh, "that Satan's bid for our souls is predicated on the debasement of our humanness as early as possible in our childhood."

He is saddened that Heather Mitchelson had so little chance in life—that she was, from the earliest moment, exposed to such danger.

"After the exorcism I visited her several times and found her at peace," he says. "However, it's quite a distance from Belfast to Balbriggan, and for that reason I could not visit her regularly enough, so I passed her into the care of another minister who lived closer."

The canon pauses. He looks wistful and downcast.

"Oh, how I wish I could say that the dear girl found peace in this life! She was very, very unfortunate—from the beginning of her life right up to the end. "Six months after the exorcism she died, you see. By her own hand. It was her third attempt at suicide and this time it was successful. Joe wasn't there that day. There was no one who could stop her, reason with her, give her the assurances she craved. She hanged herself from the light fitting in her bedroom. She strangled herself.

"So, in the end, sadly, the grandmother did indeed have her way."

THE HOUSEWIFE AND THE DEMON DUBOIS

On the face of it, there is nothing magical about the Ouija board. It has no powers, either good or evil. It is simply a rectangular tablet of wood, much the same size as a Monopoly board. It has a long history, extending back to the ancient Romans, perhaps even predating Christ. Its present form emerged in the nineteenth century and was patented by the Baltimore inventor and attorney Elijah J. Bond. Although many of the earlier boards were elaborate affairs that included angels, swastikas, and signs of the zodiac, the modern variant is relatively simple. It is printed with the letters of the alphabet, the numbers 0 to 9, and the words YES, NO, and GOODBYE.

The "game" is played by two or more persons. Somebody will pose a question, which the board attempts to answer. It does so with the aid of a planchette, literally a "little plank." Again, designs vary considerably, but generally speaking, the planchette, or pointer, is a small, triangular piece of wood or plastic that moves smoothly over the surface of the board. Often it has a "window" of clear plastic, by which a letter or number is framed. Each player places a fingertip on the planchette. The board responds to a question either by moving the pointer to YES or NO or by spelling out the answer by choosing a sequence of letters.

This is the first contentious aspect of Ouija. Who—or what—is moving the planchette? Those who have used Ouija relate with awe how the pointer moved of its own accord. Participants will swear to their fellow players that they did nothing to influence the pointer's progress, and indeed most believe this to be the case. Ouija users often describe it as having "a life of its own."

Yet skeptics dismiss this. They speak of "ideomotor" action: unconscious muscular activity by which minuscule movements are made without a person being aware that they are making them. Since it takes very little effort to set the planchette in motion, this theory might well be valid.

And yet, it is less important who or what moves the pointer than where the game leads and the uses to which it is put. Some use the board to look into the future; others to make contact with the dead; still others as a means of experimentation in a spirit of fun. Ouija as board game—as innocent as a round of Risk or Trivial Pursuit. All might be well, were it not that dabbling with Ouija seems to have had disastrous consequences for many users.

Canon William H. Lendrum suggests that all right-thinking people should shun it completely. He believes that Ouija is a portal by which malignant forces can enter this world and cause great distress, even insanity. He recalls one of his most upsetting cases, that of a County Antrim woman whose life was turned on its head from the moment she dabbled with Ouija. The "game" was to cause her fifteen years of great distress and torment—one of the longest cases of demonic attack on record.

Julie's ordeal began on a cold and wet November afternoon in 1980, when her son Gordon came home from school in high excitement. The boy had learned of a new game. It required no board, nor indeed any outlay at all. One needed only to divide up a sheet of paper and write the letters of the alphabet on the pieces, as well as numerals, and the words YES, NO, and GOODBYE. Gordon had played it with his school pals.

They had put questions to the board, and it appeared to be able to foretell the future. It knew who would marry and when, what somebody would do on leaving high school, what they would do in later life, whom they would work for, if they would be successful in their career. It was uncanny.

His mother knew at once what he was referring to, though she did not know Ouija by that name. She had come across it from time to time in the rural area where she grew up. The country people had called it the "talking board." They would play the game, with or without an actual board, to while away a long winter's evening. To the best of Julie's knowledge, it was simply harmless fun. She followed her three children into the living room and prepared the pieces of paper accordingly, and they settled down to an evening's amusement.

The game began as solely that: an innocent diversion. Following Gordon's instructions, each of the four placed a finger atop an upended tumbler. Somebody—Julie herself or one of the children—posed the first, formulaic, question. "Is there anybody there?"

No one had expected the glass to respond, and so it came as a surprise to Julie when it moved almost at once to the YES. There was the customary reaction from the participants, each accusing another of cheating, of sneakily moving the glass. But everyone protested their innocence.

"Who are you?"

The second reply came as swiftly as the first, even though the spelling out of the word took a little more time. The glass glided about the table again.

S-E-A-M-A-N

Julie frowned. It was the last thing she had expected.

"You're doing that!" one of the younger children accused another. "Mom, he's moving the glass."

"Am not!"

"Children, behave." She did not know what to make of the strange message—if a message it was.

"What kind of seaman are you?" Gordon asked. He had the usual boy's fascination with the sea: the romance of it.

N-E-L-S-O-N

Gordon was perplexed. He was about to ask for clarification when, seemingly of its own volition, the glass progressed across the tabletop again. Five pairs of lips quietly vocalized each letter it paused at.

H-M-S V-I-C-T-O-R-Y

And so began an eerie communication. Although the "visitor" did not identify himself by name, he gave the family to understand that he had once been a lowly seaman on board Admiral Nelson's celebrated warship. The glass sped rapidly over the dining room table, spelling out the letters of each word communicated by the man who claimed to have lived and died centuries before. He related how he had fought in a number of sea battles, and how he had perished at Trafalgar in 1805, when Nelson himself lost his life. And, throughout the telling, the mysterious mariner used an antique English, peppering his "speech" with "thee" and "thou" and phrases such as "It be said."

The children were delighted. It was *Treasure Island* and Horatio Hornblower come to life.

"I remember when the Ouija was telling us those things," Julie says, "a coal popped out onto the hearth, and we all jumped. And I thought at the time that I shouldn't be dabbling in such things. As a practicing Christian I'd been brought up to believe that fortune-telling, like tarot cards and tea-leaf reading and the like, was wrong. But I didn't really believe it was dangerous."

Nonetheless, she packed away the "game" and called it a night.

But the next day it rained again, and the children—her younger son and daughter especially—persuaded their mother to repeat the game. With some reluctance, Julie cleared the dining room table, Gordon helped distribute the pieces of paper, and they settled down to another session of fortune-telling.

Almost immediately, they made "contact."

J-E M-A-P-P-E-L-L-E D-U-B-O-I-S

This time it was no English seaman but a Frenchman, who went on to identify himself as Pierre. Pierre Dubois; it was the French equivalent of John Smith. An alias? No one could say. But the visitor almost immediately lapsed into simple English, full of misspellings. He had, he claimed, died at the time of the French Revolution. Without being questioned at all, the glass continued to move from letter to letter, spelling out what the newcomer wished to tell them about his life.

Julie and the children learned that he had been a blacksmith in a small town called Lessay in northern France; he communicated details of his family life, and "spoke" of matters relating to his era. It was all very absorbing, but Julie still had her reservations. Then, without warning, the messages being transmitted via the glass began to address themselves to her alone.

"Julie," the glass spelled out, "I like stay here with you."

She was shocked. Yet she plucked up the courage to ask why. The glass explained.

"I am tired wandring and need rest.... I was with relations in Suth Africa but not wanted there."

Julie did not know what to make of it. And she remained skeptical, still believing that either Gordon or his younger brother was moving the glass. "Pierre" was to convince her otherwise. The glass began to spell out a most unusual message.

"Julie go in kitchen and shut window," it read. "Rain comes in."

To her astonishment, she found this to be the case. The wind had blown open the kitchen window and rain was soaking part of the floor and countertop. She could not have known this; none of them could. From the dining room it was impossible to hear or see what went on in the kitchen....

Matters took on a more serious aspect at about 5 p.m. Julie's husband, John, came home from work to find her and the children still engrossed in their game. He was a nurse attached to the emergency room at the county hospital, and often did night duty. On this occasion, he was working a double shift and wished to catch an hour's sleep before leaving again. He came into the dining room, looked at the table, and frowned.

"What's that you're doing?"

"Ouija, Dad," Gordon piped up. "It's great fun."

"It's a load of old nonsense," John assured him with a wink.

"I'll get dinner," Julie said. "And change out of those things. You're soaking."

But no sooner had he left the room than the glass—entirely of its own accord—began to spell out a message. It was for Julie.

"John does not believe in me," it read. "But I will come to him in night as ghost."

Julie was terrified. "Oh, please don't!" she cried. "Go away."

She gathered up the pieces of paper and flung them into the fire. They burst into flame at once, then browned and blackened. All, that is, except one, which fell, face down, on the hearth step. Julie bent down to pick it up. Without thinking, she turned it over—and immediately wished she had not. For it seemed that the Ouija had given its response to her plea.

The paper read NO.

She was greatly shaken. "No more of this, children. It's no fun anymore. Time for homework."

That night Julie was unable to sleep. Alone in bed, hearing the rain buffeting the window, she found her thoughts straying to the silly "game." It remained for her a game; despite the enigmatic messages from Monsieur Dubois, despite his apparent ability to see through walls—and even to know her name—she was as yet unconvinced of the seriousness of Ouija.

Her husband returned from the hospital in the early hours. He kissed her cheek and inquired after the children.

"I hope you stopped playing that silly game," he said. "That Ouija nonsense. You'll be giving the kids nightmares with that spirit stuff."

She was still a little nervous. She reflected that the children were less afraid of the "spirit stuff" than she was. She had looked in on them earlier and all were sleeping soundly. She tried to make light of what the mysterious Frenchman had told her.

"You're the one who should be scared, John," she said with a grin. "The Ouija said it was going to come to you tonight as a ghost."

Her husband chuckled, turned over on his side, and was soon asleep.

Not so Julie. Her ordeal was about to begin.

She drifted into an uneasy sleep, but not for long. Half an hour later she was wide awake again. Something was wrong; a change was coming over the bedroom. Julie describes experiencing "a sense of dread." She sat up, fully alert, straining her ears for the slightest untoward sound, but all was silent except for the little trusted noises of the night: the ticking clock by the bedside, her husband's light snoring, the steady rain, a car hissing past on the road.

But she noticed something odd: an unnatural coldness was stealing over the room. The heating had been on for a good five hours and had only just switched itself off. How could it be so cold? She shivered and ducked back under the covers, tugging them more snugly about her.

It did not help; the cold kept increasing.

She pulled the covers over her head, chiding herself for being silly and willing herself into sleep. But the terrible dread kept gnawing at her. She tried to think pleasant thoughts, tried to ignore her thudding heart, and tried to pray. Her attempts brought little comfort; the fear continued to build. She sensed that something frightful was about to happen. She held her breath and waited, not knowing what to expect, but in the conviction that the Ouija was making good its threat.

Before too long, she heard a sound: the unmistakable creak of the doorknob. The spring bolt was sliding back with tiny clicks. She froze.

Very slowly, the door began to open.

They had no pets. Nor could it be one of the children; they never came into their parents' room without permission—even the youngest was too big for that.

Julie still had the covers over her head. An inner voice was urging her to remain so, not to look in the direction of the door.

Her fear quickened further as she heard the tread of heavy, booted feet approaching the bed. She wanted to call out to John, but some alien force was willing her to silence. She felt helpless in the face of that power.

The bedclothes were no defense against what happened next. To her horror, she felt a man's body pressing down on hers. It was cold and heavy, stifling her, almost suffocating her. And still she could not cry out. She had the sensation of a face against her own, could feel the roughness of unshaven cheeks, could hear the rasp of labored breathing. Yet she saw nothing. Later, Julie would describe how loathsome and overpowering the stench was; she likened it to the odor of decay given off by a dead creature. And she could identify another smell, commingling with it—that of burning coal or soot.

Then began the assault.

"It molested me sexually," she says frankly. "You wouldn't believe how long it took for me to actually come out and say that to anyone...not even my husband. I was so ashamed."

She tried to rouse her husband, but her arms as well as the rest of her body were frozen into immobility. Nor could she speak. Frantic thoughts were churning about in her head. When she tried to pray, the words kept slipping from her as if they were in some alien language. She had never been so frightened in her life.

She is unsure how long she lay there, pinioned to the bed. She believes that she passed out, to regain consciousness hours later as dawn was breaking. By then, the coldness had lifted. The stench in the room was now only just perceptible. She experienced what she describes as a sensation of "lightness," and knew at once that the unholy visitor had gone.

Only gradually did the paralysis leave her. Feeling returned first to her fingers, then to her hands, then to the rest of her body. She was in a cold sweat, and utterly terrified. When John woke next to her she remembers him commenting on an odd smell in the room—"like a campfire," he said—and concluding that someone nearby must have been burning garbage, or perhaps had "lit their chimney." She recalls feigning sleep, afraid that if she spoke, he might notice something that would betray what she had been through.

She heard him go downstairs to make breakfast. Next thing she knew, he was waking her with a cup of tea. She managed to tell him that she was feeling unwell and needed to sleep more. He left the tea on the nightstand.

"That's all right, love," he said. "I'll see to the kids and take them to school."

Half an hour later, Julie heard them leave. She remained in bed, feeling wretched. She had ample time to consider what it was that had come to her in the night. When examined in daylight, the visit appeared as unreal as a bad dream. Perhaps that's what it was, she thought—a bad dream. She got out of bed, feeling a little better.

"I really did believe it had all been a nightmare," she says. "The more I thought about it, the more logical it seemed. But God, when I went to the bathroom and looked in the mirror, I nearly died of fright."

The glass reflected all too clearly the terrible truth. On the left side of Julie's face—the side that had been in contact with the unshaven visitant—was an angry red rash. Horrified beyond words, she backed away from the mirror and fell against the bathtub. Nightmares were not supposed to intrude upon one's waking hours, and certainly not in such an utterly ghastly way.

If the County Antrim housewife thought then, in that fall of 1980, that the experience was an isolated incident—one that would teach her a salutary lesson about the dangers of Ouija—she was very much mistaken. Julie Neville was to endure many long years of the company of the creature who called himself Dubois. He would return again and again. There was no fixed pattern; his visits seemed random. Sometimes he would haunt her every night for a week; sometimes weeks—and even months—might separate his visits. But, like some infernal bad penny, he never failed to turn up.

Julie's tormentor was conforming to the nature and behavior of the incubus—literally "one who lies upon"—a male demon said to sexually assault women in their beds. Although the entity is generally believed to visit its victim in nightmares, there have been reports of women experiencing the assaults while in the waking state. The succubus is the female equivalent.

The entity would intrude most often while Julie was alone in her bed, but he came also while her husband slept soundly beside her. All her attempts to banish Dubois through prayer would have no lasting effect. Whenever she thought she had got rid of him, he would return with a vengeance. He gave her to understand that he was not prepared to go quietly, and were an attempt made to cast him out, Julie would have to come with him.

But that was later.

The night following the first assault, as ill luck would have it, Julie had to sleep alone; John was again at the hospital. In desperation she had pleaded with him to cancel, to get someone to cover for him. She was not feeling well, she said. Anxious. He told her not to worry; Gordon was there to protect her. Besides, he had used up all his free time. He would see her the next day.

She got the children off to bed early and retired to the living room. She intended to stay up as late as possible, in order to postpone the dreaded hour. Her Methodist upbringing had impressed upon her the importance of regular Bible study, and she turned to the Good Book now.

"The Lord is my shepherd; there is nothing I shall want." She whispered to herself the ancient words of praise, willing them to bestow upon her the peace they had seldom failed to deliver in the past. "He leadeth me in the paths of righteousness for His name's sake. Yea, though—" She stopped.

Behind her, the door was opening.

Julie gripped the Bible more tightly. She thought it might be one of the children, unable to sleep. At the same time, she wondered why she had heard no footsteps on the stair. She stood up and turned to face the doorway. She did not know what she might see.

The light in the hall was on, but there was no one there. She strove to remain calm. It had opened by itself, she reasoned; the door handle was always faulty anyway. With this thought uppermost, she went and shut it, returned to the sofa, and continued reading.

"Yea, though I walk through the valley of the shadow of death, I will fear no evil; for you are with—"

It happened once more.

This time she was more irritated than frightened. She strode across the room to shut the door again. But, as she did so, as her fingers gripped the handle and turned it... she felt the handle being grasped from the *other* side. It was turning back all by itself. The door could not be shut; a countering force was pushing it open again.

"I fear no evil; for you are with me... *God, please!*" Julie cried out. The opposing force was winning; she could not shut the door. Her strength was failing.

"For you are with me, *please, dear God, please!*"

The Bible fell from her hand. The door flew open, its impetus sending her reeling across the floor and sprawling into an armchair. She struggled to her feet again.

The horrid stench and the coldness were back. "It" was in the room. The thought terrified her. "It" could attack her anywhere. Where could she run to? It was two in the morning. The children were asleep; she could not leave the house. Nor could she go outside to await the daylight; it was unthinkable. Julie felt crushed. She climbed the stairs again to her bedroom, Bible in hand. With great deliberation, she placed it on her night table.

It cannot have been easy for Julie to draw back the covers, return to bed, and face the darkness. Yet she did, and she lay there, praying and sobbing and waiting...simply waiting.

"I had the mad idea that if he saw me crying, he'd take pity on me and leave me alone," she recalls. "How innocent I was! I know now that these things feed on your fear. The longer it went on, the more fearful I became, and the worse it got."

Through her quiet weeping, Julie heard what she was dreading. The door began to ease slowly open.

One might wonder why she did not run screaming from the room at that moment, but Julie states that, with the opening of the door, a peculiar numbness crept over her, rendering movement impossible. She describes the feeling as similar to being conscious under anesthetic; her mind was alert but her body seemed paralyzed. The entity appeared to have the power to immobilize her from a distance.

Again she was aware of the vile odor suffusing the room. She heard the dull footfalls crossing the carpet. Moments later, the crushing weight was upon her; the stubbled cheek bore down on hers. She thought she would go insane. Her ordeal began anew, and the hours dragged past. At some stage, through terror-induced exhaustion, she blacked out.

She awoke in a worse state than on the previous morning. She was shattered, could barely speak. She made other arrangements for the children and went to see the family doctor. Although his practice was two streets from her home, Julie arrived there on the verge of collapse. She recalls that she had to stop twice on the way and lean against a wall for support.

As it was, the general practitioner confessed bafflement. He could find nothing physically wrong with her, though he was dismayed by her appearance; her two nights of terror and insomnia showed. She seemed to be teetering on the verge of a nervous breakdown.

She told him as much as she dared. To her surprise and relief, the doctor did not dismiss her story out of hand. On the contrary: he asked if she had ever had a brush with the paranormal. He wondered aloud if perhaps she might be "acting as a medium." She had been doing nothing of the sort—nor had she any wish to—she told him in no uncertain terms. In the end, he prescribed a course of Diazepam, and suggested that she keep up her prayers. There was, as yet, no talk of exorcism.

Julie returned home that day, invigorated by the doctor's support and sympathy. She commenced the course of antianxiety medication at once. She had hoped that they would help. In fact, things grew worse.

"My life and my home were never the same after that day," she says. "I felt uncomfortable, especially when I was alone. I began singing French songs and the French national anthem, even though I had never learned French. Every night I'd sit up as late as possible because I was so terrified of what was going to happen. Even when I tried sleeping in another room, it would still come for me. I hinted to a few friends that I was hearing things in the house. I asked if they believed in ghosts, that sort of thing. But I couldn't come right out and tell them.... I just *could not* bring myself to tell anybody, not even John, about the sexual assaults, about what was really happening to me. It was a living hell."

The months passed and the hauntings continued. Having her husband beside her at night helped somewhat. But John was no defense against the evil that lurked in the darkness of the bedroom.

"Through time, I was forced to accept my suffering. There was nothing else I could do. The more I prayed, the more I was tormented. If he didn't come for me before I fell asleep, I'd wake up to find him pressing down on top of me. He was determined that I had no peace, no peace whatsoever."

She was startled into wakefulness one night, as if from a "falling" dream. Dubois had changed tack.

"It felt as if an invisible fist was pounding my pillow," she says. "I can find no better way to describe it. The pounding was so fierce that my head was bouncing off the pillow. It went on for a whole minute, maybe two. Then it stopped altogether. I was asking myself if I hadn't dreamed the whole thing. So I tried to get back to sleep again; I was really tired. But whatever it was that was hitting the pillow obviously didn't want me to sleep, because the next thing I knew the bedclothes were whisked off me—in one fell swoop—and dropped at the foot of the bed."

It was the start of a new phase in the attacks. As time went by, the pounding on the pillow and the removal of the covers became such routine occurrences that they failed to unnerve her; she would simply leave the bed half-asleep and rearrange the covers.

Pierre Dubois had taken up residence in the Neville home. More odd things began to happen—occurrences that could not be explained away by logic or science. Lights would flicker for no reason; water taps would turn themselves on, then off. There were minor anomalies in her bedroom, little changes that only she would notice. She would sometimes find the items on her dressing table mysteriously rearranged. On several occasions she discovered her perfume hidden in a corner of the closet. One night she drew the curtains, went to the bathroom, and returned to find them pulled open again. The children began to complain of hearing mice in the night, but Julie was certain there were no mice in the house.

Often, when she had friends and neighbors over, they could very clearly hear floorboards creaking upstairs, as though somebody was walking about. The children heard the creaking too but, as is often the case with children, they got used to it, and to the other noises and unexplained presences.

Julie urged them not to speak of those things at school or elsewhere. It was bad enough that she was subjected to the disturbances and torment; the last thing she wanted was to attract undue attention to her family and herself. People do not, as a rule, react compassionately to reports of preternatural infestation; many tend to suspect that the victim has somehow, whether by word or deed, "brought it on herself."

It reached the point where Julie could no longer be alone in the house during the day. The uninvited "lodger" was no respecter of the daylight hours; he could appear at any time.

"I was faced with a choice," she says. "I could stay in the house and go out of my mind, or get out as often as I could."

She decided to go to work again, and found employment as a shop assistant. It helped.

But working by day served only to postpone the nocturnal ordeal; Dubois would be there on her return. In the evening, as soon as she turned the key in the front door, she felt that someone or something had been waiting for her. There was the pervasive smell of burning coal and a heaviness in the air.

Monsieur Dubois was watching her.

The years passed. The entity continued to keep its nighttime appointments with Julie. It was a battle she fought practically alone. She kept it from her husband; she kept it from her children.

It is interesting to observe how quickly the abnormal can become a commonplace in a person's life when paranormal activity takes hold. It seems that, as was the case with Julie, and in the absence of rational explanations or solutions, the beleaguered person is forced to accept this unorthodox situation and somehow learns to live with it.

"I know how strange that might seem to a lot of people," she says. "But, you see, I was prepared to put up with it because there seemed to be nothing else I *could* do. In the course of time I saw a pattern to it. Whenever I prayed really hard to be rid of Dubois, things would get worse and he'd attack me even more—try to suffocate me, or worse. Those times I didn't pray, I found that he'd be just a presence in the house. I'd hear him walking around upstairs, or sense him standing in the corner of the bedroom or on the landing."

Julie was coming to a better understanding of the entity's motives, what Dubois was trying to do to her. He was attacking her very faith.

"I know now what his plan was. That I'd give up my religion and go over to him. It took me a while to see this, even though all the clues were there. For long periods I stopped going to Sunday worship or saying prayers at all, simply to get some peace. Now I know that that's how demonic oppression works. By getting me to give up on God, the demon was priming me for something altogether more horrific, but I couldn't have known that at the time."

Julie's "more horrific" development occurred at the beginning of 1992. The manner of the haunting shifted dramatically. The experience left her with the conviction that Pierre Dubois was intent on much more than molesting her at night. He wished to possess her—body and soul.

A single incident was enough to convince her of this. One night, she awoke to the familiar pattern of oppression: the paralyzing weight, the obnoxious smell, the stubbled cheek. But this time there was an additional torment. A hand was tightening about her throat; she could barely breathe. Dubois was attempting to throttle her. Her battle with the entity had become a fight for survival.

Unable to move her limbs, she sought in desperation for sacred words that might thwart the demon. At last she remembered the prayer a Catholic friend had instructed her to say if she ever felt threatened.

The words came to her, but the pressure on her throat was so great that she could hardly give voice to them. "In...the name...of...of Jesus... *Christ!*" The pressure lessened. "Get out of my life!"

Sure enough, the exhortation proved to be very effective. Julie felt the fingers relinquish their stranglehold. She was free.

She gave thanks to God, convinced as she was that her speaking the name of Christ had saved her. At the same time, she knew from bitter experience that Dubois would not take her victory lightly. Sooner or later he would seek vengeance.

He did so within the hour—just when she thought the coast was clear and was drifting into sleep again.

This time, there were no footsteps, but a low "zooming noise," as Julie puts it; one that grew as it approached the bed. She remembers sitting up to investigate, only to be pushed back down again by a hand pressing against her chest. She was attacked again, not throttled, as before, but by increased pressure of the crushing weight upon her body. So great was the pressure that she was certain that the entity was trying to crush the life out of her.

The housewife had never been willing to fully face the true nature of the creature that called itself Pierre Dubois. A part of her had been willing to accept the lie it fed her: the story of the Frenchman and his concocted history, the ruse by which a malevolent force had inveigled its way into her home. Now she felt certain that "Dubois" had never walked the earth as a human being, never been a blacksmith, never drawn breath. He—*it*—was a demon. And now it wanted her dead, so that it could drag her off to whatever dark region it inhabited.

She summoned the strength to resist as best she could, willing her arms to move and to push the vile thing away from her.

"I'd never really feared death, but I did then," Julie says. "The terror of that, the fear, is impossible to put into words. I was fighting not only for my life but my soul as well. I was convinced that if I died, I'd be brought face-to-face with that thing that had tormented me for so many years. I'd be lost forever."

She pleaded with her Maker. "Dear Lord, don't let me die," she implored. "I don't want to see its face. Please, Lord, please!" Anything was preferable to that. Julie uttered one final, desperate entreaty.

"In the name of *Jesus Christ*," she cried out once more, as loudly as she could, "*get out of my life!*"

Again, the weight lifted from her, and again she braced herself for the counterattack.

Strangely enough, it did not come. She switched on the bedside lamp and sat up, gasping for breath.

"I dearly wished I had not put that light on," she says. "But by then it was too late."

A shadow was rearing up at the foot of the bed. Julie describes it as "a blob, like a smoking black cloud, not the shape of a person—just a thing, but a terrible thing. The absolute evil that came from it was overwhelming. I was so gripped with terror, I could not move, and I knew that if it came towards me I'd be swallowed up…destroyed, and that would be the end of me.

"Imagine what it feels like to know that you're going to be killed, and the person torturing you is deliberately making you suffer beforehand. That's how it was. I felt a level of fear that is beyond words. I implored the Lord to keep it away from me and, thank God, it stayed where it was. Then I heard the voice."

For the first time ever, her tormentor actually *spoke* to her. There was no French accent but plain English, as though the entity realized that the game was up, as though it knew that it no longer could hide behind the deception that it was the spirit of Pierre Dubois, once a living human being.

The male voice was hoarse, stertorous, angry almost.

"Be quiet!" it commanded. "Go to sleep."

Julie did exactly that. She was instantly asleep—chilling testimony to the control the demon had over her. When she awoke the next morning, however, it was with the possibility, and the hope, that the end of her long ordeal might well be in sight. She felt ready to finally speak of her torment to someone else.

She threw caution to the winds. She was past caring that the demon would exact vengeance if it thought it was threatened. She confided in the most devout believer of the family—her sister. Margaret advised her to see a minister at once. She persuaded her that an exorcism, carried out in the home, was her only recourse. Before Julie left, Margaret gave her a framed picture of Jesus with the inscription CHRIST IS THE HEAD OF THIS HOUSE, THE UNSEEN GUEST AT EVERY MEAL, THE SILENT LISTENER TO EVERY CONVERSATION. Julie hung it in her bedroom.

Having shared her burden with her sister, she felt some relief. She still could not confide in her husband but hoped that soon her troubles would be at an end. Margaret was eager to help her find a suitable clergyman. There were bound to be many, she said, who were proficient in the deliverance ministry.

"I was very much mistaken," Julie says. "I went first to my own minister. He told me he'd never done an exorcism, but he gave me the name of another man. I went to him, only to be told the same thing. I must have gone to five or six, and none of them felt able to help me. I really think when they heard what I'd come through, they were too afraid to even visit my home. Honestly, I was really beginning to despair."

During her search for a suitable exorcist, the siege of her home continued. The incursions could assume a variety of forms.

"There was one night in particular," Julie recalls. "I was on my own in bed again, and some sort of loud noise woke me up. I was only half-awake, wondering what the noise was. I don't know why but I thought it might have been a dog barking. I waited for it to bark again. But we had no dog; nor did the neighbors on either side. I told myself that I'd imagined it, closed my eyes, and tried to get back to sleep. Then I heard the sound again—the one that woke me up."

She knew at once that it was no dog, or indeed any earthly creature. Julie remembers it still with a bone-chilling clarity and dearly wishes that she could forget it—forget both the sound and the malignancy that pervaded the bedroom when it had died away.

"It was a man's laugh," she explains, "a horrible, mocking, evil laugh. It filled the room, but it was inside my head at the same time. I remember putting my hands over my ears to try and block it out, but that didn't stop it. I couldn't get out of the bed, I was just powerless to escape it."

In the dim light from the street, she saw, on the far wall, the picture of Christ given to her by her sister. It was hard to make out the features, but Julie had contemplated it so often while at prayer that she could call it unerringly to mind.

"I started to pray out loud to the image of Jesus," she says. "But Dubois was not amused."

The entity vented its fury in yet another demonstration of its power. As Julie concentrated on the face of Jesus, unseen hands gripped the picture, lifted it from the wall, and smashed it to pieces on the floor.

We have seen that, throughout the many years of her ordeal, Julie Neville had somehow managed to keep her children in the dark with regard to the demon Dubois. They were aware of *something*, of course—the noises and the taps turning themselves on and off were hard to ignore—but the two boys and their sister were never privy to what went on in their mother's room when she was alone.

"I could put up with the torture so long as it didn't go near the children," she says. "I knew deep down that I should never have allowed Gordon to play with the Ouija in the first place. And as a mother, I had to take responsibility for my son's mistake. I was paying the price, but I promised myself that if it ever *did* attack one of them, I'd have to take action at once."

Eventually, what she feared most came to pass. In the summer of 1994, John and Julie went on vacation with the younger children, leaving Gordon in charge of things.

He was looking forward to the freedom of the house and having his friends over. He was ill prepared for the phenomena he was to experience.

Gordon, now in his thirties, recalls that harrowing time.

"The first night wasn't so bad. I did feel kind of uneasy. I remember it being very cold, especially on the landing and in my bedroom, and turning up the heat. But I thought it was just me, being on my own in the empty house for the first time. On the second night I made the big mistake of sleeping in my parents' bedroom. I thought it would be more comfortable. Well, 'sleeping' actually isn't the right word, because I didn't get any sleep."

It started—as such phenomena often do—with an apparent accident, a fairly trivial occurrence as far as Gordon was concerned. A little wooden cross fell to the floor.

It had hung on the far wall, in the place left vacant by the picture of Christ, the one Dubois had destroyed. Gordon had not known of its existence. He would, in any case, have considered it to be no more than an item of idolatry; he was not a believer.

His mother had compensated for its loss with the cross, found when she cleared out the attic. Gordon had his back to it when it fell. It made only the dullest of *thucks* as it struck the carpet. He turned, bemused but by no means alarmed. Perhaps he should have been.

"The strange thing was," he says, "that when I went to hang it back up again, I discovered that it couldn't have just fallen unaided, because the nail that held it was still in the wall and the loop of cord on the cross wasn't broken."

Gordon got into bed.

"The cross shook me up a bit," he says. "But I told myself I was just being silly, and after a while I dozed off."

Not for long, though.

"I woke up because I heard this creaking sound coming from the wall on the left. My mother had a wardrobe on that side of the room, a big, heavy thing stuffed with her clothes and shoes and things. And there would have been a gap of about four feet between it and the bed. Anyway, I sat up to see what was going on and I just couldn't believe my eyes."

The heavy wardrobe appeared to be growing in size, its dark bulk rising toward the ceiling. Gordon, still drowsy with sleep, blinked to focus his eyes. Bafflingly, the wardrobe continued to grow. It was filling his vision. It was making noises too; they sounded, for all the world, like a great beast groaning in pain. And all at once he knew the truth. The wardrobe was not growing. It was toppling slowly forward, its triangular pediment seemingly set on a collision course with Gordon, *as if somebody was pushing from behind.* The groaning changed to a deep bass sigh as the wardrobe's feet gave way beneath the weight.

Gordon sprang from the bed. The wardrobe crashed down.

"I tell you, I never moved so fast in my life," he says with a shiver. "That thing was so heavy I thought it had crushed the bed itself. Later on, when I discovered what my mother had been going through for so long, I really freaked, because I realized that Dubois didn't like the fact that I had taken over her bed and was actually trying to kill me."

Gordon spent the rest of the week at a friend's house.

When Julie learned of her son's experience, she knew that she could no longer keep her secret from the family. If the demon could attack Gordon, then why not his brother and sister? She was greatly afraid for them. She called the family together and revealed all, for the sake of the children omitting the most disturbing details. Dubois had occasioned enough sleepless nights in the Neville household.

John Neville was shocked and horrified; throughout the long years of his wife's ordeal he had remained blissfully unaware of the demonic presence in his very bedroom. To be sure, he had suspected that all was not as it should be, but had attributed Julie's troubles to depression. He was determined that she suffer no longer. He joined her in the search for a churchman who could put an end to her misery.

One man's name kept coming to the fore—that of Canon William H. Lendrum. Those whom the couple spoke to were loud in their praise of this man's qualities. Their search seemed to have borne fruit. It was February 1995.

Finding the exorcist had proved easy; getting hold of him was another matter. Julie believes that shadowy forces were at work to thwart her, that Dubois was determined that the exorcist would not cross his path.

"I tried the canon's number every day for a week," she says, "but the phone just kept ringing unanswered. I checked with the operator, and I did have the correct number. But each time, it would ring out. The canon told me later that his phone hadn't been ringing at all at the times I said. He told me that this was a common feature in his experience. The evil spirit, knowing it's about to be cast out, will do everything to stop it happening."

Canon Lendrum proved to be a gentle, soft-spoken man, who received Julie with great compassion and understanding, putting her immediately at ease. He arranged to visit her home the following evening—and perform a deliverance. There would be no preamble, no more time wasting; she had suffered enough, and for far too long.

"I thought I'd feel great relief when I heard that," she says, "but instead I remember this feeling of absolute dread coming over me."

The canon appeared to read her thoughts. "Don't worry," he said, "your troubles will soon be over. Have faith. But yes, it most likely *will* step up its activities now that plans are afoot to cast it out."

Those words proved chillingly correct. On returning home, Julie was assailed by a terrible atmosphere in the house. The foul odor that had become synonymous with Dubois's presence was overpowering. The demon was indeed mustering its forces for the coming battle.

She threw open all the windows and started to clean the house, but the unpleasant smell persisted. Nevertheless, fortified by the canon's words, she determined that she would not be driven out of her home in broad daylight. When she had finished dusting, however, the stench was so overpowering that it made her sick. She rushed outside and retched. It took courage to return indoors. The last chore was the vacuuming.

But Dubois held a card or two in reserve, and was about to play one. Julie suddenly recalled the old dictum *Cleanliness is next to godliness,* and all at once she divined its deeper meaning. Dubois was about to show her its opposite. Before she could finish, the note of the vacuum cleaner changed eerily.

"It began to groan and squeal," she recalls, "like a trapped animal. It was horrible. I had no choice but to turn it off. When the kids came home from school, I phoned John at the hospital to tell him we'd all be staying with Margaret that night. No way was I going to risk it."

At eight the following evening, Canon Lendrum arrived at the Neville home, accompanied by two assistants. He remembers the expulsion of the demon that called itself Pierre Dubois as a trying affair.

"Having lived in Julie's house and oppressed her for so long, it felt it had the right to stay put. Always difficult," he says now, looking back.

We are having tea in the parlor of his south Belfast home. The jovial, octogenarian exorcist is the antithesis of the doleful demon hunter that Hollywood would have us believe is the norm. His spirited demeanor and optimism belie years of having fought and routed the darkest of foes.

"When these things manifest themselves," he continues, "they should be stamped out as soon as possible. The longer a person waits, the more entrenched the malignancy, and then the harder it is to shift."

The canon describes his encounter, beginning from the moment he arrived at the Neville house. When he entered, the oppressive presence was almost palpable.

"It was worse than I thought," he says. "There was a very peculiar atmosphere in the house. I suppose I would describe it as 'hostile.' The smell of burning and the coldness were very strong, especially on the stairs and in Julie's bedroom. But one's faith never wavers in a situation like that. The power of the Lord is always present."

Julie, her husband, and Gordon gathered in the living room for the ceremony. Brief introductions were made. It could begin.

Canon Lendrum donned his surplice and laid out on a table the sacred objects for the celebration of the Eucharist: a simple cross on a stand, the Communion paten, a chalice, two candles in silver holders, and a bottle of holy water.

"I hear the private confession of those who live in the house," the canon explains, "before the service begins. This is a very important part of the ritual. If anyone declines—and most especially the person who is being oppressed—it generally means that they have something to hide, and in all likelihood the exorcism will not be successful. In my experience, a severely demonized person will find the act of repentance very difficult, if not intolerable, and from their behavior you very quickly come to realize you're dealing with the exorcism of an individual, as opposed to a home."

"Thankfully, that was not the case with Julie," he continues. "She had been oppressed by that demon and suffered it so long that she was more than eager to be rid of it. She willingly rejected all associations with Ouija and the occult, and recommitted her life to the Lord."

Once Julie had formally, and in the presence of witnesses, re-dedicated herself to Jesus, Canon Lendrum was ready for the service of the Eucharist.

The group arranged themselves on a row of chairs facing a makeshift altar. The assistants sat on either side of Julie, with John and Gordon flanking them. The canon extended his hands over the Holy Book, and read from Luke's Gospel.

"The seventy returned again with joy, saying, 'Lord, even the demons are subject to us in your name.' And he said to them, 'I saw Satan fall like lightning from heaven. Behold, I have given you authority to trample on serpents and scorpions, and over all the power of the enemy; and nothing shall hurt you.'"

The canon joined his hands and bowed his head in silent prayer. The participants did likewise.

It had been raining steadily for most of that winter afternoon. Now the wind was up. It could be heard whistling and sighing at the window. Julie was reminded of a similar winter's evening all those years ago—an evening when a much happier but gullible young woman had placed her finger on a glass and allowed something unclean to intrude upon her life. She shivered at the memory and at what might lie ahead. Would the demon Dubois put up a fight, make her suffer further? Or would this kind man of God be able to drive the horror from her life for good?

Canon Lendrum blessed the bread and wine, and distributed them among the participants.

The Eucharist is an intrinsic part of an exorcism, the canon explains. Every Eucharist is a proclamation of the death and resurrection of Jesus. It therefore celebrates his absolute, complete, and total victory over Satan.

He returned to the altar and, extending his hands over the Holy Book, gazed heavenward. "Strengthened and refreshed by the Body and Blood of Christ, we are now ready to exercise the authority and power of Jesus Christ against whatever evil is disturbing this place."

The wind blew more fiercely at the window. It seemed to shriek and howl like a demented animal. Julie was reminded of the groaning sounds she heard coming from the vacuum cleaner the day before.

"But, strangely enough, when I heard it I wasn't afraid," she recalls. "I knew that God was in the room and I felt totally safe."

"We rejoice in your great love," the canon's voice rang out with confidence, "and in the victory of your son Jesus Christ over sin, death, and hell. We pray you send angels to gather to this place any spirits that may have been active here."

Overhead the lightbulb flickered, then dimmed. John kept his head bowed, too afraid to look up. Gordon, on seeing his father's response, likewise buried his face in his hands. Of the three, Julie was the one who remained calm. She sat with her hands folded in her lap, gazing serenely at the cross upon the altar.

"Spirit, I address you now in the name and with the authority of Jesus Christ," Canon Lendrum continued undeterred. "I have power to bind you and power to release you. I—"

The light went out. The room was in darkness, save for the candles on the altar. "I command you to go immediately to the place that Jesus has—"

Slowly, the door was opening. Gordon and John looked wildly about the room. On seeing that the others did not share their consternation, they bowed their heads again, a little embarrassed.

Canon Lendrum waited. One of the assistants went and shut the door. "I command you to go immediately to the place that Jesus has appointed for you!"

The wind stepped up its howling. The window blew open. Strangely enough, the candles did not die. Again, the assistant rose; he secured the sash. "You will go and you will not return to this place again ever. The angels appointed by God will take you to your own place and there you will remain."

The exorcist paused and bowed his head again. As he did so, the wailing at the window began to subside. The presence was departing. He spread his hands and gazed upward. "Father, we thank you that this spirit is now leaving and going to where you want it to be."

The light in the room flickered into life again. John and Gordon looked up with relief. They seemed no longer afraid. "We ask you to cleanse this house from all defilement, that it may become, for those who dwell here, a house of peace."

The canon sprinkled holy water at different points in the room. His voice was gentle, no longer that of the scourge of demons. "Send your angels to guard this house and protect those who dwell here. Unite them in love and draw them to yourself, so that they may rejoice in you as their Savior and Lord forever."

Even before Canon Lendrum had ceased praying, the atmosphere in the room was changing. An air of dread and danger was giving way to peace.

The service ended with the Lord's Prayer and prayers of thanksgiving. Afterward, the canon requested that the others remain kneeling while he and Julie went from room to room and he blessed the house.

Holy water is important to every exorcism. It is symbolic of baptism and the three benefits Jesus promises through its use: forgiveness of sins, defense against the wickedness of Satan, and the gift of divine protection.

"There was a strange thing when the reverend was blessing the kitchen," Julie recalls. "We discovered that the window above the sink was open. I was really uneasy when I saw it because I knew for certain I'd locked it. It was the same window that blew open all those years ago when me and the children were messing with the Ouija and Dubois told me to go and close it."

So what was the canon's reaction?

Julie smiles. "When I saw it I nearly jumped out of my skin, but he didn't even flinch. He just smiled and went and closed it again, and said something that really made me laugh: 'Well, that's the end of *him*, Julie. Pierre Dubois has left the building.'"

At a little after ten that evening, the exorcist and his assistants took their leave. All were conscious of a prolonged battle having ended, an evil firmly routed.

It was over.

The demon—the entity that complained of being tired of wandering and was in need of rest, the entity that had been to South Africa and was not wanted there, that had come to a town in County Antrim and for fifteen years held to ransom the life of a vulnerable, God-fearing woman—that terrible entity had finally departed.

One wonders where it went afterward, if it had indeed obeyed the command of the exorcist and returned to its "own place." Or if, once loose again, it felt free to roam. If perhaps, at some later date, another poor, unsuspecting individual, whether by chance or design, placed a planchette on a Ouija board—or a finger on an upturned glass—and in so doing gave refuge to the demon that called itself Dubois.

THE BOY WHO COMMUNES WITH DEMONS

⬥

When Gary Lyttle was ten years old, he met the Devil. To be sure, the Devil did not introduce himself as such, and the boy was too young to recognize him for what he was. Satan, the fallen angel of Revelation, is believed to come in many guises, assuming many names. Most churchmen hold that the Devil, the Adversary, presides over a host of lesser demons, and that each demon has its own diabolical attributes, its own means of corrupting souls. Whatever the truth, the following is an account of how an evil entity appears to have gained a foothold in a young boy's life.

Gary lives in a sleepy town in County Donegal. Not much happens there, which is no bad thing. There are no murders, rapes, or random acts of cruelty and mayhem. Senior citizens do not feel threatened, and the police are rarely called upon to investigate serious crime. The other side of the coin is that the town has little to offer an adolescent boy who craves excitement in his life.

In the spring of 2004, Gary was making his way home from school. As usual, he took a shortcut that follows an unpaved footpath, cutting under a bridge and leading along a small river, before joining another road. The path is in frequent use—by schoolchildren, young lovers, and the occasional angler trying his luck at the bream and carp that can still be found in the river, despite the light pollution generated by a chemical plant some four miles upstream.

Gary does not know why he chose to venture away from his customary route homeward, but had the distinct impression that something was "telling" him to leave the track and inspect a sandy patch of earth and undergrowth. There were objects strewn there, many unfamiliar. The fifth-grader thought at once of "treasure." Not treasure in the sense of booty, though—more the sort that enriches a boy's imagination. But a quick examination told him that he had chanced upon an illicit waste dump. It was not unlike the rubbish to be found in much of rural Ireland: broken household appliances, old shoes, items of clothing, and other detritus dumped by the inconsiderate. Somebody had buried the lot, but it seemed that another had tried to dig it all up again. It might also have been a scavenging dog, lured by an odor still clinging to a cooking utensil. Gary was disappointed.

Until, that is, his eye was drawn to what appeared to be a large rectangle of wood—a slim panel—half buried in the ground. He shrugged off his schoolbag and hunkered down to inspect his find. He frowned. It resembled some kind of household ornament, a picture done on wood. But it might equally well be a board game, he thought—one of the old-fashioned kind he had seen in a friend's house. He tugged at the panel and it came loose.

Gary was thrilled. It was a Ouija board. This he knew because he had seen them in movies. He recognized it by the arrangement of numerals and letters, the words YES and NO. It seemed to be very old and was decorated with engravings. There was a sun and a moon, both drawn "with funny faces." At the bottom of the board, to the left and right of the word GOODBYE, were "dark ladies." "There were two black babies floating behind them," Gary says, "and angels with wings."

The boy is unclear as to what happened when he pulled the board free of the earth. He claims that something "flew up in the air." But the object refused to obey the laws of physics; instead of falling to earth at once like a tossed stone, it remained suspended in the air for a few moments before floating gently down and settling on the board.

The object turned out to be the planchette, or pointer, belonging to the Ouija. It was made of the same wood as the board and shaped like a triangle with rounded apexes. There was a circle of clear glass in the center. Gary picked it up and wiped away the soil.

He returned his attention to the Ouija board, laying it flat on the ground. Carefully, he cleaned it of all traces of dirt, intending to bring it home with him in his schoolbag—if it would fit, that is. He glanced about him. He was alone by the river. By this time, all the other stragglers from school had disappeared; there was no sign even of a hopeful angler.

Then, without warning, as Gary sat innocently gazing at the board, something incredible occurred. He experienced what can only be called "a vision." In the earth beneath his feet he felt a violent tremor. When it ceased, he heard voices: men and women's voices moaning and shrieking under the ground. Some were crying out. "They were all shouting something like 'bim eye ah,'" Gary says. "Or it could have been 'bam eye ah.' I didn't know what it meant."

The boy was terrified and attempted to get up but instead was thrown back into a sitting position. He was being held captive for a reason. Slowly, the ground in front of him began to open up, and Gary found himself on the rim of an enormous cavernlike space. Down in its depths he saw a throne. There was a figure seated upon it, but Gary insists that "it wasn't the Devil," that it was an entity that would make itself known to him by and by.

But his attention at that moment was not on the enthroned figure, for from all parts of that great cavern, beings with wings began to rise. He identifies them as "demons." They were flying up toward him, hundreds of them. Even at that great distance, the boy could make out their eyes; all seemed to be focused on him, as though a signal had been given and all were launching themselves simultaneously into the attack.

It was an apocalyptic vision such as those experienced by mystics throughout history. In 1550, St. Teresa of Ávila (1515–82) recorded a scene displaying many similarities. No one can say with certainty where such visions emanate from—whether they are a by-product of our upbringing or memories of illustrations seen in sacred books, stained-glass windows, and the like. Or even, in Gary's case, images recalled from straight-to-video horror movies.

The last explanation would be perhaps the most obvious and plausible, were it not rendered null and void by what was to happen later that day. Gary tells how he recovered from his "trance," seeming to reawaken many minutes later in the same spot. There was no longer a fissure in the earth, no more moans and shrieks from souls in torment. There was only the Ouija board, lying where he had dropped it, amid the illegally dumped household garbage. He picked up his schoolbag and took to his heels, running home as fast as he could.

This is Gary's version of events. He is supposed to have fled the scene, leaving the board behind. But, as his account progresses, so also does the likelihood increase that he either took the Ouija board with him or concealed it by the river.

Gary arrived home in great distress, according to his mother, Jessica. He went upstairs to his room, and when he came down again a half hour later, he was still nervous.

"What's wrong with you?" she asked.

"Nothing."

"Don't tell me there's nothing, Gary. You're white as a sheet."

She had a thought. "Were you fighting with somebody? Is that it?" She inspected his face for bruises. It would not be the first time he had come home from school bearing the scars of "battle." Nothing serious; simply boyish exuberance. "Did somebody pick on you?"

"No. I'm going to do my homework."

He left the kitchen and she heard him climbing the stairs again. She was shaking her head in resignation when she heard a scream. It was so shrill and so unexpected that she hardly recognized it as having come from her own son.

She found Gary halfway up the stairs. He was gripping the rail as if his fingers were welded to it and staring open-mouthed. She had never before seen him look so terrified. Kelly, her eight-year-old daughter, was immediately at her side.

"Gary?" she called out.

But Gary seemed unaware of her presence. His eyes were directed at something at the top of the stairs. Whatever it was he was seeing, it was frightening him to such an extent that he could not move.

"What is it, Gary?" she asked again.

But he shook his head, refusing to answer.

His young sister giggled. Gary turned at the sound and fixed the girl with a look that Jessica had never seen before—at least, not in Gary. It was a look that took her back to the bad old days of her failed marriage, when her "differences" with her husband had become truly irreconcilable. It was a look of hatred and contempt, and it had no place on the features of a ten-year-old boy. She hardly recognized her own son.

Jessica is quick to point out that, in the past, Gary never gave her cause for concern. She was forever thankful that he had turned out so well, so "normal." To meet him is to confirm this seeming normality.

There is very little about Gary's appearance or demeanor that marks him as unorthodox, or even unusual; one could pass him in the street without a second glance. He is of average height, with green eyes and tightly cropped black hair. Already there is the promise of his growing into a handsome and athletic young man. He shares the interests of most seventh-graders. He enjoys football, is developing a liking for rock music, plays computer games, and watches DVDs whenever he can. Of the last, his tastes lean toward science fiction, as well as the gory and macabre—in his own words: "scary movies." Also in this respect he is no different from so many preteen boys.

For these reasons, Jessica had never considered her elder child "a worry." She was grateful that he had avoided bad company, had never been in trouble with his teachers; and there had likewise been no visits by police to report a misdemeanor—as was often the case with young boys in their housing development. Gary was turning out to be a model son; Jessica was proud of him, and not a little proud of herself too, for having done such a fine job in rearing him.

Now he seemed so different; she felt she no longer knew him. She glanced from one child to the other. Without knowing why, she took little Kelly roughly by the hand and rushed her back to the kitchen. Gary had frightened her, filled her with an inexplicable and nameless fear.

The little household fell back into its everyday routine. One week following the incident, Jessica had forgotten it, and Gary seemed to be his old self again. It was with great surprise, then, when Jessica heard the commotion from upstairs.

"Get the f*** out of here, Kelly! Get out or you're dead!"

She hurried up the stairs. On the landing, her younger child stood with tears flowing freely down her cheeks. She was nursing her left arm.

"What on earth …?"

"Gary twisted my arm," Kelly wailed. "He *hurt* me."

She found Gary in his room, sitting on his bed with his headphones on. He looked at her without interest. She raised her voice. He seemed to be defying her. She went to the bed. Gary must have sensed her fury because he snatched off the headphones. She could hear faintly the upper registers of a heavy-metal power solo.

"Did you hurt your sister? Did you twist Kelly's arm?"

"No." More defiance.

"She says you did." Jessica was unaccustomed to lies from her children. "What's going on, Gary?"

"Nothing."

She hauled him from the bed and marched him to the landing where Kelly still stood, tearful and nervous.

"Why did you do it?"

"She was annoying me."

"How, annoying you? She's never annoyed you before."

This was true. The two got on exceptionally well. The incident was a new development and Jessica did not like it one bit.

"Tell her you're sorry."

"I'm ... er, sorry, Kelly."

Kelly did not seem convinced. She was looking at her brother with something close to fear.

"Tell her it'll never happen again."

"It'll-never-happen-again."

But it did. Two days later Jessica heard another commotion from upstairs, and more wailing from Kelly. This time, Gary had punched her, almost dislodging the last of her baby teeth. It was about to come out anyway, and Kelly was expecting a bigger reward than ever from the tooth fairy. Instead she got *this*.

"What has gotten into you?!" Jessica screamed at her son.

As before, he glared at her in defiance. She lost her temper and did something which she seldom had to resort to. She slapped him hard across the face.

What next occurred astonished Jessica. Gary pulled back his fist and made as if to hit her. His face was dark with anger. She was genuinely frightened of him.

But the moment passed quickly. Gary relaxed and seemed to revert to his usual affable self.

It was a false dawn. The next morning at breakfast, Gary suddenly convulsed. In front of his startled mother and sister, he fell from his stool and onto the hard kitchen tiles. His limbs began to jerk violently, writhing and twisting like those of an upturned bug seeking to right itself. Within moments, the fit subsided and the boy went rigid, as though paralyzed; his eyes were staring straight up at the ceiling. He looked terrified.

"Gary!"

Jessica bent over him, cradling his head in the crook of an arm. His eyes were still open and staring; they seemed to be glazed over. She gently slapped his cheek. There was no response.

"Is he dead, Mommy?"

"Run next door to Mrs. Sharkey, will you, Kelly? Ask her to come quick."

The neighbor was there within seconds and was startled to see Jessica attempting to bring Gary around. There was no change in him.

"Has he fainted?"

"Yes. Can you call Dr. Flynn, Carmel?" Jessica pleaded. "Say it's urgent."

When the doctor arrived some thirty minutes later, there was still no change in Gary. He was reluctant to move the boy, fearing that any sudden motion might trigger a fresh seizure. At last he removed his stethoscope and turned to Jessica.

"I'll have to send him in for tests, Mrs. Lyttle."

"What is it? What's wrong with him?"

"I'm afraid I don't know. It could be a mild form of epilepsy, but it's too early to say. We'll know when we get him to the hospital." He looked at his watch. "My brother-in-law is the neurologist there. I'll call him now and make sure he's there to take the lad as soon as he arrives."

That day, Gary was subjected to a series of tests. They included a blood test to search for low blood sugar or even diabetes. The neurologist ruled out both. He considered the possibility that the boy might have a weak heart, but a cardiogram showed otherwise. Gary had a robust constitution.

There remained the final possibility: epilepsy. Jessica was truly alarmed by the prospect. Even though she knew very little about the affliction, she understood the dreadful implications. He was just a child; what sort of a future would he have? It was too hard to even think about.

There are two principal factors that can trigger epilepsy: it can be inherited or can result from brain dysfunction, commonly called a seizure. As far as Jessica knew, there was no history of epilepsy in her family; and it was likewise unknown in her ex-husband's line.

The neurologist ordered an electroencephalogram (EEG). If there were patterns of abnormal electrical activity in the brain—epileptiform abnormalities and the like—then epilepsy was a distinct possibility. The scan, however, revealed no such irregularities; the boy's brain was completely sound. An epileptic fit is usually of short duration, on average five minutes. Gary's lasted almost an hour. Epilepsy was therefore ruled out.

When he was discharged the following day, no one was any the wiser as to what had happened to him in the kitchen. He himself had very little memory of the seizure. All he could call to mind was being seized by a great fear. Then he blacked out, to regain consciousness in the hospital. He thought of it as a great adventure—especially the brain scan. He had likened the huge machine to something he had seen in an episode of *Star Trek*.

"Like the Borg were experimenting on me," he told his mother excitedly.

"If you say so, darling. You just try to rest now."

Understandably, Jessica was beside herself with worry. She suspected that something was terribly amiss with her son but could not even guess at the cause. Her thoughts returned to that day, two weeks earlier, when she found him seemingly in a trance, halfway up the stairs. She was not satisfied with the explanations he had given; she wished to learn the truth.

She waited until Gary had recovered from his ordeal and was back to normal—insofar as she could ascertain. School was out of the question; he would not return for another two weeks, on Dr. Flynn's orders.

"Gary," she began, "we have to talk, you and me."

She switched off the television, much to Kelly's annoyance. The little girl slunk off to her room.

"Gary, I want to know what happened that day—the day you saw something on the stairs. Would you like to tell me now?"

"It wasn't anything."

"Yes, it was. And I want to know what it was. When they were treating you at the hospital, Dr. Flynn asked me if you'd had this sort of thing before, and I told him about that day. He says the two things must have something to do with each other. Now, have they?"

Gary shrugged, unable to meet his mother's eye. She pressed on.

"Kelly says you have a new friend. Is that true?"

"Yes. And it's none of her business."

"Is that why you were fighting with her? That wasn't nice. You never used to fight with Kelly." She sat down next to him. "Who is this boy? Do I know him?"

"What boy?" Gary asked, in seeming innocence.

"Your new friend!"

"He's not a boy. He's a man."

Jessica swallowed hard. This was the last thing she wished to hear. Only that week there had been extensive media coverage of a child-abuse scandal in England. Thoughts of how an adult could manipulate a child—she remembered they called it "grooming"—were still strong in her mind. The reports had alerted her to the vulnerability of children; that it could happen to anybody's kids. Even hers.

"What's this man's name, darling? Do I know him?"

"His name's Tyrannus."

"Tyr— What sort of a name is that?"

"I dunno."

"Where did you meet this man?"

"At the river; it was the man I saw on the throne," he said, his words tumbling out in a torrent, "the one that was like the Devil, only it wasn't the Devil; it was Tyrannus. He was on the stairs, and he was huge; he was ten times bigger than me."

Jessica could only stare.

Tyrannus is not a name one comes across very often. One of the movies in the *Star Wars* series had a minor villain named Darth Tyrannus, and a recent television series set in ancient Rome featured a gladiator named Tyrannus. Jessica was familiar with neither character. To the casual eye, Tyrannus seems to contain elements of "tyrant" and "tyrannosaurus"; it could be argued that both words would hold a fascination for a ten-year-old boy. In fact, Tyrannus is a Latin name, derived from the Greek *tyrannos,* meaning "sole ruler." It is not difficult to see how "sole ruler" could come to mean "cruel despot," as *tyrant* does today.

In literature, we encounter the name in a play by the tragedian Sophocles: *Oedipus Tyrannus*. It is more usually entitled *Oedipus Rex* or *Oedipus the King*. What is not widely known is that a man named Tyrannus is mentioned in the New Testament. Paul the Apostle had been preaching in the city of Ephesus:

> But when divers were hardened, and believed not, but spake evil of that way before the multitude, he departed from them, and separated the disciples, disputing daily in the school of Tyrannus. (Acts 19:9)

This brief allusion is all we have to go on. There has been speculation as to who Tyrannus was, but it remains speculation; nothing about this Greek schoolmaster has come down to us. It might be thought that Gary had picked up the reference somewhere or other; Sunday school comes to mind. And it is a fact that the boy has a Protestant background.

Jessica recalled vividly that afternoon she found him frozen with fear, staring open-mouthed at something at the top of the stairs. He had spoken of the stairs again. She wondered if they held the key.

"So this Tyrannus was in our house, Gary?"

He nodded, increasing her fears.

"That day? The day you ..."

"Yeah. He scared me. He was *huge*. A big man, dressed in black, and he was covered in stuff."

"What kind of stuff?" she asked, not really wanting to hear the answer.

"Rotten stuff. All dirt, like he'd come out of the ground, and he had wounds and big cuts all over him, but he was laughing at—"

"That's enough!" she snapped. "You've been watching too many horror DVDs at my mother's. By heavens, I'm going over there tomorrow and—"

"No, Mommy!" Gary cried. "It wasn't the films; it was the Ouija board."

And then he told her of the board, of the entity on the throne, of how it seemed to have followed him home.

The more Jessica heard, the more troubled she grew. She wondered why Gary would suddenly invent such things. It was not like him. Her good sense advised her not to give his story approbation by appearing to believe it. An active imagination was all well and good, but this particular fantasy seemed downright unhealthy. She said as much to Gary, fed him a good, nutritious dinner with plenty of greens—on the doctor's orders—and banished the entire disquieting affair from her mind.

She consoled herself that the new "friend" was not the pedophile she had feared but a creature of boyish make-believe.

She wondered if "Tyrannus" was not a character in *Star Trek*, a "Borg"—whatever that might be.

Gary returned to school the following week. But he was not the Gary of old; he had altered radically.

Reports began to reach his mother of a change in his behavior, indeed in his general demeanor. She learned of bullying, of using bad language, of treating his teachers with gross disrespect. It was as though he had undergone a complete change of personality. She could not understand it, asked herself if she were to blame, if her parenting skills were faulty.

On the Monday following his return to school, he came home late again. It was October and the evenings were longer; it was dark by the time Jessica heard his key turn in the front door. She was torn between anxiety and annoyance. He should have known better.

His excuse was that he had been "fooling around" by the river. The river again! She demanded to know more but Gary refused to tell her. She had to reprimand him for swearing: "I won't have that kind of language in this house." Again he picked a fight with his unfortunate little sister.

Calm was eventually restored. Gary still had a lot of catching up to do, and she left him to his homework. But later that evening, as she was cleaning the bath, she heard Kelly call out from the living room. She sounded frantic. Jessica wiped her hands and hurried down, thinking that Gary had again attacked his sister. He had not.

He was again lying on the floor. His lips were blue, his eyes were glazed over, and his body was locked once more in the mysterious paralysis.

Again she called Dr. Flynn, and once again he hurried to her summons. He was in a quandary. He telephoned his brother-in-law at his home. The neurologist could offer little practical advice; the EEG had, after all, ruled out epilepsy, and the other tests showed that Gary was physically healthy.

"I'm afraid I can do nothing more with him, Mrs. Lyttle," the general practitioner confessed. "I'm going to have to refer him to a psychiatrist."

He saw her anxious look.

"Don't worry," he said. "I don't think there's a serious mental problem. It's probably the onset of puberty. Some boys react to it more strongly than others. All those hormones leaping about in there." He smiled. "Enough to drive anybody a little bit batty."

"But what about medication, doctor? Something to calm him down?"

"That's the very reason why I wouldn't like to prescribe anything of that nature. You never can tell with puberty. The wrong drugs could be disastrous. Besides, I don't believe in sedating children. As far as I'm concerned, parents who go down that road are giving up accountability. Antidepressants are no substitute for love and understanding, which is all a child needs."

And so began what would prove to be an extended course of psychiatric treatment. The therapist, a child psychiatrist and consultant to Letterkenny General Hospital, embarked on what she called "Gestalt" therapy. Dr. Sally Mulgrew wished to focus on Gary's "self-awareness." Jessica understood little of what the woman told her, Gary even less. But Sally was persuasive, and the boy seemed to take to her; there was an excellent rapport.

On her advice, Gary saw Sally once a week. Each session lasted a hour, and the therapist was happy with his progress. Jessica noticed the change too. He was returning to his old self, the sweet-natured Gary she knew.

It was therefore with great dismay that Jessica, in early spring, took a phone call from her son's headmaster.

"Gary's had an attack of some sort."

She feared the worst, sensing what was to come.

"You'd better come over, Mrs. Lyttle. It happened midway through a geography lesson." (Jessica, even in her anxiety, asked herself why the man deemed this an important piece of information.) "We've alerted his doctor."

As if that were not serious enough, Gary suffered a second seizure that very week. It came, as did the others, without warning. He was recovering from his ordeal at school and was stricken in much the same manner as before. With one important difference: this time, neither Jessica nor Kelly witnessed the seizure. It was Carmel Sharkey, the neighbor from next door, who reported it. She had been "babysitting" Gary while his mother went shopping.

"Jessica," she said when Dr. Flynn had departed, "you're not going to like what I have to say to you."

"Don't tell me any more bad news. I can't take it."

"No, dear, that's not it. I think you should take Gary to see a priest."

Jessica was stunned, as any mother would be. The neighbor was suggesting that her son was somehow *unclean*, in the biblical sense—touched by evil. No mother could countenance such a thing. The stigma is too great.

"What are you saying, Carmel?"

"For his own good. I think you know full well what I'm saying."

"Well, maybe I do. But Lord save us, Carmel, not a priest. He wouldn't go near a priest."

"How can you say that? Have you asked him?"

"I just know, that's all. Carmel, you're scaring me."

"You'll have to face up to it, though. That stuff you told me about the Ouija board—I heard about a woman in England who had a lad who was messing around with a Ouija board. All sorts of things began to happen. They're bad news, Jessica, so they are."

"Ah, please, Carmel! Don't start that old nonsense with *me*."

Jessica was accustomed to her friend's pietistic ways. She humored her, although privately she felt that Carmel Sharkey's devotion to statues was no better than the idolatrous practices of the more primitive African tribes. In the Sharkey home there were more statues to Christ and the Blessed Virgin than Jessica had seen in respectably sized churches. There was a bewildering assortment of effigies of saints, whose identities could only be guessed at. Carmel did not wear her faith on her sleeve; she decorated her home with it. Yet, in all the time that Jessica had known her, she had never once tried to impose any of her beliefs. Until now.

"Half the world doesn't think it's nonsense, Jessica," she said then, hurt.

"That may be, but I won't have the likes of Father Sheridan putting ideas into my son's head. I don't like that man. He seems to me to be too fond of the good life for his own good. Why would a priest need two cars anyway?"

"I wasn't thinking of Father Sheridan. There's a lovely old man I went to before. He's in a Cistercian monastery over in Tyrone. I'm sure you know it."

"I do."

"He's a healer. They say he—"

"Ah, please, Carmel!" Jessica cried again. "It's bad enough I'd take Gary to a Roman Catholic monastery, but to a *healer*. Come on. What is he, some sort of witch doctor, or what's this they call it—a shaman?"

Carmel was shaking her head with vehemence.

"Father Dominic is nothing of the sort. You'd like him, Jessica. He's a kind, gentle soul. And he's genuine." She took her friend's hand. "Do it for Gary. What have you got to lose?"

She made an appointment that day. A two-hour drive took them to the monastery on the shores of Lough Neagh. Gary said nothing as his mother parked the car close to a large and rambling Georgian building. Jessica was nervous as she pushed open a door that seemed to have been built for the passage of giants.

They found themselves in an echoing hall with a high ceiling, bare except for a long, pewlike bench, a table, and old portraits of popes upon the walls. There was a small room off the hall and a sign saying RECEPTION.

"We've come for Father Dominic," Jessica told a smartly dressed young woman.

Minutes later, the monk entered the hall by another door. He was a big man, bearded and dressed in the robe of the Cistercians. Jessica put his age at seventy or more. He barely looked at them as he crossed to yet another door. He pushed it open and beckoned.

But when all were seated in the little sitting room, Father Dominic showed himself to be the kindly soul described by Carmel Sharkey. He spoke softly, smiled a good deal, and did not pry into areas that were of little relevance. He listened to Gary's tale, eyes shut, nodding from time to time.

To Jessica's surprise, she heard her son speaking of matters he had confided to no one else. In the wake of his third seizure, she had sent him to stay with her mother for a few days. She recalled that he returned home, if anything, more nervous than he had ever been. He refused to be drawn out then, but now he was telling the priest what had befallen him. Jessica mused that Catholic confession must work in a similar way.

"I couldn't sleep at Grandma's," Gary was saying. "I kept seeing things."

"What sort of things?" Father Dominic asked.

"Bad things. Shadows. Big, black shadows."

"In your bedroom?"

"Yeah. I knew there was somebody there but I couldn't see him properly. He kept changing. There were noises too."

"In your room as well?"

"No," said Gary with determination. "They were all over the house. It was—"

"It's an old house, Father," Jessica said.

"I kept hearing them at night," Gary went on. "They were up in the ceiling and in the walls. Real scary stuff. Like there were animals there. But Grandma doesn't *have* any pets. I had to have the light on all the time."

Father Dominic had gone silent. Jessica saw that he was looking into Gary's eyes with consternation.

"Tell me about this Tyrannus," he said.

"He shows me stuff. He showed me what I'll be like when I'm grown up, when I'm twenty-eight or twenty-nine. I'm in an office with a big desk. Tyrannus says that if I come over to him I'll be very rich."

"'Come over,'" the priest repeated quietly.

"He says I'll have great power in the future. And loads of money. But I must do what he wants."

Let us examine Gary's account. He claims that Tyrannus showed him his future as an adult. Evidently Gary was to become a successful businessman. That, in itself, is most unusual. When small boys dream of their future they do not see themselves sitting in offices. Offices are boring. They see themselves as major-league football players, or rock stars, or astronauts—the glamorous jobs. Gary's account is without doubt highly unorthodox.

Having listened to Gary's story, Father Dominic took the boy's wrist firmly in his big hand. From a pocket of his habit he drew out a small object: an oval-shaped silver casket with a glass window. Behind the glass a fragment of something old and yellowed was visible. Jessica knew it to be a relic; Carmel had several. The priest pressed the little casket lightly to Gary's brow and murmured a prayer.

Next, he taught the boy to say another prayer. It was framed in simple words that a child would have no difficulty remembering. Before they left, he took Gary's mother aside and gave her a leaflet containing a simple prayer to be said daily.

"I think you should know, Mrs. Lyttle, that you did well to bring the boy to me today. I don't like what I see in him. There's evil at work, I'm afraid."

Jessica was stunned by his directness. She fumbled for words, unwilling to accept that Carmel had guessed the truth and that the monk was confirming it.

"But he's only a child, Father."

"Indeed. Children know the difference between good and evil by an early age. Five or six, mostly—if not before. Your son is choosing evil. He is entertaining this 'demon.' I've seen its like before and I know it for what it is."

She turned to look at Gary. He was still seated on the chair that was too high for him, legs swinging in impatience as his eyes roved the dark paneling of the room and its somber paintings of ancient martyrs. Evil? She saw no evil there.

"He's going to have a very difficult and painful life if he doesn't resist this thing now," the priest said. "It's imperative that he fight it, and you have to help him in that fight."

His words dismayed Jessica. But she was angry, too, at the ugly picture being painted for her. In what was becoming a perverse situation, she felt the need to assert what *she* believed.

"Listen, he's fantasizing!" she said defiantly. "Nobody believes in demons anymore. We live in more modern times, Father."

"Indeed," Father Dominic continued calmly, "but I assure you they are not a fantasy. The Devil and his fallen angels exist, whether you believe in them or not. Not believing in evil means you are not armed against it. For whatever reason, your son has become a prime target. God is requesting that you turn back to him. It is up to you to help Gary come to this understanding."

Jessica felt defeated, hopeless. She wanted to cry.

"I want you to promise me something," the priest said gently, sensing her despair.

"Yes, Father?"

"I want you to promise me you'll have him say those prayers to the Blessed Mother every day. She has such great power over the evil one," he added enigmatically. "She'll protect you. Prayer is the only way to fight against this. And I want you to bring Gary to see me again. Shall we say this day fortnight?"

Jessica agreed. By the time they got home again, she felt that she needed a strong drink. She had much to mull over, and most of it was decidedly unpleasant.

Under his mother's supervision, Gary recited twice a day the short prayers that Father Dominic had taught him. He continued to visit the hospital in Letterkenny, and Sally reported steady progress. Jessica brought him to see Father Dominic again, and continued to do so every other week. After each visit it seemed that a little more of Gary's old self was being returned to him. Jessica felt that a bleak period was ending, that whatever it was that had come into the boy's life was leaving him in peace.

But Gary skipped his prayers one day, and another day soon after, and before long he had let the habit slide. Jessica had never held with prayer at the best of times, and perhaps for this reason did not mind too much. And everything was fine again, was it not?

She had lulled herself into a false sense of stability, so much so that when the next untoward manifestation took place, she found herself totally unprepared for it. It happened one evening as Kelly and Gary were doing their homework. Once more, it was Kelly who alerted her.

"Mommy, Gary's going all funny again!"

She turned, to find her elder son staring into the middle distance, seemingly oblivious to his surroundings. His left hand was moving rapidly over his copybook. That was the first indication that all was not well.

Gary is right-handed.

Jessica watched with astonishment and a creeping disquiet as her son's pen traveled over the page. The words he was writing—though English they were—made no sense at all.

"What's he writing, Mommy?" Kelly asked nervously, sharing his mother's unease.

"I don't know.... Gary?"

Gary did not reply but continued to write frantically. Then all at once he stopped. His body seemed to relax and he calmly turned to the next page. Jessica went to snatch the copybook away, but before she could reach it, his body had tensed again and the frantic writing continued. She tried to lift his wrist, but was shocked to discover that his arm and the hand that held the pen were quite immovable, as if "made of rock."

She watched in horror as the writing, clear and then illegible by turns, started pouring out filthy words and phrases that had no place in a ten-year-old's vocabulary. There were drawings too: little designs resembling signs of the zodiac and five-pointed stars. She knew they were not idle doodles but had darker connotations.

In such a bizarre situation, she did the only thing she could. Grasping Gary around the waist, she pulled the chair from under him and hauled him away from the table. Incongruously, his body remained in a rigid seated position as though the chair were still in place, while the hand clutching the pen continued to make frantic writing motions in midair. Jessica lowered Gary to the floor. He collapsed, seemingly in a dead faint.

"I was sick with worry," she says. "It was too much to take. I never saw the like of it. I couldn't understand any of it; it was crazy. I thought Gary was going to die. But a few seconds later he was all right again. He opened his eyes and looked around. The first thing he said was, 'What happened, Mommy?' He didn't remember a thing. Nothing."

Jessica tore the pages from the copybook, ran into the living room where a fire burned in the grate, and tossed them onto the coals. She averted her eyes as the pages burst into flame. She could not bring herself to look at the strange lines written by her son's hand. Nor did she wish to know where the garbled words and sinister pictographs had come from. Of one thing she was certain: they had not come from Gary; the words had not been his. More unnerving still, the handwriting had not resembled her son's. It was too elegant, as if from the hand of an artist.

When she returned to the kitchen, Gary was again seated at the table, wearing the same glazed look. She shook him; she was angry. He seemed to come to his senses. But then he looked her in the eye, and Jessica will never forget his words, so utterly out of character and so unexpected were they.

"*F*** you*," he spat and ran from the house.

Jessica believes that her mind was fully made up at that moment. She was finally acknowledging that she was up against a very powerful force, one that could induce a sweet, mild-mannered fifth-grader to change utterly. The change was frightening. Jessica had feared it before; now she was in holy terror of it. She asked herself what could happen next.

She thought of God. Her visits to Father Dominic in his monastery had, to an extent, turned her thoughts to the Lord, yet she had to admit to herself that it was a deity unfamiliar to her. The monk's religious world, with its statues and incense, was not the one she had known as a child. She told herself now that it was silliness, that God did not change but his worshipers did. Christ was Christ, whether worshiped in a vast, thronged Roman basilica or in a plain and unadorned Lutheran chapel.

But these were rational considerations. Her heart told her that she must seek out the help of a priest of her own faith. She withdrew to the quiet of her bedroom, picked up the phone, and called John Ashwood, an Anglican vicar.

He came to visit her that same evening. He was sympathetic on learning of her difficulties and at once recommended the services of an exorcist.

"What!" She was incredulous. "Are you telling me Gary needs to be *exorcised?*"

"I do. From what you tell me, it sounds as if there's an unclean spirit at work. I'm not saying that it's controlling Gary; I'm saying that it's influencing him in some way. And it's time to send it back to where it came from before it does any more mischief."

Her son needed an exorcism. She turned the curious word over in her head. Its associations seemed too outlandish by far. But she had to face facts and take the minister's advice seriously.

"All right, Vicar," she said at last. "If you think it'll help Gary. When could you do it?"

"Not me. I haven't the experience. But there's a good man who does: Canon Lendrum. He's retired now but still very active with deliverance." He patted her wrist. "Leave it to me. I'll get in touch with him. If anybody can help, it's William Lendrum."

Jessica and her son arrived by taxi at the Lendrum house in south Belfast on a wet, March afternoon. It was Gary's first visit to the city. From the bus he had seen the twin cranes in the old Harland & Wolff shipyard, "David" and "Goliath." They loomed majestically on the skyline, bright yellow against the gray. He wished to go there at once, see the giants close up. "Later, dear," his mother promised him. There was more urgent business to attend to.

Canon Lendrum studied the boy—perhaps the youngest "visitor" he had ever welcomed into his home. He hesitated before thinking of Gary Lyttle as a demoniac, one suffering from demonic oppression. During his long ministry he had encountered several such unfortunates. None had appeared as normal—or as bright—as did Gary.

He impressed the canon with his spontaneity and precociousness. He answered all questions put to him seemingly without guile. There was no sign whatsoever of the willfulness that Reverend Ashwood had spoken about on the telephone, and certainly no trace of the bad language. Gary seemed to him to be a well-adjusted boy.

"So you haven't been to school lately?" he said.

"No, Mr. Lendrum."

"How long is that now?"

"Three months."

"Three months tomorrow," Jessica said. "I daren't send him back. They think he's a lunatic or something. It's very trying."

"I've no doubt." He turned back to Gary. "Your mother tells me you fight a lot with the other boys."

"They're always picking on me. They call me names."

"What names might they be?"

"They call me a devil."

"But you're not, are you?" the canon said with smile. "You're a good boy."

Canon Lendrum did not doubt it. What he saw before him was a boy of ten, dark-haired, good-looking—as normal a youngster as one could hope to meet.

"I was struck by the way he answered my questions," he tells us. "Gary was confident, intelligent, articulate, and in no way intimidated." And seemingly guileless, too—until, that is, one looked into his eyes.

The canon finds it difficult to put certain matters into words. Not that he is short on descriptive powers; he is an excellent eyewitness with seemingly flawless recall. Yet he is unable to portray in full what it was he saw that day when he met Gary's gaze. The closest he can come to an adequate description is that the boy's look was "old beyond his years—older than mine even, and I'm eighty-two."

The canon can only describe the phenomenon in terms of emotion, for he is speaking of something that he believes lies outside the world of rational thought, beyond the human. He is convinced that, for a moment at least, it was not *fully* the boy who gazed back at him but a part of another personality entirely. For want of a better name he calls it "Tyrannus," and he believes it was the demon that was seeking to dominate the boy. (He is careful to avoid the word *possession*, preferring to speak in terms of *control* or *affliction*.)

But the moment passed and Gary was "himself" again. The canon continued as though nothing untoward had occurred.

"Tell me about the Ouija board," he said. "Where is it now?"

"At the river."

"Really?" It seemed unlikely.

"I hid it."

"Do you still play with it?"

"Yeah."

"Often?"

"Two or three times a week. It tells me stuff."

"Stuff?"

"Yeah, about how I'll be when I grow up."

"Tell the reverend about the Bible, Gary," his mother prompted.

"It says I shouldn't read it. It says it's rubbish."

"Mmm. How does it do that? How does it tell you these things?"

The canon had chosen his words with care. He knew as well as anybody that Ouija does not make pronouncements of its own accord but simply replies to questions asked of it. He wondered about the nature of the question that had elicited the condemnation of the Bible. Gary's next words supplied the clue.

"I ask it questions the voice tells me to."

"Whose voice?"

"The man's. Tyrannus. He says that I shouldn't go near a church. He says bad things'll happen to me if I do. And he says I should stay away from the Bible."

"Does he indeed? And do you agree with him, Gary?"

"I don't know."

"Answer me this, Gary: do you want to be free of this evil?"

"Yes, Mr. Lendrum. I do. But Tyrannus doesn't want that. He says if I don't do what he says he'll make me feel so bad that I'll want to kill myself."

"Never mind what Tyrannus wants, Gary. It's what *you* want that matters."

"But he can stop me doing what I want."

"Only if you allow him to."

Canon Lendrum rose then and crossed to a little table by the window. On it were his Bible and a cross attached to a weighted base. Taking the book, he went to Gary and stood over him.

"I can take away any power that this 'man' has," he said.

Suddenly Gary shrank back. He looked distressed.

"What is it?"

"He's laughing," the boy said. "I can hear Tyrannus laughing. He's laughing at *you*, Mr. Lendrum."

"Pay no attention, Gary. Put your trust in the Lord Jesus Christ."

Canon Lendrum held his palm aloft. He raised his voice.

"I bind you, in the name of Jesus Christ, and by the power of the Holy Spirit, I strip you of your influence over this child!"

Gary began to shake. His mother, who was well used to his making jokes, at first mistook it for laughter. And in a sense it was. But the laughter was not Gary's; later he would say that it was "Tyrannus" laughing and trying to induce Gary to join with him in the laughter, to show him the absurdity of this elderly ecclesiastic with his Bible and his medieval beliefs. But Gary says that at that point his overriding emotion was one of fear.

The laughing of the demon ceased. The boy had stopped shaking. His eyes were shut.

"It's up to you now, Gary," the canon said. "*You* have to make the decisions now, you understand? No one else."

Gary said nothing.

"You must ask Jesus to help you."

"Say it, Gary," his mother instructed. "Do what Reverend Lendrum says."

It was clear to the canon that Gary was unused to prayer. Nevertheless, the boy joined his hands as instructed, shut his eyes, and spoke in a loud voice.

"Please help me, Jesus!" he cried.

"Very good," said the canon. "Now, repeat after me: I put my trust in you, Jesus ..."

"I put my trust in you, Jesus."

"... and I invite the Holy Spirit into my heart and into my life."

"I invite the Holy Spirit into my heart and into my life."

Gary opened his eyes. Did Canon Lendrum see within them a normal ten-year-old, free of that entity he had witnessed earlier? He is not certain. But there was one more thing the boy must resolve to do, one final act that would serve to ensure his deliverance.

"Gary, I want you to go with Reverend Ashwood and find that Ouija board. Will you do that for me?"

The boy nodded.

"Then I want you to burn it. Is that clear? I'll be giving Reverend Ashwood a call next week, and I want him to tell me that the board has been burned."

"It will be," Gary assured him.

But Gary failed to keep his word. When Reverend Ashwood accompanied him to the river, there was no sign of the Ouija board. Either it had gone missing or Gary had secreted it in another place. Either way, Gary was not saying.

A week later, his grandmother started experiencing paranormal activity in her home when Gary stayed over. It took the form of strange noises and shadowy manifestations; they were present in his bedroom and in other parts of the house. They caused the grandmother so much distress that she too submitted herself to a rite of exorcism with Canon Lendrum.

At this point in time, in 2007, Gary's mother seems powerless to effect any change in her son's behavior. It would appear that she has relinquished control of her son. She prays for him and clings to the one positive note in Father Dominic's assessment. "Gary is very special. Some of our greatest saints suffered frequent attacks from the Devil so that their souls might be purified. God is testing him."

The priest might well have had St. Teresa of Ávila in mind when he said that. Certain aspects of the life of the sixteenth-century Spanish mystic who founded the Discalced, or Barefoot, Order of the Carmelites show interesting parallels with young Gary's experiences.

She was shown visions of hell, saw demons of "abominable form," heard voices, suffered severe mental anguish, and had frequent seizures, which could last longer than an hour. About one such seizure she wrote the following:

> On another occasion the Devil was with me for five hours, torturing me with such terrible pains and both inward and outward disquiet that I do not believe I could have endured them any longer. The sisters who were with me were frightened to death...for the Devil had made me pound the air with my body, head and arms and I had been powerless to resist him. But the worst thing had been the interior disquiet. I could find no way of regaining my tranquility.

When we spoke with Gary, we inquired about his continued use of the Ouija board. It is understandable that he should try it once, particularly as he had discovered it in such unusual circumstances; it was less clear why he should have gone back to it again and again, given the mischief it caused. Gary made the same reply each time: "I was bored."

Preteen boys should not be so jaded by life. Yet Father Dominic suspects that Gary's boredom is a symptom of our times. It is a topic he has touched on more than once. "In the past, religion created a moral code of ethics and acceptable modes of behavior in society," he says. "Twenty years ago children knew right from wrong. Today, self-interest dominates our thinking, and moral criticism is considered old-fashioned, so that children are allowed to do whatever they please and therefore have no defenses against evil. How else do you explain the rise in binge drinking, drug addiction, teenage pregnancy, and violent crime? How else do you explain the anarchy in schools, the lack of respect?"

"Oh, the Devil is very clever in his methods," he goes on to say. "By making God look archaic and outmoded, he creates a vacuum in the lives of the susceptible, which he, the Enemy, can then move in to fill."

The word *vacuum* is interesting in this context. We never learned what first led Gary to become so frustrated and tired of life. As outsiders, there were only so many personal questions we could ask. But it is clear that his boredom was born of a need for diversion; there was a vacuum that needed filling.

"Grown-ups have no end of diversions these days," Father Dominic says. He sighs. "At times I think half the world only wants diversion. I know this sounds like preaching, but I wouldn't be the first priest to say that the Devil makes work for idle hands. I see the truth of that in the rise in drug abuse, alcohol abuse, pornography, violence. It all starts as diversion, a way to relieve boredom."

"Children don't have these things, but they do have magic," he says. "They love magic tricks. Show a boy a bit of magic and his boredom lifts immediately. So what better way to ensnare a little boy than to show him *real* magic?"

When Gary unearthed the board by the river that day, and saw the planchette leap into the air, he could have run away. He chose not to. It was magic. By tarrying to see what would happen next—to see what the conjurer had up his sleeve—he showed himself to be receptive, and thereby exposed his vulnerability.

Father Dominic and Canon Lendrum are agreed that the processes of oppression and possession can only be understood in retrospect and verified by those individuals who have undergone successful exorcisms.

The process of surrendering to evil is twofold. First, the mind must be rendered receptive; the will then becomes amenable to acting upon that which is being offered.

Enter the Ouija. Elsewhere in this book we examined the disturbing repercussions of the "game," principally the case of Julie Neville, the County Antrim woman who was tormented by a demon for fifteen years. There are a great many such tales of misadventure. For instance, it is not widely known that the "talking board" figured large in the true-life case on which William Peter Blatty based his novel *The Exorcist*. The demonized youngster was in reality a boy named Robbie, and the exorcism took place in 1949 in his hometown, Cottage Hills, a small community in the state of Maryland. The boy was thirteen at the time.

The family was from St. Louis, Missouri, and an aunt would visit from time to time. She was a medium who, among other things, used the Ouija board extensively to contact the spirit world. Robbie learned the "art" from her and continued to employ it without adult supervision. When his aunt died suddenly in January 1949, the boy tried to communicate with her. That was when the manifestations—which would lead to his demonization—started in his parents' home. Minor and seemingly innocent at first, they grew in time to be unmistakably malignant.

This appears to be a common pattern where the Ouija is concerned. Most modern commentators on the use of the boards will warn that they should be approached with extreme caution. One churchman likened playing Ouija to allowing a child to build sand castles on a beach primed with land mines. The sensible advice is perhaps to avoid the Ouija altogether. The boards have too much unfortunate history.

It was not too long ago that the board was freely available in Ireland. The producer of the most popular version was the Waddington toy company, based in Leeds. But the company withdrew it from the market in 1970, principally because of a petition drawn up by a number of Christian churches. It was found to have disturbing effects on those who used it. At the time, the Reverend George Tarleton of South Woodford Congregational Church, London, voiced the concerns most vehemently. "Ouija always affects a person spiritually," he stated with conviction. "*Always*, without any shadow of doubt."

A Leicester toy manufacturer took over the distribution of the controversial board game, despite the protestations of British clergymen and concerned parents. There were calls for it to be banned, especially when a survey taken by a Leicester vicar, the Reverend Peter Anderson, revealed that 80 percent of the schoolchildren interviewed had consulted Ouija at one time or another. He pointed to a tragic case of a young boy who threw himself from a fire-station tower following extended sessions with the board. The dead boy's father subsequently left home, and his mother was declared insane. It was revealed that both had consulted the Ouija on numerous occasions.

The British tabloids had a field day with the sensational findings, and it was not long before the Irish media picked up the story. The resulting furor, while not leading to an official ban, ensured that Ouijas in any event disappeared from toy stores. The "game" had lost all pretense of innocence.

It was going to fall out of favor anyway. By the mid-1970s, few boards were being produced in Ireland and the United Kingdom. Grown-ups and children were making alphabets from pieces of paper instead and using an upturned glass to move between the letters. It would not be until the 1990s that the traditional "talking board" began to make a comeback.

The board had a less stormy history in the United States. From the time it was patented, in 1891, it was popular, both as an aid to divination and as a game. Two world wars helped to stimulate its popularity as a "spirit" medium—understandably when so many young Americans were in deadly danger a long way from home. Parker Brothers bought the patent in 1966, as well as the rights to the name. In the present day, the "official" board is made by Hasbro, Inc., and marketed throughout the world.

With the turn of the millennium, a new generation would come to recognize the Ouija from its recurring appearances on the big screen. Among them was Gary Lyttle. Those who approach his story with the intention of obtaining evidence of falsehood or fraud, however, may well come away empty-handed. Though it is true that Gary *might* have been acquainted with the case of Robbie "Doe," the boy who inspired *The Exorcist*, it seems unlikely. Book and motion picture date from the 1970s. Nor is it likely that he could have faked what was to follow.

The name "Ouija," assigned by a man who marketed an early version of the board, was derived from the Moroccan city of Oujda. But it was not long before a different explanation entered the public domain: that the name was a juxtaposition of the French word *oui* and the German *ja*, translating to "yes, yes." It is a fitting interpretation, for it suggests that each time the board game is played, the participant consents to accept whatever may intrude. And he agrees to accept the consequences of having made the invitation—for good or ill. In so "consenting," Gary Lyttle unwittingly opened the door to Tyrannus. Now he seems unable to free himself of what appears to be a baleful, subjugating influence. Thus are circuits of dependency created.

The longer this state of affairs is tolerated, the harder it is to dismantle it. Often, when attempts are made by the victim to renege on his former decision and escape the nightmare, tremendous pressure is brought to bear by forces outside or within himself. They frequently take the form of terrifying visions, inner voices, physical torments, and thoughts of death as being the only means of escape.

At the time of *The Dark Sacrament* going to press, Gary appears to have his demons still. He fears them and appears to be in thrall to them—perhaps in the old, literal sense of the word. To be "enthralled" meant to be under the control of another; it was sometimes applied to the victims of witches and sorcerers. In exceptional cases, it was applied to the victims of demons.

No one but Gary has ever seen—or heard—the demon who calls himself Tyrannus. It would be easy to dismiss him as a figment of a youngster's active imagination, an imagination fed on a diet of cheap Hollywood straight-to-video motion pictures. More difficult to dismiss are Gary's seizures, witnessed by members of his immediate family and his doctor. Neither a neurologist nor a Gestalt therapist could find a satisfactory reason for them, either physical or psychological.

There are very disturbing signs that point to a problem of a spiritual nature. Gary has now developed a full-blown hatred for anything sacred. Nothing will induce him to enter a church; he has stopped praying. He suffers from depression and has suicidal thoughts. He attacks those closest to him. He seems "content" to be in the company of his demon, or demons.

Those clergymen involved in the exorcism and deliverance ministries speak with one voice with regard to the amendment of one's life and repentance. "The hardest part for me," an exorcist tells us, "is that which comes after the exorcism, when I must impress upon the delivered person the need to turn to the Lord for guidance and to lead a better life. Someone who hasn't been brought up with God-centered values really cannot appreciate the importance of prayer and repentance. In that sense, they truly are lost souls. In such circumstances, there is nothing much an exorcist can do."

"Gary must desire to be delivered of his 'controllers,'" Father Dominic stresses. "If he chooses to hold on to them, there is little point in prayers said by me or anybody else." As long as "Tyrannus" holds the reins, he concludes, no other power can intervene.

THE UNQUIET SPIRIT
OF CHILD SARAH

❖

The little gift store was about halfway along a line of shops, sand-wiched between a fashion boutique and an upscale bakery. Stepha-nie Rooney, a petite twenty-four-year-old, had not noticed it before; her trips to Derry rarely brought her to that part of town. She was curious. She was also fired up by the acquisitive passion of the new homemaker, never letting pass an opportunity to add to her growing collection of bric-a-brac. She pushed open the door. She was half-expecting the jangle of an old-fashioned shop bell—it was that kind of place—and was delighted instead by the melodious tinkling of what could only have been Tibetan wind chimes.

The store's interior was heavy with cinnamon, vanilla, apple, lavender, and a myriad of other luscious scents. Stephanie hardly noticed them at first because there was so much to please the eye. There were statuettes whittled from dark wood, each with the like-ness of an African deity; there were elaborate carvings from South-east Asia showing elephants intertwined with luxuriant foliage. She marveled at crystals and hefted small Chinese spheres that seemed to hum with esoteric music.

Then the burlap bags caught her eye.

They were ten in number, and each was no bigger than a grocery bag. Each was unfurled to reveal its contents of wooden marbles, smaller than ping-pong balls. As Stephanie drew closer to the bags, she realized that the scents that had so delighted her emanated not from potpourri, as she first thought, but from those curious little wooden balls.

"They're a popular line," the assistant told her. "Especially the strawberry. I have them all over the place at home."

Stephanie picked one up and held it under her nostrils.

"They're divine," she said.

"Buy ten, get two free," the girl told her. "I forgot to put the sign up this morning."

"In that case I'll take a dozen of the strawberry," said Stephanie, counting them into a tiny wicker basket provided for that purpose. She brought them to the counter.

"Hmm, you've got thirteen here," the assistant said with a smile.

"Oh, right. Sorry."

"Oh, don't worry about it. Sure we won't quibble over one extra. You can have it for luck. Isn't that what they say—thirteen, lucky for some?"

"Thanks very much," said Stephanie. She fished in her purse for some small change. "Yes, we can all use a bit of luck, can't we?"

She was still musing on luck and its many and varied interpretations as she emerged from the little gift store. Stephanie considered herself a very lucky woman at that time, on Tuesday, September 16, 2003. The sun shone brightly on the city of Derry, and the carefree post-office assistant was enjoying a free afternoon. She was happy. Just six months married and already occupying a brand new home (or "desirable residence," as her mother called it) on the outskirts of town, she felt that life could not get much better.

Her priorities had shifted since she and Declan had moved into 8 Cedar Close, Dungiven. There had been a time when much of her income went to clothes, makeup, and evenings out; now all her spare cash went toward making her new home as cozy and attractive as possible. She thought a bowl of the scented balls would look pretty on the hearth and create a lovely perfumed atmosphere in the living room. It was, after all, the room where she and her husband spent much of their leisure time.

She found a porcelain bowl, a half-forgotten wedding gift from a young niece, dusted it off, and arranged the scented balls. She placed them on the living room hearth, stood back, shut her eyes, and reveled in their fragrance. Their magic, she thought, was working already.

Declan noticed the wonderful scent as soon as he came home. He thought his wife was baking a strawberry pie or making a dessert of some kind, until she explained about her little purchase and brought him into the front room. He nodded his approval.

"Hmm, that's odd," said Stephanie, puzzled. Three of the scented balls were lying loose on the hearth. "I put them all in the bowl. I know I did."

She shook her head, scooped up the stray balls, and held them out for Declan to savor. "Smells good enough to eat," he said. "Now, what's for supper? I'm starving."

But how, Stephanie was asking herself, did the scented balls get out of the bowl? They had no children, no pets. She thought of mice and shuddered. But logic told her that one did not, as a rule, find mice in new houses. In the country, perhaps, but not here in town. Bemused, she replaced the balls and followed Declan into the kitchen.

"I'm still wondering about the wooden balls," she said later. "How could they leave the bowl all by themselves? How could they do that?"

Declan stomped twice with his heel on the kitchen floor. Like that in the living room, it was of pine, beautifully polished; it was brand new, unblemished, without a scratch.

"Y'know, them wooden floors have a spring in them before they get bedded down," he said. "Probably you walked out of the room in a hurry and the vibration upset the bowl. It's a shallow bowl, light too."

Stephanie was thoughtful. She wanted to go to the living room at once and test his theory, but something dissuaded her. What if he was wrong? What if the wooden balls had somehow left the bowl all by themselves? She did not wish to consider this possibility and all that it might imply. She had to see to supper and was looking forward to settling down in front of the television later on. They were showing one of her favorite Johnny Depp movies. That would certainly take her mind off things.

Several days passed and Stephanie thought no more about the scented balls. Her best friend, Michele, was celebrating her twenty-fifth birthday that Saturday, and they were invited. The Rooneys remember that birthday party with absolute clarity, perhaps because the carefree atmosphere and the good time they had that evening contrasted so sharply with what awaited them on their return home.

It was 2:15 a.m. when they arrived back at Cedar Close. Declan went upstairs at once, leaving Stephanie to switch off the standard lamp in the living room. They tended to leave the downstairs lights burning for security reasons, even though burglaries were rare in the neighborhood; it was one of the reasons they had chosen it.

Stephanie was stopped in her tracks. The French traveling clock in its gilt case occupied the central position as usual, flanked left and right by Belleek china harps. But the photographs—the three framed photographs, one of Stephanie and Declan, two of family members—had been turned to face the wall.

"Declan!" she cried, backing toward the door.

He came down the stairs quickly but with some annoyance, his toothbrush still in his hand. "What's the matter?"

Stephanie was pointing at the mantelpiece. He saw that her hand was shaking. He stared in disbelief at the picture frames. There really was no logical explanation. Declan knew that all windows had been firmly secured and doors locked before they left the house. How could the framed pictures have turned themselves around? He was prepared to believe that their footsteps across the new wooden floor might have jolted some of the scented balls free of the porcelain bowl, but this was a phenomenon of a different order.

"Look, we'll talk about it in the morning," he said gently, trying to reassure Stephanie. "There's always a rational explanation for these things. Always." With that, he shut the living-room door and took the added precaution of locking it; they retired to bed.

They were tired. Declan fell asleep almost at once, but Stephanie lay awake for a time. She tried to quell her disquiet by rerunning scenes from the birthday party, smiling again at Michele's awkwardness when she introduced the new man in her life. It helped. Stephanie felt herself drifting off. But, without warning, something jolted her wide awake again.

She sat up. She was sure that she had heard a loud thud from downstairs. It had come from the living room, which lay directly below the bedroom. She shook Declan awake.

"Listen!" she whispered urgently. "I heard something downstairs."

"What?" He sat up, drowsy. "I locked all the—"

"Shush!" Stephanie was trembling. "The living room."

They sat in the darkness without speaking. They heard nothing more.

"Look, you only imagined it," whispered Declan wearily.

"Maybe."

But, just as they were about to settle down again, they heard it: the unmistakable thud of an object falling from a height.

"Oh, my God!" gasped Stephanie. She switched on the bedside lamp. Declan sprang out of bed.

"Where are you going?"

"Where d'you think?" Declan tried to keep the fear out of his voice. He could see how frightened his wife was becoming. For her sake, he simply had to remain calm and seemingly in control.

"You can't go down there! What if . . . ?"

"—what if it's a burglar? If it's a burglar I'll deal with him."

He reached into the walk-in closet. He had been putting up shelves and knew instinctively where to find his tools. He picked up a hammer.

"I'm coming with you," said Stephanie. Despite her fears, she could not allow him to venture downstairs alone. She switched on the lights. All was quiet; they heard nothing but their own rapid breathing.

Gingerly Declan turned the key to the living-room door. In one deft movement he flung it wide; Stephanie threw the light switch. They stood in the doorway, staring in astonishment. The traveling clock and the china harps lay on the hearth rug. On the mantelpiece, the three framed photographs, which Stephanie had righted not an hour before, were again reversed.

A locked room. There was no sign of forced entry, no sign at all that anybody had been and gone—only the items arranged so bizarrely. The fright the couple experienced in those moments can only be guessed at. Fifteen minutes later they were dressed and in Declan's car. They would go to his mother's house. Remaining in Cedar Close that night was unthinkable.

The following day, Sunday, following a fitful night's sleep, the couple returned to their home. It was around noon. Everything was as they had left it, and for the remainder of the day they experienced no further disturbance. Encouraged by this—after all, it might well have been an isolated incident—they stayed the night. On Monday morning each left for work as usual.

But Declan's newfound optimism was shattered that evening on his return home. He usually arrived about six; on this occasion he was much earlier. He turned the key in the front door and let himself in.

The living room seemed in order: the framed photographs were in their customary places on the mantelpiece, as was the traveling clock. On closer inspection, however, Declan noticed something amiss. He checked his wristwatch. It was four thirty, but the clock read a quarter after three. Odd, he thought. The clock was new and always accurate. Of course, it was entirely possible that the battery had run down.

But the clock was ticking very audibly and not missing a stroke, as far as he could tell. The battery could not be at fault. Puzzled, he set the time and went to check on the other clocks in the house. To his astonishment, he found that each one read a quarter after three—and all, like the traveling clock, were still ticking. With a mounting sense of unease, he reset them all and returned to the living room.

The travel clock had reverted to three fifteen.

Now Declan was filled with disquiet. Of one thing he was certain: he would say nothing about the clocks to Stephanie. If she noticed them, so be it. Her car was in the shop that day, and he had promised to collect her from work. He had an hour to kill.

An hour. He was thinking of time again, and thinking of time caused him to look at his wristwatch—and the clocks. He was going crazy; he could not stay in the house. He still had time for a beer. He felt he could use one.

They got back to Cedar Close a little after 6 p.m. Declan need not have worried. All the clocks were showing the correct time again. Thank God for that, he thought. With any luck that would be the end of the latest mystery. He kept quiet about the clocks.

All returned to normal—or so it seemed. Later that same evening, however, it was the turn of the scented wooden balls again. Declan recalls that he was lulled into a false sense of security; the house seemed more peaceful than ever. The street was silent. No sounds intruded from outside. After supper, they settled down to watch some television before going to bed. Stephanie dimmed the lights in the living room and they sprawled, as they always did, on the big couch.

But no sooner had Declan poured himself a beer than they heard a loud, sharp report on the floor directly behind them, followed by the sound a rolling marble makes. It was one of the wooden balls from the hearth.

Stephanie was startled, though still not persuaded that something unnatural was taking place in her home. Looking back now, she admits she was in denial. "I thought right away that Declan was messing around. I don't know; he has a sense of humor, likes a laugh. I thought: it would be easy for him to put one of the wooden balls in his pocket; then, while we were watching TV, he could throw it over his shoulder. The room was dark and I wouldn't see him doing it."

But one look at her husband's face was enough; he was as frightened as she was. An unknown agency had tossed the ball.

"We're getting out of here," Declan announced.

They left immediately and again spent the night at the home of Declan's mother. They did not know it then, but this pattern of staying overnight with relatives would soon become routine. Whenever they returned to Cedar Close, something would happen to drive them out again.

"The house," Stephanie says, "was telling us something. At first we thought it wanted to get rid of us. In fact it was drawing attention to itself. It was saying: 'Look what *I* can do.'"

Much of the paranormal activity was centered on the wooden balls. They would execute maneuvers that left the Rooneys perplexed. At times there seemed to be no design or purpose; they seemed to be acting at random. At other times they had, according to Stephanie, "a mind of their own."

They would spring out of the ceramic bowl of their own volition, form patterns, hide in different parts of the house, then reappear later in the middle of the living-room floor. Often a single ball would go missing. Other times one would roll after Declan as he walked down the hall to the kitchen. It would stop abruptly, then reverse back up to the front door—and launch itself into a potted palm that stood there. Sometimes the scent of their perfume would become overpoweringly strong.

Declan turned to his father for advice. Mr. Rooney seemed to know the answer. "Do you know what I think, son? And your mother agrees. I think it's only a poltergeist."

Only a poltergeist. It might be useful at this point to examine briefly what is meant by poltergeist activity. There is a consensus among modern investigators of psychical phenomena that such paranormal manifestations are not in fact spirits, but evidence of "psychokinetic"

energy at work. It is generally believed that this energy resides in the person who is undergoing the haunting.

The trouble with the psychokinetic (or PK) theory is that the phenomenon has never been scientifically proven. There is, to be sure, a vast body of research, most conducted since the 1930s. This is not to say that the human body contains no energy. It does, and experiments show that our bodies can generate enough static electricity to power a lightbulb. What is more, if the body is subjected to a high charge of electricity, this is sufficient to cause the same lightbulb to glow when held a centimeter or two away from the body.

But this falls far short of the phenomenal amount of energy one would require to propel that same bulb through the air without the use of one's hands. Nor does the theory explain how larger objects can fly about a room or transport themselves from place to place. An energy source is needed in each case, and the first law of thermodynamics states, in brief, that the universe contains a constant amount of energy; in order to move an object, energy must be converted from one form to another. Although the human body can store about eighty watts even when in repose, the brain itself uses on average only twenty watts. Anyone who has tried to read by the light of a twenty-five-watt bulb will appreciate that this is a minute amount of energy. The notion that a human brain can move objects, unaided by the rest of the body, seems absurd.

Frequently, investigators of poltergeist activity will allude to the onset of puberty in one of the principals. We are asked to believe that a hormonal change in the body of a boy or girl will somehow release sufficient energy to send pictures toppling from walls or electrical appliances running berserk. It seems so implausible. Puberty is no more than that period in a child's development when the body begins to produce hormones—testosterone in boys, estrogen in girls.

Generally speaking, puberty affects the body. The child's demeanor is also affected, causing moodiness, as any parent with moping and listless pubescent children will confirm. But there is no truly dramatic upset to the young person, and certainly not enough to send objects hurtling about the home.

To speak of poltergeist activity in such terms, then, seems to be yet another ploy to explain the inexplicable. The truth is that no one knows what it is, what causes it, or the nature of the forces at work behind it. It is also true that such activity does not confine itself to the places where there are pubescent children. In the case of the Rooney house, there were none.

"We ought to try and catch your poltergeist in the act," Declan's father said.

To this end, they devised a means of "observing" the phenomena at work. They would leave a tape recorder switched on overnight. It would be voice activated, so any sound louder than the ambient noises in the living room—the ticking of the clock, the hum of the water-heating system—would trigger the recording mechanism. There was the added possibility that, were a prankster at work, his footfalls would be recorded as well.

The experiment was a success. Every morning, when the tape was rewound, the *clack-clack-clack* of the wooden balls bouncing on the wooden floor was clearly audible. But that was all; if a human agent was at work, there was no record of such activity on the tape. Far from bringing reassurance to the Rooneys, the recordings only increased their anxiety. Something *very* strange was going on.

In time, things began to happen upstairs as well as down. The Rooneys would hear the bedroom doors being opened and shut again; bathroom faucets would turn themselves on. More than once, they discovered drawers pulled out and their contents disturbed. It was as if someone was searching for something.

The couple was distraught. Their work was suffering, and they were reluctant to come home in the evening. The house in Cedar Close, the dream home they had sunk all their savings in, was becoming a liability. What could they do? They asked themselves whom they could turn to.

"When this sort of thing happens to you," Declan says, "the last thing you want to do is let on to the neighbors. If you do, then word gets out that your house is haunted, and nobody wants to come near it. We were going out of our minds, but we had to keep it all to ourselves."

It was hard to know whom to turn to for help. A physician can cure disease through surgery or medication; a psychiatrist may soothe mental anguish through therapy and pharmaceuticals. But who can attend to that which appears to be not of this world, that which lies beyond our understanding? The Rooneys faced a choice: they could enlist the help of parapsychologists—what Declan deprecatingly called "ghostbusters"—or they could turn to religion. Stephanie's mother urged them to seek help from their parish priest.

The young couple, though brought up in the Catholic faith, were not especially devout. Like so many of their contemporaries, they did not take religion very seriously; they prayed only when occasion demanded it. They took no active part in parish affairs and were therefore on little more than nodding terms with their parish priest, Father Duncan O'Malley.

The good father, a brusque man in his sixties, wasted no time in concluding that their lack of faith was causing "the bother," as he put it. He spent almost an hour lecturing them on the consequences of "neglecting their duties" before blessing the house. The couple was pleased that he had at least acknowledged the graveness of their predicament. He left them a prayer to Michael the Archangel and counseled that they say it every morning and last thing at night.

It is perhaps important to mention how this prayer (reproduced both in full and in abbreviated form in Appendix 2) came into being. It was written by Pope Leo XIII soon after he experienced a traumatic vision. On October 13, 1884, he collapsed unconscious while attending a meeting of his Curia. The comatose pontiff was shown a vision of hell and of the archangel Michael overcoming Satan and his legions.

"Saint Michael the Archangel," Father O'Malley declared grandly, "our greatest champion in the face of the Enemy. Write it out, learn it, and place a copy in every room in the house."

Stephanie was examining the text of the prayer with a mixture of gratitude and unease. "You don't think, Father, that it's ..." She blushed, unable to say the dreaded word. "That it's *him?* I mean—"

"The Divil himself? Aye, who else would it be?" the priest thundered, frightening the pair even further. "The Divil, Oul' Nick, Satan himself. He slithers about like a snake in the grass, waiting for his chance to strike!"

"Prayer and repentance," he urged again, getting up to take his leave. Then, on seeing Stephanie's distress, he swiftly changed the subject. "I see ye play the Scrabble," he said eyeing the cardboard box under the television set.

"Haven't played it for a while, Father," said Declan, trying to keep calm. He was annoyed at Father O'Malley's boorish attitude and lack of sensitivity.

"I don't think he really believed us," Stephanie said, when the priest had left. She was gathering up the teacups in the living room.

"I know what you mean. Pity something didn't happen when he was here."

"Oh, my God!"

Declan heard a cup shattering on the pine floor. He turned from the window, to find Stephanie staring at the hearth. It was once again the unfathomable. There on the step, neatly lined up at equidistant intervals, were three sets of Scrabble letters.

RUN HIT HIDE

Intriguingly, the Scrabble box itself appeared undisturbed.

Whom and where to turn to now? Declan's first impulse was to appeal to Father O'Malley. Stephanie was of two minds.

"Look," she said, "if we tell him about the Scrabble, he'll be very disappointed that his blessing didn't work."

"Yeah, and wouldn't it serve him right? Coming in here and as good as accusing *us* of causing all the bother. He wouldn't be so high and mighty if—"

"That's hardly the attitude, Declan! Maybe if you had a bit more faith, the blessing would have worked."

"Oh, right, so *I'm* to blame now, am I?"

"No, I'm not saying that…. Oh God, I don't know *what* I'm saying. There's bound to be more priests around who can deal with these things. But where do you begin?"

Two days later, the answer presented itself. Stephanie was in a stationery store, looking for a birthday card for a nephew, when she was drawn to the books section. On a shelf labeled MIND BODY SPIRIT, a title seemed to allude to what she and her husband were experiencing. *Confronting the Paranormal* was a slim volume by a certain W. H. Lendrum. She picked it up and read the cover blurb. The author, she learned, was an Anglican minister from Belfast who had many years' experience in the deliverance ministry. Over the years, he had brought his unusual skills to bear on troubled situations, some involving individuals afflicted by unwelcome entities, others involving places beset by poltergeist activity.

She bought the book immediately and read it that evening in one sitting.

Canon William Lendrum is well used to the ringing of the telephone. His services have been in demand for many years but more so in the past decade. He is not surprised by this increase and contends that "the turning away from God by the masses in Western society has made natural man vulnerable to attacks by spiritual forces."

He is careful to keep an open mind whenever a fresh instance of paranormal manifestation is presented to him. He is not a man who sees demons everywhere. He questions relentlessly and does not jump to conclusions. A deeply spiritual and caring man, he has the emotional welfare of the individual as his main priority.

As Declan Rooney related his catalogue of strange events taking place in the house in Dungiven, the canon's first thought was "child's play." The activities—the scented balls being bounced around the floor, the Scrabble letters arranging themselves into words—all struck him as being the pranks of a mischievous "spirit" child.

At the same time, he believes that it is wise to nip such activity in the bud. He is keenly aware that, left to itself, such activity—child's play or not—can quickly get out of hand. He arranged to visit the Rooney home without delay.

Shortly before nightfall the following evening, Canon Lendrum and his wife, Alison, drew up at 8 Cedar Close. They were surprised to find a large number of people—family, near and distant—gathered for the occasion. That fact alone put the canon on his guard. In his long experience, the afflicted did not, as a rule, "shout from the rooftops" about their paranormal encounters, nor did they, in the initial stages, invite whole gatherings to witness events.

His puzzlement grew after he had spoken at length to Declan and Stephanie.

"I began to wonder if they hadn't got their priorities a little bit skewed," he says. "They seemed to want to talk about the shenanigans of the scented balls and precious little else. But, for me, those were only minor phenomena. The Rooneys were glossing over the real issue: the phenomenon that set this case apart from most of the other cases I'd been called in to help with down the years. I was more interested in that sinister aspect: the reversed photographs."

Nevertheless, he listened to a tape recording of the balls being tossed about the room and was shown photographs of them arranged in various patterns. He concluded that such "evidence" could easily have been faked, but for the time being kept his suspicions and doubts to himself.

For all that, Canon Lendrum was prepared to accept that the phenomena were genuine, and so acted accordingly. He celebrated what he recalls was "a beautiful Eucharist," one throughout which "the Lord was verily and powerfully present."

The canon left the house in Cedar Close, satisfied with a mission well accomplished. Indeed, in the weeks that followed, he learned through regular contact with Declan that his home was peaceful once more.

The Rooneys got on with their lives and endeavored to put the troublesome episodes behind them. As the weeks passed without incident, and weeks turned to months, they felt tremendously grateful for the peace the canon had restored to their home. But they were heedful, too, of what Father O'Malley had said at the time of his visit, and they took his advice about praying regularly. They recited the prayer to Michael the Archangel every night. Stephanie copied it out several times, as the priest instructed, and placed a copy in each room of the house.

A full nine months went by, and all was normal. Then a change occurred—one that, in Declan's words, "ratcheted things up a notch."

Josie and Noel Brady live at 10 Cedar Close, the property adjoining the Rooneys'. Josie, a no-nonsense woman in her late thirties, had been aware of "problems" with the couple next door, but she prided herself on not getting caught up in the gossip that seemed such a part of community life. Unlike her other neighbors, she was new to the area and therefore did not feel it was any of her business to interfere in the lives of others. She had heard the rumors about number eight but chose not to believe in "all that malarkey." Ghosts and spirits, in Josie's book, were merely superstitious nonsense circulated by those who had nothing better to do and who likely wished to draw attention to themselves. She found Declan and Stephanie a pleasant young couple but rarely saw them, except on weekends or when they had time off work.

On Wednesday, May 5, 2004, she was upstairs in one of the children's rooms, collecting laundry, when she heard something unusual. She remembers checking the time on her daughter's Barbie clock. It was 12:30 p.m.

"As I was making the bed I heard an almighty hammering on the party wall," she recalls. "In fact it was so sudden and fierce, it made me jump."

Josie immediately thought that Declan was doing some home improvement. But she was sure she had heard the couple leave that morning. She went at once to the window. She was correct; their cars were gone. Never mind, she thought, perhaps they had employed someone to do repairs in their absence. Without giving it further thought, she heaped the laundry into the basket and went downstairs.

Several days passed and Josie forgot all about the disturbance. Until a similar incident occurred.

She was upstairs again when she heard a rapid thumping on the wall. She looked at the clock and froze. It was 12:30—the same time as before. But now the noises seemed more urgent and were somehow more deliberate and purposeful. There was something eerie about the pattern of sound as it traveled to various points on the wall, each time repeating a succession of what she could only describe as "hammer blows." Josie was becoming uneasy. She hurried from the room, slamming the door shut behind her.

Once downstairs, she berated herself for being so silly. There was only one thing to do: knock on the door of number 8 and find out who was making all that racket.

It was a still, mild day, and Cedar Close appeared to be otherwise deserted when she pushed open the gate to the Rooney house. She had an odd sense of foreboding. The feeling was made all the more powerful when, just as she was about to ring the doorbell, a magpie swept down as if from nowhere and landed on the doorstep. Josie jumped back, her hand to her heart. In her fright she trampled on some geraniums. The bird took flight.

An old wives' tale common to many parts of Ireland suggests that it is unlucky to espy a lone magpie. In order to dispel the misfortune, one is encouraged to wave or to salute the bird. This Josie knew; the vestigial echoes of superstition from a rural childhood would never quite disappear. She made the prescribed gesture in the wake of the fleeing bird.

The sense of dread had not left her. She rang the doorbell. There was no response; she heard no sounds from inside the house.

She rapped on the stained-glass door panel and waited for a few moments more. Still no response. Josie was undeterred; she went around to the patio doors at the rear and tried again. Still there was no answer. She stood perplexed. Perhaps the handyman was a shy person who did not like to be disturbed. As she was turning to go, however, something in the kitchen caught her eye.

The kitchen was similar to her own. The patio doors allowed a great deal of light to bathe the area, revealing a sizable area of floor space to someone looking in. Josie also had a view of the hallway and staircase. But her attention was on the kitchen floor and something quite remarkable.

Shielding her eyes against the glare of daylight and peering more closely, she tried to come to terms with the inexplicable. Plumb in the middle of the pine floor was a lighted candle in a small brass holder, and next to it an open book. Its bulk and the red silk ribbon lying askew across the pages told Josie it was a Bible.

But the house at number 8 was not done with surprises. She discerned movement on the staircase. What she took to be a bright orange "ball of light" was swiftly descending. "It certainly wasn't the reflection of the sun," Josie says, "because there was no sun to speak of that day. It moved with such speed anyway. I got really scared because I thought I was going to see it at the glass. I never ran so fast in all my life."

Back in the safety of her own home, she recovered by and by, and went to put the kettle on. She thought a cup of tea might settle her nerves. But the calm did not last long. From upstairs came the unmistakable hammering on the shared wall again.

Josie Brady grabbed her coat and car keys and left the house in haste.

A few hours later, Declan and Stephanie pulled into their driveway. The first thing they noticed was the unlatched garden gate.

"Bloody postman," complained Stephanie. "I know who it is, too. Lar Stewart. He's in a back-to-work program and he doesn't much care what he does."

"I know how he feels," said Declan, locking his car. "I remember when I was unemployed they made me do that nonsense as well. Slave labor if you ask me. They put me picking mushrooms for an old creep outside Claudy. God, he was a tight old—"

"Yes, Declan." Stephanie was in no mood to listen to a story that she had heard countless times before. "Just look at our geraniums. That's Convery's bloody dog—or Stewart's big feet. I'll tell you something: I'm going to read him the riot act tomorrow."

"Er, it wasn't the postman," he said. "Look—no letters."

"Who was it then?"

"The ghost?"

"Please, Declan! Not even in jest, okay?" And she went upstairs to change.

From the time their troubles began, the couple had made a habit of locking all the doors before leaving for work. At the same moment that Stephanie was putting her key in the bedroom door, Declan was unlocking the door to the kitchen.

Upstairs and down there was evidence of fresh mischief.

Stephanie was staring at the drawers of her bureau. All had been pulled open and the contents rifled. The window was shut tight, just as she had left it. There could therefore be no doubt—their otherworldly visitor had returned.

Downstairs, Declan was struggling to come to terms with the burning candle and the Bible.

Curiously, in those moments, both decided that they would not alarm the other by telling of what they had seen.

With quivering hands, Stephanie rearranged her effects and quietly closed each drawer. Meanwhile, Declan picked up the Bible. It was open at Proverbs. He slammed it shut, afraid to read what might be written there, and stowed it away in a kitchen cupboard. He blew out the candle. If he tossed it into the garbage can in the yard, he reasoned, Stephanie would never know.

He was sliding back the patio door when a thought struck him. Perhaps this was someone's idea of a practical joke. After all, he was sure that the whole neighborhood and beyond knew about their "problems" by that stage. But he was remembering something else.

Declan was in the habit of stopping for a beer on his way home most Fridays. The local men had gotten to know him. He was friendly with them all, with the exception of one individual: Scottie Byrne. No one seemed to like Scottie. He worked in a shoe-repair shop in town, but he also cut keys. The word was that he could not be trusted. With his knowledge of locks, who knew what he might be capable of?

He had met Byrne the previous Friday, as he was leaving the bar. Scottie was a little drunk.

"Hey, Rooney," he said with a smirk, "did that ghost of yours ever come back?"

Thinking back on it now and still puzzling over the strange tableau on the floor of his kitchen, Declan was asking himself if the unsavory Byrne might not have something to do with it.

He returned indoors and tucked the candleholder away in the back of a drawer. He hoped his wife would not notice it. He would clean up later. He needed time to think matters through. He made coffee and carried the tray into the living room.

"What's that smell?" Stephanie asked, coming downstairs.

"Smell?" Declan had not reckoned on the smell. He wished he had sprayed some air freshener.

"A burning smell. Like candle wax."

"I think it's coming from outside," he said. "I opened the back door to put something in the bin and it got in. Somebody burning rubbish or something. So how was your day?" he added, quickly changing the subject.

Much later that same evening, Josie Brady was telling her husband about *her* strange day. "It's not like you to go snooping around neighbors' houses," he said.

"But it was awful! You'd have done the same, Noel. There's something not right about all of this. We should do something."

"What do you suggest we do?"

"Well, you could talk to them. Say there might be burglars in the neighborhood."

Noel checked with the Rooneys and came away satisfied that Josie had indeed been imagining things. No, the Rooneys had not employed a handyman. Furthermore, they assured him that the house was locked between 7:30 a.m. and 5:30 p.m. and that they held the only keys. Noel, in his wisdom, said nothing about what his wife *thought* she saw: the orange light on the staircase, and the Bible and candle. He would have felt a bit stupid relating such things. Even if Josie was mistaken—and he believed that she was—he had no wish to upset the young couple further.

The Rooneys closed the door on Mr. Brady's retreating back and looked at each other in dismay.

"My God, Declan, it's coming back!" Stephanie was devastated, close to tears. In her confusion and anger she did not know what she dreaded more: the return of the manifestations or the whole street knowing about them—and suspecting it was somehow the Rooneys' fault, that they had done something to invite this thing into their home. If Father O'Malley could think it, then why not others?

Declan tried to console her. "Look, maybe that woman was hearing things. You just don't know with people."

He thought again of Scottie Byrne and his brief encounter with him the previous week. What if Byrne was behind it? Byrne was laughing. Was he laughing at his own sick joke? Declan did not doubt that Byrne could gain access to his house via the rear entrance; the man was forever bragging that he could pick a lock faster than any burglar and leave no trace. What if he was responsible for that trick with the candle? Why not run upstairs and hammer on the wall for a laugh as well? Annoy the neighbors. Annoying others seemed to be his stock in trade. It was a crazy idea, but Declan thought Byrne was a little crazy.

He decided to share his suspicions with Stephanie. She was not convinced. "That wouldn't explain the drawers in my dressing table."

"Oh? What about them?"

"You might as well know," she said with resignation. "They were all pulled open when we came in. Just like before!"

"Well, there you are then. What was to stop him, after hammering on the wall, messing with the drawers on his way out?"

"I suppose he could have," Stephanie slowly conceded. "But why would he do a thing like that? We've never done him any harm. It just doesn't seem logical. For heaven's sake, I've never even spoken to the man."

"I know. But even so, there are some very strange people in this world. Characters who get a kick out of seeing others upset. I've never liked Byrne. Wouldn't trust him as far as I could throw him."

This much Declan said to Stephanie. He was being less than honest, though. He did not believe that Scottie Byrne was the culprit. Nor was he prepared to face the possibility that there were paranormal forces at work. Wooden balls bouncing about the room were one thing; lighted candles and open Bibles in the kitchen were something else again. Ghosts and poltergeists, in Declan's book, did not do such things—people did. He was considering a number of possibilities. He was asking himself if he or Stephanie had made an enemy of someone without being aware of it. He was asking himself if somebody was trying to frighten them into leaving the house in Cedar Close. For what purpose? Was there perhaps something buried on the site? Stolen money? Something more sinister?

Declan was determined to solve the mystery. He would unmask the intruder. Before going to bed that night, he put his new plan into action. Over the pine floorboards in the kitchen, he sprinkled a fine covering of salt. If somebody entered the kitchen, he or she would leave footprints in the salt, proving that intervention of the human rather than the ghostly kind was at work. He made sure to lock the patio doors, and took the added precaution of locking the kitchen door as well.

While Declan was engaged downstairs, Stephanie was kneeling at her bedside, praying fervently to Michael the Archangel for protection. At the same time, she was hoping that her husband's supposition was correct, that all this was somebody's idea of a joke. If that were so, she vowed that the creep would pay the price. Nobody was going to drive her from her own home.

But something woke her in the early morning, in the predawn.

Stephanie sensed that a voice—a child's voice—had spoken to her, though she heard nothing further. She lay very still, hoping to hear the voice again. Strange to say, considering her fears of the night before, she did not feel frightened. She heard Declan breathing lightly in his sleep and had no wish to rouse him. Perhaps she had simply been dreaming. She lay awake, wondering about the child's voice. Though her eyes were shut, she was aware of the first light of day beginning to seep in at the window.

Idly she began to think about children and how fine it would be to have a child of her own. She and Declan had discussed it from time to time. The plan was that, in a couple of years' time, when they had enough money saved, they would start a family. Like so many young women, Stephanie hoped that her first child would be a girl.

She was picturing a delightful little girl in a frilly pink dress and auburn pigtails: a little girl not unlike the toddler she had once been. She saw her clearly in her mind's eye. The child was running to meet her, laughing and reaching out to be hugged.

What happened next was extraordinary.

Stephanie felt what could only be a small hand squeeze her upper arm. She was wide awake immediately. She sat up in bed and switched on the bedside lamp, even though it was dawn by then. Her heart pounding, she peered at her bare arm, expecting to see a mark there. There was nothing.

She was convinced, nonetheless, of a presence in the room. She sensed that the little girl was still there, gazing at her and her sleeping husband. Gone was Stephanie's fear; tenderness for the child had replaced it. She sensed a need.

"Who are you, sweetheart?" she managed to whisper. "What do you want?"

Stephanie waited with a hand on her heart. There was no response, but still she sensed the presence nearby. Declan stirred in his sleep.

The atmosphere in the room was subtly changing. Stephanie, for reasons she could not understand, was drawn to the rattan chair beside the bed. Something was telling her that the "spirit child" was seated there.

"What do you want, sweetheart?" she asked again. "What's your name?"

This time, a response came.

"Sa–rah." It was the voice of a little girl, a half-whisper of a voice that filled Stephanie with sadness and poignancy.

"I want to help you, Sarah," she said, near tears. "What can I do?"

She waited and waited. But no answer was forthcoming.

Minutes later, Declan was awakened by his wife's loud sobbing. He understood none of it. Eventually, as he helped her down the stairs, he learned what it was that had upset her so much.

He unlocked the door to the kitchen.

"Coffee," he said, since there was not much else he could say. "I'll make it."

By this time, it was fully morning. When Declan pushed open the door, the sun was bathing the kitchen in bright light.

Stephanie said nothing. She remained in the doorway, staring with open mouth at the floor. Declan's plan had worked—perhaps too well. But there were no footprints in the salt he had scattered.

"God!" Stephanie had found her voice at last. "Oh, God."

Scrawled in the salt, in a childish hand, was a single word.

SARAH

Declan experienced a terrible sense of dread. But anger quickly took its place. He had had enough.

"Who the hell *are* you?" he yelled. "Why are you doing this?"

The following day, the couple moved out of their home again and went to stay with in-laws.

When Canon Lendrum encounters a particularly difficult case, as the Rooney case was proving to be, he calls on the help of a close friend of many years' standing. Florence Miller possesses what is known as the "gift of discernment" and, being a deeply religious and devout lady, uses it freely to help others.

Florence accompanied the canon and his wife on their second visit to the Rooney home. As they journeyed there, the trio prayed for a successful outcome. Canon Lendrum was disappointed—and a touch surprised—that his first attempt had not borne fruit. It had seemed to be a fairly low-key haunting, the sort of paranormal scenario he frequently encounters. As Florence prayed, she began to receive a vision. She saw an old fireplace. She did not know what it meant, but knew the design was from another era, perhaps the late nineteenth century. She hoped that its significance would become clearer on their arrival at the house.

Canon Lendrum was dismayed to see how distressed the couple were. Stephanie appeared to have lost weight, and she and her husband looked tired and drawn. Present also at the house were Declan's parents. In fact, it was his mother who had persuaded him to engage the canon again; she, more than anybody else, was convinced that something unholy had entered her son's home.

The group settled down in the living room and, over tea, the visitors listened as Declan and Stephanie told of the catalog of manifestations that had plagued their home.

Florence is a quiet woman who prefers to take a back seat at such times. She tends to listen, awaiting signs and indications of extraphysical presences. She held her counsel as the Rooneys spoke of the new developments. She was waiting for what she terms a "signal." She explains that the signal is a communication, whether auditory or visual, from the "other side." It helps her to establish who—or what—is creating the disturbance. As yet, nothing had come to her. She allowed the couple to finish their account, then posed a single question: "Is there an old fireplace in this house?"

The Rooneys assured her that there was not. In fact, only one room had an open fire—the room they were seated in. The fireplace in the living room was—as one would expect—of contemporary design.

Canon William Lendrum, for his part, was most intrigued by the name traced in the salt.

"What do you think it means?" he asked the Rooneys.

Declan confessed bafflement. He knew nobody named Sarah, he said—not unless they could include a girl by that name he had dated when a teenager. The canon pressed him further. Declan trawled his memories.

Florence, in the meantime, was noticing a change coming over the room. It was a sensation she had experienced on numerous occasions; she describes it as a kind of "tightening apprehension," akin to what one might feel when a thunderstorm is brewing. She could hear Declan's voice receding, as if someone was turning down the volume on a radio. She waited for what she calls "the happening."

All at once it came. At another mention of the name Sarah, a pebble flew through the air and landed at their feet on the hearthrug. It had entered through the open doorway of the living room.

The pebble had obviously come from the driveway. But how, with the front door shut, had it managed to materialize inside the house, alone and unaided?

"Somebody's playing games," Canon Lendrum announced.

It was the first time he had witnessed an incident of this nature in the Rooney home. Like everyone else, he was puzzled, but the occurrence reinforced his initial theory that a child was playacting, teasing the house's occupants. He prepared to celebrate a second Eucharist. Since the pebble had been thrown into the living room, he judged that it would be the appropriate focus for the sacrament.

As on the first occasion, the Eucharist progressed without incident. Nothing untoward occurred to disturb the liturgy; no more pebbles were flung. After the service the canon went from room to room, cleansing the house in the name of the Lord.

As a rule, Florence never discloses anything of her experiences to the victims directly, fearing that they may hear things that would undoubtedly cause further distress. Only afterward does she discuss her observations with the canon, and together they look for connections that may prove helpful.

On the return journey to Belfast, Florence shared what she had experienced. She had had two psychic encounters.

The first occurred as the canon's car approached the Rooney home. She had the distinct impression that the area—the entire estate—was filled with what she called "territorial spirits." She claims that she could see them everywhere. Yet the interesting part of her vision concerned the Rooney house itself. Of all the homes in Cedar Close, it alone was being protected by a "ring of angels." She saw them circling above the roof of the property.

Her second vision occurred while the Rooneys were speaking with the canon and the pebble landed on the hearthrug. Florence had looked, as everyone had, to the open doorway. But no one else could sense what she sensed. She had the compelling impression that they were in the presence of a spirit child—a little girl.

Canon Lendrum had suspected it in the first instance; now they felt certain that the "playful" activity was the work of the mysterious spirit child. He was glad, and for good reason. Florence's vision had helped in establishing that there was no evil at work in 8 Cedar Close. A full exorcism would not be necessary. The best course was to pray for the child, that her spirit might find rest.

He counseled the Rooneys to do likewise.

Declan could rule out Scottie Byrne or a mischievous neighbor. In the days to come, he was almost sorry he had entertained either possibility. When he thought about it, it appeared increasingly unlikely that human agents were behind the disturbances. Declan was of two minds about this. Like everyone who comes face-to-face with the inexplicable, his need to rationalize became paramount. If he was being asked to believe in ghosts—if there was a little girl named Sarah, who was somehow connected with an antique fireplace—he wished to know *why* she was troubling his home. He wanted it all to make some kind of sense.

He started to make inquiries. For a long time, they appeared to lead nowhere. But on October 10, 2004, five months after Canon Lendrum's second visit and a full fourteen months after the Rooneys' problems began, Declan made a breakthrough. He had been hunting down facts that might have a bearing on the case and had examined countless documents in local and national archives. In the history department at Queen's University Belfast, he turned up something of great significance. In the nineteenth century, two children went missing close to what would become Cedar Close, in the area known as Ballylouth. The little girls, nine-year-old Mary Magee and Sarah Logan, age ten, were never found.

So there she was—Sarah, the mysterious child Florence had seen. Declan experienced a tremendous sense of relief on unearthing this information. The pieces of the puzzle that had haunted him and his wife for so long were finally coming together. He hurried home in high excitement and related the good news to Stephanie.

They knew the identity of their ghost. They could pray for her now.

Stephanie went to Father O'Malley and arranged for a Mass to be said for the little girls. She anticipated that the priest would have no objection, and this proved to be the case. She felt it was prudent, too, to say nothing about the intervention of a priest of another faith.

On Father O'Malley's recommendation, the Rooneys began a nightly recitation of the rosary for the repose of Sarah's soul. Nor did they ever neglect the prayer for the protection of Michael the Archangel. Since the onset of their troubles, it had become a routine part of their lives. They knew it by heart and no longer needed to refer to the written version. Nevertheless, Stephanie was reluctant to remove those copies of the prayer she had placed in every room.

Over the previous months their house, understandably, had become a repository of sacred objects. The Rooneys and their relatives had come to the conviction that such objects were talismans against the unknown. The crucifix was now a permanent fixture on the living-room wall. A holy picture or novena hung in every room.

One thing remained to be investigated: Declan still had not satisfied his natural curiosity with regard to the fireplace that Florence had seen in her vision.

"It must mean something," he said to Stephanie.

"I wish you'd leave it alone. What's the point in stirring it up again?"

"I think it's important that we know, Steph. Why would Florence Miller see a fireplace?"

Declan had a hunch that the answer lay on his property. He sought out the contractor who had built the development. But Mr. Heaney seemed reluctant to discuss the matter. Yes, there had been a block of old row houses. So what? No, he did not know who the "previous owners" were. Did Rooney think he was chairman of the archaeological society or what? He had bought the land to build houses on, not for the purpose of digging up the past.

Declan asked around. Somebody must know something, he reasoned. And somebody did. In exchange for a beer or two, Kevin McTeague, one of Heaney's former employees, divulged some interesting information. He claimed that the Cedar Close development was built on the site of a fairy fort.

This gave Declan more pause for thought. He knew a little about fairy forts. There are perhaps 40,000 all told in Ireland. Most are knolls or dunes, either naturally or artificially constructed. The fact that the provenance and purpose of these mounds were unclear to the country folk gave rise to the belief, in less enlightened times, that they were the homes of the "little people," or fairies. The superstition persists that if anyone disturbs such a site, great misfortune will befall him.

"That area beside your house is where it was," McTeague told him. "Heaney had it leveled, but made sure he didn't build on it. He wasn't taking any chances."

"Oh, that's just great! Now I'm hearing this when it's too late. It would have been nice to know this before we bought the place."

"Depends on whether you believe in all that fairy stuff," said McTeague. "But I remember when we were working there, it took ages for us to get the bloody job finished. Everybody took sick, one after the other. Then deliveries would be delayed; calls that Heaney made went astray. He lost a lot of money on the project. We were happy to see the back of Cedar Close, I can tell you. When I heard about your troubles, I wasn't surprised at all."

Declan was not in the least superstitious; he had never believed in ghosts. Yet events over the past year had caused him to look closely at his skepticism. If the spirit-child theory was correct, and it had the appearance of being so, then why not the fairy story?

But what to do with such information? They could hardly sell the house, not after barely two years. Besides, even if they did sell, it would probably fetch a much reduced price, given the talk in the neighborhood. McTeague had demonstrated to him that even casual acquaintances knew about the phenomena. No, Declan decided, selling was out of the question.

If Canon Lendrum was to be believed, then the problem of the spirit child could be solved through prayer and faith. But the fairy fort? Nothing could be done about it, short of having Heaney bulldoze the site—an unlikely, and absurd, scenario. Declan's only consolation lay in the fact that he had not been responsible for disturbing it in the first place. Perhaps McTeague's story was true, insofar as Heaney and his workforce were culpable.

Declan shared his concerns with Stephanie.

"Look," she said, "so far, for a whole six months, we've had no trouble—fingers crossed. So long as we keep praying for that little Sarah, things will be okay. God knows what happened to the poor wee thing."

"I know. But what if it all starts up again? All that spirit stuff."

"It won't!" she snapped. "I wish you'd have a bit more faith, instead of listening to old pub talk. I don't believe that fairy fort nonsense.

Fairies are what alcoholics see when they've got the DTs, so I'm not surprised Kevin McTeague believes in them. He's never out of the bloody pub."

And that seemed to end the discussion. They said their prayers and retired.

It may have been coincidence. Stephanie is not so sure. Her own feeling is that Declan's inquiries had somehow opened a door on some secret or other and in so doing had left both of them vulnerable to aggression from "the other side." Whatever the cause or motivation, that night Declan was physically attacked. Of that there was no doubt. He awoke the next morning to find that scratch marks had mysteriously appeared on his torso.

A rubicon had been crossed; war was declared. From that night on, events took a turn for the worse.

Physical injury to a person by a paranormal agency is rare. According to psychic researchers, when physical interaction is present in a haunting it generally takes the form of touching, squeezing, or the sensation of an oppressive weight, none of which, in the main, leaves marks on the individual. The aggression to which Declan was subjected signaled a very worrying development. These were no longer the antics of a "playacting spirit child." The rules of engagement had changed radically.

Over the coming days and following from the physical attack, the Rooneys would come face to face with something they had dreaded from the outset. The entity would demonstrate, by targeting the sacred objects, that it was antireligious. When this occurs in cases of paranormal activity, when consecrated, protective objects come under attack, one must face the possibility that evil forces are at work.

The couple vacated their home yet again. Each day, they would look in after work—and each day would be confronted with incontrovertible evidence of evil intent. Over the course of a week, all the religious objects in their home were targeted.

It started with the crucifix above the fireplace. They discovered it lying on the hearth, where it had evidently been hurled with some force. What is more, the Fatima rosary that adorned it had been pulled apart and its beads scattered.

On at least two occasions, they fled the house crying out in shock and physical pain. Incredibly, the holy water in the font by the front door was so hot that it burned their fingers. They had made a habit of crossing themselves on leaving the house. Something was trying to prevent them from continuing the practice.

Water from the French shrine of Lourdes, which Stephanie kept on her nightstand, inexplicably turned to ice. More holy water was emptied onto the kitchen floor, and the bottle that contained it was flung under the table. A novena prayer to St. Jude was removed from its frame, torn into tiny pieces, and strewn about the bedroom floor.

But perhaps the most startlingly malign incident—and one which confirmed for the Rooneys that demonic influences were at work—involved the prayers to Michael the Archangel, which Stephanie had placed in five separate rooms. She found the words HIDE HERE NOW scrawled in a child's hand on the reverse of each prayer. Interestingly, the Scrabble letters had spelled out RUN HIT HIDE.

"'Hide,'" Declan mused. "Maybe the two wee girls are playing hide-and-go-seek together."

"And maybe I'm going out of my f***ing mind, Declan," said a distraught Stephanie.

He looked at her with concern. She never used that kind of language—not unless she was *truly* upset. Yet he could not let go of the idea that the phantom children were playing games again. It was better to believe *that* than to question the nature of an entity that seemed to take delight in, by turns, boiling and freezing sanctified water.

The new cycle of manifestations increased in frequency and grotesqueness. The prayer leaflets became the focus of something even more sinister and alarming. Mysterious symbols appeared one day on the walls of the living room, kitchen, and hallway.

One, drawn at head height—about five and a half feet from the floor—resembled a staring eye. The symbols did not appear to have been applied with a writing implement, such as chalk or felt-tip marker, but seemed smudged, as if a finger had been dipped in a dark pigment of some kind. Declan thought at once of runes or hieroglyphs, but the drawings were like nothing he had ever seen before, whether in books, magazines, or TV documentaries.

A curious odor pervaded the house, as of charred paper. The couple noted that it was stronger on the staircase. They hurried upstairs and inspected the bedrooms. Every copy of the prayer to Michael the Archangel was burned. They concluded that the ash had been used to daub the graffiti on the walls downstairs.

It was time to seek help again.

Canon Lendrum is understandably disappointed but never dispirited when he learns that his efforts at cleansing places or individuals have not been entirely successful.

"We don't know why one deliverance works immediately and another takes longer," he says. "But I believe that it's all a matter of faith. The unshakable faith of the deliverance minister must be matched by the unwavering faith of the afflicted."

Strictly speaking, in the Protestant ministry there is no formalized ritual for exorcising places. Nor is there a biblical reference to the purification of dwelling houses. The deliverance minister is therefore free to act at his own discretion. Rome's chief exorcist, Dom Gabriele Amorth, describes how he and his fellow priest Candido Amantini go about this task:

The Rituale [Romanum] includes some ten prayers beseeching the Lord to protect places from evil influences. They include the blessing of houses, schools and other buildings. We intone several of these prayers. Then we read the first part of the First Exorcism of persons, adapting it accordingly. Next we exorcise each room, in much the same way we would bless a house. We follow with another circuit of the rooms, this time dispensing incense. We end with more prayers. After the exorcism, it is very efficacious to celebrate a Mass in the house.

"Very often the blessing of a house and a service of the Eucharist will be enough," Canon Lendrum adds, "but there are those cases that demand more robust measures. The infestation of the Rooney household was one such case."

When the canon visited the house for the third time—again accompanied by Alison and Florence—he was struck by the threatening atmosphere. It was almost tangible even as they entered.

"Evil invariably comes with a coldness," he says. "Science has never been able to explain why this is so. I was not aware of it on the first two occasions, but I had the impression—and Florence confirmed it—that the child spirit had been replaced, or to be more accurate, 'used,' by sinister forces to gain access to the house."

He celebrated another Eucharist in the presence of the Rooney family. More prayers were said; the rooms were blessed a third time. As before, the canon and his party left Dungiven in the belief that whatever it was that had laid siege to the house had departed, never to return.

"We felt liberated then," says Stephanie. "We felt that a door was shut."

It was a door that had been opened by the restless spirit of a little lost girl named Sarah and used as a portal for evil to enter and disrupt the lives of an innocent young couple.

We wonder about the scented wooden balls that started it all. Where did they end up?

"Oh, we burned them a long time ago," Stephanie says. "No more of that for us. We see them from time to time in the shops, and most people would say they look pretty and smell nice. But Declan and me, whenever we see them, well, a shiver runs through us. And who can blame us for that?"

LITTLE LUCY AND THE
PHANTOM FAMILY

❖

The Gillespie farmhouse, a gray stone, two-story structure, sits in thirty or so acres at the end of a narrow, meandering lane in the lake-rich countryside of County Fermanagh. It was built two centuries ago by an ancestor of the present family. The visitor will find nothing remarkable about the property; there is the customary yard with its barns and outbuildings, dotted with farm machinery standing idle or at the ready, depending on the season.

Ian and Linda Gillespie are a handsome, hard-working couple. He is a businessman and farmer; she is a former teacher. Their three children are beautiful, intelligent, and well mannered. The family seem to embody the benefits of wholesome country living. It is hard, then, to imagine extramundane forces intruding upon this idyll, yet that is what occurred in the autumn of 2002. During September and October of that year, the Gillespies' youngest child, eight-year-old Lucy, was the focus of a number of very unusual visitors.

It began one evening when Lucy was playing in the yard with her sister, eleven-year-old Sandy, and brother Darren, age ten at the time. Their parents were outdoors as well, herding cattle from a back field toward one of the barns.

It was growing late, and all at once Lucy felt the cold. She bounced the ball back to her siblings and told them to wait while she fetched her coat. She sped through the open door of the farmhouse and down the hallway to the back room. This room, once a store-room, had become the playroom; the children listened to their music and watched videos there.

Lucy's coat was hanging inside the door, which stood open—as it generally did. She stopped abruptly, pulled up short by a most incongruous sight. There was "a lady" in the room. She was bent over the coffee table by the far wall, her back to Lucy. She seemed to be arranging the videotapes.

The girl was transfixed. Not through fear, it must be said, but because of "something" that held her in the doorway, something that was urging her to take careful account of every detail of what she was witnessing. For Lucy was in no doubt that the lady was not like other women. She knew of the existence of ghosts—or perhaps more accurately the *possibility* of their existence. What child does not? Lucy sensed that she was seeing one, in daylight, in her very own home. She had what she calls a "clear" view of the lady, though the lady herself was not quite as clear as a normal human being. She was "fuzzy round the edges."

Lucy could not see her face but had the impression that the lady was around her mother's age. She was tall and well built and wore a long, gray, straight skirt and a burgundy shawl. The clothes were definitely from another century—even young Lucy knew that. Most bizarrely, the stranger appeared to have no feet. The hem of her skirt seemed to hover about three or four inches above the ground. She was so intent on tidying the tapes that she did not register the presence of the child—not that Lucy wanted her attention. She hurried back down the hallway, coatless and breathless, to relate what she had seen to her brother and sister.

"There's a ghost in the playroom!" she blurted out.

Darren and Sandy, still bouncing the ball back and forth, did not pause their game. Lucy grabbed her sister's arm and shook it hard.

"Sandy, there's a ghost in the playroom!"

"A what?"

"A ghost!"

"Yeah, right!" Darren stopped the ball with his foot and rolled his eyes. "And your head's a bubble."

But Sandy was not amused. She was looking quizzically at her sister. It had been instilled in the children from an early age that fibbing was a sin. It was wrong. Sandy sensed that Lucy was telling the truth; her whole demeanor said so.

"Are you sure?"

"Quick, come and see." Lucy grasped Sandy by the arm and propelled her toward the front door. "She might be still there."

Darren, not wishing to be left out, reluctantly followed the pair down the hallway. But when they got to the playroom door, they found it shut.

"It was open the last time!" Lucy whispered desperately. "She must still be in there." She put her ear to the door; she could hear shuffling sounds. "I can hear her lifting the videos. Listen."

Sandy put her ear to the door. She, too, could hear noises from within. She looked through the keyhole but saw nothing in the darkened room.

"What are you three up to?" It was their mother. "Come on, upstairs. Bedtime."

"Lucy saw a ghost, Mum," Sandy cried excitedly. "It's in the playroom."

"Nonsense!" Linda had had a long, hard day. Ghost stories were the last thing she wished to hear so close to bedtime. She needed her sleep as much as the children did. A ghost. Such things were known to keep the children awake at night—with all the consequences for her own sleep and peace of mind. She had to put out this fire right away. "Nonsense," she said again. "There's no such thing as ghosts."

"But it's true!" Lucy protested. "She's in there sorting the videos. I saw her, Mum. I'm telling you, I did."

Linda considered her daughter's anxious little face and the earnestness with which she spoke. She felt a slight shiver of unease.

"I hadn't said anything to the children," she tells us. "Or no-body else. But the truth of the matter is that I'd had a brush with something myself a couple of weeks before. I don't know if you'd call it a 'ghost.' I got this feeling there was a presence in the house. It seemed to be a woman's presence, and I felt it most strongly in the girls' bedroom. It was a little bit scary, but I'd kept my fears to myself. I'd no wish to alarm the children."

"Very well, Lucy," she said, "we'll have a look. And if she's there we'll have a little word and ask her what's she's looking for. And if she's not there, it means that you only *thought* you saw her. Fair enough?"

With that, Linda took her courage in both hands, flung the door open, and switched on the light—taking care to keep her eyes averted from the coffee table where the videotapes were stacked.

"There...see. No ghost!" She entered the room and spread her arms wide. The children hung back in the doorway. "See?"

The children's attention was on the coffee table. Young Lucy was pointing.

"But the videos—"

"Now look, there's *nothing* here!" Their mother's tone told them she would tolerate no contradiction. "Upstairs, all of you, this min-ute. And I don't want to hear another word about it."

That seemed to end the matter. Linda got the children to bed and went back downstairs to put the kettle on. She heard her hus-band Ian come in and switch on the television. He would be catch-ing the nine o'clock news, as was his habit. Before joining him in a cup of tea, she went to check the playroom again. She had been putting it off, but it had to be done, if only to set her mind at ease.

Linda had long given up tidying and putting things away in the playroom. It seemed a futile task. But, at that moment, she found herself fervently wishing for disorder; she prayed that she might see the usual mess: the videotapes strewn willy-nilly over the coffee table. That would prove Lucy's story groundless. She opened the door and switched on the light.

Her heart sank. The twenty or so tapes were neatly stacked—as neatly as a display in a store. Not only that, but all had been slotted carefully into their individual boxes—boxes that, in the ordinary run of things, Linda would find discarded underneath the coffee table and elsewhere.

With trembling fingers she examined the top row. Each movie was in its correct box. There they were, neater even than she would have arranged them herself: *James and the Giant Peach, Babe, Monsters Inc., Muppets in Space.* The fifth box, however—*Spy Kids*—was empty. She looked about the room but could not find it. She went to the VCR and pressed the eject button. The machine was empty.

I don't have time for this, Linda thought. Perhaps the dog carried it out to the barn—he was known to do things like that—or perhaps one of the children had lent it to a friend at school.

Without quite knowing why, she hurriedly removed all the tapes from their boxes, tossed some of the boxes back under the table, and generally returned the playroom to its usual, untidy, state. In the morning the children would see that it had all been one great joke.

She was not smiling, though—far from it. As she pulled the door behind her, she had the feeling that another door was opening into another place, a place she had no wish to confront, or even consider.

She decided, then and there, that she would not burden her husband with her suspicions just yet. He had enough to deal with, what with a full-time job from eight to five and the additional farm work in the evenings. Besides, Ian was a skeptic; he would not take it seriously. She would wait and see how things developed. With luck, there would be no more to it.

In the days that followed, life returned to normal. The children went to school as usual; Ian went off to work; and Linda, with much to occupy her during the day, tried not to dwell on the strange phenomenon. Being a religious woman, she resolved to pray more with the children at bedtime. It gave her peace of mind, and it seemed to soothe them.

A week later, however, Lucy had her second vision.

It was about four o'clock on a calm, bright Friday afternoon. Linda was in the kitchen washing the dishes. Sandy and Darren were at the table, still busy with their homework, and Lucy, who tended to finish hers before the others, was outside at play.

The first thing that a visitor to the Gillespie homestead notices is the silence that envelops it. The house lies some distance from the main road and neighboring farms, and the silence is potent. Linda, being at home for most of the day, is especially attuned to this quietude. The noises that disturb it are almost welcome: the hum of a far-off tractor, Ian's car as it turns in at the gate, the playful shouts of the children, the barking dog that heralds a visitor.

The scream of a terrified child is something else entirely.

Linda dropped everything and ran outside, with Sandy and Darren close on her heels. Lucy was racing up the lane toward the house. She fell into her mother's arms in great agitation. While Linda did her best to calm her, the child kept pointing back the way she had come.

"He was there!" she cried, indicating the wild garden on the left. "A minute ago, Mommy… a man."

Linda took her by the hand.

"All right, dear," she said, "we'll go down and have a look."

But there was no sign of the mysterious man. He seemed to be as nonexistent as Lucy's "lady" of the previous week.

"Look, there's no one there, sweetheart."

Linda was perplexed, unsure what to think. Her daughter was behaving very much out of character. She rarely, if ever, made things up; it was not in her nature.

"There's nobody there, Lucy," Sandy assured her.

Lucy began to sob. "But he *was* there. I saw him. I swear he was there!"

Linda could read the child's anguish. She was torn between chastising her for being silly and believing her. She dismissed both as unhelpful. Linda knew that her children were not given to attention seeking. She thought it better for everyone's sake to remain neutral and simply to allow Lucy to have her say.

"All right," she said, "let's all go inside and have some orange juice. Then you can tell us all about it."

Once settled and calmer, Lucy related what she had seen. As she was skipping down the lane past the garden, she saw a figure standing just inside the gate: a man. He was of average height and wearing a black, hooded cloak. His hands were clasped chest-high in an attitude of prayer. He was "like a monk," Lucy said. He did not move or look at her, but seemed to be gazing fixedly down the lane. The words *look* and *gazing* are probably incorrect in this context, because the monk had no features as such. A "peachy haze"—Lucy's charming description—filled the space where his face should have been.

Linda listened with mounting dread. What on earth was happening? Ghosts appearing in broad daylight, inside the house and out-of-doors. She wanted desperately to discount the whole affair. Yet, of her three children, Lucy was the least excitable; she was a calm, level-headed little girl. Why this sudden change? Linda was growing very concerned. She resolved to visit her doctor and seek his advice.

The doctor's diagnosis held no surprises. Children have fertile imaginations, he told Linda, especially at Lucy's age. They have difficulty distinguishing fact from fiction. What they see in movies can sometimes seem very real.

There was nothing new there, but his next words angered Linda. He wondered if the child perhaps felt she was not getting enough attention. The "visions" might well be her way of refocusing her mother's regard.

Linda could not concur; she treated her children equally. But the visit to the doctor had eased her mind to some extent. Lucy was sleeping well and her schoolwork had not suffered. The general practitioner assured the mother that it was just a phase, that things would calm down.

And they did.

"Three whole weeks went by with nothing happening," Linda tells us, "but you know, deep down I knew it was too good to last. And the reason I say that is because, even though Lucy wasn't having any more visions, I knew, *I just knew*, that the strange woman was still in the house. I'd sometimes feel her on the stairs or the landing, but what really worried me was that she was strongest in the girls' room."

While tidying up in there one morning, she noticed something odd. The children always made their beds before going to school. It did not require much skill—straighten the duvet, plump the pillow, and place it on top. But now she noticed that Lucy's bed was made differently. The pillow had been placed beneath the cover. Linda shook her head in mild bemusement, left the room by and by, and thought no more about it.

Until it happened again—and again. She was seeing it every day. She questioned Lucy. "I always put it on top, Mommy. I thought *you* were changing it."

The three children were sitting down to tea, having just got home from school. "Maybe it's the lady," said Darren, tucking into a slice of cake. He grinned.

"Now stop that! There's no lady in this house—and don't speak with your mouth full."

"There is, Mommy," Sandy announced bravely. "Lucy saw her twice—and we *feel* her in the bedroom as well."

"What!" Linda was stunned. "Is this true, Lucy?"

The child nodded.

"Come with me. Take your tea with you if you like."

She brought Lucy into the front room and shut the door. It was time to have it out with the girl.

"Now, I won't say anything about you being naughty, all right? You just tell me what happened. Right from the beginning."

The story came out. "I saw her when I was in the bath on Monday night," Lucy began. "She went past the door because the door was open…and she…She stopped and looked at me, but she had no eyes, Mommy, because her face was all fuzzy like the monk's."

Linda stared at her daughter and feigned a smile. She had no great wish to hear any more of this, yet knew she must.

"And the second time, dear?" she managed to say.

"The second time was yesterday when I was putting out the bin. She was...she was in the backyard. She was praying, Mommy."

"How do you know that?"

Lucy screwed up her little face, irritated that her mother should ask such a silly question. "Because she was kneeling behind the wall and she had her hands joined...and she had a brooch on."

"A brooch?"

"Yes. It was gold with a red diamond in the middle."

"Why did you not tell me this before?" Linda's concern was growing.

"I didn't want to upset you, Mommy."

"I'll not be upset, Lucy." Linda tried to keep her voice calm. "Now promise me, sweetheart, the next time you see a strange woman or man, you must call me immediately. I want to see them as well, and I want to ask them what they're up to."

Lucy nodded.

"And there's no woman in your bedroom. It's the mirror inside the door." Linda had placed a cheval mirror that had belonged to her mother in the girls' room. Because of its age, it tended to swing too freely in its bracket. "Any time I walk into your room, the mirror moves, because it's an old mirror. It's not because of any strange lady. Even a bird flying past the window gets reflected in it, and you'd think it was a person."

The child seemed content with this explanation. She finished her tea, did her homework, and went out to play with the others.

Perhaps the most unusual aspect of Lucy's case is the extraordinary variety of her visions, coupled with the fact that they could appear at any hour of the day, nearly always in broad daylight and usually when she was engaged in some activity or other. Her encounters appear all the more baffling when one considers that over 80 percent of ghostly apparitions are seen at night, commonly when the observer is in a relaxed state, either having woken from sleep or about to fall asleep. Technically, these twin states of consciousness are known respectively as the hypnopompic and hypnagogic. Extensive studies have shown that an individual can experience odd phenomena when in either state. They may take the form of visions and other imagery; a frightening aspect can be a paralysis lasting minutes or even a loss of speech.

Lucy was, of course, wide awake when she observed her "ghosts." Her brain was active and therefore entirely able to distinguish truth from illusion. Daylight also lent clarity and relative unambiguity.

Her next vision made its presence felt one evening at around seven—once again before night had properly fallen.

Lucy was in the room she shares with Sandy. Their beds stand about four feet apart. The door was fully open and the landing light was on. Lucy sat down on her bed to slip into her sneakers. She had just laced them up and was about to rise when, in her own words, she "was made to sit down again."

There was a man standing just inside the door.

She tried to call out to her mother but discovered she was tongue-tied. Again she had the sensation of being "held" in the one spot.

The man was tall, about six foot; he looked to be in his thirties and was clad in a dark green uniform with matching beret. Around his waist he wore a black belt and across his left breast pocket was a military ribbon rack. Unlike with the lady and the monk, there was no "fuzziness" about this figure—Lucy saw his face clearly. He was stern and very pale, with sharp features—long nose, thin lips, and small, narrowed eyes—and he moved his head from side to side as if peering from one corner of the room to the other. He did not look at Lucy—at least, not as far as she could tell.

The most significant thing about him, however, was his right arm. It ended at the elbow, and the sleeve was pinned back and secured at the shoulder. Because he was standing behind Sandy's bed, Lucy could not see his feet. But she had seen enough and at last felt able to shout for her mother. As she did so, the "soldier" disappeared.

Linda arrived breathless at the top of the stairs, to find a distraught Lucy once more insisting on the veracity of what she had just seen.

Later that same evening, when she had finally gotten the children settled in bed, Linda decided it was time to tell Ian. Knowing him to be a skeptic, she did not expect much understanding. He was unwinding in the sitting room after a long day, watching the sports channel with his feet up. Bad timing, she thought, but he has to know; I can't shoulder all this on my own.

As she had anticipated, Ian saw little cause for alarm. "After all," he assured her, "ghosts never harmed anyone. Lucy will grow out of it. It's just a phase."

"But, Ian, these visions seem so *real* to her! We have to do something about them."

"Look," he said, "your mother was psychic and you're psychic. Lucy's inherited the 'gift.' More like a curse, if you ask me."

Her husband spoke the truth. Linda did indeed share a most unusual "gift" with her mother: an ability to perceive things that others could not. At times, she could almost guess what another was thinking, and she frequently knew what people were about to say before they said it. And Ian was correct: it was more of a curse than a blessing.

"She'll grow out of it," he said again. "And anyway, *I* haven't noticed any change in her. She seems perfectly all right to me."

"But, Ian, you don't see her from one end of the day to the next. I do. And I'm really worried about her. She's just not herself."

"Well, if it puts your mind at ease, go along and see that parish priest of yours. Priests seem to be good at driving out ghosts and things, if them Hollywood films are anything to go by."

She was a bit miffed by his flippancy, for it hit a sore spot. Ian is Methodist and Linda is Catholic. When they married, each retained his or her respective beliefs, but Linda agreed to the children being brought up in her husband's faith.

"Look, it's not funny!" she said.

"Sorry, love. I know it isn't." He yawned. "God, I'm tired. Bedtime, I think."

Linda knew there was no point in further discussion. She got up as he switched off the TV.

"It's interesting about that soldier, though," he said as they climbed the stairs. "That set me thinking, so it did."

Linda turned, startled.

"Why's that?"

"Well, during the First World War there was an army battalion stationed on this land. My grandfather used to tell me stories about them when I was a wee one."

Not surprisingly, this information gave Linda no comfort whatsoever. She knew little about ghosts, had never seen one, and, like many people, only half-believed in them. Ian was a doubting Thomas, but she herself never shut the door on the paranormal. But one thing she knew of ghosts: they were frequently the souls of men who had met violent ends—like some soldiers do. Lucy's vision was of a battle-scarred veteran; Ian's words were causing Linda to think that the man might well have suffered a violent death on her property.

The notion appalled her. She resolved to go and see Father Lawless the following day. Clearly, this was a case of a restless soul—possibly more than one—and surely a Catholic priest was ideally placed to offer help on the plight of souls.

As it turned out, Father Lawless saw little cause for concern.

"Oh, we don't take such things seriously anymore, Mrs. Gillespie," he said. "Maybe a couple of hundred years ago, but not in these more enlightened times. Children have very active imaginations these days. All that rot they see on TV and the films has a harmful effect. Pray more, and sprinkle some holy water; that's my advice. I'll get you a bottle."

He left the room and returned a few minutes later with the holy water and a prayer leaflet.

"Now, I'm giving you this Divine Mercy Chaplet to say. It's very powerful altogether. It reminds us that God's love is unlimited and available to all of us. It's good to get into the habit of regular prayer; that way, you'll feel God's protection and won't be too fearful of these paranormal things. The chaplet affords you great security. Say it every day—and have little Lucy say it also. In no time, all this will clear up. You'll see."

The Divine Mercy Chaplet has an intriguing history, as Linda would learn. Its message and devotion stem from the writings of a Polish nun. Born into poverty as Helen Kowalska, the third of ten children, she would become known as Sister Faustina.

On February 22, 1931, when Helen was twenty-six, Jesus appeared to her in a most singular vision. He was robed in white. Rays of light, some red and others white, emanated from his heart. An inner voice—she believed it to be the voice of her Savior—explained that the rays represented "the blood and water that gushed forth from the depths of my mercy when my agonizing heart was pierced on the cross. The pale rays symbolize the water, which cleanses and purifies the soul."

The vision continued to reappear. Sister Faustina kept a record of these mystical encounters, which would run to over six hundred pages. The message is always the same: that God is merciful, that he is love itself poured out for us, and that he wants us all to turn to him with true repentance while there is still time.

The nun was given to understand that she was the recipient of a new mystic image of Jesus and its accompanying message, one that would take its place alongside that of the Sacred Heart. This was a momentous revelation, yet it would be many years after Sister Faustina's death in 1940 before it was recognized and accepted by the Vatican. She herself foresaw its proscription, imposed in 1959 by Pope John XXIII. Apparently, poor and misleading translations of her diary would circulate, whereby the revelation would become corrupted. The Vatican would impose a ban. She wrote that it would remain in place until "suddenly the action of God will come upon the scene with genuine power, to bear witness to the truth."

It was not until April 1978 that the ban was lifted. The man responsible was the archbishop of Sister Faustina's home diocese, Karol Wojtyla. In October of that same year he would become Pope John Paul II. Sister Faustina was canonized in April 2000.

Linda felt better after her visit to Father Lawless. His words had reassured her. He seemed to believe that regular prayer was the remedy. Perhaps it's all that's needed, she told herself: a little more faith and an adherence to the godly.

Back at the farmhouse, she decided to perform her own "cleansing" using the holy water. She would have the house to herself for the best part of an hour before the children returned from school.

She went from room to room, downstairs first, then upstairs, sprinkling the water and urging the spirits to go to their eternal rest in the peace of God. She left the girls' room until last.

When she entered, she found that the presence of the "lady" was almost palpable. But it was not unpleasant, not threatening in any way. Linda blessed every corner, sprinkling the water more liberally on the spot where she felt the "visitor" to be standing. She knew with near certainty that she was there; it was much the same sensation as that of another person being in the room. She almost felt she could speak to that "other." And no, there was still nothing threatening about the presence, not even after she had sprinkled the holy water. Nevertheless, Linda resented another encroaching on her private space, her home, her children's privacy.

"Go!" she ordered. "Go in the name of God." Then, feeling more annoyed than courageous, she said: "This is *my* house, not yours. Whoever you are, you're not wanted here."

Linda fetched her rosary, got down on her knees by Lucy's bed, and recited the Chaplet of the Divine Mercy, gazing all the while at the picture on the prayer leaflet that the priest had given her. To her relief, she felt a change coming over the room. There was the sense of a presence departing.

There followed a period of peace and quiet. Lucy saw no more phenomena, and Linda inwardly thanked God. Father Lawless's advice had borne fruit. She berated herself for not putting more trust in him; she prayed each morning and night with the children, hoping that the peace would last.

It did not. Three weeks following her visit to the priest, Linda's confidence took a knock when Lucy had her sixth vision. In fact, it was as if the respite had been sent to tease and taunt. Lucy was to experience five more apparitions, a fresh one appearing every other day.

The first three were of an extraordinary nature, and again all were seen during the day, after Lucy had returned from school.

The first occurred when she was playing with Sandy and Darren. They were out in the lane jumping rope. Lucy and Darren were holding the rope while Sandy took her turn. On the eleventh stroke, Lucy stopped. She had gone a little pale.

"Look!" she cried, pointing to the tractor-trailer at the end of the lane. As before, her brother and sister saw nothing.

But Lucy did, and what she saw astonished her. Laid out on top of the trailer, some twenty feet away, was a youth. She was near enough to see him clearly. He was perhaps sixteen, nude, and his body seemed to be outlined in a shimmering, golden light. His eyes were open and, as the girl watched, he very slowly rose and hovered above the trailer before disappearing. Lucy says that the vision lasted some thirty seconds.

The next two manifestations did not involve human figures as such. At breakfast one morning, Lucy saw what she describes as a thin "string of smoke" coming in at the kitchen door. She thought it was dust at first, until without warning it grew denser and thicker, as it formed itself into "a rope shape" and turned white. This "rope of smoke" slowly coiled itself about Sandy's head, then Darren's, girdling them in a figure-eight shape. Lucy said nothing, but continued watching, perplexed, as it leisurely uncoiled itself again and disappeared back out through the door.

"Are you all right, sweetheart?" Linda was observing Lucy as she prepared their lunches. She thought the child might be daydreaming, sitting as she was with her spoon poised above her cereal bowl, staring into space. But then again …

"I'm fine, Mommy." Lucy resumed eating. "I thought I saw smoke round their heads, but it's gone now."

"Nonsense. You know Daddy and I don't smoke."

"I know." Lucy sensed that it was probably not the right time to tell her mother what it was she had seen. But later that evening she told all. Linda was dismayed. Whatever it was that had been troubling her daughter was back in earnest—despite her prayers and the sprinkling of holy water.

Lucy's next experience was the most bizarre of all. We will let her describe it in her own words.

"I was in the shower one afternoon, and I saw something through the glass door, lying on the floor. I couldn't see it right because the glass was all steamy, so I cleaned a wee hole and I saw this chest, like a man's chest, cut off at the waist with no arms or a head. It was all a pale color."

If there was blood present, Lucy did not wait around to check. She was terrified; she jumped over the ghastly torso and ran naked and screaming to her mother.

Linda was desperate. Up until then, Lucy seemed to be coping reasonably well with the phenomena, but the torso had truly frightened her. What on earth might the child see next? Linda decided not to bother Father Lawless again. There was another man of the cloth who might be able to advise her: Dr. Nigel Lomax, the minister attached to Ian's church. She went to see him that very evening.

Dr. Lomax was distressed to hear of Lucy's predicament. She was one of his favorite parishioners, and he was eager to do all he could. Yet he confessed to having very little experience of what he termed "the paranormal." He did, however, know a man in Belfast who perhaps could help: Canon William H. Lendrum. He gave Linda an address and telephone number, and wished her well.

That night, little Lucy slept fitfully. Her mind was replaying over and over the horrid shower scene. Sometime close to midnight, she gave up her attempts at sleep; her darkened bedroom, with its shadows and hints of danger, was making her uneasy. She slipped into her parents' room and roused her mother, who made room for her in the bed. Eventually she drifted off to sleep in the comfort and security of Linda's arms.

But at about six o'clock, she found herself wide awake. Light was peeping in at the window and she no longer felt sleepy. She eased herself quietly from the bed and padded to the door.

She checked on her brother and sister and was disappointed to find them fast asleep. Lucy was at loose ends. She had no wish to return to bed, sensing that she would be unable to sleep. She was hungry but was reluctant to go down to the kitchen. The downstairs bathroom, where she had seen the gruesome body part, lies just off the kitchen, and she was afraid of going near there. Were she to see the torso again, at that hour of the morning, she knew she would scream and wake everyone up. She put on her bunny slippers and went to one of her favorite places: the top of the stairs. Ever since she was a toddler she had liked to sit there, where she could watch people coming and going down below.

All was quiet, save for the snores coming from the open door of her brother's bedroom. Through the glass-paneled front door, the dawn sun was gradually filling the hall with a golden light, bringing the house's interior to life. Lucy felt safe. She rested her chin in her hands and gazed down at the phone table, the coat stand, and the doorjamb of the parlor door at the foot of the stairs, its high-gloss varnish reflecting the light. All those familiar things were real, and therefore comforting. They would not suddenly vanish, to manifest again and upset her.

It was while Lucy was gazing at the doorjamb of the parlor that something magical occurred. Without warning, a little girl's head popped out from behind the door, smiled up at her, and disappeared back inside.

Lucy was not scared—she was fascinated, and wanted to see the little girl again. Her wish was granted; seconds later, the child reappeared. But this time she stepped out from behind the door and came to stand on the bottom step of the stairs.

"She was like a wee Victorian doll," Lucy says, "because she had on a pink frilly dress and, like, frilly legging things. Maybe she was about four or five, and"—Lucy giggles at the memory—"she started playing peek-a-boo, jumping off the step and covering her eyes, and popping in and out from behind the door."

She was delighted. Since Darren's room was closest, she called out to him to come and see what she was witnessing. There was no response. Well, then, it was Darren's tough luck for being a sleepy-head and missing all the magic. Lucy returned her attention to the little girl.

"But when I looked again," she recalls, "I saw this big hole, like a big oval shape opened in the wall on the stairs, and it was all filled with fuzzy bright colors. And I saw the wee girl coming up the stairs and standing beside it. Then she just went into a mist, like a smoky thing, and the smoky thing went into the fuzzy hole in the wall, and then everything went away, so it did."

Like Alice through the looking glass.

Lucy was saddened by the disappearance of her spectral play-mate. She felt cheated—the little girl was the only apparition that had actually engaged with her in any way.

Or had it? The ghost appeared to Lucy to have been aware of her, had played peek-a-boo with her. And yet, on consideration, all Lucy had observed was an apparition that *seemed* to be looking at her, as if the ghost were seeing her too. The question therefore arises: had Lucy not been sitting on the top stair, might the phantom child have appeared in any case and gone through the same motions as she did with Lucy? In other words, there is no good reason to believe that this new apparition was in any way different from the others Lucy had seen.

Two days later, on the evening of Thursday, October 17, 2002, Canon Lendrum was scheduled to perform his cleansing of the Gillespie farmhouse. On that very morning, Lucy was to see her ninth ghost.

Unlike the other manifestations, this one appeared to her shortly after she had woken up, at roughly 7:30. Sandy was still asleep in the adjacent bed, but standing behind the bed was a figure.

"She was like a maid," Lucy tells us, "because she had on a black dress and a white apron and a frilly cap, and she was carrying a big silver tray with cups on it."

While Lucy stared in wonder, the maid began to move. As she did so, a pool of gold appeared to advance before her. Lucy describes the pool as a circle of gold, "like the sun, but you could look at it, because it wasn't dazzling."

"Sandy, Sandy, wake up!" she yelled. "Quick, wake up!"

Sandy sat up in bed, startled. Her sister was pointing at the wardrobe. It was to be the only time that she would share one of Lucy's enigmatic experiences. She saw "a black-and-white cloud," almost like the static seen on a badly tuned television set. It hovered for a moment or two above the wardrobe, then vanished.

Thus did the final day of phenomena begin.

We thought we might test Lucy by asking a trick question. Earlier, she had told us that the maid appeared *behind* her sister's bed. What, we asked presently, was the maid wearing on her feet? Lucy threw her eyes heavenward and replied immediately: "I told you, didn't I, that she was standing behind Sandy's bed, so I couldn't *see* her feet."

It has to be said that, throughout our conversations with little Lucy, we were impressed by her absolute honesty. She neither embellished nor exaggerated, even when pressed. The most skillful prosecutor would doubtless be no match for her. We came away from the Gillespie farmhouse with the conviction that we had made the acquaintance of a very special young girl.

"The Gillespie case," Canon Lendrum says, "was extraordinary because of the number of manifestations, and the fact that they were so unusual. But there was nothing evil about them, thank heavens. One of my less disturbing cases, I'd say."

He goes on to explain that little Lucy's phenomena seemed to conform to what is known in psychical research circles as a "residual" or "mental imprint" haunting. The manifestations generally occur at the site of a highly charged emotional event—for example, a battle or a murder. It is believed that the discharge of enormous amounts of emotional energy by such events can cause the scene to be imprinted on its surroundings. At significant times—for instance, on the anniversary of the death or deaths of those involved—the occurrences may somehow be reenacted. One can think in terms of a three-dimensional film, in effect a moving hologram, the images being projected not onto a flat screen but onto the very air itself.

A number of other factors seem to bear out the "residual imprint" hypothesis. Such hauntings tend to occur in old houses or historical buildings. The Gillespie farmhouse is over two hundred years old. Lucy's ghosts tended to hover a few inches off the ground and walk through walls; it might be conjectured, then, that they continued to follow floor plans that existed in earlier times. They seemed oblivious to the presence of the living—even though it could be argued that the little girl on the stairs was attempting to interact with her. It is believed that the psychic energy such apparitions emit can be picked up by individuals who are psychically "sensitive." Lucy's mother is of the opinion that her daughter is psychic, and that this gift, or indeed peculiarity, has been passed down the maternal line.

"Such phenomena usually disappear over time," Canon Lendrum asserts, "although there is the risk that repeated sightings by the living can revive the psychic energy that keeps them going. There is also the danger that evil entities will use the opportunity to gain access, and cause great distress and upset. So it's always best to cleanse the site as soon as possible."

We are curious to know what, in his opinion, triggered the manifestations in the first place. Prior to Lucy's experiences, there was no history of sightings. We wonder if it was a case of somebody dabbling in the occult. Over the course of our research and following numerous interviews, we concluded that anything connected with the occult—Ouija boards, horoscopes, seances, tarot cards, fortune-telling, witchcraft, and so on—can sometimes serve as a portal for spirits to enter an individual's life.

"I'm glad you asked that," the canon says. "Yes, something the mother told me set the alarm bells ringing. Two things, in fact.

"Mrs. Gillespie's own mother had died in April of the year the manifestations started. They had made a pact, you see. While the mother lay dying, Linda asked that, when she got to the other side, she send her a sign that she was all right. The mother agreed. When a month passed and nothing happened, Linda became anxious and started ringing psychic phone lines, hoping that a fortune-teller could tell her something.

"What she heard from one of them was very strange. The medium asked her to go outside, because she saw the mother in the yard standing beside an orange duck. Linda thought this was bizarre. The family did not keep ducks, but she decided to check anyway. She found Lucy outside and, odd as it seems, the orange plastic duck she played with at bath time was lying at her feet. Lucy claimed she hadn't taken it from the bathroom, and her mother had no reason to doubt her."

Did this occurrence confirm for Linda that her mother had indeed made contact?

"No. She said the experience upset her, but that same evening something else happened that satisfied her that her mother had succeeded. She was resting on the sitting-room sofa when a circle of golden stars appeared in one corner of the room, whirled around for a few seconds, and then disappeared."

"I didn't like the sound of any of that," Canon Lendrum continues, "even though Linda was acting with what she believed were the best intentions—caring about where her mother might be. Make no mistake: such naiveté can be used by discarnate entities to disturb and disrupt lives. It was after that occurrence that Lucy began having her visions."

The canon goes on to cite the incidents in Scripture that record the living making contact with the dead. He views those examples as warnings and holds that they are as pertinent today as they were in biblical times.

In the First Book of Samuel, King Saul requests that the witch of Endor, a woman possessing a familiar—a demon that does her bidding—commune on his behalf with the spirit of the dead Samuel. She succeeds, to her surprise, and it seems that it was the demon that made the contact possible. It is also interesting to note that Samuel is none too happy at his rest being disturbed.

Also, in Luke's Gospel, Jesus tells the story of the rich man and Lazarus. The former is suffering in hell and asks that Lazarus, the poor man residing in heaven, be sent back to earth. The rich man fears for his five surviving brothers, and asks that they be warned of the torments that await them if they do not mend their ways. His request is refused on the grounds that the living have the word of Moses and the prophets to persuade them. They should have no need of the testimony of dead men.

And this is the nub of it, according to Canon Lendrum. Those who turn to the occult for answers are demonstrating a lamentable lack of trust in God.

He reminds us of a passage in Deuteronomy: "Let no one be found among you who practices divination or sorcery, interprets omens, engages in witchcraft, or casts spells, or who is a medium or spiritist or who consults the dead. Anyone who does these things is detestable to the Lord."

They are also asking for trouble, the canon feels. Doors into the unknown can open. The Gillespies were fortunate that their particular door seems to have opened onto one of the more benign regions of extraphysical existence.

We ask about the nature of the exorcism itself. It is our understanding that it was more a cleansing of the house than a deliverance of Lucy. "Yes, indeed. One can speculate that the lady whom Lucy had seen three times had possibly the greatest emotional attachment to the place. Probably suffered a good deal during the war. The armless soldier could have been the husband; the body part in the shower, the naked boy, possibly sons who died violently. Interesting that Lucy first saw the mistress tidying the videotapes. Asserting ownership, I'd say, then her praying by the wall and the monk praying also...trying to come to terms with the tragedy."

We wonder if any of Lucy's apparitions congregated for the blessing, whether the canon was aware of any "presences."

He nods. "I did feel a presence, which I suppose could have been that of the mistress. I sensed that if I laid her to rest, the others would follow in due course. I celebrated a Eucharist with the family and prayed that she'd go in the peace of the Lord, where she could meet her loved ones again in the light of God's love. Then I blessed each room in the house and the outbuildings as well."

"So all in all, everyone was happy," he concludes. "It is wonderful to participate in such a healing victory. Experiencing the power of God's love in these situations is something neither I nor those afflicted ever forget."

The effects of Father Ignatius McCarthy, used during an exorcism.
Father Ignatius requested anonymity, and so is not pictured.

PART TWO

THE MONK: FATHER IGNATIUS McCARTHY

A native of County Clare, he is eighty years old and has been a clois-
tered monk for fifty-three of those years. Despite having left the
county of his birth some five decades ago, he has never lost the accent.
He speaks softly, and one has to listen closely to catch his words. Yet
his gentle demeanor masks an iron will and a fierce intelligence. There
is also an air of another time about him; one suspects that the saints
and Christian martyrs of antiquity looked and sounded a lot like Father
Ignatius.

His call to the religious life came when he was still a child.

"I was enthralled by the whole solemnity and pomp of the Mass,"
he recollects. "While other boys were most likely bored by that Sunday
ritual, I was enchanted. I remember asking my mother what a priest
did besides offering Mass, and she said: 'He dresses in black clothes
and prays a lot.' I think maybe she didn't want me getting ideas in that
direction."

But the young Ignatius's dream of becoming a priest did not di-
minish as he grew older. "I suppose when I got into my teens I became
aware of what I'd be giving up, what the monastic life would involve,
and that worried me. I'd be burning my bridges, and there would be no
turning back. But, fortunately, God's call was louder and stronger than
all those petty considerations."

At age seventeen, he entered Maynooth Seminary in County Kildare to begin his seven years' training.

Following his ordination, he joined the Redemptorist Fathers and served as a missionary in Africa. Ill health forced him to return to Ireland before his five-year tenure was completed. He joined the Cistercian order in 1948 and has been with that community ever since.

"I always had the idea that monks were a lazy crowd who sat about all day thinking deeply about things," he says with a smile, as he gives us a tour of the grounds. "I got a rude awakening when I came here. Much of the work consisted of heavy farm labor. There are over a hundred acres of arable land surrounding the monastery, and most of it was under crop every year back then. Apart from that, we had a dairy farm with a milking herd of seventy or more cattle."

The tough labor that characterized his early life has now been replaced by a gentler routine, yet when it comes to spiritual matters, the rigid disciplines remain firmly in place and are embraced with as much fervor as ever. Prayer and meditation are the order of the day.

His day begins at 3:45 a.m., when the Great Silence—imposed at 9:15 p.m. the previous evening—is broken by the tolling of the chapel bell.

Vigils, the first office of communal prayer service, start the day. They are followed by Lauds, the second office or morning prayers, at 7 a.m., after which Father Ignatius prepares to say morning Mass. At 8:15 a.m., midmorning prayers, or Terce, are said. This is the shortest office of the day. At noon, midday prayers, Sext, are followed at 2:30 p.m. by None, midafternoon prayer, and Vespers, or evening prayer, at 5:30 p.m. The day ends with Compline, the final office. In between these seven prayer periods, Father Ignatius eats three light meals, reads, and spends time with those visitors who come seeking his help. He retires at 9:15 p.m., entering the Great Silence once more, and sleeps for four to five hours.

His first encounter with the demonic occurred in the 1960s, in a most unlikely place: within the very walls of the monastery.

Brother Francis was a young man in his twenties when he joined the order. Father Ignatius recalls him with sadness. "He was the proud-

est person I'd ever met … terribly self-centered and covetous. There was an air of danger about him, and when he'd get angry—which was very often—you really feared for your own safety. I remember him throwing a can of oil at me for no reason at all and then laughing when it hit its target. He loved seeing people upset; he seemed to thrive on it. I've noticed that a marked immaturity lies at the heart of all evil, and that there needs to be a degree of dysfunction already in the individual before evil can take hold. Brother Francis ticked every box.

"On several occasions, I noticed his light on in his room in the middle of the night … and in one of his rare moments of calm I asked him about it. He told me that in the dark something would visit him and press down on his chest. I offered to pray in the room with him. He asked me what good that would do, and in no time he was back to his usual, angry, self."

After a year Brother Francis was asked to leave.

"He ended up a homeless deviant," Father Ignatius continues, "and was charged several times with sexual assault, on both women and men. These days he spends his time wandering the roads, I believe. A lost soul in every sense of the word. I always remember him in my prayers, though. Where there is life there is still hope."

Father Ignatius's introduction to exorcism occurred quite by accident. A fellow priest, Father James, a friend from school days who had been allocated a new parish in the west of Ireland, visited him one day with an unusual story.

He explained that, since moving into the parochial house, he had been having some very strange experiences. On several occasions he had awoken in the early hours to find a young woman standing by the foot of the bed. She was dressed in clothes from ancient times and was badly disfigured down one side of her face. The priest, sensing that she was a lost soul, began praying for her. Within a matter of days, the visions ceased. However, things took a more sinister turn when one morning he found his breviary not on his study desk where it always sat but lying face down on the floor. From then on, other religious objects in the house came under attack.

"He was terribly troubled when he came to see me," Father Ignatius recalls, "and asked me if I would come to the house and pray. I did, of course, without hesitation. Father James reported that my intervention proved successful, and after that word spread. I was called upon to assist in other such cases. I take no credit for these successes," he continues modestly. "We priests are simply channels through which God does his work. Our job is to remain firm in faith and never fear, because the Devil is as nothing in the face of God the Almighty."

Father Ignatius has always believed in the existence of evil.

"I'm from the old school," he asserts, "however antiquated that may sound. As a Catholic priest I believe in the Gospels, in Jesus's life as the supreme example of how we should live. Jesus cast out many demons during his ministry and spoke persistently about the Devil and his works. The fact that Jesus spoke so clearly about the reality of Satan is the most powerful evidence we have. So we priests are duty bound to continue his work. We can't cherry-pick those aspects of Jesus's ministry we choose to accept as gospel and ignore the idea of Satan simply because it is distasteful to our so-called modern minds."

He has seen a rise in the instances of demonic oppression over the past few years—but is not surprised.

"Materialism and consumerism have eroded spiritual values," he concludes, "but they don't deliver the peace and happiness people crave. We satisfy our egos at the expense of our souls. The result of all this moral decay means that Ireland may now be the second-richest country in Europe, but at what a cost! We have the highest incidence of alcohol abuse, drug abuse, and teenage pregnancy in Europe as well. Pope John Paul II, when he visited Ireland in 1979, warned of this moral decline. He said: 'Your country seems in a sense to be living again the temptations of Christ. Ireland is being asked to prefer the "kingdoms of this world with their splendor" to the kingdom of God. Satan, the tempter, the adversary of Christ, will use all his might and deceptions to win Ireland for the way of the world.... Now is the time of testing....'"

These days, this humble, devout man leaves the monastery only to deal with those cases that have defeated other priests—in particular, when a haunting takes on an antireligious character, indicative of the work of hostile spirits or demons.

He spends most days in solitude and prayer, yet is forever willing to receive those who come to the monastery seeking his prayers and wise counsel.

Truly this man is "in the world" but not "of the world."

It is said that all it takes for evil to flourish is for good men to do nothing. The charge of inaction in the face of spiritual danger is not one that can be laid at the door of this devout and dedicated monk.

The following five cases complement those of his Anglican counterpart, Canon William Lendrum. Father Ignatius regards each of them as a cautionary tale, but all serving to remind the reader of the formidable power of prayer.

THE PIT BENEATH
THE HEARTHSTONE

❖

CONNEMARA, COUNTY GALWAY, 1974

A blue Vauxhall Astra sits idling by a farmhouse gate on a hot Sunday morning in mid-June. At the wheel is a young man, one elbow resting on the door frame, whistling to himself as he gazes beyond the windshield. Occasionally, he flicks a glance at the whitewashed cottage but, as yet, there is no sign of life. He sounds the horn a second time: one short, sharp blast that shatters the quiet of the countryside. But still nothing stirs. He lights another cigarette and sighs.

Dan McBride has been ferrying the Dwyer brothers to and from Mass every Sunday for the past eighteen months. He is not particularly fond of the pair, but his mother feels sorry for them. Both are bachelors in their late seventies, taciturn men who rarely venture beyond the confines of the twenty-acre farm that sustains them.

Dan grows impatient. He tosses the half-smoked cigarette into the hedge and is about to step out of the car, but at that moment, he hears the front door of the cottage opening. He watches Edward and Cornelius Dwyer emerge into the sunlight and shuffle up the path. Edward, as usual, is carrying a plastic gallon container.

The men climb into the car and mumble a greeting. Their routine never varies. They wear the same clothes, nod politely, and use the same words of greeting before falling silent. Cornelius settles himself in the backseat and lays the two missals on his lap. Edward rides in front with the container between his knees. They are ready to leave.

The tires of Dan's car crunch over the rough graveled lane, which winds for a good mile to the main road. He remarks on the weather and is answered by a grunt from Cornelius.

On arriving at the church, Edward makes the same puzzling request of Dan that he has been making every Sunday: "You wouldn't get that filled with holy water while you're waiting?"

"Right-o," says Dan.

While the brothers attend the forty-five-minute service, Dan fills the container from a barrel of holy water by the sacristy door. His chore done, he passes the time by reading the newspaper and smoking a couple more cigarettes.

On this particular Sunday, however, Dan's curiosity gets the better of him. Back at the Dwyer cottage, he decides to ask the question that has been gnawing at him for the longest time.

"Tell me something," he says, as the men are getting out of the car. "Why d'you need so much holy water every Sunday? D'you make the tea with it, do yous?"

The brothers turn as one and eye him sourly. "You needn't give us a lift again," Cornelius says.

"No, you needn't give us a lift again," Edward repeats. "We'll get somebody else to take us to Mass from now on."

Dan can only stare after the pair as they shuffle back down the path, Edward carrying the container of holy water in his right hand, Cornelius gripping the missals in his left.

"That's gratitude!" Dan shouts after them. Angry, he guns the engine and turns in the yard. His final glimpse of the brothers is in the rearview mirror as they enter the farmhouse without a backward glance. He will never see them again.

Six months later, both Dwyers are dead, having passed away within weeks of each other.

There were nine siblings in the family, four of whom died in infancy. Cornelius and Edward were the eldest. Two sisters had married and were living in England. Shane, the sole surviving brother, was also married with a young family and lived close to the paternal home.

It seems that there was bad blood in the Dwyer line. Shane discovered, on his brothers' demise, that the unthinkable had happened: they had bequeathed the family farm to neighbors. He had taken for granted that he would inherit. He was shocked. Land that had been in the Dwyer name for generations now belonged to outsiders.

He vowed to buy it back, if only to restore the good name of the Dwyers and their standing within the community. But, as the years passed, the demands of his own family took priority.

Shane always felt keenly the loss of the land. Partly to heal the hurt, he threw himself into the education of his eldest son, Shane Jr., believing that the boy, by excelling in college, would win back the self-respect taken away from the father. But, even after decades had passed, the dispossessed man still hankered after the "home place," as he called it. His dying wish was that Shane Jr. might close the gap that his brothers had so cruelly breached.

In January 2002, that wish was fulfilled. His son bought back the land. He built a new home on the footprint of the old cottage in memory of his dear father and, in so doing, restored the family name to that little patch of Connemara that had always belonged to the Dwyers.

The modern, two-story dwelling occupies an enviable position within the shadows of the Twelve Pins mountain range. It is a peaceful place, far from the main road and embraced to some extent by the rough natural beauty of Ireland's western seaboard. There are no other homesteads in sight.

We are sitting in Shane Dwyer's kitchen as he relates his story. He is thirty-four, a tall, lean, dark-haired man with alert brown eyes and an easy manner. He and his wife, Moya, are both high-school teachers. They have two children: Emma, age nine, and Rory, five.

"Yes, it is very quiet here," Shane agrees, when we comment on how fortunate he is to be living amid such tranquillity. "But don't let that fool you. The past two years have been anything but peaceful."

He is confirming what has already been told to us. We are here in this isolated part of County Galway because the events that took place in the Dwyer home caused alarm among quite a few clergymen.

It began on June 10, 2004, the day the family took possession of their lovely new home. It was so much more spacious than their old one, a row house in Clifden. One would have thought, then, that everyone would be pleased, but that was not the case.

"I well remember the day we moved in," Shane tells us. "I felt that Moya wasn't happy, but I put it down to the change of scene."

While the children played outside in the yard, the parents spent that first sunny afternoon unwrapping bric-a-brac and hanging pictures. They concentrated on the two small rooms to the front of the house, the "green room," or lounge, to the left of the front door and the "red room," or parlor, to the right.

Unlike the rest of the house, these rooms are small. They faithfully follow the floor plan of the old cottage. In fact, the rooms, together with the hall and pantry, occupy the exact area on which the original Dwyer home stood. The couple had received a heritage grant to preserve this historical feature.

"Granny's Bible, where do you think?" asked Shane, hefting the heavy, leather-bound book in both hands.

"Oh, the parlor. Don't want the kids to get their hands on it." Moya took it. "Here, I'll do it."

She carried it down to the red room. Despite the heat of the day, there was a cold feel to it. She remembers that there was something about the room that made her uneasy. It may have been the thickness of the walls; the old cottage walls were designed to provide shelter throughout the long, damp Connemara winter. Moya stood up on a chair and placed the Bible on a high shelf to the left of the fireplace. As she did so, she heard the door shut softly behind her.

"Shane, is that you?"

No answer.

Again, a slight shiver ran through her. She had the sensation of someone, or something, having entered the room. She rushed to the door and pulled it open. But there was no sign of Shane. Instead, she found him in the kitchen.

"Why did you do that?" she asked.

"Do what?"

"You shut the door on me. In the red room."

"I didn't."

"Yes, you bloody well did! And it's not funny."

"Look, the wind must have done it."

"The wind. Look at those trees, Shane!" She went to the window. "They're as still as statues. There's not a breath of wind today, and besides, the windows at the front *are not open*."

"Well, maybe it just swung to. New doors sometimes do that."

"Yeah, right. If it happens again I'll want a better explanation." She busied herself unwrapping another item.

Shane said nothing. He knew his wife was not too happy with the move to the country. Born and raised in the lively, bustling town of Clifden, she had relinquished a whole way of life to live in "the back of beyond," as she called it. Shane was fulfilling his dead father's wish, and he felt guilty that Moya was part of that wish too—whether she liked it or it. He had noticed that every time they visited the house during its construction, Moya's mood changed. On the return journey she would say hardly anything at all, and it would take a while for her to become "herself" again.

He hoped that things would settle down once they had moved in. But here they were, barely two hours in the place, and she was accusing him of mischief. The signs were not good.

"I'll make some coffee," he said, trying to lighten the atmosphere.

Moya was not listening. She was looking thoughtfully at the picture of the Sacred Heart. Shane had just hung it near the stove, as his parents had done in their old home.

"I don't want it there," she said abruptly. "I want it over the mantelpiece in the red room." She reached into a box on the floor and hauled out a crucifix. "And this in the green room, on the back wall. Can you do that? *Now,* please?"

He nodded. He was unsure of what to say. "Moya knew better than I did that something was wrong with the house. She told me later that she got an inkling on that first day, the day we moved in. She didn't use the word *evil* but I knew what she meant. She felt that the holy picture and crucifix should be there. She didn't know exactly why she felt that, but I trusted her intuition."

The months passed. The house became a home. Shane was gratified to be able to fulfill his father's dream of having the land restored to the Dwyer family. As time wore on, he grew to love the house, to feel that he belonged within its walls. Moya had overcome her initial disquiet. Emma settled into the local school and made friends. They were living the idyll.

But, before too long, there were signs—nothing overt, but small signs—that things were not quite right. The trouble began with three-year-old Rory.

Emma and Rory each had a bedroom on the first floor. It was Shane's habit, having tucked in the little boy, to check for the boogeyman. It was something he had always done; he supposed he would be doing it for quite some time to come.

That particular evening, a little after seven o'clock, he made a great show, as usual, of crouching and peering under the child's bed.

"Nope, no boogeyman," he assured Rory, getting to his feet again.

"But the boogeyman's not down there, Daddy!" The boy was looking fixedly toward the other side of the room. "He's standing at the window."

"Right, I'll open the window and throw him out."

He made a great show of striding purposefully across the room.

"It's all right now, Daddy. He just went into the wall."

Shane smiled, remembering his own childhood and the host of imaginary friends he had—the fairies, the hobgoblins, and creatures slight and small. Yes, children have rich imaginations, he mused. A pity they lose it all so quickly, when boring adulthood kicks in.

He gave it no further thought. He continued to check under the bed each night for the boogeyman—and Rory continued to insist that "the bad man" was actually by the window. Then the child announced one night that he could dispense with his father's sentinel services.

"There's no need, Daddy. Michael comes in and sends him away."

Shane smiled, ruffled Rory's blond curls. "Who's Michael, then?"

"He sits on the roof and he's got wings…and…and when you go out, he comes in and he sends the bad man away."

Again, images of elves and fairies came to mind. Shane filed "Michael" away as yet another denizen of a little boy's fantasy world. At the same time, minor incidents were occurring in the Dwyer home. Each by itself was trivial, but taken together they were forming a pattern.

"Items would go missing or get misplaced," Shane explains. "You might set your coffee cup on the table, then go to get something in another room, come back, and discover that your cup had been moved to the draining board. Or we'd find the telephone off the hook for no good reason. At first we blamed each other, then we blamed the children."

The trifling anomalies were to give way to something more ominous. It occurred during the approach to Christmas.

"It was bizarre," Shane says. "Moya had put the Bible in the red room. Three mornings in a row we found it lying smack bang in the middle of the floor, and always opened at the same pages: Isaiah twenty-eight to twenty-nine."

He sees our look of bemusement. He fetches the Bible and turns to the chapters in question. "It seems to be all about the fall of Jerusalem and the demon drink," he says. "And before you get any ideas, I never touch the stuff. Never have."

He reads a verse or two.

Woe to the crown of pride, to the drunkards of Ephraim, whose glorious beauty is a fading flower, which are on the head of the fat valleys of them that are overcome with wine!

Behold, the Lord hath a mighty and strong one, which as a tempest of hail and a destroying storm, as a flood of mighty waters overflowing, shall cast down to the earth with the hand.

The crown of pride, the drunkards of Ephraim, will be trampled under feet....

"We couldn't understand what any of it meant," Shane confesses, "but it was leading up to something, and we soon found out. That Christmas, all hell broke loose."

The phrase is an apposite one. The first holiday season in their new home would herald a catalog of events so terrifying, so extraordinary, and of such frequency, that one is left wondering how anyone could endure it and remain mentally and emotionally unscathed.

Christmas Day itself passed peacefully. Moya's parents came for lunch, exchanged gifts, and left around nine o'clock. The children were put to bed soon after. The Dwyers watched a movie and retired at 11:30.

But at midnight they found themselves wide awake and hurriedly switching on the bedside lights. Somebody was knocking on the front door.

"Maybe it's your parents," Shane offered, on seeing his wife's look of alarm. "They might have broken down on the road." He got out of bed.

"Hardly, they left ages—"

Her words were cut short by another burst of knocking, this time louder and more furious. Shane hurried downstairs. He threw the switch that turned the porch light on.

"I'm coming!" he called out. He drew back the bolt and flung the door wide.

There was no one there.

Perplexed, he went outside and stood on the step. Snow had been falling gently but steadily all evening. The garden and pathway were covered. The tracks made by his parents-in-law and their car tires were obliterated—and there were no fresh tracks to be seen. All about there lay a deathly silence.

As he stood there trying to make sense of the mystery, a sudden fear gripped Shane. He slammed the door shut as Moya was coming down the stairs.

"Children awake?"

"Sound asleep." He saw that she shared his unease. "I *knew* there was something awful about this place from the very beginning."

"I think you're exaggerating, love. Maybe we imagined it."

But no sooner had he said the words than the frantic knocking started up again—this time on the back door. Shane rushed down the hallway to investigate but, as he did, the clamor at the back ceased and immediately resumed at the front.

"It was then I had to admit we were dealing with something completely unnatural," he tells us. "It was as if ten sets of knuckles were rapping...rapping really hard. And that's the way it went on—stopping and starting. Back door, then front—back and forth, back and forth. Then together, at the same time."

The situation was too preposterous for words. They did not know what to do. They hesitated in the hallway.

"Jesus, we'd better get out of here!" Shane said finally.

"I'm not going anywhere!" Moya was shaking visibly. That surprised him; she was a strong-willed woman who did not scare easily. She started slowly up the stairs. "It's outside. If you open the door again, it'll come in. I *know* it will!"

He followed her. All at once, the knocking ceased. There was silence. They stood for a time staring at each other.

"It's over!" Moya whispered. "*Listen!*"

Feeling a little more confident now, they tiptoed up a few more steps, each sharing an irrational notion (they confided to each other later) that the slightest sound might trigger the terrible disturbances again. But just before they reached the top stair, they were pulled up short. Moya gripped her husband's wrist hard. The front door was opening.

It swung fully open. An icy blast swept into the house, making everything about them tremble and flap.

"It blew open!" said Shane, seeing Moya's terrified face. "The wind blew it open, that's all. I'll close it."

Steeling himself, he prepared to go back down the stairs. But, before he reached the bottom, the door had swung shut again, all by itself. He hesitated on the stair. He heard something. He felt something, too; it caused the blood to drain from his face. It was not his imagination—heavy footsteps were slowly crossing the hall, in the direction of the stairs.

Shane hotfooted it back the way he had come. Moya reached out and grasped his arm, pulling him toward the bedroom, as one would pull a man out of the path of danger.

"Oh, Jesus, Shane—*quick!*"

They stumbled and half-fell into the room. Shane locked the door. Moya fell onto the bed, crying uncontrollably.

"Shush." He wanted her to stop. Even through the closed door he could hear the unseen intruder mounting the stairs, so loud were the footfalls.

"They were the steps of a heavily built man wearing boots," he says. "You could hear the stairs shake with every step he took."

The footsteps continued to climb the stairs. Shane put his ear to the door and listened, hardly knowing what was louder, the thudding of his own heart or the lumbering tread of the phantom boots.

At the top of the stairs they halted. Moments later, they crossed the landing. Shane caught his breath—the children's rooms were on that side. His terror was supplanted by the overriding urge to protect his children at all costs. He unlocked the door.

"What are you doing?"

He told her.

"Oh God, Shane!"

They found the landing deserted, nor was there any sound from the children's rooms. Rory was sleeping undisturbed, as was his sister, Emma.

The house was silent. Whatever had intruded seemed to have left them in peace, if only for the time being. Moya fetched the holy water she kept on a windowsill and gently blessed the children as they slept.

"Let's say a rosary as well," she said.

They knelt in their own bedroom and began the prayers. "Our Father who art in Heaven ..." The words were soothing. "Lead us not into temptation, but deliver us from evil..."

Moya held up a hand. "No, not 'evil.' 'The Evil One' is what we should be saying. 'Deliver us from the Evil One.' There's an evil presence around this house. I can *feel* it."

"Look, you were the one who didn't want to leave," Shane said untactfully.

She started crying, and he wished he had kept his mouth shut. His nerves were taut; he was not thinking straight. The uncanny occurrences had frightened him more than he was admitting to her.

"It's stopped now anyway," he said gently. "Let's finish the rosary. It'll be all right."

The silence held. They knelt again and resumed the remaining decade. But hardly were they halfway through when Moya stopped again.

"Shane, there's someone outside the window!"

He was growing exasperated. After all, they were on the upper floor; in order to reach the window, an intruder would need a ladder. And the blinds were drawn. He had no idea what Moya was talking about.

"I *heard* something," she insisted. "Listen!"

But there was no sound apart from the ticking of the clock on the bedside table. The night was unusually quiet—as nights are when a fall of snow lies on the ground.

"Very well," he said, getting up, "if it puts your mind at rest."

He raised the blind and peered out. He had left the gable light on. Snow had started falling again. There was no trace of anybody near the house. He saw the distant lights of a car out on the road, but that was all. He left the window.

"Nothing there," he said. "What did it sound like?"

But she did not need to answer because it came again, and this time it was loud enough for Shane to hear. He recalls it as sounding like a low whimper, followed by moaning.

"The wind."

But it was not—and he knew it. The moaning grew steadily louder and higher in pitch. There could be no doubt: the Dwyers were hearing the wailing of a grief-stricken woman.

"Oh, my God!" Moya cried. "What *is* that? Who's doing that?" She was still on her knees by the bed, twisting the rosary beads around and about her fingers. She tugged at Shane's sleeve. "Let's just keep praying!"

He got down on his knees again. Although he tried not to show it, he was as terrified as his wife.

They tried to pray more loudly, to drown out the woman's voice and their fear. And yet, the more they raised their voices, the more the wailing intensified. In the end, a frightful, high-pitched screaming was drowning them out. They had a wild conviction that something or somebody was attempting to stymie their prayers.

But they would not be deterred. Sheer terror spurred them on, and prayer seemed the only course to adopt. They wanted desperately for their prayers to be effective against the evil—they felt certain it was evil—that was encroaching on their home.

They began a second rosary. Hardly had Shane recited the opening words than the banging on the front door started up again. He flinched. Even upstairs, the blows were deafening, seeming to resound throughout the house. They stopped, but the screeching from outside the window continued unabated and undiminished.

And then, momentarily, it died away. Now it was replaced by a frenetic rapping at the window. It was too much; they had to abandon the rosary. The "intruder" had won.

The couple hurried to look in on the children again, believing that the racket was bound to have awakened them. But, incredibly, as before, they slept on undisturbed. Shane could only conclude that some force was exercising control over their waking and sleeping.

The siege of the Dwyer home—the screaming and wailing, the urgent rapping on windows and doors—continued all through the night.

"It would switch itself off and on every half an hour or so," says Shane. "The wailing in particular alerted us to the possibility that it might be a banshee, so I telephoned my family to check that everyone was okay."

It is perhaps only natural that the Dwyers should draw this conclusion, for the myth of the banshee runs deep in the Irish psyche. In Irish and Scottish folklore, she is a female spirit who attaches herself to families, especially those whose surnames begin with *Mac* or *O*. Her wailing is said to presage the death of a member of the family. Irish mythology paints the *bean sí*, or "fairy woman," as a beautiful creature with long, flowing hair and eyes reddened from weeping. She is variably dressed in a green or white gown. But, although many claim to have heard her, actual sightings of this elusive creature are rare.

According to Scottish tradition, the banshee is also known as the *bean nighe*, or "washerwoman." The legend runs that she anticipates the violent death of a family member by appearing to wash his blood-stained grave clothes in a river or stream. Unlike her more beautiful counterpart, the *bean nighe* appears as an ugly, deformed creature that exudes malevolence.

Shane only half-believed the legend. But he was taking no chances. The horrendous events of the night had convinced him that paranormal forces were arrayed against him and his family. If *they're* real, he thought, why not the banshee as well?

He telephoned his young brother Andy in Australia. Andy had called on Christmas Eve to wish them well, and had told Shane he would be traveling between Adelaide and Sydney on December 27—that very day, allowing for the time difference. He knew he would never forgive himself if Andy were to have an accident because he had failed to warn him. He also called his mother and sister, both of whom lived near Clifden, and persuaded them to come over.

"There was a need to get others to witness what was happening," he says, "and so prove that we weren't going crazy. The puzzling part was the children. They were sleeping, oblivious to the whole thing, which was just incredible, because the noise was deafening. I remember when I was phoning my Mum, she didn't need much convincing, because she could hear the commotion down the line."

Mrs. Dwyer and Maura arrived at 4 a.m. They could tell at once how upset the couple were; Mrs. Dwyer commented on how haggard they looked. No sooner had they crossed the threshold than the wailing began, much to Maura's consternation. Moya saw her cross herself. Without delay, Mrs. Dwyer suggested that all four say a rosary together in the red room.

"Why there?" Shane asked.

"I don't know, son. Maybe it wouldn't do any harm to recite it where this thing started."

They had to raise their voices to make the prayers heard above the screeching from outside and the almost incessant pounding on the doors, back and front.

"My mother was a tower of strength," Shane tells us. "She seemed to take it all in her stride. At one point during the prayers, the Bible was flung again from the top shelf by the fireplace. It came down on the carpet in front of the fireplace, and it fell open at exactly the same place: Isaiah twenty-eight and nine. I don't think she believed me when I told her about it before, but she did then, that's for sure."

At around 4:30, the howling and banging, which had begun a full six hours earlier, stopped as abruptly as it started.

"You need to get the priest in," Mrs. Dwyer said, when they had completed the rosary. "Give him a call first thing."

"But it's Stephen's Day, Mom."

"Sure, don't worry about that. He'll come."

And he did. Father Dorrity answered the summons promptly, losing no time in coming to bless the house. He could only speculate, but in his considered opinion the root of the problem was "a wandering soul—or souls maybe, more than one." Perhaps it was Shane's uncles, the previous inhabitants, he suggested. He urged the family to pray for them.

The Dwyers felt reassured after the priest's visit. Mrs. Dwyer and Maura stayed on that day to keep the family company and give support. Maura did the cooking. They left in the early evening, having assured the couple that they would be in touch before the New Year. When Shane and Moya retired for the night, exhausted by the night's ordeal, they felt that their troubles must surely be at an end.

Moya checked the children and sprinkled more holy water. She was not in the habit of shutting the bedroom doors, but that night she shut Rory's, remembering with a shudder the sound of the phantom footfalls entering his room. It was her way of assuring her little son's safety, even though, in her heart of hearts, she knew that a closed door would offer no resistance to a ghost.

Tuckered out, the couple fell asleep almost immediately—only to be awakened again after a minute or two by a noise that made their flesh crawl. It was the unmistakable sound of a door opening, and it was coming from across the way.

"Oh, my God," whispered Moya, "I shut Rory's door a few minutes ago and he was fast asleep."

"I'll go," Shane said.

He switched on the corridor light. The door to Emma's room stood open, as expected, as did the door to the bathroom, which was rarely shut. But the door to Rory's room was open a fraction. Shane's heartbeat quickened. Moya said she had closed it. Someone had gone in there. It was the only explanation.

"What is it?" Moya had followed him out. She was standing, shivering, more from fear than from the cold. Shane put a finger to his lips.

"It must be in Rory's room."

He went cautiously to the door and eased it open. The bedside light in the child's room was always kept on. It showed clearly that the bed was empty.

Shane heard a little cry from the corridor and Moya hurrying down the stairs. At the bottom, curled up in a little ball, lay Rory.

"He's asleep," she said. "He's fast asleep."

"I don't understand. Was he walking in his sleep?"

"It's not like him." She had the child in her arms. He had not woken up. "He's never done that before."

"I know," said Shane. He also knew that Rory had not opened the door. He had never done that before either; from the time he was a baby he had always slept the night through.

They carried Rory back to bed and knelt to say a prayer of thanksgiving.

They had only just made the sign of the cross when, as on the previous night, a loud hammering sounded on the front door. It was followed almost at once by screams at the bedroom window. The haunting had resumed, as though the priest had never come, as though his blessing meant nothing.

Terrified, they packed up as quickly as they could, bundled the children into the car, and fled the house.

They spent New Year's with Shane's mother. She assured him that they could stay as long as they wished—she appreciated the company. But the couple were keen to return home as soon as possible. It was bad for the children, Moya insisted; they needed the stability.

"What's so stable about a home that's under attack by banshees and God knows what else?" Mrs. Dwyer countered.

"So what would you suggest we do, Mom?" Shane asked.

"Have a word with Father Dorrity again."

As it happened, the priest had recently attended a talk given by a man who had successfully performed exorcisms in South Africa. Patrick Monroe was a Baptist minister and missionary; he would be in Ireland for some time more, and Father Dorrity promised to get in touch with him right away. The phone call was made, the day decided on. The missionary arrived at the Dwyer house in mid-January. Together with Father Dorrity, he effected a cleansing of each room in the house. Prayers were said in English and Latin.

It was not a solemn exorcism, but it had the desired effect. A peace descended on the farmhouse in the shadow of the Twelve Pins. The family could return and get on with their lives again. All was well; the ghosts were banished. Or so it seemed.

"About three weeks later," Shane says, "it started again. At times like that you just want to say, 'To hell with it!' We seriously considered clearing out, putting the house on the market, moving in with my mother until the sale went through.

"But we didn't, because it didn't seem too serious at first. We had the nonsense with the Bible again. It'd fall—or be thrown—and, sure enough, it'd be opened at Isaiah, per usual. We'd find it on the rug in the red room. But we could live with that. So we just ignored it. But then 'it' started appearing, and that's something we couldn't ignore."

The "it" was a manifestation totally new to the sequence of hauntings. One night, Shane awoke to find a tall, hooded figure standing in the corner of the room. A full cowl threw the face into shadow; the arms were crossed over the chest. The creature's hands were hidden in the deep folds of its garment.

"I was bloody scared because it was so real," Shane tells us. "You know—like a solid person. There was no fuzziness or anything ghostly about it. I had to wake Moya, and she nearly had a seizure. We shouted at it to go away, but it wouldn't budge. It just stood there, even when we'd switched the light on. So we thought, if it's not going to leave the room, we will. But when we got to the landing, there it was again, standing at the bottom of the bloody stairs."

The couple did not know what to do. The safety of the children was uppermost in their minds. They could not leave them unattended while the *thing* was in the house.

"Moya got Emma, and I got Rory. We carried them into our room. They never woke up through all this—which was just as well, because I don't know what we'd have done if they'd seen that thing. It would have given them nightmares for the rest of their lives."

They locked their bedroom door. Shane is the first to admit that it was more a psychological measure than a means of keeping the thing out. The hooded entity had demonstrated that doors and walls were no obstacle.

"We lay awake most of the night," Shane recalls, "with the kids fast asleep between us in the bed. We were prisoners in our own bedroom, I suppose, because we were too afraid to go downstairs. It was as if the thing didn't want us to leave the house. But we dozed off eventually."

As daylight broke at the window, Shane was the first to awaken. He knew at once that something was wrong. Emma slept soundly at her mother's side—but little Rory was missing.

He cursed himself for having fallen asleep. Trembling, he left the bed without rousing Moya. The door was still locked. He hardly dared think about what he might find outside. He refused to accept the possibility that their son could be lost to them. It did not bear thinking about.

But Rory was safe. As before, the child lay fast asleep, curled up on the stairs. On this occasion, he had been placed halfway down. From then on, the children would sleep at their grandmother's home.

It was becoming apparent to the Dwyers that their tormentor was singling out their son for its attentions. Twice, the child had been taken from his bed, yet no harm had come to him. They asked themselves if it might be a warning of some kind, if Rory might, in some way, be linked with the other phenomena—the thrown Bible, the hammering on the doors, the ghostly footsteps, and the eerie wailing of the woman.

With the coming of the hooded figure, the couple decided it was time to seek the Church's help again, and Rory was to play a decisive role in uncovering the nature of the hauntings.

Father Dorrity came to their aid a third time. This time, he visited the house alone. In the red room, he offered a requiem Mass for the repose of those souls "who may be in danger," as he put it. The service passed off without incident.

"Everything went well," Shane tells us, "and by that I mean nothing weird happened during the Mass itself. It was only afterwards that the trouble started. It didn't even seem like trouble at the time."

Rory is a shy little boy, he explains, and certainly not given to talking to visitors. It came as a surprise, therefore, when the boy ventured into the red room while the Dwyers were having tea with Father Dorrity. The priest was preparing to leave and offering the couple some advice. Rory went to him and tugged urgently at his sleeve.

The priest put aside his cup and saucer and patted Rory's head. "What a big boy you're getting to be," he said.

"Michael put the bad man in the fire." The child wore a very serious expression.

The priest was nonplussed. He smiled. Shane, for his part, was recalling a night, many months before, when he was putting the child to bed. "Michael" had been spoken of then, too.

"Did Michael put him into that fire?" the priest asked, pointing to the hearth, where a log fire crackled.

Rory shook his head. "No, the big fire down *there*." He bent down and splayed his little fingers on the rug.

"And how did Michael do that, Rory?" Father Dorrity was looking perplexed.

"With a big sword," the child said solemnly. And with that, he left the room.

"We were all very disturbed," Shane says, "because he was only three. He'd never seen any pictures of St. Michael the Archangel; we had none in the house. He'd been taught the names Jesus and Mary, and he knew about God because we prayed with the children every night. But that was it. Also, the fact that he went right up to the priest like that while he was speaking very seriously to us. This is a kid who'd hide behind his mother whenever a stranger came to the door. That in itself was very unsettling."

Father Dorrity shared Shane's concern. He took him aside before leaving. "I'll come again tomorrow and say some special prayers in that room. I don't have them with me now. To tell you the truth, I've never been called on to use them. Until now, that is." He seemed distracted. "Yes, I think that would be best. You see, Shane, children are very sensitive to things in the 'other' world. That's why I'm rather worried about what the child said."

He returned the following day at 6 p.m. and led the Dwyers in a rosary in the red room. That completed, he asked them to remain kneeling. He had with him the set of prayers he had alluded to the day before. They were handwritten, and each sheet bore the heading *The Litanies of the Saints.*

"If you both do the responses," he instructed, "where you see the *A*'s." He placed a purple stole about his neck and knelt down beside them. "Now, if anything happens while we're praying, just try to ignore it and keep going."

These were ominous, disquieting words. Before the couple could ask what he meant by them, Father Dorrity had begun.

"Do not remember, O Lord, our sins or those of our forefathers."

"And do not punish us for our offenses," Shane and Moya answered.

They then recited the Lord's Prayer together, and the priest began reading from Psalm 53. "The fool hath said in his heart, 'There is no God—'"

On the last word, the Bible fell from the topmost shelf of the bookcase and landed, open, on the rug. "Corrupt are they, and have done abominable iniquity...." The priest ignored it and continued reading.

Shane and Moya could only stare at the book. This time, it had not opened at Isaiah. Before their astonished eyes, the pages began to turn, *all by themselves,* from right to left, as though invisible fingers were leafing through them.

"... there is none that doeth good. God looked down from heaven upon the children of men, to see if there were any that did understand, that did seek God." Father Dorrity completed the psalm, ending with the words, "Save Shane and Moya, your servants, O Lord."

The Dwyers were late with the response; they were still staring in dreadful fascination at the Bible. As if by sorcery, it was again opened at Isaiah 28 to 29.

They turned their attention back to the page. "Because we hope in you, my God," they answered.

"Be a tower of strength for them, O Lord."

"In the face of the Enemy."

Father Dorrity paused. He was gazing fixedly at the sofa along the back wall. They could see the page in his hands quiver slightly.

"Let the Enemy...have no victory...over them."

From somewhere beneath the sofa came a deep rumble. The vibration was so powerful that they could feel their legs tremble. It was as though a huge generator had started up. The priest got to his feet and went to stand before the sofa. He motioned for the Dwyers to continue the responses.

"And let the Son of Iniquity not succeed in injuring us."

The shuddering ceased.

"Send them...send them help from the Holy...from the Holy Place, Lord." Father Dorrity's voice was faltering. He stood with his back to them, head inclined. They knew he was staring at the sofa.

"And give us Heavenly protection," the couple answered quickly.

An atmosphere of menace and threat seemed to pervade the room. The air felt charged. They wanted the prayer to end swiftly and to make a bolt for the door.

"Lord...." The priest sighed heavily. Another tremor came from the floor beneath the sofa. They saw him sway slightly, then right himself immediately. "Lord...hear my prayer."

Shane and Moya glanced at each other. They wondered if they should go to his aid but did not feel they could interrupt the prayers. "And let our cry reach you—"

They stopped. Father Dorrity was flung backward, as if someone had pushed him in the chest. He fell into an armchair.

"Are you all right, Father?" Moya asked. He was ashen faced and perspiring. Shane went to assist him.

"Fine ...," he said, recovering himself. "I'm fine! Just keep kneeling. I need to finish." He got up and returned to the same spot. There was evidently something there, something dangerous that he had disturbed.

"... God and Lord of all creation! You gave power to your Apostles to pass through dangers unharmed. Among your commands to do wondrous things, you said: Drive out Evil Spirit. By your strength, Satan fell like ... fell like—"

Once again he was thrust back into the armchair, and once again the Dwyers tried to help, but he checked them with a wave of his hand. They resumed kneeling.

He got up and continued on from where he had left off. "By your strength, Satan fell like lightning from Heaven. With fear and ... and trembling."

The couple could see that the priest was indeed trembling. The pages he held were shaking. His voice was cracking.

"I pray and supplicate ... your Holy Name. Give me constant faith and power, so that ... so that ... armed with the power of your holy strength, I can attack this cruel Evil Spirit—"

The pages fell from his hands and fluttered to the floor. He slumped onto the sofa. The Dwyers helped him to his feet.

"I'm sorry, I can't do this!" he gasped. He had the air about him of a man defeated.

"Don't blame yourself, Father," Moya said kindly.

"I'll try to find someone else who can help you."

"God, I hope so," Shane said. "I really do."

They went to the kitchen. Father Dorrity was clearly shaken, but, after a restorative cup of tea and glass of brandy, he was himself again. He tried to make light of the incident, told them not to worry, that he had a bit of a cold coming on and had not eaten since breakfast. Shane accompanied him out to his car.

"I didn't want to say anything in front of Moya," the priest said. "I didn't want to frighten her, but was there anything of the old cottage left in that room we were in?"

"I don't understand, Father. All that was left was the bare foundation stones, and we built on those."

"Are you sure now? Nothing left along that gable where ye have the sofa?"

It was then that Shane remembered.

"Well, come to think of it, there *was* something. The hearthstone. It was such a heavy thing—so heavy, in fact, that we couldn't move it. So we just left it and built over it."

Father Dorrity was thoughtful. "I see," he said, almost to himself. "Yes, it's becoming clearer now. That's where it lives."

"What? What d'you mean, 'it'? What are you talking about, Father?"

"I don't want to alarm you, Shane, but I'm not an exorcist. And that's what your house needs: an exorcism. I'll need to ask the bishop. Not every priest can do that kind of thing, you see."

"But what is it? What's causing all of this, Father?"

Father Dorrity avoided answering. He got into his car.

"I'll phone you at the end of the week," he said, starting the engine. "By then, we should have the name of a good priest for the job. In the meantime, keep up the prayers—and sprinkle holy water as often as you can."

With that, the good man sped off, leaving Shane in the yard feeling more uneasy and confounded than ever.

Despite the priest's portentous words, the Dwyers had a further two weeks free of any paranormal incident. Looking back on that period, they almost found themselves believing that the forces ranged against them were deciding on what to send next to torment the family. A fresh phase of manifestations again saw a change in direction. It was as though what lay beneath the hearthstone was demonstrating the variety of phenomena it could conjure up.

On February 2, 2005, Moya was awakened by what she took to be the cries of a child. She sat up in bed, startled and at once alert. Was it one of the children? Shane continued sleeping. But when it came again, she realized that the weeping came not from inside but from *outside* the house.

She went to the window and pulled the curtain aside, but could see nothing. She went quietly out onto the landing—and was abruptly brought up short.

At the far window stood the figure of a woman, wearing what looked like a white nightdress. She was gazing down into the back-yard.

Moya did not know what to do or think. Was she hallucinating? Then she heard the unmistakable sound of weeping again. This time, however, it was not the cries of children, nor was it coming from outside. The woman by the window was weeping.

She hurried back and woke Shane. She needed him as a witness; maybe she was seeing and hearing things.

"Right, I'll have a look," he said sleepily.

The apparition was still there. And the sobbing had intensified. Now a plangent wailing filled the house.

"Don't go near her," Moya whispered, clutching Shane's arm.

"Why not? I'm sick of this bloody nonsense. And anyway, I want to see her face." A mane of dark, shoulder-length hair hid the woman's face from view.

"For heaven's sake, don't go near her!" Moya warned again.

But Shane was already approaching the woman in white. She stood as still as a statue, albeit a translucent statue, with hands joined in an attitude of prayer.

"I don't know what it was," Shane tells us, "but something about the woman made me think I knew her, that I recognized her from somewhere. Only when I got up really close, almost close enough to touch her, did I see it. It was my granny."

Shane's grandmother had died when he was eight. But the figure of the woman was much younger than he remembered his grandmother to be. This was a younger version. It was as though a ghost from another time was being shown to him—a time long before his own birth.

"Granny, is it you?" he asked. He did not feel in any way threatened.

But the figure still did not move; it seemed quite oblivious to his presence. He put out a hand to touch her. As he did, she dissolved into "a kind of mist" and was gone. The weeping died away.

The couple went back to bed. Emma and Rory were—as usual—staying over at their grandmother's, and consequently under no threat. In all honesty, the Dwyers did not regard the apparition as being in any way threatening. Neither had any great urge to leave the house—not at that time of night and without good reason. They went back to sleep.

But, at around 4 a.m., they were wide awake again. They heard, plainly, the mournful cries of the woman. This time they were coming from the yard.

"It was terrible," Shane tells us, "because we could hear children crying too. I thought of the four Dwyer children who had died as babies. They were calling out, 'Mommy, Mommy!'"

Moya suggested that the children and the wailing woman were somehow connected. It almost seemed as though she were crying out for her lost children, and that they in turn were searching for her. It seemed to Moya that all were searching in vain, making their respective wailing all the more poignant.

"It went on for ages," Shane says. "We felt helpless to do anything. We just sat there in bed and spent the rest of the night praying for them."

There was to be a further development. On inspecting the red room later that morning, they discovered something decidedly ominous. It likewise involved children, and it shook Moya to the core. The framed photographs of Emma and little Rory had been turned to face the wall.

They were reluctant to bother Father Dorrity again but felt they had no choice. The parish priest expressed his sympathy "for your troubles," and promised he would send his curate to celebrate another Mass. He told the Dwyers that he had apprised the bishop of their situation. They learned that the wheels had been set in motion: a suitable exorcist was being sought.

Two days later, the curate came. Another Eucharist was celebrated and the house blessed a third time. But the manifestations continued undeterred.

The hooded figure began to appear more frequently, always at night and always in a corner of the couple's bedroom. The screaming at the windows and the hammering on the doors resumed. It was too much to take—the family was forced to move out again.

With some reluctance, Shane made the decision to consult other clergymen. He did not doubt Father Dorrity's sincerity—the man had, after all, put himself in the firing line on their behalf—but he could not wait forever for the bishop to respond.

An aunt of his had befriended a Presbyterian minister who was well acquainted with the paranormal. He was happy to help and offered his services at once.

"He performed what he called a 'deliverance,'" Shane recalls. "He was reluctant to call it an exorcism but I suppose that was what it was. But whatever the name you want to give it, it was very effective. The house was definitely better after it. We had no more bother for a long while."

The minister followed it up with weekly prayer meetings in the red room, attended by Shane's mother, his sister Maura, and a number of other relatives.

For three whole months there was peace. Then, as bad luck would have it, the minister was called away on missionary work. Before leaving, he stressed the importance of the weekly prayer meetings.

A few days following the clergyman's departure, Shane received a perplexing telephone call. That call was to herald a new and bizarre phase in a haunting that had already thrown up some of the most perplexing manifestations ever witnessed in that part of Ireland.

"My name," the caller said, "is Vincent Davage. You don't know me, Mr. Dwyer, but I know about your predicament."

It was early June, and Shane had taken the call at work. The stranger spoke with a cultured Galway accent. Without much preamble, he was offering to help "where others have failed." Shane was mystified.

"Excuse me," he said, "I don't know who you are and I don't know how you got this number—and furthermore, I don't know what you're talking about."

The only people outside the family circle who knew about his "predicament" were the religious. He had been led to believe that their discretion could be relied on.

"Oh, but I think you do know what I'm talking about." The voice took on an authoritative edge. He was reminded of a clergyman, an elderly clergyman perhaps. "I have knowledge of these things, you see. I know about the manifestations in your home. I had the same trouble myself. I'm offering my services, and they come with a blessing."

Shane was mystified. "Are you a priest?" There was a marked silence on the end of the line. "Hello, are you still there?"

"No, not a priest...." He received the impression that Mr. Davage found the question amusing. "But I come with a special blessing."

"Well, I put my trust in the Church, if it's all the same to—"

"But your Church is not having any effect now, is it?" the caller interrupted. "I'll come at a time of my choosing. Good-bye."

The line went dead.

Shane was deeply disturbed by the call. He considered phoning Father Dorrity, or perhaps his mother. He decided against it. He thought it best to keep it to himself. He would not even tell Moya. There was no reason, he decided, to bother her with something that in all likelihood was a hoax. She had enough on her plate.

The following evening, however, just as the couple finished supper, an unfamiliar car pulled into the yard. The children were at their grandmother's as usual.

"You expecting someone?" Moya asked.

"Not that I know of." Car doors slammed. Shane parted the net curtain and looked out. A man and three women were surveying the house. He thought there was something unsettling about them and the manner in which they strode purposefully toward the house, as if on a mission. There was none of the hesitancy one would associate with newcomers.

The women were youngish, early twenties, perhaps. They were attired in clothing that was almost of an "ethnic" nature: long cotton skirts, hand knits, and headscarves. The man was dressed casually.

Shane immediately thought of the curious phone call. He looked at Moya, but she only shrugged. The doorbell sounded. He took a deep breath and prepared to answer it.

The man who stood on the doorstep was middle-aged and of slim build. Shane stared at the close-cropped blond hair, the gray eyes, and the sickly pallor. The visitor held out a hand. "Vincent Davage. We spoke yesterday."

Shane opened his mouth to say something, but before he knew what was happening, Davage and his entourage had pushed past him and were walking in single file down the hallway in the direction of the red room.

"What in God's name d'you think you're playing at!" Shane called out. Moya was on his heels. "No one invited you here."

"No," Davage said, "but nonetheless you need me."

Two of the women arranged chairs, while the third drew the curtains. The room was plunged into semidarkness.

"This room is the focus," Davage announced. The four arranged themselves around the table and linked hands. "This is where it lives."

"Look, we want you out of here *now!*" Moya cried, her anger rising. "Do you hear me? And if you're thinking of having a bloody seance in here, you'd better think again. We're not into that nonsense. So kindly get out, please."

"I'm calling the police," Shane said, making for the door.

Davage turned in his seat, still linking hands with the women on either side. His voice was calm and decisive. "I wouldn't do that if I were you, Mr. Dwyer. You might end up worse off than you are now. I am here to calm the evil that is in your midst. Last night, the gates of hell opened up once more. I was shown what must be done. It is advisable that you and your wife heed what I say. We are here to help."

The Dwyers were stunned. Abruptly, the dynamics of the situation had changed—changed utterly and in the most chilling way. Shane tried to speak, but the words simply would not come. There was a tense silence.

"Shut the door, please," Davage ordered, "and we can begin." He bowed his head and the women did likewise.

"All right. Very well." Shane was choosing his words carefully. Something was cautioning him not to inflame the situation further. It's for the best, he was telling himself; if this arrogant man can achieve what he says he can, then why not let him try? "But we pray first," he insisted. "That's the deal. Then do what you have to and just go."

"We don't pray." One of the women had spoken for the first time.

"No, we don't pray," echoed Davage; "we connect. You pray if you wish. It won't affect what we do, one way or the other."

Greatly alarmed, the couple found their rosary beads and knelt down by an armchair. They focused on the Sacred Heart picture above the fireplace.

"I believe in God the Father Almighty," they began, trying to pray as vigorously as possible, in order to mask their distress, "Creator of heaven and earth, and in Jesus Christ, His only son, Our Lord ..."

Halfway through the first decade, however, they were forced to stop. Davage had begun speaking in a strange language. The women appeared to be chanting; their heads were no longer bowed but raised up and tilted to one side. Their eyes were closed.

"I really couldn't tell what kind of language he was speaking," Shane recalls. "It didn't sound like Latin. God knows what it was: Coptic, Hebrew, Aramaic... take your pick. We'd never heard it before and we sure as hell never want to hear it again. Then, during it, the very same thing happened as when Father Dorrity was praying. That rumbling sound, only this time it was louder and it didn't stay under the sofa. It started to move across the floor. We could actually feel the floor vibrating under us—like there was something moving under the floorboards, very fast. And after about, say, a minute, it went out under the door and into the hall."

The Dwyers were terrified, more so than when the unseen entity had assaulted the priest. This was paranormal activity of a different order. They had never seen the like of it. It seemed to them that Davage and his band had brought a new menace into their home, one that was gaining ground by the minute. They had nothing but prayer to hold it in check; they prayed more loudly than before. But Davage's voice kept rising progressively, the words spoken in the strange language vying with their prayer. Then, all at once, he stopped.

"Our guest in the hallway wishes to come in now," he announced. He turned to the Dwyers. "You do not have to look at it if you don't want to. In which case, it would be best to keep your eyes closed."

"I can honestly say that, until that night, we thought we'd experienced enough horror to last us a lifetime," Shane says. "But when Davage said that, the pair of us just went into shock. We knelt there, just stiff with fear. We couldn't move. We couldn't speak. We tried to pray again, but it was as if we were struck dumb. All we could do was shut our eyes tight and wait."

They heard the group direct some mysterious command in the direction of the door. For a few moments, there was nothing unusual.

"That changed," says Shane. "There was this gradual coldness in the room. It crept up on you. It chilled you to the bone. I kept my eyes closed, and I know Moya did, too."

They heard the doorknob turn and the door slowly open. The cold intensified, but there was something else: a truly vile odor was pervading the room.

"It"—or indeed "the guest," as Davage called it—was now in the doorway.

"The smell of it was horrible. Really, really bad, like burning hair. I tried to hold my nose, but it was useless. Both of us started to feel really sick. But there really was nothing we could do. The urge to run out of the room was very strong, but that would have meant opening our eyes, and we couldn't bear to look at it. Besides, it was blocking the doorway—that's how it seemed. Something was telling us that, if we looked at it, we'd probably never recover from it...that we'd be part of it—if you can understand that. It's very hard to describe. It was just surreal, terrifying. I never want to go through anything like it ever again."

Did he have the impression that this presence had human form?

"It's very hard to say. It was huge, that's for sure. And it rustled...like it had wings or suchlike...." He stops and chooses his words carefully. "I now know that it was...that it was a demon. What we've learned since then bears that out."

Davage began addressing the creature in his arcane language. They could tell by his voice that he had turned in his chair and was talking to it, as if he were "having a conversation with someone."

Astonishingly, the presence began answering in the same, strange-sounding language.

"But the voice was disembodied," Shane explains. "A man's voice, very deep, but it was coming from all around the room. From the ceiling, the floor, everywhere. Sometimes we'd hear it right behind us, then in front...then from the armchair that we were kneeling beside."

Both voices grew in volume. They seemed to be arguing. Shane wanted desperately to glance at his wife to check if she was all right. He was terrified. How must *she* be?

But he knew he dared not look. He could feel her arm against his, trembling. He felt certain he could hear her teeth chattering, not only from abject terror but from the subzero temperature in the room.

Suddenly, the deep-throated voice broke into English.

"Give me what I want and I will leave!" it bellowed.

"No, you *cannot* have him!" Davage snapped back.

"I will not leave until I have him!"

Davage lapsed into the sinister language once again, speaking very rapidly, like a judge lecturing a criminal in the dock. The exchange continued thus, as if the two were trading insults.

Eventually the rumpus ceased.

"Now, return to your pit!" Davage ordered.

They waited for the door to open and for the presence to leave. But nothing happened for several moments. By and by, they could feel the coldness and the horrid odor dissipating, then the swish of something passing them and making its way toward the sofa along the gable wall. They heard the rumbling sound again under the floor.

All at once, the room was quiet. It had gone. The curtains were being pulled open and chairs scraped back.

"You may open your eyes now," Davage said.

Before they could get to their feet, the group had left the room. Shane hurried after them and caught up to Davage before he reached the back door.

"What the hell was all that about?" Shane's fear had turned to anger again.

"You heard, didn't you?"

"What in God's name did you bring into our home?"

"Oh, not me, Mr. Dwyer. I didn't bring anything in. It was there long before I got here." He pulled a crumpled page from his pocket and handed it to Shane.

Shane looked at a series of squiggles running across the page.

"What the hell's that supposed to be?"

"Go inside and hold it up to a mirror. The names on there sent me here. I received messages from them."

Shane was torn between hitting Davage full in the face and doing what he was told. He chose the latter course, if only to satisfy his curiosity. He went inside and held the paper up to the mirror.

He stood staring, dumbfounded. The reversed writing suddenly made perfect sense. There were three words.

Edward and Cornelius

"How did you know my uncles?" he asked in disbelief. Davage was still on the porch.

"I didn't know them in life, but I met them in spirit. I talk to the dead. Or rather," he continued with a chuckle, "they talk to me." He looked up at the house. "This was their home. They never meant your father to have it, but you have it now. Perhaps that's your mistake. Perhaps you must pay the price. It's dangerous to meddle with the wishes of the dead."

Shane was stunned. How could this stranger know so much? He had never met him before that day.

By now, the three women had returned to the car.

"It lives—" Davage began. The car engine started. "Sorry, I have to go now."

"What the f*** are you talking about, 'it'? What the f*** is 'it'?"

Davage stepped back, wincing. "I do not care for your language Mr. Dwyer."

"And I do not care for your brazen cheek! Now what the hell was that in the room just now?"

"A spirit, Mr. Dwyer. An evil spirit—a demon, some might say. It lives under the hearthstone in that room. That's its pit. It goes to ground there whenever you bring clergymen in or when you're saying prayers. But prayers are useless against it."

Shane did not know what to make of it all. What he was hearing went beyond his comprehension. He recalled Father Dorrity mentioning the hearthstone, too.

"What does it... what does it ..."

"What does it want?" Davage finished the question for him. "Oh, it wants *you*—or your soul, to be more exact. Pray all you want, but it won't do any good. You are paying the price for your trespass. I came here tonight to buy you more time. But I can't protect you much longer. It's very simple: you sell the house and leave, or stay put and risk damnation. It's up to you."

With that, he was gone. The car sped off, leaving a trail of dust and a great deal of panic in its wake.

No sooner had Shane shut the door than he heard a crash. It came from the green room. Moya was there before him. She was pale. On the timber floor lay the shattered remains of the crucifix that he had hung there so many months before. He wondered about the premonition Moya had had that first day, how she could have sensed that all was not right with the house.

There came a second crash, this time accompanied by the sound of breaking glass.

In the red room, the room they had just vacated, the picture of the Sacred Heart, the focus of their prayers, lay broken and ruined on the floor.

"Jesus!" was all Shane could say.

The destruction of the images marked the beginning of a spate of such attacks. From that day on, no picture, crucifix, or other sacred object was safe. It was as though the visit of the strangers had unleashed the fury of something unholy.

The Dwyers had had enough. They could not even ensure the children's safety in daylight. They themselves could no longer spend the night there. They moved out.

Father Dorrity briefed Father Ignatius McCarthy as fully as possible about the case. In total six clergymen, of various faiths, had attempted a deliverance, and none could procure more than a temporary respite. It was time to draw on the solemn rite of exorcism as outlined in the Rituale Romanum. Father Ignatius prefers to use the Latin version, believing it to be more effective.

"This was no restless soul," he tells us. "The repeated hurling of the Bible onto the floor, the broken crucifix...the Sacred Heart being dashed to the floor. All these things pointed to the likelihood that an evil spirit was at work."

Why the Dwyer family? We wondered if it was something in their past, something about the old cottage and the uncles. Was it possible they resented the house returning once more to the family?

"God only knows," he says with a sigh. "God alone has all the answers. All we can do is speculate. I'm sure Shane told you about Cornelius and Edward's habit of getting the holy water every Sunday. Who's to say but they put up with this demon most of their lives, and the holy water was their way of dealing with it. They couldn't tell anybody—they were too afraid—so they learned to live with it, God help them."

"And when you look at it that way," he continues, "you get an inkling as to why they left the land to outsiders. It wasn't out of spite. They wanted to spare their youngest brother, Shane's father, the horror of discovering the truth about the old place. You know they say that St. Patrick himself could not convert the tribes in that part of Ireland. The hold of the Druids was too strong; desperate things went on, by all accounts." He grimaces. "And, given the Dwyers' experiences, who's to say the stories aren't true? Heaven knows what happened on that land in days gone by. We never know what we're inheriting, do we, now? It is strange how things work out. Had young Shane not insisted on buying the farm back, he would have been spared this whole sorry business."

And Vincent Davage. What is the verdict on him?

"A very strange character, from what I gather. Certainly he dabbles with the darker side of things. Did he make the situation worse? Undoubtedly so. The attacks on the holy objects started soon after he left. But, God willing, all that is over now."

Before we take our leave of Shane, he brings us down to the red room. After all that he has told us, it is not easy to feel comfortable there. He points out the sofa along the far wall that sits over the dreaded hearthstone, and the bookcase where they kept the Bible. The compassionate gaze of the Sacred Heart above the mantelshelf looks down upon us. We do not wish to tarry in that room for too long; there is an uncanny air about it. The modern furnishings sit uneasily there, seeming to mock the cramped space. Perhaps it was never meant to be lived in, to be used as an ordinary room.

We are grateful for the outdoors, as Shane walks us to the car.

"The house has been on the market for almost a year now," he says. "We haven't had one single bid in all that time. Word gets out; people talk. What can you do? We sank all our savings into this place and now it looks like we're stuck."

We bring the conversation back to his uncles and the holy water. Did they ever say why they needed it in such quantities?

"Yes, before Edward died my father asked him. He gave a very odd answer. 'For the hearthstone,' he said. Then added, 'To put the fire out.' I thought it was the raving of a dying man."

Shane Dwyer looks back at the house and sighs. "Unfortunately, I know now, to my sorrow, what it was he meant by that. Old Edward meant it literally, may God have mercy on him."

MR. GANT AND THE
NEIGHBOR FROM HELL

———————— ✦ ————————

Malachi Gant and Charlie Sherrin had never quite been friends, yet they had an understanding. Charlie is a neighbor who shares a quiet road in a quiet town in the northwest of Ireland.

Malachi is retired now, and has been for a good ten years. He was always a hard worker, and in the course of four decades or more had built up a very successful hardware business with a presence in three midland towns. When he sold the stores and retired, he had enough left over to realize a lifelong ambition: to see as much of the world as he could within two years. His wife, Blainead—"Blenny" to all who know her—was delighted by the prospect. She had rarely ventured far from her native Sligo.

First, they flew to America. Malachi's younger brother lived in Boston. They stayed with the family for a month, then rented an RV and set out in the direction of San Francisco, taking in no fewer than sixteen states in their leisurely progress across the continent. They devoted four more months to exploring California and Arizona, before traveling on down to Mexico and South America. A year later they found themselves in Florida, booking a cruise to Egypt.

It was 1996; it would be some years before the attack on the Twin Towers induced Americans to stay at home and in particular to avoid the Middle East. The passenger list was full when, at the beginning of October, the liner set sail out of Fort Lauderdale. Two weeks later, the

Gants' party arrived in Alexandria, wended its way slowly down the Nile to Cairo, and at last landed in Luxor. It would be the finale of the Egyptian sojourn, before they moved on to a resort by the Red Sea.

The cruise company had prepared a special treat for that evening. As dusk settled over the Nile, the Gants and the other guests were escorted by uniformed guides down the long Avenue of the Sphinxes that connects Karnak and the temple of the old gods. There they were, those gods, scores of them: ram-headed, floodlit, and magnificent, crouching stark against a background of palms and a sky the color of cobalt. Costumed light bearers had been stationed at intervals, each holding aloft a flambeau. It was kitsch but it was breathtaking. It was calculated to set the mood for the remainder of the evening.

Aperitifs were served in the colonnaded temple. Thereupon the guests entered the magnificent open-air dining area and were seated at tables laid with white and gold linen. Candlelight bathed the scene, and the floodlit, ancient columns formed a stunning backdrop on three sides. The air was laden with rich spices and the aromas of the East. Waiters in traditional costume glided from one table to another, serving a four-course dinner as music emanated from a classical quartet.

"This is the life, eh?" someone said. "Sure beats an all-you-can-eat shrimp supper down at Al's Seafood Diner." His friends chuckled. The food was excellent, the company convivial. The wines, too, were fine and copious.

Halfway through the meal, however, just as the musicians had ended one piece and were about to embark on another, the tranquil atmosphere of the evening was shattered. A terrifying scream rent the air, sending a chill through the assembled diners.

"It was like a wounded animal, not human at all," Malachi recalls, "and it frightened the life out of everybody, because everybody stopped eating at once. You could've heard a pin drop, as they say."

All eyes were fixed on a solitary man at one of the tables. He seemed oblivious to what he had just done and sat staring into the middle distance, at something it appeared only he could see. Moments later he got to his feet, letting the chair fall back with a clatter. Malachi recognized him; he had spoken with him earlier—the usual friendly chitchat. His name was Walter Ehrlich and he seemed an amiable sort. He had been to Egypt on a previous occasion, he said, many years before. His wife had been with him then but she had died in 1978. This year, he had come alone.

Perhaps that brief conversation had endeared Malachi to Ehrlich, because he now appeared to single him out. Slowly but deliberately, he approached the Gants' table, a glass of wine in his hand. The other guests could only stare; some were frightened, others uneasy. Their hosts seemed unsure of what to do.

"Where did you say you were from?" Ehrlich asked, fixing Malachi with a look of mild aggression.

"Ireland."

"Catholic, right?" He emptied his wine glass and replenished it at once from a decanter. In a loud voice he said: "All you Irish are Catholics, that right?"

Somebody tut-tutted. Mr. Ehrlich was introducing a very sour note into what should have been a perfect evening.

He pointed directly at Malachi and lowered his face to meet the Irishman's eyes. For a fleeting moment, Malachi could not believe what he was seeing. Even now, years later, his voice quavers as he recalls the incident.

"God Almighty, I'll never forget that face," he says. "Blenny saw it too and she was very upset."

The face before him was no longer that of Walter Ehrlich. The features had transmogrified into something thoroughly freakish, a mask of utter malevolence. The lips were pulled back in a terrible grimace. And the eyes—they were no longer the eyes of a human but hooded, like those of a cold-blooded creature predating mankind.

"Let's go, Malachi," Blenny urged.

He felt her hand on his wrist. She was trembling. But he was already recoiling from that awful face. He felt that he could not get far enough away from it.

Walter Ehrlich was not through with him just yet, though. As quickly as the dreadful, reptilian aspect had taken hold of his features, so did it seem to leave. The face returned to normal. Walter straightened and stepped back from the table.

"*F*** you!*" he roared. He looked fiercely about him, and Malachi will never forget the shocked expressions of the other diners. "F*** you all! *We* f*** you all, and to hell with the lot of you. There's no God here. Your God is dead!"

To everyone's astonishment, the troubled guest emitted a loud squeal, ran in the direction of the pillars to one side of the temple, and vanished into the darkness beyond.

All present—dinner guests, organizers, waiters, musicians— were appalled.

"Alcohol," muttered the Egyptian maître d', shaking his head, his Islamic sensibilities repelled by the display. "To drink so much, not good."

"I don't think so," said a white-haired man, turning to Malachi. "No, I don't think it's alcohol. There are demons at work there."

"You're joking," said Malachi.

"No joke." He was frowning. Blenny had exchanged pleasantries with the man's wife during the cruise. She had learned that he was a pastor of some kind, retired for many years. "That's demonic. I've seen it before, lots of times. When a man starts using that kind of language—and referring to himself in the plural—it's pretty clear that there are demons at work."

The dinner was upset but not ruined. The quartet struck up again, playing a lively set. A waiter righted the fallen chair and removed what remained of Walter's meal. Malachi Gant was intrigued; he wished to learn more from the retired pastor. He was disappointed; the man was reluctant to discuss such matters. He murmured something about "leaving well enough alone," and went on to ply a neighbor with golf stories.

The next morning, Malachi and Blenny found the "demoniac" at a poolside table. Walter looked pale, red-eyed, and nervous, and was—even at that early hour—nursing a cocktail of some description. He studiously ignored Malachi, and for that matter everybody else in the party. The Gants never saw him again. According to the tour guide, Mr. Ehrlich had cut short his cruise and caught a plane back to Atlanta, his hometown.

Malachi and Blenny returned to Ireland in 1998. They had visited four continents. They had seen more sights than some will see in a lifetime. They brought back with them many wonderful memories, but Malachi is keen to stress that not all their memories were pleasant ones. Blenny and he had seen the world in all its facets, and some were unsettling, even gravely disturbing. He cites the Luxor incident involving Walter Ehrlich as being the most disturbing of all.

Today, at seventy-five and having endured four torturous years of demonic oppression, Malachi is forced to admit that the event in Egypt haunts him still. In hindsight he sees it not as an isolated, random occurrence but as part of a whole—the sinister beginning of his troubles.

"What if I hadn't gone on that cruise?" he asks despairingly. "It was as if that 'face' followed me all the way home. I've never been the same since."

Malachi is a nervous individual. This seems at first out of character because he is an imposing man: well over six feet tall, broad in the shoulders, with a grip like a blacksmith's. He towers over Blenny, who, having brought coffee and cookies, leaves Malachi to his story.

"She knows something of what I'm going through," he says, "but I keep the more frightening bits to myself. I can't have her getting upset."

His hands shake as he stirs his coffee. He seems genuinely frightened of something. We are here on the referral of Father Ignatius, who has told us only a little about the case. It may well be that he wished us to hear the details from the "sufferer's" own lips, so we could arrive at a more objective analysis. Malachi seems hesitant about sharing his experience. He reminds us from time to time that he is speaking of it "only because Father Ignatius asked me to."

202 | THE DARK SACRAMENT

His story centers on his neighbor, Charlie Sherrin. He is a widower, some thirty years Malachi's junior, who lives down the road with his two teenage daughters.

Malachi has known the Sherrin family all his life. He went to school with Charlie's father; he watched the sons and daughters grow up and one by one leave the parental home. Charlie was the oldest; he remained. He is good with his hands, Malachi tells us. He practically rebuilt single-handedly the house he inherited, doubling its floor area and in so doing quadrupling its market value.

When Malachi ran his hardware business, the Sherrins were among his regular customers. He remembers how Charlie's father would come to him for everything from a nail to a bench grinder.

"Dan was a creature of habit," he says. "If he bought from you once, he was a customer for life. He did a lot of odd jobs for people in the town here, mostly in the evenings and on weekends. I'd hire big things out to him: generators, sanders, that kind of thing. Charlie got a lot of that from the father. Terrible good with his hands. Never idle."

On retirement, Malachi disposed of the business but kept some stock. He extended his garage to accommodate it all. He is an altruistic individual and well liked in the area, not least because of his habit of lending power tools and the like to friends and neighbors. When his daughter married, he helped her to buy her first home and even lent a hand with the decorating. His son-in-law got on well with Charlie Sherrin. They drank together, moved with the same crowd.

All that ended six years ago, however, on a summer's night when Charlie showed his dark side. The incident is an open secret in the street—yet nobody mentions it, not even Blenny.

"We don't talk about it," Malachi says. "We never discuss it. As far as she's concerned, it's over and done with. That's how she likes to keep it."

So what did happen on a balmy June night in 2001? What was it that transformed Malachi Gant from a healthy and vigorous man into a nervous wreck? The answer must lie a few hundred yards farther along the road, behind the well-kept hedges of the Sherrin family home. But Charlie is saying nothing. It is also futile to question the other neighbors, including Malachi's son-in-law, who was an eyewitness to what occurred. What is left is circumstantial evidence—which is nonetheless compelling—and Malachi's own harrowing account.

Charlie Sherrin came over at about ten that evening. It was dusk and still warm. He was returning a hedge trimmer that Malachi had kindly lent him. They strolled back together from the shed. Malachi suggested a glass of whiskey. He had "the remains of a bottle" in the house and, as he himself was not much of a drinker, did not want it "going to waste." Charlie readily agreed.

"But no sooner had we made ourselves comfortable in the parlor than he started," Malachi says. "Complaining about everybody and anybody, so he was—the children, his in-laws. But that's the way he was: always finding fault. I think he must have had a run-in with everybody he met that day. Maybe the weather had gotten to him. It was a very hot day, and I remember he was still in his shorts when he came round with the trimmer."

Malachi was not surprised to find Charlie in such a state. He hoped the whiskey would calm him.

"He carried so much hatred in him," he tells us. "Or maybe it was bitterness; I don't know. He was forever running people down and he had such a vicious temper."

The temper is something that Malachi returns to time and time again. He recalls Charlie's behavior toward his children as they were growing up.

"They were great kids. But he'd often throw stones at them in a temper. Big stones. I'd see him at it and think, if one of those stones was to hit that little girl it'd do serious injury."

He goes on, painting a picture of a strangely unpleasant and volatile man.

"He'd lose it completely. I remember one time I was helping him mix some cement for the floor of a conservatory he was building.

Something went wrong with the mixer—I don't know what, but the cement was coming out all lumpy. Now, anyone else would have switched the thing off and had a look at it. Not Charlie. He starts kicking the thing and cursing. The language was terrible, very obscene. He ended up destroying the mixer, so he had to pay for it in the end. That's the sort he is—he just goes into a blind rage and doesn't know *what* he's doing anymore. I pity the daughters, always have."

For years, Malachi has been concerned for their welfare. Nor was it only their father's violent temper they had to fear; it seemed to Malachi that Charlie's relationship with the children was always a little suspect.

"He never got on with one of his daughters," Malachi confides. "The oldest one. I don't know what was going on there. It could be anything. He'd talk about things in front of the girls that wouldn't be nice among adults. He'd always have language that wasn't good, or yarns and dirty stories, always of a sexual nature. Given what he did to me, I would say that it wasn't only physical abuse those children suffered at his hands. He could be terrible obscene. I don't know how many times I saw him even going to the toilet in front of his daughters."

Malachi sees our confusion. He explains.

"I'd be in his back garden. In the summer, like, maybe he'd have a barbecue." He shakes his head sadly. "He wasn't *all* bad, you know. But he'd be after drinking I don't know how many cans of lager and be wanting to go to the toilet. So in front of the girls he'd open his pants and let go against the hedge or something. It was a strange thing to do, but Charlie saw no harm in it." Malachi pauses, reflecting. "Or maybe he did know it was wrong, and did it out of divilment. He was like that. The children were afraid of him. They were always very quiet, never a peep out of them."

He continues his account of the June evening in 2001. Charlie Sherrin had appeared to be his customary complaining self, but there was nothing out of the ordinary that Malachi could see. They had drunk a glass of whiskey and Malachi had poured another, finishing the bottle. He turned to fetch the water jug. Then something happened that made his blood run cold. All at once, he was right back in Egypt, hearing once again the ear-splitting howl of the demoniac, Walter Ehrlich.

Charlie Sherrin was squealing like a pig.

The pig has had a hard time of it throughout history. In at least two major religions, the animal is looked upon as an "unclean" creature whose flesh is denied to the faithful. There is no satisfactory reason for this, despite repeated attempts by Jewish and Islamic scholars to justify the proscription on the basis of biological or nutritional science. Yet pigs crop up often in cases of demonic disturbance.

In addition, devils and satyrs were traditionally depicted with cloven, piglike hoofs. No doubt the oft-quoted biblical story of the Gadarene swine did much to associate the pig with the demonic in the Christian consciousness. The fact remains, however, that pig sounds are identified with several of the most notorious episodes of diabolic infestation. They were reported in one of the most shocking: the Smurl family in Pennsylvania, a haunting that lasted many years. At the height of the disturbances, porcine noises were heard coming from within the walls of the family's home.

Malachi froze on hearing the blood-curdling squeal. But, before he could react, he felt a tremendous blow to the back of his skull. Only later did he conclude that Charlie Sherrin had struck him with the empty whiskey bottle. He passed out.

When he recovered consciousness, he was lying outside on his front lawn. Evidently Charlie had dragged him there.

"He proceeded to kick me. He kicked me very badly," Malachi recalls.

In fact, the attack was so vicious that the victim required six days of hospitalization. Malachi, dazed and bewildered, lay screaming on the grass as the neighbor assaulted him most brutally. He was dimly conscious of Blenny emerging from the house, of his neighbors, Jim and Margaret, running down the garden path that separates their property from his own. He remembers all three attempting to pull Charlie off him. It proved impossible. He seemed to have the strength of ten men. Malachi heard Blenny scream as she was flung across the grass. Margaret and Jim suffered a similar fate.

But Malachi's nightmare was only beginning. His hands are shaking as he relives that terrible night and relates what occurred next.

"Charlie pulled the clothes off me," he says. "I couldn't believe what was happening. It was like it was happening to somebody else. He tried to have sex with me—there's no other word for it. He was trying to have sex with me. I was semiconscious, and I couldn't move. The weight of him was indescribable. It was like I had the weight of a big plow horse lying on top of me."

Then the unbelievable—and truly terrifying—took place. As Malachi lay on his front lawn, in great pain and with his clothing in disarray, he was aware of something extraordinary happening to the ground itself, within a radius of three feet of him. It was slowly splitting open.

"When Charlie was on top of me he kept trying to force my face into the ground, but I managed to keep my head up so that my chin got buried instead. That way I was just about able to breathe. With my head in that position and my body paralyzed, the only part of me I could move were my eyes, or so I thought. I could see this big curved gash opening up in front of me, and I knew something dreadful was about to appear. I tried to squeeze my eyes shut, but I couldn't...I just couldn't."

The vision that Malachi was forced to witness was indeed more dreadful than anything he could have imagined. Five objects began to rise slowly out of the earth. They formed a rough semicircle about him and the man who was trying to sodomize him. Though maddened by pain, Malachi was in no doubt as to what the objects were. They were human heads.

"They were terrible looking. It was the grotesque face that I'd seen in Egypt multiplied five times—only worse. These faces were disfigured: all sores, terrible teeth and mouths, and they were all biting, like biting towards me. It was like a vision from hell, worse than anything you could ever dream about, and the stench coming from them was terrible. They just rose up out of the ground, staring at me, trying to attack me—but they couldn't because they had no bodies that I could see. Just the heads. I'll never forget them. I thought I was going to die at that moment. I was calling out to my wife and Jim and Margaret. The heads were shrieking. It was as if they were waiting for Charlie to kill me. Like I was some sort of offering that he was making to them."

It is an astonishing account of a near-apocalyptic vision, the agony of a severely traumatized man. But, leaving aside for a moment the most bizarre aspect—the nightmarish heads—the account is shocking. On a calm summer's evening a neighbor suddenly goes berserk. Without provocation, he attacks a man who has always been kind to him; he drags him out in front of his home, strips him, and tries to rape him in the presence of his wife and next-door neighbors. It defies belief.

Malachi remembers that, for a moment, the great weight pressing down upon him relaxed. He found his voice.

"Jesus, help me!" he cried out. "Jesus, help me!"

At the sound of his entreaties, Charlie Sherrin abruptly left off his attack. The ghoulish heads, their mouths still opening and shutting obscenely, began to retract into the earth. Malachi felt the weight on his body ease a little further. But his ordeal was not yet at an end. Suddenly, the hair on his scalp was being yanked upward with great violence. Before he knew what was happening, his abuser was crouched down in front of him, their faces almost touching.

But the face that confronted Malachi was no longer that of his attacker. He was looking into features that resembled those of the hideous heads. He began to scream uncontrollably. Charlie thrust his victim's face into the earth to muffle his screams and turned to address the onlookers.

"We're not finished yet!" he crowed. "We're going to make an example of Malachi." In an eerily calm voice, he told them in obscene detail what he intended to do.

Malachi was reminded of another frightening parallel with the Egypt incident: the use of the word *we*. He remembered the pastor's words: "When a man starts using that kind of language—and referring to himself in the plural—it's pretty clear that there are demons at work."

The pastor had good grounds for saying this. The Gospels of Luke and Mark record how Christ came upon a possessed man who evidently lived in a cemetery. On being asked his identity, he replied, "My name is Legion." Luke explains the curious name: "He said Legion because many devils were entered into him."

Charlie Sherrin returned his attention to his victim and attempted to enact that which he had just described. Malachi shakes more than ever as he recalls the brutal rape. Mercifully, it seems to have been over quickly. At last, his terrible work done, Charlie left without a word. When the coast was clear, Blenny and the others rushed to Malachi's side and helped him into the house.

"They got me in the door," he says. "I couldn't get up the stairs and lay there very badly broke up. Blenny got the doctor for me. He took me into hospital."

Malachi told the doctors and nursing staff that he had fallen down. No one believed him; his injuries were not consistent with a fall. It was evident that he had been attacked. They asked him if he knew the identity of his attacker. He lied. They asked him again. Somebody wanted to alert the police but Malachi stubbornly refused to involve the authorities. Even in his suffering—and despite the appalling sense of shame and outrage the assault had engendered—he still had consideration for Charlie Sherrin's daughters, and had no wish to cause them hardship.

As Malachi lay recovering in the hospital, his mind was a riot of thoughts, all frantically trying to explain his neighbor's atrocious and thoroughly unprovoked conduct. He could find no explanation.

It did occur to him, however, that it might not have been the first time that Charlie had assaulted a man in this way. The more he thought about it, the more little memories of him began to stir. He was remembering certain words and actions and hints dropped by the children and others....

Yet Malachi is an unusually forgiving and understanding man. When, three days following the attack, Charlie came to visit him in the hospital, he received him without rancor. Charlie, for his part, denied any recollection of the incident. He looked with dismay at Malachi's bruises, some healed, many not. Malachi insists that he almost saw compassion in that look—compassion mixed with remorse.

"I don't remember a thing," he said.

"Well, *I* do!" Malachi told him. "Why did you do it, Charlie?"

"I honestly can't remember a thing," he insisted. And with that he jumped up from his chair and hurriedly left the ward. That was the last time Malachi spoke to him. Six uneasy years have now passed.

"My trouble didn't stop there," Malachi Gant says. "The heads gave me an awful turn and I couldn't forget them. They kept returning to haunt me."

It is undoubtedly the motif of the grisly heads that transforms the case of a man being attacked by a deranged neighbor into something altogether more sinister. One's initial response to such outlandish accounts must be to query the state of mind of the narrator at the time. Certainly Malachi, by his own admission, was in no fit state to think clearly. He had been knocked senseless by a blow to the head, dragged from his home, and kicked mercilessly in the head as well as the rest of his body. He was dazed. In such a state of disorientation it is easy to imagine things. Yet a vision of ghastly heads, such as Malachi claims to have seen, seems to belong more properly to the realms of drug-induced hallucination than a vision brought on by pain. Not even the horrors reported by those experiencing delirium tremens come close to this description. It has more in common with the terrible visions recounted by the saints and mystics of antiquity.

In short, the heads are the false note in the story. The vision is easily discounted—and would have been, had Malachi's story ended there. It did not. Some weeks after the attack, when he had recovered from his injuries, he had another ordeal. Fearful though it was, it was infinitely more benign than the first.

Father Ignatius McCarthy's monastery is in the next county. Over the years, Malachi was a frequent visitor. He would give his services freely to the monks when they needed odd jobs done or—as was often the case—when they required the use of a power tool.

He was drawn to that place for two reasons: he found spiritual renewal there, and he could look in on an old school friend, Brother Canice. The two were very close. In adult life the monk had become Malachi's confidant. Whenever Malachi experienced a crisis of faith—no matter how big or how insignificant—Brother Canice would unfailingly set him on the right path again.

Brother Canice died on New Year's Day, 2000, a few minutes after midnight. Malachi was glad that his old friend saw a "little bit of the millennium." "He was fascinated by the idea. It meant more to him than most of us. He loved the notion of Jesus going into a third millennium. It's what he'd always prayed for."

Since the incident in his front garden, Malachi had been tormented by memories of the terrible heads. He had nightmares about them, and on occasion would awaken to find that the horrible vision was still with him, the tableau of the ring of heads appearing suspended in the air above his bed. He prayed often and long for deliverance from them. One night in early September 2001, when the nightmare had seemed more real—and more threatening—than ever, something roused him.

"I was staring in terror at the heads above me," he says, "when I realized there was a figure standing by the bedside. I looked up and saw Brother Canice. He was as real as you are now. He was looking down at me and smiling. I think he had a pair of rosary beads in his hand. When I looked again, the terrible heads were gone, and from that time on I never saw them again. That was all due to Brother Canice. I'm sure of it."

The attack in June was proving more devastating than Malachi had imagined. Not only did his mental health suffer but there was a physical deterioration as well. It was as though something was attacking his entire person, as a virus will enter the body and work its deadly way through the various organs and cell systems. That summer, Malachi was laid low with a raft of minor ailments, from head colds to muscle pains to inexplicable rashes. He had always had a strong constitution and was dismayed to find himself visiting his doctor sometimes twice a week. Dr. Moran could find no immediate cause beyond what he called "the onset of old age." Perhaps of most concern was Malachi's sudden weight loss. He had lost more than twenty pounds in eight weeks.

"'Wasting disease' was what I kept thinking of," Malachi says. "I read it somewhere, and those words kept coming back to me. I didn't understand it at all. I was eating the same as I always did—Blenny saw to that. In the end Dr. Moran sent me into hospital for tests. I was there two days; they looked at me from top to bottom. Couldn't find a thing wrong with me."

He was discharged and advised to have lots of bed rest. But this was to prove impossible. His arrival home coincided with the onset of a series of paranormal events that served to drive him further into despair.

"It was the second night I was home. I was sleeping on my own because of my illness, and I wakened to see something happening to the picture of the Sacred Heart which hung on the wall. It was suspended in the air at the foot of the bed. And as I was lying there trying to figure out if I was seeing things, these two hands appeared either side of the picture and turned it back to front. God, it had a terrible effect on me."

In Malachi's eyes, the sight of the disembodied hands was frightening enough. Yet what caused him the most torment was the idea that Christ was—almost literally, as he saw it—turning his back on him. Malachi felt that he was being sent a very clear message.

He increased the frequency and intensity of his prayers, but seemingly to no avail. Whatever it was that was haunting him was not to be put off so easily. It stepped up its nocturnal visits.

"I'd see nothing," Malachi says, "but I'd always feel an evil presence in the room, near my feet, at my shoulders. I'd get stone cold in my feet and legs, so cold. I couldn't move. I'd wake up and feel it coming into the room. Sometimes I'd feel it on my chest—this terrible weight. One night it was so bad I screamed."

Blenny Gant awoke with a jolt to find Malachi in a very distressed state. She could not discern a cause; there was nothing out of the ordinary that she could see. The crushing weight had lifted at the moment Malachi cried out. Not wishing to frighten her, he pretended he had had a nightmare. But Blenny *did* notice something odd: a smell of burning in the room. She described it as being "like the smell of a fire in a gypsy's camp."

"From then on, I'd only smell it in the middle of the night when she'd be asleep," Malachi recalls. "I'd wake up to the terrible smell and I knew it was the thing again. I knew it was standing beside the bed and I'd just lie there terrified. I felt that if I turned on the light I'd maybe see it, and I just couldn't face that."

But face it he must, as he discovered. Malachi could just about endure the frightful apparition in the dark of night, but when it began attacking him in broad daylight, his torment became unbearable.

"Sometimes I would feel it moving through the house. God, it terrified me. I always knew when it was coming for me because my body temperature would drop. The temperature in the room wouldn't be any different; it would just be me. I'd start to shiver and turn blue from head to toe—really freezing cold. God, it was terrifying. I'd concentrate on Brother Canice, sort of talk to him in my head. I'd ask him to help me. I believed his spirit was somehow watching over me, and that was a comfort."

Nevertheless, the "presence" in his home refused to leave. Almost every day, he had the unsettling and constant feeling of being under observation.

"One time when I was driving I looked in the rearview mirror and felt it on the back seat. I nearly crashed the car with the shock of it. After that I stopped driving. It was just too dangerous."

Malachi's son-in-law and daughter would take turns accompanying him whenever he made a long journey. He found himself visiting the monastery less often than he would have liked. At the same time, he sensed a power of some kind attempting to come between him and his religious faith.

"There was a time when I couldn't say my prayers," he confesses, "and I was somebody who prayed often. I couldn't say my prayers or read my missal. I'd have the book in my hands and wanted to tear it up several times. I couldn't read anything anymore—my missal or anything else for that matter, not even a paper. I felt I was being worn down. Whenever I tried to go to Mass, some kind of force seemed to be preventing me. I'd get terribly agitated and confused on a Sunday morning. Those times I was well enough to go, it would be pushing against me as soon as I got through the church gates. It hated anything holy."

The last should have alerted Malachi to the true nature of his torment. In fact, he concedes that it did. Yet he was trying to convince himself, in the face of all evidence to the contrary, that it was a battle he could fight alone. He toyed with the notion that his problems were psychological, that it might all be in his head. For all he knew, he might be imagining everything. He might even be going a little insane.

He decided to seek medical advice and went to his general practitioner, Dr. Moran. Malachi had been seeing him off and on for many years, and the doctor was well acquainted with his medical history. Dr. Moran had been unable to ascertain the cause of

Malachi's physical decline in the wake of the Sherrin attack. Now his patient was coming to him with a story so fantastic it beggared belief. Moran was being asked to make a leap of faith in order to explain the inexplicable.

"I told him everything. He had no trouble believing me because he knew I was a man who didn't invent things. At the end of it all he said, 'It's not a doctor you need, Malachi. It's a priest.'"

It was a highly unusual statement for the doctor to make. Most victims of demonic oppression report that they encounter a wall of skepticism when they confide in their doctors. It is understandable. Few members of the medical profession are willing to allow that a patient's difficulties may have a spiritual, as opposed to a psychological, cause. It is perhaps an indication of enlightenment and insight that Malachi's doctor recognized the presence of something unclean behind the attacks.

So a priest it had to be. Malachi turned to the obvious: the monastery.

It is situated on the outskirts of a small town, no more than a large village, in County Sligo. It is reached from the road by a driveway that meanders between pasturelands where many cattle once grazed but that are now bare, save for a small flock of sheep. In its heyday, the monastery housed a community of over two hundred men; now there are fewer than thirty, the numbers dwindling inexorably with the passing years, as the old monks die off and no young novices come to take their places.

Malachi had a friend drive him there. He had no fears as they negotiated the familiar driveway. He had driven it countless times, knew every bend and pothole. The nearer they drew to the big house, the more at ease he became. On rounding the final bend, he caught sight of the chapel with the monks' quarters to the rear. Adjacent was the house itself. It is a fine building in the Queen Anne style, once the home of a prominent Anglo-Irish family. The last heir, a convert to Catholicism, died in 1912 and bequeathed the house and lands to the religious community. Over the past two decades, the monks had disposed of much of the original acreage, as well as hiring a farm manager from the area, the first time the business of running the agricultural wing of the establishment had been entrusted to a layman.

There was only one other car in sight as they drew to a halt on the gravel in front of the entrance. It belonged to an elderly woman, who emerged from the little shop that sold religious goods as Malachi's driver cut the engine.

He had a four o'clock appointment with a certain Father Ignatius. He only knew the good man by sight, but a younger brother at the monastery had recommended him as an individual distinguished by his purity, his piety—and his reputation as an archfoe of the demonic.

"But I nearly didn't get to see the priest that day," Malachi says. "When I approached the door there was a pressure like a wind. Only it wasn't a wind; it was something like it, trying to stop me from entering. It was like walking against a very strong gale. It was like what I used to experience going through the church gates of a Sunday—but worse, much worse. Something didn't want me to see that priest."

"Father Ignatius thinks that Charlie Sherrin is possessed," Malachi says. "He came to that conclusion at once. He asked me about the family, about Charlie's daughters. He was also keen to know about Charlie's father."

Father Ignatius would indeed have identified, from Malachi's account of his neighbor, several of the hallmarks of the possessed. During the furious sexual assault, Charlie Sherrin revealed what could be construed as evidence of a demonized personality. Charlie used the plural pronoun when referring to himself. His face assumed, if only fleetingly, bestial characteristics. He was capable of "possessed gravity"—that is, of acquiring immovable weight. Malachi likened the weight on top of him to that of "a big plow horse." The attacker emitted inhuman sounds: the piglike squeal. Furthermore, Malachi often felt repulsed by Charlie's behavior around his own family, including violent outbursts at minor upsets and lewd talk and behavior in front of his offspring. In the aftermath of the assault, when he visited Malachi in the hospital, he claimed to have no recollection of what he had done.

Finally, there was the hellish vision of the disembodied heads. Not only had the preternatural broken cover during the assault but further phenomena were continuing to oppress Malachi.

What Malachi recounted in the course of a number of interviews is harrowing, for want of a better word. The events reduced a once-robust man to a nervous wreck, a man who dares not be alone for more than a few minutes at a time.

As we take our leave at his front door, our eyes are inevitably drawn to his garden. There are seven species of roses growing there, in colors ranging from saffron to an almost purple red. Somebody has trained a wilder variety to climb the brick wall almost to the second-story window. Across the way, the green fields have been earmarked for a new shopping mall. For now, it is a tranquil place, far from the main road. We hear only a dog barking off in the distance. Malachi nods in the direction of a patch of grass under his living-room window.

"I don't like that spot in the garden," he says with sadness. "I only mow it. I thought of digging there last year, to lay a little ornamental pond, but I couldn't do it. I broke out in a sweat at the thought of it. I wouldn't put a spade in that now if you paid me."

There is a great deal unresolved in this case, yet Father Ignatius has total confidence in Malachi's ability to heal his spiritual self. "He has come through this ordeal a stronger and wiser man," he says. "That is the compensation for enduring great evil. It forces us to learn great lessons. Malachi's faith was always strong, but since this dreadful episode he's had to draw on the power of God more and more. That is the victory."

Would that the same could be said of Charlie Sherrin. "Charlie needs an exorcism, but he must want it himself," says Father Ignatius. "It has to be his decision. And he's not ready yet to make that decision."

An acquaintance agrees, but feels that the civil authorities should be alerted. "Malachi ought to have gone to the police as soon as that happened," he says grimly. "It's a criminal matter as well as a spiritual one. He still can. It's only five years, and the hospital will have records. I have the feeling that more people are in danger. I have the feeling that Charlie's done this sort of thing before."

Having listened to Malachi's appalling account and observed his ongoing suffering, we are prompted to ask a very pertinent question. Why does he continue to live so close to the man who caused him such anguish? Surely it cannot be pleasant to look out—every day of his life—at the garden in which the ferocious attack took place. Malachi answers without hesitation. "Oh, but I could never leave this house," he says. "My grandfather built it. It was his home and he was very proud of it. I'd be letting him down if I left. Charlie Sherrin has taken a lot from me but he's not going to drive me out of here."

When put in those terms, his reasoning is hard to fault. He is a courageous man, and his faith is strong. His battle is not yet won, but he believes that good will triumph over evil in the end.

"I go to Father Ignatius whenever things get really bad, and he keeps me on the right road," Malachi tells us. "I've asked him to do an exorcism but he says I'm not the one who is demonized. He prays with me and for me, and I'm praying the thing won't win. But it keeps on trying. Whenever I go to see Father Ignatius there'll be that same wind again, trying to keep me away from the monastery door."

He reaches into his shirt and brings out a little silver chain. There is a medal attached; it is circular and displays a bearded saint in a monk's habit. "It's St. Benedict," he says. "Father Ignatius gave it to me." He points to a large cross on the reverse, around which are arranged a number of letters. "Latin. It means: 'Get thee behind me, Satan! Do not tempt me with vain things. You offer evil? Drink your own poison!' Father Ignatius says it's the only Catholic medal with an exorcism on it. He says it's very powerful against evil spirits."

"I still have the presence in my room at night," he continues. "I'll wake up to find the awful stench, that burning smell. I still get the pressing weight on me, but it's not so often now, thank God! Sometimes when I go to the monastery, I'll be attacked that very night. Father Ignatius always asks me the same question. He asks if I can forgive Charlie, and I'm always honest with him. I say, 'Father, there are times when I can, and other times when I could kill him and be done with it all.' Father Ignatius says those times when I feel the most hatred against Charlie Sherrin are when Satan's in his element. He loves to see us in despair, to give up hope and live tormented. That's his goal, you see: to wear us down so that suicide becomes an option. And the more I'm able to look at things in that way, the more I'm able to forgive Charlie and feel better. I know he wasn't in his right mind when he did that to me. That's the only way I'm ever going to have any peace. So I pray now for the strength to forgive. And I pray also for his children."

It is tragic that a man like Malachi has been left in old age to carry such a burden. How could he have known, as he traveled the world with Blenny, that those two glorious years would be followed by five years of torment? In Egypt he accidentally stepped into the path of evil in the form of Walter Ehrlich. No one could have foreseen that, upon the Gants' return, that same evil would manifest itself on the very road where they live.

The Egyptian episode continues to intrigue us. We wonder if it was in some way linked to Malachi's 2004 experience. Father Ignatius does not dismiss the notion. "It's entirely possible," he says, "but very difficult to establish. Do not forget that evil is to be found just about everywhere in this world of ours. It's also true to say that men like Malachi Gant—spiritual men—will always be more susceptible than most people to attack from evil forces."

On leaving Malachi's home, we draw level, some distance farther on, with the Sherrin house. We cannot help pausing to steal a look. In the garden there is a man with his back to us, off to one side, clipping a hedge. At the sound of the car, he turns slowly to stare at us, but we do not linger. The weight of Malachi's testimony proves too much; we have no inclination to examine at close quarters the face of evil.

THE HESSIAN WHO RETURNED TO HAUNT

———— ✥ ————

The following events, which occurred on the Downey fruit farm between August 2004 and January 2005, were recreated through interviews with Patricia Downey, the owner's wife, her daughter, seventeen-year-old Katie, and a deposition written by Mirjana, a twenty-one-year-old foreign worker.

Mirjana does not like to see the sun sink and darkness stain the sky. She continues to work, even though it is ten o'clock and the boss's wife, Mrs. Downey, has told her it is time to stop. Even though she has worked a nine-hour day and is exhausted, still she works. The red Braeburn apples feel cool in her chapped hands as she plucks them from the tree and places them in the basket.

She misses her family back home. This is her first time abroad, but soon the fruit-picking season will be over, her work in Ireland at an end, and she will be returning to her village in Bosnia-Herzegovina.

"Mirjana!"

"Yes, Miss Tricia, now I finish!"

Reluctantly, she carries the basket to the trailer and tips it in carefully. She is the only female employee left on the fruit farm. Her co-worker, Marta, took sick a week ago and had to return home to Eastern Europe. She misses her very much, and most especially when darkness comes.

Today, the women in green did not appear in the orchard. Perhaps tonight they will not come.

She waves to her employer and makes her way down the winding lane to the old cottage. Her heart quickens as she nears the front door. She would do anything rather than enter. But she is tired and needs to sleep. Besides, there is nowhere else to go.

In the bedroom, she undresses and lies down, holding her rosary beads to her heart. She concentrates on the picture of the Virgin of Medjugorje—Our Lady Queen of Peace—and hopes and longs and prays, just as she has over so many nights, that the sounds from the far corner will not come....

Always, there was something not quite right about the farm, as far back as anyone could remember. It was the land, not the homes that had been built upon it in the course of five centuries or more. Neighbors and friends suggested that the land was cursed. Tricia Downey did not rule this out.

"I never would've believed it myself," says the mother of four. "That wasn't how I was brought up. We're Catholics and we believe in what the Church teaches us. But, given what we've been through, I keep an open mind."

The Downey farmhouse is in County Wexford, and lies roughly midway between two sites of great historical significance. Vinegar Hill and Oulart Hill are battle sites. In the spring of 1798, each was the scene of some of the most ferocious fighting ever witnessed in the country.

At the first, overlooking the town of Enniscorthy and the Slaney River, the rebel army suffered a great defeat. They were the United Irishmen, spurred to revolt against English rule in their country by the successes of the American and French revolutions. Oulart, some miles to the east, was the place where that same ragtag militia saw its greatest triumph. Among its captains was the fighting priest Father John Murphy, whose brief but valiant military career is celebrated in the ballad of *Boolavogue*.

These ancient facts, as we shall see, would come to have a bearing on a prolonged assault on the Downey family.

The name Oulart derives from the Gaelic word for orchard, *úll-ord*, literally "apple field." Today, apples still grow on Oulart Hill, but they are of the wild and inedible variety. Better, luscious varieties grow in the orchards owned by the family. Hugh Downey is the proud owner of close to a hundred acres given over to apple and pear trees. Although much of his produce is bought by Irish supermarkets and cider makers, he also exports fruit to foreign markets. The business is thriving and the family is among the wealthiest in the area.

It was not always so. There is a house very near to the Downeys' own. It is a long, one-story cottage that speaks of harder times. It is, we learn, more than 250 years old; in fact, it was standing here at the time of the Rising of 1798, when the Irish made a valiant but unsuccessful attempt to end British rule. The Downeys occupied the old house up until a few years ago. This fact, too, has a bearing on the case.

The family has lived in the area for generations, Tricia Downey tells us.

"I'm from County Kilkenny myself," she says, "but my husband's people are here five hundred years, if not more. They go back a long way."

Tricia is a pretty, well-groomed woman of forty-one. She speaks with the residue of an English accent, picked up during years spent working as a secretary in London. It was there that she met her future husband, Hugh. They married in 1988 and have four children: two boys and two girls.

Every year, they employ a small workforce of men and women—immigrants, mainly of East European origin. The women are quartered in the old one-story cottage, the men in an adjoining building.

"That house was rebuilt three or four times," Tricia tells us. "It still had a thatched roof when I moved in. I liked it, though. There was something very quaint about it, even though it was a bit cramped. But Hugh insisted on building a new house. He'd lived in the old one all his life, so I suppose it was understandable he wanted a change."

Mirjana hears the rustling in the corner. She clutches the rosary beads more tightly to her chest. She wants to switch the light on but knows she cannot. The boss does not allow it. The light disturbs the guard dogs in the yard and makes them bark. She cannot afford to wake the family. She cannot afford to lose her job. She holds her breath and waits . . . and waits . . .

In October 2003, construction work on the new Downey home was completed. The family moved in toward the end of December, when the fruit harvest of that year had been picked, packaged, and dispatched to the respective buyers.

The room we are sitting in has a huge picture window that looks out over a good portion of the Downey land. The sun is low and slants between neat rows of apple trees, now bare of fruit. The seasonal workers all have gone. The place is quiet.

"That's how it was too before it all began," Tricia says. "It started in a very quiet way. Just after my sister passed away."

Tricia's sister, Claire, was only thirty-five when she died of ovarian cancer. It had been diagnosed late and was too far gone for treatment to be effective. Claire had never married, so it was left to Tricia to either consign her to a hospice or make her final days comfortable in her own home. She chose the latter. Claire was moved into the old house a few weeks before the new one was ready, and when the family made the move she went with them. It was agreed that she should have the room that daughter Katie had earmarked for herself. It is on the ground floor, across the corridor from her sister Eilish's room. Katie did not object; she loved her aunt dearly.

The family is unusually devout, and their home reflects this. It contains many examples of religious iconography. We know of several priests' houses that have far fewer images of Jesus, Mary, and the saints, or statues to the Child of Prague, Michael the Archangel, St. Martin de Porres, and many other holy men and women we cannot readily identify. There are prayers also: hand-stitched samplers calling on the Lord to "Bless this House" and to protect its occupants against danger of an otherworldly nature.

Throughout the months of her sister's terminal illness, Tricia had prayed for her recovery. She led her family in countless rosaries, said novenas at home, and petitioned the nuns in a nearby convent to do likewise. Despite all this, Claire died early in the evening of July 6, 2004. Tricia was at the bedside up until the last. "I was holding her hand as she was dying," Tricia recalls. "Her last words were, 'It's getting dark, oh so dark!' and I remember assuring her she was going to God's light and to just let go."

Ostensibly, there was no link between Claire's death and what was to ensue in the Downey home. In reality, however, there *was* a link, and that link was prayer.

The prayers for Claire did not end with her death. Like all committed Irish Catholics brought up to believe in the importance of prayers for the dead, the Downeys—if anything—increased the fervency and frequency of their praying. Day after day, evening after evening, the house rang with Our Fathers, Hail Marys and other supplications to the Almighty, that he might look favorably on the dearly departed.

"It started with the eggs, would you believe," Tricia says, "a few weeks after Claire's death."

Tricia rose earlier than usual, roused the others, and went to fix breakfast. She opened the refrigerator in the utility room to get the eggs and bacon. There were no eggs.

"Did you move the eggs, Katie?" she called out.

"Not me."

But they were there—out of sight in the back of the fridge, where eggs had no good reason to be. Tricia, still consumed with grief, thought no more about the incident. She had any number of things to occupy her.

But the following morning the eggs had again gone missing. They were nowhere to be seen in the fridge. Tricia was vexed now. She immediately blamed her offspring.

"This is no time for stupid games!" she said. "Whoever's messing around with the eggs has to stop it right now."

But none of the children seemed to be responsible. It was, Tricia reflected, a trivial thing. But, later in the day, when she was preparing to do the laundry, there they were—all eight eggs in a neat pile in the drum of the machine.

Eleven-year-old Paul was the joker in the family. When he came in from school, despite his hot denials, she grounded him for the evening. That would teach him. Before going to bed, she locked the eggs in the store cupboard and put the key under her pillow. Surely that would be the end of all the childish devilment.

But, alas, it was not the end but rather the beginning of devilment that would prove far from childish. The next morning, she did not need to check the storeroom; lined up on the kitchen table were the eggs. And the storeroom remained locked.

"I knew then there was something very strange going on, but I'd never really experienced anything paranormal. Well, I say never really—there was just one incident when we were living down in the old cottage. One night I woke up to find two women, an old one and a young one, standing in the corner of the room. But that was the only time."

A month passed without further incident. A memorial Mass was said for Aunt Claire in the parish church, attended by the Downeys and a number of relatives. By this time, all the dead woman's effects had been removed. Katie had made the room her own.

On September 28, shortly after she had gone to sleep, the fifteen-year-old was wakened by a series of loud poundings and scratching noises on the ceiling. She could not tell where they were coming from. She left her bed—and met her parents on the stairs. They were agitated.

"Were you making that racket?" Hugh asked sourly. Katie's room lies directly under theirs.

"No, Dad. I thought it was somebody else."

They found all the ground-floor lights on and no one about. Tricia asked who was last downstairs, if perhaps somebody forgot to switch off the lights. But Katie was the last and she swore she had turned everything off.

Things went downhill from then on. There was an almost tangible presence in the Downey home. In Tricia's words, "a thing had started to visit."

"You'd hear it at all hours of the day and night," she recalls. "You'd be sitting and you'd hear it shuffling about. Not footsteps as such, but rustling and shuffling. You couldn't see anything, though. Not at first."

As the days passed, the presence gradually made itself known. Again, there was nothing threatening. Tricia decided to resume the rosaries they had dispensed with a month after Claire's death. "Looking back on it now," she says, "I think maybe that's what made matters worse."

Around the middle of October, the Downey household was awakened by a scream in the night. Katie burst into her parents' room, crying and shaking with fear. It was just after two in the morning.

"Mom, there's something in my room!" she sobbed.

They were shocked at the state she was in. Tricia got out of bed and put her arms around the girl. "Look, love, you've had a nightmare, that's all."

"No, Mom, it was real. I swear it was real!"

"I'll go down and check," Hugh said. "Like your mother says, it's just a bad dream. You'll see."

He returned shortly, shrugging his shoulders. There was nothing. By this time, Katie had calmed down sufficiently to give an account of her experience. "I woke up because I felt something on my back," she tells us. "It was pushing me out of bed. I looked round because I thought maybe it was Mom or Dad wanting to wake me up for school. But there was nothing there."

It felt as though somebody was trying to eject her from the bed, as if she did not belong there. She thought that somebody was playing a joke on her. Then suddenly the duvet was whisked off the bed, leaving her shivering.

"To be honest, I thought it was 'night fears' and that she'd dreamt it," Tricia explains, "but she was very sure of what she felt and saw. Of course Hugh saw nothing in the room. The duvet thrown on the floor, but that was all."

Katie was the first victim. Before long, the rest of the Downeys were to discover that her night fears were more than mere illusion. For the time being, though, the manifestations were innocent, playful almost. The episode with the eggs was followed by others of a similar nature.

"When I came home from school I'd notice things moved in my room," Katie recollects. "Things being left open—drawers and things. I thought maybe Eilish was doing it. I knew it wasn't my imagination, because a couple of times I made a note of something I closed, and when I looked five minutes later, sure enough, it would be open again."

In the night, she would hear noises, "a lot of running and banging upstairs in Mom's room, and scratching." But Tricia, for her part, thought the disturbances were coming from Katie's room.

The rustling in the corner ceases. Has it gone? Mirjana is very frightened and very tired. She lies in the darkness willing herself to sleep. But even if she does sleep, she knows they can wake her up again.

She concentrates on the face of Gospa—Our Lady—and thinks of her many visits to the shrine at Medjugorje, as she counts off the names of the visionaries on her rosary beads. One of them even has her name: Mirjana. Yes, Mirjana, Ivan, Jakov, Marija, Vicka, and Ivanka. She pictures herself climbing Mount Podbrdo with her mother—the mountain where the Virgin first appeared. Every week her mother visits the shrine and follows the Lady's counsel with regard to Satan, and the five weapons to use against him: prayer, Mass, confession, fasting twice a week, and fifteen decades of the rosary every day.

The rustling in the corner starts up again. Mirjana tightens her grip on the rosary and prays.

Tricia is of the opinion that the night she heard the horses was the night "the molester" entered her home.

"I was woken up around four," she says, "by the sound of horses' hooves out on the road. It was like there was a cavalry of horsemen passing. Hugh heard it too."

The Downey house lies close to the road. It is a minor road that has been there a long time. When the old house was built more than five centuries ago, there was a road running past it, connecting the town of Enniscorthy with the coast.

But horsemen no longer travel the roads of Ireland; horse trailers are used instead. Nor do horsemen ride at night. Hugh Downey drew back the curtains and looked out. The lamps on the gateposts were bathing the roadway in a soft light. There were no horses. The road was deserted.

"It was astonishing," Tricia continues, "because when we opened the window, the noises just got louder. There was this babble of voices, men shouting at each other. We couldn't understand what they were saying. To be honest, I couldn't even tell if it was English. But, as they passed and the commotion was dying down, we heard like one horse rearing up and whinnying, like it was being turned against its will. Next thing," Tricia puts a hand to her heart at the memory, "next thing, we hear it galloping up the avenue to the house and the rider letting out this terrible howl. God, it was awful! Like some sort of war cry."

Moments later, there was a single, ferocious thud on the front door. "Like a battering ram were being used against it." The house shook with the impact. The whole family woke up.

The next day, the children were too tired to attend school. That night, everyone retired to bed earlier than usual. Everyone slept soundly—everyone, that is, except Katie.

She was roused from sleep because she heard noises in the room. She could breathe only with difficulty. The cause was not hard to discern: somebody was lying on top of her. She could not move a muscle.

"I was terrified," she says. "I couldn't see his face but I knew it was a man's body." We see her embarrassment and understand what she means. "He was grunting and panting. Not like an animal, but like a person, someone demented. It sounded sexual, really horrible."

She attempted to call out but it was as if her vocal cords were frozen. Soon the grunting stopped and gave way to labored breathing. The horror-stricken teenager could sense a face very close to her own. Still she could see nothing; the room seemed darker than ever. She tried to scream.

In the room across the way, her seven-year-old sister, Eilish, the youngest child, slept soundly. As did the rest of the family on the second floor—Katie's parents and her brothers, Paul and Liam. No one had heard the unearthly sounds emanating from whatever it was that was pinioning Katie. And no one heard her scream because she was unable to. "I was numb from the weight on top of me, but not only that. It was as if the bed was outside in the yard, the room was so cold. Like an icebox."

For how long she lay there, stunned and immobile, she cannot say. Nor does she remember going to sleep that night, but she did. She appeared at breakfast white faced and shaken.

"I can't go to school today either," she told her mother, breaking into tears.

"I couldn't quite believe what she was telling me," says Tricia. "Really, I'd never heard anything like it, and at the same time I wondered why on earth she would make up such a thing. The next night we moved her into Liam's room, and he doubled up with Paul."

"Everything was all right the first night after that," Katie explains, "but the second night I was disturbed again. Not by the thing on top of me, but by someone sawing wood—well, that's what it sounded like. I put the light on and I couldn't believe my eyes. The wardrobe doors were open and the drawers were being pulled out and in... out, in, out, in, really fast."

Katie sprang from the bed and rushed out into the corridor. She was surprised to find the rest of her family, with the exception of little Eilish, assembled there. Her mother saw her fright.

"It's okay now, love," she said. "It's gone."

She saw Katie's puzzlement. "What's gone?" the girl asked.

Paul was in floods of tears. Crying was something her know-it-all young brother rarely did.

"Paul thought he saw a black thing when he went to the bathroom," Tricia explained. "But it's gone now."

Katie decided to keep quiet about the drawers; her mother was upset enough and would never sleep. But she could not keep it to herself. What happened with the wardrobe was unnatural. It also proved to her that she was definitely not dreaming. The things were real; they were under attack. She told her mother at breakfast the next morning.

Mirjana is awakened by a loud thud in the far corner of the bedroom. The women in green have appeared. There is the old woman with the long, gray hair falling over her face. The younger one, wearing heavy boots, with a dark stain down the front of her dress. They stare at her.

"Go away," Mirjana pleads, but they do not move. She fears the old one more. "Please, Gospa," she implores the holy picture, "please, make them go away!"

But they do not go away. Instead, the old one is coming toward her with arms outstretched. Mirjana wants desperately to switch the light on but knows she cannot. The dogs will bark.

She runs to the door but finds that it is locked. She cannot get out. Terrified, she looks around; the crone is now back in the corner. There is no choice but to return to bed. She pulls the blankets over her head and starts to pray. All is quiet for a time.

She lowers the covers a fraction. Eyes set deep in an ancient, wizened face are staring into hers. The old lady is leaning over the bed.

Two days after Katie's experience with the drawers, Tricia was forced to accept that it was true. "I was in her bedroom tidying up when I heard the strange sawing sound, exactly the way Katie described it. I turned round and couldn't believe my eyes—the four drawers were being pulled out and in, all by themselves. I nearly fainted. I knew then that I'd have to call on the parish priest."

Father Frank McMenahan, a personable young man, new to the parish and the county, came to bless the house the following evening. He assured Tricia that a blessing would put things right.

All the family gathered in the Downeys' living room, which looks out over the orchards. The priest prepared for the ceremony by lighting a candle, blessing two basins of water that Tricia had made ready, and reciting several prayers of protection with the family.

He then motioned to Katie to take the lighted candle and follow him; her brother Paul was to take along one of the dishes of water. The priest filled a plastic squeeze bottle with some of the water. Katie and her three siblings could barely contain a smile. They had been brought up accustomed to solemnity in the Church. Incense was dispensed from a brass censer, Holy Communion from silver and gold vessels. To see a plastic squeeze bottle being prepared for the sprinkling of holy water was highly unusual.

And it was more than sprinkling. The house was to be thoroughly drenched. So thoroughly, in fact, that water ran down the walls. They went from room to room, Father Frank making the sign of the Celtic cross on each lintel and window. It was a cross enclosed within a protective circle. Its significance was not lost on the Downeys.

"The moment I went into Katie's room," Father Frank tells us, "the hairs rose on the nape of my neck. A feeling of icy coldness cut right through me. I almost lost my balance with the force of it. There really was no logical explanation for it."

We wonder if it could have been suggestion. After all, both mother and daughter had described in detail what had taken place in the room. It would have been fresh in his mind.

"Suggestion?" he says. "There's always that possibility. But it was too real for that. I'm a skeptic at heart where such things are concerned, but that really shook me."

The priest blessed the room, sprinkling—if anything—even more holy water than he had used elsewhere. He left the Downey home, confident that whatever it was that had "visited" the family had been expelled.

He could not have been more wrong.

"After he blessed the house, it went crazy," Tricia Downey says with a shudder. "It was growling and banging, not only during the night, but in the daytime as well—upstairs and downstairs."

Mirjana does not know how many hours she has slept. Yet, as always, she knows that the visitors have been and gone. She awakes to find that the bedroom door—locked by unseen hands some hours before—is now open. She sees her rosary beads discarded on the floor.

Everything is in disarray. She finds her shoes on the kitchen table, her clothes under the bed; all cupboards in the kitchen lie open, their contents on display.

She makes breakfast quickly and leaves for the orchards, glad to be gone from the house.

The thing Katie described has all the hallmarks of the incubus.

The incubus—the name derives from the Latin *incubare*, meaning "to lie upon"—is, according to traditional belief, an evil spirit or demon that takes male form to have sexual intercourse with a sleeping woman for purposes of procreation. Its female counterpart is known as the succubus.

There is reason to believe that the notion of the incubus was founded in misogyny. As early as the fifteenth century, the Church showed an unhealthy interest in female sexuality. The hunt for witches became an instrument for the further suppression of women. To many, it was inconceivable that a woman should have sexual desires of her own. Should a woman be seduced, willingly or unwillingly, then the blame might be laid at the door of the incubus. The *Malleus Maleficarum* of 1486, that notorious handbook of the witch-finder, recognized three categories of suspected witches: those who submitted voluntarily to evil, those forced by other witches to sleep with incubi, and those assaulted by incubi against their will.

Descriptions of the entity were not in short supply. "The incubus," according to Francesco Maria Guazzo, in his *Compendium Maleficarum* (1608), "can assume either a male or a female shape; sometimes it appears as a full-grown man, sometimes as a satyr; and if it is a woman who has been received as a witch, it generally assumes the form of a rank goat."

Belief in the incubus persisted up until the eighteenth century, when the medical profession at last began to question its validity. Some viewed the entity as being no more than the invention of a woman's perverted imagination. It was pointed out that the incubus could be conveniently blamed for an unwanted pregnancy or used to conceal an illicit affair.

And yet, there is a high incidence of reports of such attacks in present-day Europe and America, in communities that long ago dispensed with many sexual taboos. There seemed to be no good reason why Katie Downey should concoct an account of a nighttime visitor that corresponded so closely to traditional descriptions of the incubus. That it was singling her out for attack was self-evident.

"We were more afraid for Katie than for any of the others," Tricia tells us. "The thing only seemed to be interested in her. I mean, I'd heard noises and so did the others. But it seemed to be focusing on her. I was very worried by the sexual element. I mean, Katie knew about the birds and the bees—all the children did—but she'd never had a boyfriend. She found it very difficult to talk about what was happening to her. So why on earth would she make it up?"

Soon the unthinkable would occur. The incubus began materializing next to Katie's bed.

"The first time I saw it I was wide awake," she explains. "I'd just turned over on my side to try and get more comfortable when there it was standing beside the bed. I tried to get away from it, but as I did, I was lifted up. Then suddenly I was back on the bed and it was on top of me. I could make out this shape, the 'head' of whatever the thing was. It had a human shape, but on the top of the head there were two things—not horns exactly, more like ears of some kind. Instead of grunting and panting, that first time I saw it, it started screaming and howling, like something gone berserk. I was so scared I just passed out."

Between October and January of 2005, there was little respite for Katie. The family took to saying a rosary in her bedroom before going to bed. Some nights it worked, but more often it did not.

"Just when I thought it had gone, it would come back," she says. "My schoolwork suffered. I lost all confidence in myself. It didn't like to see me happy. I got a part-time job in my uncle's pub, just so

I could stay out late. But, on my way home in the early hours, I'd start panicking. I used to stay over with a friend, but I couldn't do that every night. Always when I'd go into my bedroom, it'd be there waiting for me. I could feel it. For a while, when it started to show itself, I didn't tell anyone. I didn't want to scare Mom. But in the end I knew I had to. I just couldn't go on."

It was a bad omen. Tricia Downey had the uneasy feeling that the sighting of the "black form" might be the beginning of another and more frightening phase of the haunting. She went to the priests' house again, taking her daughter with her.

"Do you think," Father Frank asked, "that you'd be up to spending a night in Katie's room?"

Tricia had not expected this. She had assumed that the priest would suggest a second blessing, or perhaps a Mass.

"I want to know more about what it looks like," he said. "From what Katie tells me, it sounds terrible enough. But I'd like a second opinion."

"You do believe me, don't you, Father?" Katie asked.

"I do. I believe that *you* believe what you saw. But Katie, nighttime is a strange enough time. Sometimes the darkness can convince us that we see things that aren't there, or we mistake shadows for real things. That's why I think we should let your mother spend the night with you."

Privately, the priest thought that Katie might be having psychological problems, as adolescents often do. He was also distressed to learn that his house blessing had proved ineffective.

That night, Tricia shared the bed in Katie's room.

"Why did you turn off the heat?" she asked her daughter. "It's freezing!"

"I didn't, Mom. It's up full. See for yourself."

Tricia went to the radiator. As was the case in her own bedroom, it was a double radiator. The valve was open fully. In the small room the temperature should have been almost unbearable.

"I'll have your father look at it tomorrow," she said.

"It's been like that for days, Mom. It's *him*. He does it!"

Tricia's unease was growing. She had come armed with her rosary beads, her prayer leaflets, and a St. Brigid's Cross—woven expertly of rushes by a long-dead relative. She placed it, together with a Bible, on the nightstand.

Mother and daughter talked for an hour or more, not so much because they had a lot to say to each other but because neither was in a hurry to go to sleep. Both feared what dreams might come. At last, Katie told her mother that she was ready for sleep. Tricia kissed her goodnight and began silently praying. She was aware of Katie's breathing growing shallower. After a while, she too drifted off.

Tricia awoke from what seemed like a long sleep. Panic gripped her. She found herself pinned to the bed, effectively paralyzed, exactly as her daughter had described it. Beside her, she could hear Katie's soft snores.

"It was like a ton on top of me," she recalls. "I knew it was bad—you could feel it was bad. I tried to make the sign of the cross, but it wouldn't let me. As I was raising my right hand, it was gripped at the wrist. I had my rosary beads under the pillow, so I tried to maneuver my left hand underneath to get at them, but again my arm was gripped, so I couldn't. I tried to pray, but I couldn't even speak. My tongue was frozen."

She did not see the entity that night, and for this she was thankful; her torment had been traumatic enough. Yet the fact that it had not made itself visible to her did not mean she was free of it.

On the contrary, Tricia believes that the thing took this opportunity to latch onto *her*, allowing Katie some respite. She claims that it pursued her to her own room and appeared to her the following night, while she slept in her own bed, her husband by her side. It was the beginning of a series of attacks.

"It didn't matter that Hugh was in bed beside me," she recounts. "I'd wake up and it would be on top of me. Then I started to see it. It was as Katie had described, an animal-like head, but the body of a human. It was a dense black form."

Tricia screamed, waking her husband. Incredibly, he saw the attacker and described it in almost exactly the same way Tricia did. He could not believe his eyes. But he was courageous; he saw the danger his wife was in. He sprang from the bed and rushed to the dressing table, where Tricia had placed a bottle of holy water.

"He threw it over the thing," she says, "and ordered it out of the room."

It went. Katie's father did not know it then, but as the creature vanished from the bedroom, it simultaneously materialized downstairs in Katie's room. Having been thwarted in its molestation of the mother, it launched a fresh assault on the daughter.

At the breakfast table the next morning, the family held a council of war. They needed the priest again. Forty-eight hours later, Father Frank returned to the Downey home and offered Mass in Katie's room.

Mirjana wakes. She has heard the door swing open. She looks to the far corner. The old woman and the girl are not there. But there is something else in the room. Outside it is raining. She has the impression that one of the guard dogs has just come in. She can smell the wet hair and feel its coldness. But the dogs are chained up.

Something is loping about the room, snorting and pawing at the floorboards, but she sees nothing. There is a small flashlight under her pillow. She gets up and shines it about the floor.

Something springs up onto her bed, grunting and panting. Petrified, she stumbles out of the bedroom and down the hallway. On reaching the kitchen, she feels the wet pelt of the unseen creature brush briefly against her legs as it bounds in ahead of her. It begins to squeal like a pig. Mirjana bolts back to the bedroom and slams the door.

"After the Mass we had about a week of peace," Tricia says, "before everything went crazy again. In the middle of the night, all the doors and windows would start banging—opening and shutting.

The boys started to talk about an animal in the bedroom that made pig noises. Eilish was the only one who wasn't affected; she sleeps like a log. But the rest of us were all being worn down, and it seemed the more we prayed, the worse it got. Katie and I didn't have the creature on top of us like before, but little did we know that after the Mass it went for poor Mirjana."

Mirjana lies suffocating. She attempts to raise her head from the pillow, but something is holding her down. She tries to look at the picture of the Virgin, but something is moving in front of her eyes—a black form blocking it out.

I am dying, she thinks. Please, Gospa, don't let me die.

She cannot move; she cannot scream. A grunting starts up close to her ear.

She smells wet fur; the phantom beast is on top of her. There is nothing she can do. She feels for the rosary beads at her right hand, but they are no longer there. I don't want to go to hell, she pleads with the Gospa, as tears trickle down her cheeks.

At 6 a.m., Mirjana pounds on the Downey front door and collapses into the hallway.

It is then that Tricia knows it has gone too far, and drastic steps must be taken. At her insistence, Father McMenahan moves for an exorcism. The call goes out. It is answered by a venerable monk in the northwest of the country.

"I couldn't tell you what Father Ignatius did," Tricia says. "He spent a long time in Katie's room, then down in the old house praying, but it worked. Thank heavens! We've never seen or heard it since. God willing, it'll last. He said it probably was the spirit of a Hessian, which was a new one on me because I'd never heard the word before. But then Hugh started to look into it, and what the priest said started to make sense."

The Downey land, which lies between two notorious battle sites, would have seen some of the worst atrocities and brutality perpetrated against the Wexford people. The Hessians, German mercenaries, were sent to Ireland in 1798 to help quell the rebellion inspired by the United Irishmen. According to more than one reliable account, they went on a rampage, raping, pillaging, and terrorizing the local population.

It is an intriguing explanation, not least because of the military elements in the haunting. There is the ghostly cavalry that the family heard in the night, the "battering ram" used against their front door, the sexual assaults on the females. All seem to reinforce the theory that the spirit of a marauding Hessian might have been at work.

Furthermore, the two women who appeared in the old cottage wore green dresses. It is significant that, in 1798, the wearing of the color green was forbidden by order of the English government. In County Wexford especially this order was defied almost universally by the women. They were to pay dearly for their defiance: the Hessians subjected them to the most vile and indecent sexual assaults. Many women died cruel and savage deaths.

But Hessian or not, Father Ignatius found it a very unusual and perplexing case.

"I don't rule out the presence of an evil spirit," he tells us, "but I feel that a sustained attack on the religious objects in the house would have been more in keeping with the activities of such, but no religious objects were disturbed. The Downey home had a great many holy pictures and statues, so the opportunity was certainly there. Given the bloody battles that were fought in that part of Wexford, it is possible that it was the spirit of a soldier. Like Father McMenahan, I had that same sensation when I entered young Katie's room, that sense that I was intruding, that the room was its territory. Who knows—perhaps this Hessian was slaughtered on the spot where the Downeys built their new house. The killing could have been an act of vengeance for all the terrible things he did."

And the incubus theory? Father Ignatius is noncommittal on the subject.

"The sexual element was obviously the most distasteful and frightening part for the females to have to go through," he says. "I don't come across that kind of thing very often. The incubus and succubus—are they simply myths? You know, there is the great danger in this enlightened age of ours to relegate all such ideas to the ignorance of the Middle Ages. Satan has managed to get himself out of the picture very well in these modern times of ours—and managed it very successfully, I'm sure you'll agree. He can take on many implausible forms, so why not that of the incubus?"

Before we leave, Tricia takes us down to Katie's bedroom. It is a typical teenager's room, with its collection of cuddly toys and posters. There is not a whiff of the horrors that her daughter endured.

She points to a holy picture above the bed.

"That's Our Lady of Medjugorje. Mirjana gave it to us before she went back to Bosnia. Katie and I went to visit her in May. She lives near the shrine and we wanted to go and give thanks. I got a great feeling of peace when I was there…it was a very spiritual experience. I just had the conviction that we'd never be bothered with that thing again. You know, I came across a book at the shrine, and it said when we're bothered by these things, we should give them a nickname and laugh at them. The more you fear them, the more energy you give them to attack you."

We wonder if Mirjana will be returning to the fruit farm.

"Oh, I don't think so," Tricia says with a smile. "And who could blame her, poor thing? But we'll be seeing a lot of her. I love Medjugorje and I intend to visit the shrine every year. Out of all that bad stuff came something positive. If anything, it's given me a better understanding of spiritual things. That can't be bad, now, can it?"

THE WOMAN WHO LEFT
HER BODY AT WILL

---❖---

Angela Brehen was seventeen years old when she had her first taste of astral travel. At the time she did not call it that. In fact, she could not call it anything at all, because throughout the morning following the occurrence, she was almost speechless with terror. She imagined that she had died, so frightening was the experience.

It was 1988 and Angela was a high-school student in Galway City. She was in her senior year, preparing to take her final examination. There was little to set her apart from the other girls attending the school; she was bright, but not exceptionally so. She had decided on a career: she planned on pursuing business studies and graduating from college before her twenty-first birthday, when she hoped to have a full-time job in Dublin—or England, perhaps.

On Saturday, March 19, Angela finished her homework at about eight o'clock, watched some television, and went to bed around eleven. The family home was some two miles from the center of town, the last house in a quiet cul-de-sac. Her young brothers were already in bed, and she heard her parents retire about twenty minutes later.

She awoke while it was still dark. Angela knew almost instinctively that it was long before time to get up; she did not even have to look at her bedside clock. She was lying on her back, the position she always found most comfortable. But there was something different about the room.

It was nothing visible. As her eyes grew accustomed to the darkness, she could make out the familiar contents of her room: the posters on the walls, the dresser with the mirror, her closet, the chair with her jeans draped over it. All was as it should have been. But there was something "funny" about the room, a sense that a change had taken place since she switched off the light. She closed her eyes again—and within seconds was wide awake, and very fearful.

She describes the sensation as something she "half felt and half heard," almost impossible to explain. It seemed to her that a force was approaching the place where she lay.

"It was like a storm that was coming," she says, "but not a violent one, nothing big or anything. I seemed to sense it coming to the house from a long way off. Something in my head was telling me that this force could go right through walls, and that it was coming for me."

The "force" entered Angela's bedroom; it appeared to hover some distance from the foot of her bed and several feet off the floor. She was terror-struck. She shut her eyes tight, afraid of what she might see.

In the next few moments, it seemed to her that something within her was resonating with the force that had entered her room. She felt a wave pulsing slowly up and down her body, traveling from head to toe. The sensation was, again, a heady mix of sound and feeling.

She felt the force inside her quickening, the vibration coursing up and down her body. She was terrified. And when she felt her body being launched into space, she knew the dread of death, because she was convinced at that moment that she was indeed dying, or had died already. That her soul was leaving her body.

"All sorts of mad ideas came into my head," Angela recalls. "I suppose I was a religious girl in a basic sort of way, though I can't remember praying very much outside of a church. But I did believe in God and heaven and the angels, all of that. I believed that when we die we go to heaven. I was convinced that the force I felt coming for me was the Angel of Death taking me off to heaven. But the last thing I wanted to do was die. I was seventeen, a kid. I was too young to die!"

In a strange sense, she was conscious of the "being" that was Angela, as it somehow swept up out of her body at a steep angle. Too fearful to open her eyes, she asked herself if her soul had eyes at all. Yet her frightened mind was telling her that this new "body" it was occupying was identical to the one that lay on the bed behind and below her.

And then she passed through the ceiling and roof of the house, and she could "see."

With her new eyes, she looked in awe at a sight that was new to her. Spread out below was the development where her home stood. She saw the roofs, the street lamps, the trees, roads, and swards of grass. She saw it all as if she were a bird.

In other circumstances, Angela would have been enchanted by the whole experience. Which of us has not at some time longed to freely take to the air, to experience the liberation of unassisted flight? And here she was—"flying." Not, however, in her physical body, but in something very much different. She was convinced more than ever that she had died.

This conviction shocked her into opening her eyes at last. As in the case of a "falling" dream, Angela experienced a sudden drop to earth. She was back in her bed, with the yellow light from the street picking out the familiar objects in her bedroom. Her heart was pounding, she was sweating—but she was glad to be alive.

She thought of praying, of giving thanks to God for her safe "return." But she did not really believe in the power of prayer. Her family was not devout. Each Sunday, the Brehens paid lip service by attending Mass, but for Angela religion was a school subject and little more.

She told no one about the unsettling experience, not even her best friend, Rhoda. Throughout the next day and in the weeks that followed, Angela puzzled over the bizarre episode. She had no ready explanation other than that she had been dreaming. And yet, the more she considered that possibility, the more implausible it seemed.

"I think we know when we're dreaming," she argues. "Even if it's a really vivid dream we still know it's only a dream. I was convinced that this was something else entirely. What kept on going through my head was that other people must have the same experience—that it wasn't just me. But I'd no one to turn to. I'd have felt like a right idiot even talking about it. My folks would have had me locked up."

She could not let go of the notion that she had stumbled upon the existence of a hidden faculty, one lying dormant in every human being, its presence unknown to and unsuspected by all but a few. She wished she could put a name on this remarkable capability.

The more she dwelled on it and the more she recalled the wild exhilaration of that night, the less her fear of it became. By and by, she found herself wishing that the strange "force," which had plucked her from her bed and transported her into the unknown, would visit her again.

The Leaving Certificate examination was looming. Angela and her friend Rhoda made a trip to Dublin; they needed copies of old exams to study from. Their school had distributed the copies they had, leaving a few students without papers. The girls arranged to visit the educational bookstores and procure the necessary copies; they were going to Dublin anyway, to stay with Rhoda's aunt.

The friends "got the boring business out of the way" quite quickly. Rhoda wanted to visit the clothes shops, but Angela had little interest in fashion. They parted company; they would rendezvous at the bus stop on Nassau Street. Angela returned to her favorite pastime: browsing the bookstores for bargains.

She happened upon the worn paperback in an equally worn shop down a side street. It had been placed on the wrong shelf. Its jacket showed two men of the East in silhouette and a snowcapped mountain; within the blackness of their forms a universe of stars was

visible. The title was *You Forever*, and the author gloried in the un-
forgettable name of Tuesday Lobsang Rampa. She turned it over.

> Rampa...provides step by step instructions for enhancing your
> psychic abilities. The book is designed so you can work at your
> own pace to develop intuition, see auras, travel in the astral
> plane, see clairvoyantly, and make your life happier and more
> comfortable.

She paused over that curious phrase "travel in the astral plane."
It excited her imagination. She wondered if those words might not
hold the key to her extraordinary experience on that Saturday night
in March. She flipped through the book; unfamiliar terms jockeyed
for her attention. The author was promising considerably more
than "astral travel." There was psychometry, self-hypnosis, telepathy.
Well, mused Angela, if they're all part of the package, then so much
the better. And in his foreword, the man with the wonderful name
appeared to speak to her directly, to flatter her into believing that
she was truly somebody special.

> Let's at the outset state definitely that woman is the equal of
> man in all matters—including those relating to the esoteric and
> extrasensory realms. Women, in fact, often have brighter auras
> and a greater capacity for appreciation of the various facets of
> metaphysics.

Somebody bumped up against her in the narrow confines of the
shop. The book slipped from her hands.

"Ah, sorry about that."

The young man ducked to retrieve it. He was perhaps twenty.
His long hair, unkempt beard, and sloppy clothing marked him as
a college student. He was carrying a shabby leather briefcase. He
studied the book's jacket.

"That's a good one," he said, handing it to her. "I have all his books. It's very interesting stuff."

The young man was earnest and keen. She thought she knew the type. They were given to talking too much and smoking foul-smelling, hand-rolled cigarettes. All were too opinionated for Angela's liking. Yet this individual seemed not to fit the mold.

"He's actually English," he said.

"Who?" She had not been listening.

"Lobsang Rampa. Claims he's the reincarnation of some Tibetan monk or other. And who knows, maybe he is. He sure knows his stuff, anyway." He seemed to blush slightly. "Are you interested in...eh...that kind of thing?"

"Depends what you mean by—"

"Meditation, out-of-the-body stuff." Angela must have betrayed her interest because he followed with, "Can I buy you a pint?"

"I don't drink," she said quickly. And, she was thinking, if I did I would not be drinking *pints* of beer. "And I don't even know you."

"Barry." He extended a hand. "Barry McNulty."

"Angela Brehen. I'm with a friend, though. I'll be—"

"Your boyfriend?"

"No. I haven't got a boyfriend."

The words were out before she had considered them, and she saw that the young man was interpreting them as an invitation. She was too young then to know how to respond; she had little experience with boys. Besides, Barry was not her type. She wanted to end the conversation, get out of the store somehow.

"Look, I've got to go," she said impatiently.

He looked hurt. She felt that she had to make it up to him. But he was there before her, with another proposal.

"Why don't I give you my phone number?" he said. "Next time you're up in Dublin you might give me a call."

She nodded. He produced a ballpoint and patted his pockets. He hesitated, began to open his briefcase.

"Oh, write it here," Angela said, passing him the book.

"But it's not your book," he said with a grin.

"It will be in a minute."

And it was. Barry McNulty inscribed both his phone number and address on the half-title page of *You Forever*. She left the store and left Dublin, and many years would pass before she saw him again.

For three weeks, Angela struggled with the lessons contained in the tattered paperback, following each one to the letter. None seemed to work. She had so longed to reprise her exhilarating nocturnal "flight." Dr. Rampa had as good as promised that she could release the hidden faculty whose existence she had guessed at. But she could not induce an "astral" flight through the meditation techniques he recommended. At the end of the three weeks, she had concluded that Tuesday Lobsang Rampa was a fraud. She consigned the book to a back corner of her closet and forgot about it.

Within a month of her Dublin trip, Angela's life changed utterly. Reality intruded, making her dalliances with the paranormal seem petty and frivolous. Without warning, her mother died. She had been diagnosed with diabetes, but no one had suspected the hypertension that led to a fatal stroke. Nuala Brehen lingered in the hospital bed for six days and then was gone.

Angela's father never recovered. Nuala had been his childhood sweetheart. On her death, he went into a morbid depression that refused to lift. He started drinking heavily—an unusual departure. His personality seemed to change accordingly. Within six months of Nuala's death, he was a wreck. His health declined, he lost his job, and he became a housebound semi-invalid—and a very angry one at that.

"What sort of a God is it," he would rant, "who'd take a good woman like your mother and leave the shower of wasters we have running the country? There's no bloody God at all if you ask me."

Angela's faith was likewise shaken. Although she continued to believe in God, she could not accept the seeming injustice he had meted out. By this time, she had left high school and was about to start a course in business studies at University College Galway. She canceled, put it on hold. She took a part-time job in a drugstore in town and devoted her free time to looking after her father, while keeping the home together. She found herself acting as a surrogate mother to her brothers, by then ages eight and nine.

The part-time job became full-time. Before she knew it, Angela was in her thirties, holding down a job she had no love for and caring for a father who was increasingly a burden.

Eventually he too died—by his own hand. Life no longer held meaning for him. Angela found him still and cold in his bed, early one February morning. An overdose of prescription drugs had put an end to his misery.

Angela was alone. Her brothers were living in Dublin; both were married with young families. Of the Brehen siblings, only she remained unwed. It was 2004. She was thirty-three, overweight, prematurely gray—and badly disillusioned. It was not how the bright schoolgirl of seventeen had envisioned her future.

Toward the middle of July of that year, three events took place in rapid succession. Angela could not help but conclude that all were in some way linked. The first occurred on a Sunday. Rhoda, her old schoolfriend, whom she had not seen in over a decade, telephoned out of the blue to say that she would be in Galway that afternoon. She was, she explained, "en route to Chicago," and was looking in on her mother before catching a flight at Shannon Airport the following morning.

"By this time," Angela recalls, "Rhoda was 'a woman of some importance,' as she used to joke. She was a partner in a Dublin investment firm, earning heaps of money and living the life of a high-flyer. She never married either; said she'd no time for it. So there we were, the pair of us, meeting again after all that time. Rhoda bought us lunch and afterward we went to a hotel for a few drinks."

The few drinks became a colossal binge. Angela barely remembers the taxicab that brought her home that night. But clarity was to come later on, after she had slept for an hour or two.

She awoke in great perturbation. She had had a strikingly lucid dream. It differed in almost every respect from her usual dreams, even the most vivid. This particular dream had all the hallmarks of an experience she recalled from a time long flown—from when she was a twelfth-grader preparing for her final examinations. Angela was as certain as she could be that she had undergone, in her dreaming state, an out-of-body experience.

"I dreamed that I woke up in my dream," she says, "and I was in a strange bedroom. I saw this woman in a white nightdress lying sprawled across the bed, fast asleep with half the bedclothes on the floor. Something about the room told me I'd been there before, and when I looked around me, I remembered that I'd spent so many days of my childhood doing homework with my best friend in that very room. The woman on the bed was Rhoda.

"I remember laughing, because she looked so ludicrous lying there, with her mouth hanging open, dead to the world, as they say. 'Drunken stupor' were the words that came to mind."

Then the voice came. It seemed to fill not only the bedroom but Angela's head as well, defying her to guess its origin. All the same, it was different, she thought, from the voices we sometimes hear in the course of our day: the imagined voices of our loved ones, voices remembered, voices we manufacture ourselves. We can always tell them apart from the extraneous, unwelcome voices. This voice was one of the latter. It was female, sibilant but not unpleasant, and it spoke with a strong Galway accent.

"Rhoda won't survive the week," it said. *"You won't see her ever again."*

Angela was horrified.

"If I'd been in my skin I'd have jumped straight out of it," she says with a thin smile. "But of course I wasn't. The next thing I knew

I was waking up in my own house, in my own bedroom, wondering what had happened to me. Had I dreamt it? But I knew I hadn't, because I'd been in that sort of situation before. I knew it was all real."

Her first impulse was to telephone Rhoda's house. But after consideration she dismissed the thought. Rhoda would be sound asleep—and no doubt lying in much the same position as Angela had seen her. The clock told her that it was a little before 4 a.m. Rhoda would not relish being roused at that hour, with a plane to catch later that morning. Her mother, a widow of some years' standing, was elderly and in poor health. Angela could not bring herself to disturb her. And what reason, she wondered, could she provide? "Mrs. Delany, your daughter is in mortal danger; I was in her bedroom in my ethereal body and this voice spoke to me." It was preposterous. Angela, head already beginning to throb with an incipient hangover, resolved to phone at a "respectable" hour, turned over, and eventually fell sleep.

She was awakened by her bedside telephone ringing shrilly. She cursed aloud on seeing the time. She had overslept by almost two hours. It was the drugstore wondering if she was coming to work that day. She assured them she was on her way. And suddenly, as she was hurriedly getting herself ready, the full force of that terrible message, delivered by a discarnate voice, struck her foursquare.

Rhoda was going to die.

Angela shut her eyes tight, as she did when she was a child "to make the boogeyman go away." It never worked then either. She told herself she was being silly, that she was making too much of what was—on reflection, in the sobering sanity of a Monday morning—more than likely an alcohol-induced nightmare. She hauled a brush through her hair, shrugged into her coat, grabbed her purse, and went to start the week.

Three days passed without incident. On Thursday, Angela put in a full day at the drugstore and was on hand to supervise the late closing. It was past nine o'clock when she arrived home, tired and in need of cheering up. She had a glass of wine and watched half a movie.

"I remember feeling terribly depressed. Seeing Rhoda again made me realize what a failure my own life had been. There she was, traveling the world in a high-flying job, and there I was—living alone, a lowly shop assistant with nothing to look forward to but old age."

That night, Angela did not stop at one glass of wine. She drank the entire bottle. She collapsed into bed around one o'clock. She could not know that she was about to have another out-of-body dream, more terrifying than the previous one.

The mysterious force came for her as before, lifted her from her bed, and propelled her into blackness. As was the case in Rhoda's bedroom, there was no intervening sensation of travel.

"I woke up in what I called 'the spirit,'" she says. "I found myself high above a city. It was broad daylight."

She thought at first that it must be New York. There were skyscrapers and a network of highways linking the strange city with a green and flat countryside. Then she saw what could only have been an inland sea, or indeed a lake. A voice in her head—the sibilant one with the Galway accent—was telling her that the city was Chicago.

She remembers with amazing clarity finding herself above an intersection in what looked like a business district. The light of a summer afternoon slanted between the buildings, casting long shadows. A line of cars waited for the lights to change.

Some distance away—two blocks away to be exact—there was a flurry of activity. From her vantage point, Angela had a bird's-eye view.

She saw a speeding white car approaching the intersection. The lights changed and a yellow taxicab moved forward. There was no possibility that the driver of the white car could stop in time. He tried to swerve, and the cab driver did the same. Had both not attempted the evasive maneuver, all might have been well. But the white car struck the cab on the passenger side, sending it spinning across the intersection and into the path of oncoming traffic. There was a pile-up.

Angela found herself being propelled at great speed toward the stricken taxi. She was among the first to examine the wreck. Lying in the back seat was a woman of about her own age. Her eyes were open and staring, her head twisted at an unnatural angle.

It was Rhoda, and she was dead.

Angela woke again in her bed. She was shaking with terror, her heart hammering so fast that she feared for her own life. She stumbled from the room, made her way downstairs, went into the kitchen, and poured herself a brandy. She drank it swiftly and poured another.

This time, she did not hesitate to ring Rhoda's mother. As it happened, the elderly woman slept very little and was not in the least perturbed. After all, Angela Brehen was an old friend of her daughter's.

"Listen, Mrs. Delany, would I be able to get in touch with Rhoda? Did she leave a number or anything?"

Rhoda had. It turned out to be that of a hotel in Chicago.

It was after 2:30 in the morning. Angela knew that America was several hours behind but had no idea in which time zone Chicago lay, only that it was farther west than New York. She dialed the number and was greeted at once by a pleasant-sounding woman. Yes, Ms. Delany was a guest. Could Angela hold?

Angela broke the connection a minute later. She was trying to come to terms with the impossible.

"I couldn't believe it," she says. "I still can't. But it turned out that Rhoda was killed that day at the time I saw it happen, allowing for the time difference. I saw it all like it was happening right in front of me. I couldn't have imagined it because it was only later that day that we got word back in Galway. I went round to Rhoda's mother and heard about it. And the horrible thing was, she was somehow holding *me* responsible. God knows why. After the funeral she never spoke to me again."

Rhoda's remains were flown home and laid to rest in Galway. The funeral took place some eight days after the accident. But before then, on the Saturday following Rhoda's death, Angela was to have her third odd experience. This time, however, there were no paranormal overtones—or so it seemed. It was simply a meeting between two people, in ordinary, workaday circumstances.

Angela went to her job in the drugstore as usual. She was greatly perturbed by her friend's death and the events surrounding it; she thought that the routine of work would help her cope with the tragedy.

By lunchtime she had recovered some of her equilibrium and could bring herself to chat with the regular customers. At one o'clock she grabbed a sandwich, did some desultory shopping, and was back at her post at a little after two.

To this day, she asks herself how it was she recognized the face. Sixteen years had passed since she last saw the man, in 1988. And she had been no more than a child.

"To crown it all I'd only spoken to him for about five minutes," she reminds us. "I wouldn't say I have a great memory for faces. About average, I suppose. But right away I knew it was Barry McNulty. He was much thinner than I remembered and his hair was a lot shorter, but there was something about him that I recognized. Maybe a certain look he had—a kind of intenseness."

Barry had a little boy with him, of perhaps five or six. The child looked bored and was running a sticky finger along a neat display of hair colorants. Angela saw two boxes topple. She left her station at the back of the shop.

"Angela? It is you, isn't it?"

"It is indeed, Barry—Angela Brehen. That wasn't today or yesterday."

"You didn't marry, then, I take it?"

He had lost none of his forwardness. It was a trait she found unappealing in men. She found herself staring at the child, whom Barry now had by the hand. He must have read her thoughts because he hurried to enlighten her.

"My sister's boy, not mine. He's staying with me a few days. I'm living here now, you know. Moved last month."

"That's a coincidence."

"Isn't it?"

There was something about the manner in which he said it that left her wondering.

He was glancing about the store. "So this is what you do, eh? Nice."

He thinks I own the place, Angela concluded. She had no intention of disillusioning him.

"Did you like the book?" he asked suddenly.

"Book ...?"

But she had remembered at once, as soon as he walked into the shop. She had given not a thought to it in sixteen years.

"It was okay," she said. "Well, not really. If you want to know, I didn't think much of it at all."

Something in her face must have betrayed her, brought to the surface the terror of the past days. Barry was looking at her intently.

"There's something wrong, isn't there? I've come at a bad time; is that it?"

"No, no. Well...yes. A friend died."

"I'm sorry. Were you very close?"

"We were once."

He was still studying Angela's face, seemingly trying to find answers there. "Why do I get the impression there was something very unusual about this friend's death?"

"Maybe you're psychic, Barry."

"As a matter of fact, I am." He saw her frown. "Seriously. I know things. Like that time in the bookshop; I could sense what you were looking for."

His nephew was betraying an almost intolerable impatience to leave. Angela suggested they meet that evening. She knew a quiet little hotel off Shop Street where they could talk further. Barry found her there a little after eight.

Over drinks they got better acquainted. She found him an unusually good listener—so good, in fact, that before long she was confiding in him details of the bizarre events surrounding Rhoda's death.

"I read about it in the *Tribune*," he said. "One of these freak things. We know not the day nor the hour, as the man said."

"But *somebody* knew," she countered.

"What do you mean?"

"A voice told me in a dream."

"Hmm."

"Is that all you can say—'Hmm'? I'll tell you something, Barry: it totally freaked me out, hearing that voice."

"I can well believe it. But look at it this way, when you're a remote viewer, you're—"

"Remote viewer?"

"A clairvoyant. That's what it is, you know: clairvoyance, remote viewing. When you view a scene remotely, you're entering a different dimension altogether. Time doesn't exist there—at least, not as we know it. So it doesn't matter if something is in what we call the past, present, or future; for the clairvoyant, it's happening in the here and now."

"So I can see into the future in the same way I can see the present? I thought the future didn't exist. That we have free will. That we can all make our own future. It isn't written in stone."

He looked at her keenly.

"That's only someone's theory, Angela. Nothing more. You yourself proved it wrong. You knew that Rhoda wouldn't survive the week. The voice told you so. That's as much proof as you need that you can look into the future."

"It could have been coincidence."

He laughed loudly. Heads turned. He lowered his voice.

"That's rich coming from somebody who claims to have visited her best friend clairvoyantly—twice in the one week. Angela, you know as well as I do it was the real deal. You had a premonition of your friend's death, and you traveled to Chicago to see it happen. I believe you, because I've been there myself. You have a gift, just like me: a psychic gift."

"That's not what I'd call it. I want to be rid of it, if it's all the same to you."

"No, that's the wrong attitude. You should develop it. That's where I come in."

Angela did not like the turn Barry's conversation was taking. He was altogether too sure of himself and too intrusive. She reminded herself that she hardly knew him, much less trusted him with her private affairs. And what, she asked herself, could be more private than your own thoughts, your very dreams?

"I've always been psychic," he said. "My mother was, so I think I get it from her. Over the years I've perfected the art. I help a lot of people with my gift, Angela, and you can too." He sat back in the chair. "I suppose you could call me a healer."

"Really! You mean you can heal diseases?" Angela thought it best to humor him.

"I can do anything," he announced with all the zeal of a cult leader. "I am what is known as a magician in the great Western tradition."

"You mean you're into black magic?"

"No," he quickly corrected her. "On the contrary, magic is a powerful tool that can be used for good or evil. Black magic seeks to destroy; white magic seeks to improve and heal. As I say, I use my gift for the betterment of mankind."

He raised his drink, basking in what he believed was Angela's silent admiration. She, on the other hand, could not help thinking that Barry's speech had been rehearsed, that it was a stock speech kept in readiness to impress the gullible.

"W. B. Yeats," he said, "was one as well."

"The poet? He was a magician too?"

"Yeah, the poet. He was one of the most important members of the Golden Dawn." He leaned forward, his hands clasped together. "I have to level with you, Angela. Running into you—in the chemist's—it wasn't an accident."

She felt uneasy. "Oh?"

"A little bird told me you'd be there. Well, if you must know, it wasn't a bird—it was a voice. You told me about the voice you were hearing. I have one as well. It goes with my psychic abilities. See, I knew you were experiencing this stuff even before *you* did. That's why I'm here."

She was growing nervous. "I don't follow."

"Let me get us another drink, Angela," he said. "Then I'll explain the plan to you, see what you think of it."

The "plan" turned out to be one of the most audacious ventures that Angela had ever embarked upon. Barry's initial premise was simple: they would "visit" each other clairvoyantly.

"And that was my biggest mistake," Angela sighs. "But I was lonely; I was vulnerable. I'd just suffered the trauma of Rhoda's death. My mind was in turmoil...and in a strange way I didn't want to disappoint him. From what he told me, I believed he could help me. When I look back on it now I can see it was mad, but at the time it seemed almost logical. Barry McNulty was very convincing."

They exchanged addresses and, with the aid of paper napkins, each sketched out a crude map pointing the way. "Though I doubt if you'll even need a map," he said with conviction. Barry's home was on the outskirts of the city. In passing, she learned that he was divorced, with three children who lived with their mother. He had joined the civil service on leaving college. Angela found that incongruous but said nothing.

They met again in the same hotel. They agreed on "rules."

"We promised each other that we wouldn't pry," she goes on. "That we'd respect each other's privacy. If one of us had somebody round then the other would make themselves scarce."

Barry had brought along an unusual item. It was a book on meditation techniques. It was photocopied, and she got the impression that the original was not in general circulation but a limited edition, perhaps published by the occult circle to which he claimed to belong. He urged her to study it well. It was, he said, greatly superior to her old Tuesday Lobsang Rampa book.

She was also to discover that he used drugs to help achieve what he called his "altered states." He did not come right out and admit it, but rather hinted. He suspected that Angela would shy away from the very notion of narcotics, and in that he was correct. The idea appalled her.

During that second meeting, they laid down the ground rules and fixed a date for the first experiment. Angela did not know what to expect when Barry told her he would visit at a prearranged time.

"Will I be able to see you?" she asked.

"I doubt it. The purpose of the exercise is for *me* to see *you*."

On the night in question, a Saturday in early August, she stayed up late, reading without much interest a copy of a woman's magazine. She had made herself comfortable in the living room; from time to time she would cast a nervous glance at the clock.

"I was sitting there," Angela says, "reading some silly problem page or other, trying not to get too afraid, when all of a sudden I felt this presence in the room."

She put away the magazine and turned in her chair. She saw nothing.

"I didn't have the feeling it was Barry," she remembers. "You know the feeling you get when you're in a room and there's someone behind you. It's a 'knowing' feeling, comfortable even, because you're familiar with the person who's there. This wasn't like that. It was terribly unsettling. For the short time it was in the room, I had the strongest urge to run out the door and just keep running. I remember getting up and backing towards the door, and just as I was doing that, the phone rang."

"Did I scare you?" At first she did not recognize the voice. The words were delivered in a curt, clipped manner. It unsettled her so much that she could not speak.

She thought she heard people laughing in the background. Then the question came again.

"Did I scare you, Angela?" This time, the tone was deliberately threatening.

"Barry? Barry, is that you?" Angela tried to keep her voice calm. She could barely hold the receiver steady.

"Of course it's me! Who the f*** else could do what I've just done? Now, do I have to ask you the question a third—"

"No, no!" Something told her that she must humor him, play his game. She had the unreasonable fear that the consequences of antagonizing him might be terrible. "Yes...yes, Barry, you did scare me. I—I can't describe it."

"Leave the descriptions to me," he said brusquely. "Your house is a semidetached bungalow," he continued, in a smooth, matter-of-fact voice, as though reading from notes. "There's a dining room with open-plan kitchen on the right and a living room on the left. You have a dado rail with blue flowery wallpaper and a suite of furniture to match. There are two standing lamps, one next to the TV, the other next to the two-seater."

Angela, standing in her hallway, clutching the phone, was looking through the doorway into the living room. The back of her head tingled as Barry proceeded to describe what she was seeing, as though he were standing right beside her.

"There's a coffee table with two magazines," he went on. "The *RTÉ Guide* and *Marie Claire*. The carpet is dark gray with a light blue design running through it. On the mantelpiece there are six or seven photographs. One of them is of you with an older woman in front of Tower Bridge."

"Stop!" she cried. "I believe you, Barry. Jesus, it's too weird for words."

Again she heard laughter in the background.

"I'd call that a very successful experiment, wouldn't you? Tomorrow night it's your turn. I'll be expecting you around ten."

"Barry, I—"

"Angela, you'd better stick to the plan," he said abruptly, "or you'll regret it!"

The line went dead, leaving her perplexed and not a little afraid. She wondered what it was she had gotten herself into.

The next day, she tried to reach Barry McNulty but without success. His phone was off the hook.

"I was so shocked by his manner," Angela says. "I think that shocked me more than the weird presence in my living room. I was in turmoil for the entire day, and the awful thing was, I couldn't tell anyone about it. They'd have had me certified. At the same time I tried to rationalize his odd behavior. If he was a drug user, and there was every indication that he was, then he probably wasn't even aware of having been so rude to me. In the end, I decided it was safer to go along with what we'd planned. I'd try to visit him clairvoyantly at the appointed time, then have nothing more to do with him."

At the same time, she was very afraid that her attempt at re-mote viewing would fail, and she had an irrational dread of such failure. "Something told me that if I didn't succeed he would make me suffer. I'd read his photocopied book from cover to cover and back again. I knew it like the back of my hand—but only in theory. I started asking myself what would happen if the techniques didn't work."

She had to make sure. She recalled that, prior to her out-of-body experiences involving Rhoda, she had drunk heavily. Convinced that alcohol might hold the key, she bought a bottle of brandy. She set-tled herself on the living-room sofa and proceeded to drink enough to make her woozy. She felt her muscles relax. She lay back and ap-plied the meditation techniques.

They worked. She seemed to pass out, to awaken in an altered state of consciousness. It was not a dream, but not quite reality ei-ther—not as Angela knew it. It was a trance.

Barry's map, drawn crudely on the hotel napkin, had proved unnecessary. His home was a cottage, perhaps at one time the gate lodge to an estate that no longer existed. Even in the gathering dusk she could clearly see that its roof was in disrepair; in fact, the place was little more than a barely habitable shack. Angela entered through the broken slates, rotten battens, and rafters—and was dismayed by what she saw there.

"I sort of got an inkling of why him and his wife had split up," she says. "It's possible that he was into all this stuff when they were together, but...I don't think any woman could have lived there, not without going out of her mind. It was like stepping into Marilyn Manson's den."

The interior resembled, if anything, a temple. Ranged about the main room were the trappings of magic and mysticism. Angela saw shrines to Eastern deities, statues and statuettes to the gods of antiquity, gold, black, and red candles, bowls of incense, ceremonial daggers, and—on the walls and in great profusion—drawings, prints, and paintings of characters from legend. The adjoining room was given over to books, hundreds of them. A bedroom adjoined it. Lastly there was a sitting room; it was a mess, a jumble of furniture and bric-a-brac of every description. Sprawled on a sofa set against one wall was Barry, a can of beer in his hand. He looked up on her entering. Astonishingly, he was aware of her presence. He set down his drink and raised a hand in greeting.

"You made it," he said, grinning. "Angela Brehen, you and me are going to have *fun*."

"I was not prepared for what happened next," she recalls, grimacing at the mere memory of it. "But as he spoke, his face began to contort in this horrible way. Like something you'd see in a scary movie. And he was coming for me; he looked completely different. I was so scared. All I wanted to do was get out of there. That was when I woke up with a jolt. I was back in my own house, thank God."

On her return to "reality," Angela gave herself a few minutes. They had agreed that she should telephone him at once "while it's all still fresh in your memory," but she had to compose herself first. She was still trembling as she dialed the number, not knowing what to expect—the unpleasant stranger she had seen him become, or his normal self. To her immense relief he was the latter: the customary, self-assured Barry McNulty. She tried hard not to show her fear or slur her words as she gave a description of his home. He was delighted; it all tallied. She had proved to him that his search was over.

Prudently, she made no mention of that "other" Barry. There was no opportunity to do so, because he did all the talking. He embarked upon a long-winded explanation of what they had experienced. She could follow most, if not all, of it. He called it TC, transference of consciousness. It was his own designation; he disliked such terms as astral travel and out-of-body experiences. "An OBE," he joked, "is something you get from the Queen of England." She learned that he had sought long and hard for a partner, somebody who shared his facility for TC.

The following weekend, he invited himself to her home. He said he had an important experiment he wanted her to take part in.

"I was really shocked at his brazenness," says Angela, "but knew I must agree. You're probably wondering why I didn't tell him the show was over and just end it there. But even when I tried to, I was filled with so much fear, I couldn't get the words out. It was as though he had this hold over me, some kind of power. You know, I used to think that people that fell under the spell of the likes of David Koresh and Jim Jones were just fools, but now I know different. You stay with people like that out of sheer terror. I now know that what I was experiencing were the symptoms of demonic oppression. To Barry, it was business."

Barry's "business," as he called it, was the exploration of other dimensions. Angela learned that he had accomplished much on his own, but needed a partner for what he called the "tricky stuff."

"I didn't like the sound of that," she says, "but when he explained it, it seemed okay. We would take it in turns looking after each other when one of us was out of the body. It seemed reasonable. Or rather, I kidded myself into believing it was reasonable."

Barry McNulty required Angela's cooperation in an experiment. It did not, on the surface, appear in any way sinister. In fact, it had at its heart such endearing sentimentality that she was forced to re-evaluate her poor opinion of him. She began to think that her terrible experience—her witnessing his alarming transformation—was simply her imagination playing tricks on her.

With the benefit of hindsight, however, she thinks otherwise: she believes that it was part of his attempt to exert control. Barry seemed to have an uncanny knack of knowing what she was feeling and thinking, and knew how to manipulate a situation to suit his own ends.

It was an idea he had toyed with for years, or so he claimed. Like many men who never knew their father—or who had lost him at a very early age—Barry greatly missed his, and forever sensed that an important bond had been broken. His greatest wish was to meet his father again, to relive those few short years that were little more than hazy memories, and ones that faded unrelentingly with each passing year of adulthood.

For he had loved his father dearly, and his mother reassured him throughout his boyhood that his father had loved Barry, his youngest child—loved him if anything more than his other offspring. An industrial accident had killed him, Angela learned. He had clung to life in a hospital bed for forty-two hours before death intervened. He had called out for Barry, but the boy had arrived too late—by mere minutes.

"I was nearly in tears when he was telling me all this," Angela says. "I could understand what he'd gone through because it was the same with my mother, though I was old enough to take it better. He was determined to see his father again, and I was the one who was going to help him."

It was going to be a complicated procedure. It would involve a little more than TC. By this time, Barry was so proficient in inducing TC that he saw it as child's play. Angela had seen how easily he could do it. But this was of a different order.

"Did you ever do LSD?" he asked.

"Barry, I told you what I think about drugs."

"Sorry, I forgot. Well, I did a lot of LSD. That's what got me started with this other thing. In my first year in college, a few of us were fooling around with LSD. Brilliant stuff altogether, but Jesus, if you had a bad trip then you knew all about it! But the point I'm making is that you were always warned not to go tripping on your own. You could do stupid things, get into a lot of trouble. Some guys in the States jumped off tall buildings, thinking they could fly."

"God."

"So that's why you needed what we called a 'buddy.' He'd be someone who stayed straight, didn't drop any acid. So if you started freaking he'd be able to take care of you."

Angela listened as Barry's speech seemed to revert almost effortlessly, and probably unconsciously, to the jargon and narco-speak of decades past. As he spoke, she felt relieved that the drug scene had never fascinated her.

He spoke of spontaneous clairvoyant experiences induced by LSD. They were no hallucinations, he was at pains to point out, but genuine TC. The hallucinogen appears to have triggered in his psyche the same mechanism that caused the release of Angela's etheric double when she was seventeen. Barry had no explanation for this. He did, however, discover that once the drug had facilitated TC, he could dispense with it—or so he said.

"I want to see if time travel is possible," he told her with an absolutely straight face.

"Come on, Barry, be serious. Time travel!"

But he hastened to assure her that he was using the term in an innovative sense. He was not foolish enough to believe the nonsense one came across in books on the subject of astral travel, he said—the wild claims people made of their ability to travel back in time to, say, ancient Rome, or the building of the pyramids, or even the Crucifixion. That was impossible, he said; Einstein had said so, and that was good enough for Barry. His method involved what he called "awakening in consciousness in your own past," he explained.

"I was seven when my dad died," he reminded her. "So I was conscious in the sense that I could reason, work things out for myself. There's this memory I have of being with him; it's so clear I can remember every detail. He loved sailing, had his own boat, kept it moored down at Bullock Harbour in Dalkey. It was only a tiny thing, a cheap fiberglass job, but to me it was a huge yacht. I kept begging him to take me sailing with him but he never would. He'd take one or two of the others, and sometimes my mother even, but he never took me because I was hopeless at swimming. 'But I'll wear a life jacket,' I used to say, but he still thought it was too dangerous.

"Until one Saturday morning, very early, he boots me out of bed and tells me we're going sailing. I'm telling you, Angela, that was just about the happiest day of my life. I'd just turned seven, I was on my school holidays, it was a fabulous summer—and I was sailing in Dublin Bay with my dad!"

Angela recalls Barry's expression of rapture as he spoke of that wonderful day of long ago.

"I can still remember the wind on my face, the sea spray coming up over the boat, and my father teaching me how to maintain a starboard tack. Then he let me take the tiller. It couldn't have been for more than five minutes, but by God it felt like an hour. 'Hold that heading on the Bailey, hold that heading on the Bailey,' he kept saying, meaning I had to keep the bow pointing at the Bailey lighthouse off Howth. And that's the image that's stayed with me all these years: me in my life jacket gripping that tiller, my arms on fire, my dad grinning at me and giving me the thumbs-up. He must have been as proud as I was. I want to use that as my focal point."

Barry's audacious plan was to TC into the mind of his seven-year-old self. In effect, time travel.

"I knew the idea was totally off the wall," Angela says. "But I couldn't tell him what I really thought. I was afraid of what he might do. It was safer to humor him. I kept thinking he'd overdosed on something. I was checking his eyes to see if they were normal—you know, that the pupils weren't dilated or anything. But he was serious."

"He told me that he nearly made it once or twice," she says. "He told me he was very close. He would use the mantra—he called it that—of his father saying over and over, 'Hold that heading on the Bailey.' He said he was nearly there but at the last minute he chickened out. He didn't know if he'd be able to come back."

"Then he told me about something that made me prick up my ears," she says. "He told me that a *voice* came to him the last time he attempted it. He was just about to give up when he heard the voice. It said, 'You can do it.'"

Unlike Angela's mysterious voice, heard in Rhoda's bedroom shortly before her death, the voice Barry heard was male.

"I had him describe the voice, and what he told me corresponded with what I experienced that time. It seemed to come from both outside and inside his head at the same time. He had an explanation—Barry always had explanations. He said it was his *oversoul* speaking to him."

Listening to Angela Brehen is sometimes akin to attending a talk given by a psychic or some such dabbler in the paranormal. No sooner has one digested one arcane belief than another presents itself.

Barry McNulty's "oversoul" appears to have much in common with Jung's concept of the collective unconscious. In some respects, it also seems to correspond to the Judeo-Christian idea of the soul: both are eternal; both survive the death of the body.

Barry had a further interpretation. He likened the oversoul to the Eastern concept of "masters"—masters in the sense of a group of individuals (or advanced souls, to employ the esoteric terminology)—who watch over humankind and guide the soul along the "proper" spiritual path.

"You heard your oversoul speak to you," Barry told Angela. "I heard mine." The gender was unimportant, he assured her. Her oversoul or master communicated with her using a female voice because it judged that she would be "more comfortable" with this.

It appeared to make sense.

In the quiet of Angela's home, the two embarked on a series of experiments that she concedes were bizarre. Barry would be the "traveler" and Angela his "minder."

The traveler would attempt to TC with the younger self; the minder would be on hand to deal with possible emergencies. Barry's fear was that, were he to TC for a prolonged period, a stranger—or perhaps some busybody of a neighbor—might think he was in a coma and call the paramedics.

Barry's talk and his desire to be reunited with his father had a profound effect on Angela.

"Up until that point I hadn't thought very much about my mother," she says, "but then one morning I woke up in floods of tears, and I knew that what I was experiencing was the grief of my eighteen-year-old self...of the young girl I'd been when my mother died. God, it was terrible! I was going through the whole grieving process, but this time it was worse, ten times worse. Barry came to the rescue, of course. What he said made so much sense. It was something like: 'There's only one way to heal your pain, Angela. Your mother's calling you. You must visit her on the astral plane and prove to her that you're all right.'"

Angela confesses that at that point a "reunion" seemed the answer. She felt that a meeting with her mother—however unorthodox—would lift her out of the desolation she was feeling.

"I knew I had to see her again," she says. "I'd convinced myself that talking to her, if only for a minute or two, would put things right. I wanted to tell her I was happy, even if things hadn't worked out the way she hoped they would. I suppose I wanted her to be proud of me."

So Barry and Angela each fixed their "golden moment," the target they would aim for. He went first. Angela had prepared the room, her old bedroom, where she had had her first experience of astral projection at the age of seventeen. She felt that there might be something "special" about the room. She cleared it of everything except the bed, a chair, and the night table. They drew the curtains, and Barry made himself comfortable on the bed. It gave her a strange sensation.

"I couldn't help thinking what my mother would make of me having a man in my old bed—well, *on* the bed at any rate. But, as I said, there was nothing between Barry and me. He was strangely asexual; there was always something very cold about him."

Barry assured her he would give a sign of some description if his "transfer" was successful. He could not be more specific.

"You'll know," was all he said.

"What if it goes wrong? What then?"

They had discussed this at length, yet she needed to be sure she understood him. After all, his sanity—if not his life—might depend on her correctly interpreting his signals.

"If I'm not back—if I'm not awake—within two hours, then I want you to wake me gently, okay? No rough stuff. Don't shake me; don't press. Just call my name softly. Keep calling until I wake up."

"And if you don't?"

"I'll leave that to your own discretion."

Barry need not have worried, however, because he did not succeed. He tried that night and the next. He even tried the day after, in broad daylight. "Maybe I need to be able to visualize the sun on Dublin Bay," he said. But, day or night, nothing worked. He was sorely disappointed. Or so it seemed.

It was Angela's turn.

She began in good faith and high spirits. The thought of meeting her mother had eased her grief-stricken depression considerably. Now she was determined to succeed.

She lay down on the bed, shut her eyes, and made herself comfortable, secure in the knowledge that Barry was on hand should anything go wrong.

"By that stage I trusted him," she says. "All my earlier fears gave way to...awe, I suppose. Yes, awe is the best way to describe it. He became my guru. I believed that if he could help me see and speak to my mother again it would change everything."

Angela had never before even entertained the possibility of communicating with her dead mother. She had always considered spiritualism and seances to be somehow unhealthy, if not downright wrong. She had no wish to disturb the dead. But what Barry was exploring was not the same thing at all, she reasoned; it was a matter not of contacting the dead but of returning to a time when Nuala Brehen was fully alive and vital. Surely there was nothing wrong with that.

For an hour—Barry was keeping track of time—nothing happened. Angela, as relaxed as she could will herself to be, tried to recreate that tableau from her past. The kitchen. The kitchen in 1988; not so very different from the kitchen in 2004, yet sufficiently altered to interfere with her visualization. She had had it renovated in 1998, had replaced the table and chairs, had had new fronts put on the drawers and cupboards. The walls were canary yellow now, magnolia then.

She tried to picture her mother seated with her back to the window, as she had been sitting that day. She would be nursing a cup of tea—a cup, never a mug—with a small plate of chocolate cookies at hand. She would be wearing the minimum of make-up. She needed her hair done; Angela had made the appointment for her the previous day. She had taken off her apron and was wearing her dowdy old beige housedress. She was stirring her tea; when thinking hard about something, she would spend a ridiculously long time stirring her tea.

"Don't make the same mistake I did, love," she was saying. "Don't make the same mistake I did."

It was Angela's "mantra," her equivalent of Barry's father's nautical instruction. Over and over, she had imagined her mother saying it, had concentrated on the lips moving, on the work-worn fingers gripping the spoon as she stirred her tea, on the pale yellow blind on the window, on the metronomic tick-tock of the old kitchen clock. She had become very proficient at it.

"Don't make the same mistake I did, love."

Somebody coughed softly. Angela thought for an instant that the sound came from her own throat but knew then it was Barry. So caught up had she been in her visualization exercise that she had blanked him out entirely.

She sat up, annoyed.

"Why did you do that?" she demanded.

"Look," Barry produced a pillbox from his pocket. He held out a tiny white tablet. "Take this," he said. "Acid."

"Barry, I told you before: I don't do drugs!"

"But you drink, don't you!" he shouted, his face contorting with rage. "It's the same bloody thing. And it's only half a tab."

"I was so shocked," she recalls. "The calm Barry had turned into that awful creature again, the one I hoped I'd never have to see again. He just wasn't himself. I know people say that about guys who do awful things, but in Barry's case it was literally true. I was scared of him. I knew that if I didn't take the LSD, something terrible was going to happen. I'd no option."

She took the pill and lay back down on the bed, trying not to show how frightened she was. She applied the meditation techniques, but it was hard to relax. Barry had unnerved her.

Then, perhaps a half hour later, the LSD began to take effect. It was like nothing she had ever experienced. It was as though she were stepping outside reality, entering a place that obeyed other laws....

And all at once she was *there*. It was no dream, no figment of her imagination, no restored memory. Angela had awoken in the kitchen of 1988. There sat her mother, Nuala Brehen, looking remarkably youthful—incongruously youthful, until Angela remembered with surprise that, in 1988, Nuala was about the same age as she herself was in 2004. She could very well have been looking across at herself.

"Don't make the same mistake I did, love."

"What mistake is that, Mommy?"

Angela could not believe that she had spoken the words. Yet her own larynx had formed them; she had heard and felt them emerging from her lips. Except that the lips did not belong to her, not really. They were those of a seventeen-year-old schoolgirl. She looked at her hands. They were slim and svelte, the skin smooth and as yet unblemished by "liver spots" and damage the summer sun would wreak. She raised a hand to her hair and felt it long and lank; the trips to expensive hairdressers would come later.

She was really there. She had done it. She had achieved the inconceivable: she had transferred her consciousness to the person she once had been.

"*Well done,*" a voice said. "*Oh, very well done, Angela. And there is so much more to be done. So much you can accomplish here.*"

It was the woman's voice again, the one with the Galway City accent. It was coming from everywhere and nowhere, speaking with that same sibilance and breathy quality. Her master, her guide, her oversoul.

But her mother was speaking again, cutting across the words of her spirit guide.

"I don't want you to go wasting your life, love," Nuala Brehen was saying. "Me, I didn't really have a say in the matter. But times were different then. My mother was a slave all her life, you know. She slaved for her husband and she slaved for us. She took me aside one time, the same way I'm doing now with you, and—"

"Angela!"

"—gave me the same advice I'm—"

"Angela! Angela, come back now."

272 THE DARK SACRAMENT

Her mother's face was blurring, her words growing indistinct and garbled. Angela heard them as though they were being transmitted through a tank of water. The contours and colors of the kitchen were giving way to blackness. A voice was speaking softly at her ear.

She opened her eyes to find Barry McNulty's face swimming above her own, pale in the semidarkness of the room. She was back. She felt betrayed.

"For heaven's sake! Couldn't you wait?"

As soon as the words were out, she was regretting her folly. Now she would have to face his dark side. She felt strange, too; the drug was still exerting its power. She was not herself.

But Barry showed no anger, only concern.

"Wait?" he said. "I waited nearly three hours! We agreed on a limit of two, Angela. But you looked so normal lying there. I didn't want to spoil anything."

"It *can't* have been three hours. It felt like ten minutes."

"Trust me—it was three hours."

"I want to go back."

"Angela, it's one o'clock. Maybe we should call it a night."

"To hell with that. I was doing so well, and you ruined it."

"Well, thanks very much. I was just sticking to our agreement."

"I want to try again. I may not get this chance again. I *saw* her, Barry. I spoke to her. She was as real as you are now."

"Your mother?"

"You were right all along. It *is* possible. Oh, Barry, this thing is huge! This has to be about the most important breakthrough of its kind. I have to go back there."

Angela did go back, though not that night. Try as she might, she could not recapture the circumstances of that first excursion into her past. A week went by, then another, before Barry returned to her home.

"I thought he was making me suffer because I'd been successful and he hadn't. But it was all part of the game. *I* knew and *he* knew that the LSD had enabled my transition. In the end I had to ask him to let me have more and stay by me while I made a second attempt."

When he did come again, it was with the stated objective of returning Angela to the point at which she had left off. He said that he was going to learn from her. She was the pioneer, the one who had opened the door to untold possibility.

As before, Angela took the drug and entered that state of "other" consciousness. Barry sat by the bed in the darkened room, on hand, as it were, to help in case of unexpected difficulties.

"Don't make the same mistake I did, love."

She was there in less time than it had taken before—so rapidly, in fact, that the "transfer" left her slightly dazed and disoriented.

The selfsame tableau presented itself, as though she had never left it. There was her mother endlessly stirring her tea, like some fragment of film endlessly looping. And in a sense it was a good analogy; Angela was indeed returning to a moment that would always be there, to be played back endlessly by she who had discovered the secret mechanism. Now she wished to go beyond that moment.

"I didn't, Mommy," she said, through the mouth of her younger self.

Nuala Brehen stopped her stirring and frowned. "You didn't what, Angela?"

"I didn't make the same mistake. I never married, you see. I never had children. I went out and got a job."

"What are you talking about, love? Sure you're not making any sense at all."

Angela was going to make the most of the situation; she was going to exploit her newfound power to the full. She left the table, reveling in the feel of a body that was at once alien and somehow familiar. She was moving with youthful grace and lack of effort, could feel the potency of the energy in her limbs. She had forgotten how it felt to be that age—and yet the tragedy of being that age, she knew, was that only in later life, when it is much too late, does one appreciate it.

She turned back to the woman seated at the table.

"What's got into you, Angela? You're acting very strange."

Should she tell her? Would her mother believe her? No, of course not. It was insane. She sat down again and looked long at Nuala Brehen. She felt such a surge of love for this middle-aged woman who had once been her darling mother. She could sense her thoughts and emotions, because in her "other," older existence she shared a great many of them.

For the first time ever, she sensed how it must have been to be her mother. Pregnant at seventeen and a half, married at eighteen, Nuala had never known the freedom of carefree, unattached young womanhood.

"Mommy, I want you to know that I love you. You're a wonderful woman."

Nuala stood up, hands automatically brushing her skirt for stray crumbs. Angela could sense that she had embarrassed her.

"I'll put the kettle on," she said. "Would you like another?"

"I'll do it. You sit down there now. You never relax, Mommy. You're always on the go."

Angela went to the stove, reached for the still-warm kettle, and brought it to the sink. She was smiling to herself as she allowed the tap water to gush into it. It felt so extraordinary to be there, at that time, in that place. She glanced left and right, seeing the sun come slanting in at the window, illuminating the old, worn cupboards....

But—wait a minute. The cupboards were not old and worn; they were her own modern ones. She looked to the left of the window where the sepia-tinted picture of her grandfather used to hang. It was no longer there.

Angela stopped what she was doing, perplexed, the ghost of a suspicion forming. She turned off the tap and set the kettle down. She looked again at the wall.

It should have been magnolia, not canary yellow. In 1988 the kitchen walls were magnolia, gone dull in places, grease spattered in others, smoke darkened above the stove.

But she was seeing yellow walls. A decade would pass before she had them painted yellow.

She turned and studied the back of the woman seated at the table. Nuala Brehen was reaching for a cookie—a chocolate cookie.

Two years before her death, Nuala Brehen was diagnosed with diabetes. She was immediately prohibited from eating chocolate.

"I felt a tingling all over my face right then," Angela says. "I knew there was something desperately wrong."

A moment later, she heard the mysterious voice again, which she had identified as belonging to her "oversoul." It was speaking soothingly, coming from all corners of the kitchen, even from the ceiling.

"Look again, Angela; look again," it was saying.

She looked, and the walls were no longer yellow but magnolia—good old safe magnolia. The cupboards were once again old and worn, and her grandfather's picture was hanging in its rightful place. But she was having no more of this. She sensed a terrible danger.

"I was panicking," she says. "I was afraid of what might happen to me. Maybe I felt I might die or something horrible. I started to shout. I was shouting things like "Jesus, help me! Let me out of here!" I saw my mother turn to look at me and then I was shown the most horrifying vision."

Angela falters, on the verge of tears as she tries to describe the indescribable.

"I was shown what the progression of death had done to my poor mother's body. It was done in a kind of time-lapsed sort of way, and no matter what I did, I could still see it. I could even *smell* it. I squeezed my eyes shut, but I could still see everything. Then I heard that voice again and it said...I'll never forget the words. It said, 'See, Angela: no soul, no God, no afterlife. Only death, only death!'

"I remember screaming 'no!' over and over."

Through her own frantic shouts she heard a third voice, a male voice, close at hand. It was derisive, mocking. She heard laughter and words she could not comprehend.

The bright kitchen was darkening, as though it were sinking slowly to the bottom of a murky pond. With it went her mother's eyeless corpse, still standing there, its head cocked at an angle, the ravaged lips mouthing silent words.

She felt her body grow heavy, as though it were filling up with water or some other liquid. She opened her eyes to see Barry McNulty. He was sprawled in the chair, head thrown back, laughing insanely.

Angela stumbled from the room, down the stairs, and out into the safety of the street. To this day she has no memory of what happened after that. Later, she was told that a neighbor found her wandering barefoot, shouting and screaming that the Devil was in her home.

She was taken by ambulance to the local hospital.

Angela spent three days in their care. They pumped her stomach. They told her that she had overdosed on drugs, that she was lucky she had not harmed herself, that she might have died. She was discharged with a caution and a lecture.

"I didn't dare tell them the real story. They would have had me locked up. But Barry McNulty was the one who needed locking up, not me. The first thing I did when I got home was to sit down and write him a letter, telling him in no uncertain terms that if he ever came anywhere near me again, I'd have him arrested for stalking." Angela sighs heavily. "God, I was so naive to think it was that simple. I overlooked the fact that his powers went way beyond the physical."

Her problems began soon after she mailed the letter.

"It started with little things," she says, "very subtle at first, so that I thought it was just my own forgetfulness. I'd keep losing or misplacing things, like my keys or handbag. One day I found my make-up bag in the cutlery drawer...and I really got worried. Was I going mad? Another day I came home from work to find the front door unlocked. I always double-locked it. Always.

"My first thought was Barry McNulty. Everything kept building and building. After that the nightmares started. In my dreams I kept being returned to that awful scene in the kitchen. One night I thought I saw that terrible image of my mother standing beside my bed. Then the phone would ring at all hours. Sleep became impossible. God, it was a living hell. I just wanted to die—to put an end to it all. My work suffered; everything suffered. There was no way I was going back to the doctor. I knew that medication and a spell in hospital were no cure for what I was suffering. Oh, how I regretted ever having dealings with Barry McNulty! He was grinding me down, so that I'd come to him for help."

Matters came to a head before too long. When they did, Angela was to discover just how powerful Barry was and how potent were the forces he had at his bidding. She was getting ready for bed one night. All seemed normal—until she sensed that there was something in the room with her.

"I was pulling my nightdress over my head, when all of a sudden this...*thing* was behind me." She struggles to describe it. "God, I really can't put into words how awful it felt. It didn't feel human; it felt like it was going to swallow me up. I knew, *I just knew* that if I turned around to look, something terrible would happen."

There were three other bedrooms in the house. She would sleep elsewhere. But, no matter where she went, the menace followed her.

"I knew it was Barry who was doing it. He was taking his revenge for the letter and showing how he could control me. So I started pleading with him to take it away, whatever it was he'd sent to my house. I was convinced he could hear me. I told him I hadn't meant to send the letter. I was crying and screaming for him to help me. I would have done anything at that point to be rid of that thing."

It seemed that her pleas were answered. Within minutes, as Angela lay slumped on the bed, sobbing, she sensed the presence departing.

The telephone rang. She suspected who the caller was and knew she had to answer it.

"Barry? Is that you?"

For a moment or two there was silence. Then the laughter started. It erupted from the receiver, hysterical laughter that grew louder and louder, until it filled her head and—it seemed to Angela—the house itself.

She slammed down the phone. She went upstairs, took two sleeping pills, lay down, and soon fell into a groggy half-sleep.

But her ordeal was far from over. Sometime later, she was awakened by noises outside the bedroom door. She sat up in alarm. Somebody was pacing up and down the landing.

"Pacing is maybe the wrong word," Angela explains. "It was more like someone dragging their feet...a stocky man with a gammy leg. There was wooden flooring on the landing, so I could hear these heavy boots echoing through the house."

She was distraught. She dared not put the light on, lest the sliver of light coming from under the door betray her whereabouts. In the circumstances, she did the only thing she could do. She groped her way to the door and quietly locked it.

The dragging feet could be heard at the far end of the corridor. Angela got back into bed and sat in the darkness, holding her breath. She heard the heavy boots turn and begin the slow trudge up the corridor again. She prayed that the footfalls would somehow stop at the staircase and continue down the stairs.

They did not.

"Oh, Jesus, help me!" she whispered over and over to herself.

The dragging footsteps approached her bedroom door. They stopped.

Angela clamped a hand over her mouth. Inwardly, she was screaming, but she must somehow contain her fear. Whatever it was that stood on the other side of the door seemed to know how to induce the utmost terror in her.

She waited—and waited—trembling.

All at once, there came a frenetic scratching and scraping at the door. She describes it as being "like the paws or claws of an animal trying desperately to get in." It was the last thing Angela heard.

"I passed out," she says. "Now I know what's meant by the phrase 'I nearly died of fright.' That night I came as close as anyone could to doing just that."

"You do know," Father Ignatius McCarthy said, "that it's a bad idea to try to communicate with the dead? That's why I advise people not to attend seances or that sort of thing. Jesus warned against it. You're taking a risk."

He had received her in a book-lined study in the monastery. The room, with its faded antiques and heavily polished furniture, seemed an appropriate setting for the elderly exorcist, who had made himself comfortable in a leather wing chair.

Angela confesses that she has the greatest difficulty with people's ages, but to her, Father Ignatius was as old a priest as she had ever come across still fulfilling his ministry. She had traveled a long distance to see him. At first she considered going to see somebody in Galway; but she was known there because of her job in the drugstore. She thought it wiser to seek help farther afield. She needed anonymity. A relative suggested that Father Ignatius could help. In some circles he was known to have experience of "troublesome" cases.

Angela was at pains to communicate to the priest her need of his services without delay.

"My home was under siege," she tells us. "I was a refugee in my own town. Since that terrible night, with the 'visitor' from God knows where, I'd been forced to live in a guesthouse. I dared not go home again. I went back during the day to grab some things, but I couldn't stay more than a minute. The place gave me the creeps—even in daylight."

At first, she could not come straight out and confide in this kindly stranger details of the insane enterprise—and yes, she thought of it then in those terms—that had brought her to such a pass. She cursed herself long and hard for being a fool. Her gullibility had exposed her to unknowable danger. She had come to know the nature of such danger. But, for the time being, she was content in wrapping it in terminology that only hinted at the truth. Angela was at pains to point out that she had not been a willing participant in Barry's scheme. She was the victim. She was a little vexed that he seemed not to understand that.

"I hear what you're saying, Father," she told him. "But I never went to any seances or that sort of thing. And I never *asked* for those strange out-of-the-body experiences that started this. They just happened."

"Did they, now?" The priest looked at her intently. "Fair enough. But I'm not so interested in what happened to you at seventeen. At that age we all have fantasies about flying and being astronauts and heaven knows what else. No, I'm more interested in the present. Tell me something: that first time you found yourself 'in the spirit,' as they say, in your friend's bedroom and then looking down on her body at the crash scene, what kind of state were you in—prior to all that?"

"What d'you mean, Father?" She laughed nervously but saw that he was not amused. "I was in bed asleep, of course."

"That's not quite what I mean. Would there have been drugs or drink involved?"

"Well...yes." She hesitated. "I'd been drinking both times."

"To the point where you blacked out?"

Angela could only nod a response, too ashamed to say anything more.

"I thought as much. Now, please don't take this the wrong way, Angela, but I'm wondering if you appreciate how foolish that is—that drinking to the point where you black out. Most people don't, you see. Most don't give it a second thought. But *I* do. And here's the thing: when you're out of your mind with drink, or indeed drugs—they're all the same in my book, Angela—you actually leave yourself open. And anything can come in."

Angela had never heard the like of it. It was ludicrous and she told him so. If that were the case, she argued, then a sizable swath of the population of Ireland was possessed. That was what Father Ignatius was implying.

"If you drink to excess," he countered, "to the point where you forget who you are, you leave yourself vulnerable. That's all I'm saying. More evil acts are carried out under the influence of drugs and drink than most of us like to think about."

She could not fault him on that. She hesitated. The full import of his words had registered.

"My God, Father, are you saying I'm *possessed?*" It was an appalling prospect.

"No, not possessed, but you certainly left yourself open to the possibility. You see, Angela, Satan is very clever. Not only can he use our weaknesses to fool us; he can also use our ignorance and vanity to lull us into believing falsehoods. That's the trap. Your weakness was believing you needed to contact your mother, and your ignorance in the area of occult practices led you to think it was actually possible."

"But I really *did* see my mother, just as I remember her."

"Exactly! Just as you remember her. We all carry around memories of people close to us who've passed on. I get people coming to me from time to time with that sort of story. They'll have been to this or that clairvoyant or medium, and they all come out with the same sort of nonsense. 'Oh, such-and-such told me something that only my dead husband or wife or whatever would have known.' And I tell them what I'm going to tell you now. Satan knows all about us as well. And there's nothing to stop him looking inside our heads and using the memories we have of our loved ones to fool us."

"He can do that?"

"He can do many things. He could even appear to some of our greatest saints in the guise of Our Lord or the Blessed Virgin. Why do you think the Vatican is so cautious when they hear of yet another sighting of the Virgin Mary across the world? They have to be cautious; they know the score. Out of the many hundreds, only a handful have been officially recognized."

She had to ask. It was the question that had gnawed at her for days. It would not let go of her.

"The thing that's in my house, Father...is it...is it the Devil?"

Father Ignatius gathered his thoughts before replying.

"That friend of yours—Barry. He sounds to me like he's involved in the occult in a big way. Very dangerous territory, black magic and all of that...."

Angela was opening her mouth, intent on explaining her naiveté, but Father Ignatius held up a hand.

"Oh, no doubt he told you it was white magic?"

The priest's perceptiveness astonished her. "Yes, he did. He said he was a healer, and he used white magic to help people."

"Ah yes, he would say that, wouldn't he? 'White' sounds very proper—more acceptable, you might say. That's the trap, you see. That's how the gullible get sucked into these things." Father Ignatius looked at her steadily. "There's no such thing as white magic, Angela. There is only black, and all forms of magic are practiced with recourse to Satan." He leaned forward. "Now, I don't want to alarm you, my dear, but I'd say that Barry has called up something of that nature to attack you."

"When you say 'something'..."

"An evil spirit, a demon. It sounds like it to me. Those noises you heard in the night, that inhuman presence you felt. This is done to frighten you, to cause great fear. But let me assure you that there's no more to fear; the good Lord will deal with it. We can get rid of it."

"Do you mean, Father, that you'll do a ..." She was hesitant to voice the word.

"An exorcism. That's what you're trying to say. Well, no, Angela, I don't expect we'll be doing a full exorcism. Not in the sense I think you mean it. Nothing as dramatic as that. But we shall see."

The priest patted her shoulder.

"By the sound of it, it's your friend Barry who really needs the exorcism," he said. "Not that he'd ever submit himself to one—more's the pity."

Angela had not been a practicing Catholic since her teens. For her, prayer was a distant memory; prayers recited to ward off evil belonged to a distant past. She did not know what to expect that Friday. It was October 8, 2004.

Father Ignatius was due to arrive at seven o'clock. Angela, still too afraid to venture into her home, was sitting outside in her car when the blue Vauxhall pulled up. She was surprised and slightly uneasy to see that he was accompanied by two others. He had given her to understand that he would come alone.

The driver was a burly priest who introduced himself as Liam Mulryan. He would assist Father Ignatius, Angela learned, as would the third member of the party, Sister Immaculata, a soft-spoken, elderly Carmelite.

They entered the house.

The two priests excused themselves at once, explaining that they would "have a look around the place." In truth, they were ascertaining where "presences" might be strongest.

Yet all seemed tranquil on that particular evening. Angela had half-expected to sense something, but the house gave off nothing more sinister than the disused feeling houses do when left vacant, even for a short period. All the same, she was nervous. Sister Immaculata kept her company in the kitchen as she prepared tea. She was grateful for the nun's cheeriness. She seemed intent on keeping the atmosphere light.

"People come to Father Ignatius all the time," she said, "with stories about disturbances in their homes. A lot of the time it's a case of an old house settling on its foundations, or air in the water pipes, that sort of thing. On the odd occasion it's something else entirely, and we come along to help out." She smiled.

Angela did not like the sound of that.

Presently, tea having been drunk, the two priests began their preparations. A Mass would be said in the living room. The table would serve as the altar.

Father Ignatius lit the candles and draped a purple stole about his shoulders. Sister Immaculata and Father Mulryan produced printed prayer sheets and knelt down to one side. Angela joined them. The service was about to begin.

It was nearing eight on a mild fall evening. All was quiet both inside and outside the house at the end of the cul-de-sac. The curtains were drawn against the darkness. The main light in the living room was on.

The celebration of the Mass passed off without incident. Angela was relieved, thinking all was over.

"Far from it," she says. "Little did I know it was about to begin. Father Ignatius said that he wouldn't be doing an exorcism, but that was before he saw the house. I don't know what him and the other priest saw, but it must have been enough to convince them there was something seriously wrong."

After the closing prayers, Father Ignatius announced that what he enigmatically referred to as "the blessing of the house" would commence. All made the sign of the cross. The celebrant opened his book and proceeded to read aloud.

"In the Name of Jesus Christ, God and Lord; through the intercession of the Immaculate Virgin, Mother of God, Mary, and Holy Michael the Archangel, the blessed apostles Peter and Paul, and all the saints, and relying on the holy authority of our office, we are about to undertake the expulsion of any evil spirits that are present here."

There followed a respectful silence as Father Ignatius placed his book upon the table and joined his hands.

"May God rise up and may his enemies be dissipated," he entreated.

"And let those who hate him flee before him," the nun and the younger priest said in unison. Sister Immaculata held her prayer sheet close to Angela and indicated the responses. They would be given by three voices.

"Let them be dissipated like smoke," Father Ignatius continued.

"As wax flows before fire, so let sinners perish before God," the trio answered from the text.

"Look on the cross of the Lord. Be defeated, all enemies!" The exorcist's voice was gaining in volume.

"The ancient strength will conquer, the King of Kings!" The words of the nun and young priest rang out with the certitude of the faithful. Angela strove to keep up.

The strange-sounding, medieval words were affecting her. As she spoke them, it seemed to her that they were charged with power and that she was to some degree partaking of that power. The solemnity of the occasion and the earnestness with which the three religious prayed caused her to dwell on the gravity of her situation. She was uneasy.

"Let your mercy be with us, O Lord!"

"According to our hopes in you," said Father Ignatius, concluding the prayer. All bowed their heads in silence.

From upstairs came the unmistakable sound of a door opening. Angela gasped and looked at the others, but they did not stir.

Father Ignatius took up his prayer book again.

"We exorcise you, each unclean spirit, each power of Satan—"

The words were cut short as the same door was, quite audibly, banged shut.

"… each infestation of the enemy from hell, each legion, each congregation, each satanic sect—"

Heavy footsteps, sounds produced by a number of booted feet, were crossing the landing. Several moved quickly and as one, as if marching to some ethereal command; others dragged behind as if they belonged to the wounded. They paused abruptly at the head of the stairs, marching on the spot. Angela bit her lip in fright. Sister Immaculata laid a comforting hand on her arm.

Father Ignatius glanced at the ceiling and waited for the commotion to cease.

Presently, it did. He looked back at his text and continued, unperturbed.

"In the name and by the power of our Lord Jesus Christ! Be uprooted and put to flight from the Church of God, and—"

The phantom footsteps began descending the stairs, tramping out a slow, ordered rhythm. It seemed that they paused and marked time on each and every tread. Their determined marching was like that of a platoon of battle-weary soldiers advancing in a final push. With each tread gained, the marching grew louder.

Tramp, tramp, tramp.

"Be uprooted and put to flight from the Church of God—"

Tramp, tramp, tramp.

The footsteps were drawing ever nearer. Angela let out a little cry. Of the company, she seemed to be the only one who was showing fear.

"... and from the souls that were made in the image of God and redeemed with the blood of the divine lamb."

Tramp, tramp, tramp.

The phantom army had reached the bottom of the stairs. The measured tramping of so many pairs of boots now filled Angela's hallway. All that separated the group from the horror was the living-room door. Father Ignatius took up the crucifix and pressed it to his lips. Father Mulryan remained kneeling with his head bowed in prayer. The nun passed her prayer sheet to Angela. She spread her arms wide and gazed heavenward. She was about to speak. Abruptly, the din in the hallway ceased.

The nun seized her chance. She spoke out into the tense silence, in a voice that was loud and confident. "Father, in your goodness, come to us now," she implored. "Now in our hour of need. O good Jesus, hear us. Save us, O Lord. Save us, your servants, from every threat or harm from the Evil One. We beg you, we beg you!"

Angela's hands began to tremble. The prayer sheet fell from her grasp. Father Mulryan calmly retrieved it and handed it back with a reassuring smile.

Sister Immaculata continued. "We beg you, Father, through the intercession of the archangels St. Michael, St. Raphael, and St. Gabriel to protect us now. To protect us now in our hour of need. Come, O Lord; come, O Holy Spirit; come, O Holy Virgin Mother; hear our call. Deliver us from the evil that is present here."

Father Ignatius lowered the crucifix. Sister Immaculata placed an arm about Angela's shoulders. The young priest raised his head and looked toward the door as if in expectation.

All waited. As if on cue, the next manifestation presented itself.

The sinister scratching and scuffling that had driven Angela from her home started up on the other side of the door. She began to shake and sob in terror. She was unprepared for any of this; it was to have been a simple "blessing of the house."

Father Ignatius took up the crucifix and held it aloft, facing into the danger.

"Do not dare further!" he commanded in a loud, authoritative voice. "Do not dare further to defile this place, most cunning Serpent. Do not dare further to deceive the human race."

The scratching noises grew louder.

"… to persecute the Church of God, to strike and shake the chosen of God like chaff. God the Father commands you. God the Son commands you. God the Holy Spirit commands you."

The scratching began to lessen.

"Christ orders you, he who is the eternal word of God become man. He who destroyed your hateful jealousy against the salvation of our race."

There came a frantic pounding, as if a dozen heavy boots were kicking against the door, drowning out the words of Scripture. But Father Ignatius would not be deterred. His voice soared above the cacophony.

"He who humiliated himself, making himself obedient to death. He who built his Church on a firm rock and provided that the strength of hell would never, *would never* prevail over that Church.

He who will remain with his Church for all days, even up to the end of human time."

The door flew open. All heads turned. Just as suddenly, it banged shut again. This action was repeated twice more in rapid succession, sending tremors through the room. The candles guttered wildly, then died; the bottles of holy oil and water fell over.

Angela made to stand up. She was terrified. She wanted to escape, out through the back door. The nun tightened her arm about her shoulders.

"We're nearly there," she whispered. "Have faith, child. God is good."

Father Mulryan righted the bottles and relit the candles. The exorcist took up the holy water and began sprinkling it about the room.

"The sacrament of the cross commands you! The virtues of all the mysteries of the Christian faith command you. The most exalted Mother of God, Mary the Virgin, commands you. She, though lowly, trampled on your head from the first instant of her Immaculate Conception."

Angela felt her fear dissipating under the comforting arm of the nun and the words spoken so commandingly by the priest.

He laid aside the holy water and unstoppered the bottle of holy oil. Sister Immaculata helped Angela to her feet. She and Father Mulryan each placed a hand on her shoulder. Father Ignatius anointed Angela's forehead with the oil.

"I command you and bid all powers who molest this servant of God, by the power of God Almighty, in the name of Jesus Christ our Savior, through the intercession of the Holy Virgin Mother, to leave this servant of God forever and to be consigned to the unquenchable fire, to that place that the Lord God has prepared for you."

The blessing being accomplished, he went to the door. It was time for the banishing. Father Ignatius moved through the hallway and the downstairs rooms, sprinkling holy water as he went. His voice, charged as it was with authority, could be heard throughout the house.

"Go now from this place! Death is your lot, impious one. And for your angels there is an endless death. For you and for your angels the unquenchable flame is prepared. Because you are the prince of cursed homicides, the author of incest!"

They heard him ascend the stairs.

"The head of all the sacrilegious, master of the most evil actions, the teacher of heretics, the inventor of all obscenity. Go out, therefore, impious one. Go out, criminal. Go out with all your falsehoods. Leave, therefore, now. Go away, seducer! The desert is your home. The serpent is your dwelling. Be humiliated and cast down. Behold, the victorious Lord is near and quick. All things are subject to his power."

Returning to the living room, he went to Angela and, making the sign of the cross on her forehead, said, "May your servant Angela be protected in soul and body by this sign of your name." On her chest he made the sign of the cross again: once, twice, thrice.

"Preserve what is within this person," he intoned. "Rule her feelings. Strengthen her heart."

All present again bowed their heads in silent prayer. As she prayed, Angela felt her fear drain from her. In that moment, she did indeed sense that her heart was strengthened.

Father Ignatius motioned for them, his little congregation of three, to kneel again. He extended his hands over them.

"Father," he intoned, his voice gentle, no longer that of the bane of demons, "we pray you, all-powerful God, that evil spirits have no more power over this servant of yours and in this place, but that they flee and not return. Let the goodness and the peace of Our Lord Jesus Christ enter here at your bidding, Lord. For through Jesus we have been saved. And let us not fear any ill, because the Lord is with us. He who lives and reigns as God with you in the unity of the Holy Spirit, for ever and ever. Amen."

Father Ignatius then led Angela through a profession of faith. The ceremony ended with the Lord's Prayer, the Anima Christi, and a final prayer of deliverance. The work was completed.

"It was a long night," Angela recalls. "But a long and miraculous night, that's for certain."

And, after her visitors had gone, she did something she had not planned on. She went to sleep in her own bed. She sensed that she could do so without fear, without a thought for unseen and unwelcome forces.

"Before they came, I thought I'd be leaving with them to stay at the guesthouse," she says. "That wasn't the case. My fear had vanished completely. I fell asleep immediately from the exhaustion, and woke up knowing—simply knowing—that I'd never be bothered again."

Angela Brehen still lives in Galway City. Her new home is on the other side of the river Corrib and a considerable distance from the house of her birth. She moved there shortly after the exorcism, in the spring of 2005.

"It wasn't because I was afraid of being 'invaded' again," she assures us. "No, I certainly didn't move for that reason. It was because Barry McNulty still knew where I lived, so I thought it safer to move, and I gave up my job in the shop as well. I just needed to make a clean break. My job seemed to belong to that time as well, when I was foolish and naive. I've grown up a lot since then. You know, the positive part of all of this was that it brought me closer to God. He saved me—I know he did. I'm sure of it. And the irony is that evil brought me to goodness. I had to come face-to-face with the one to find the other."

She later learned that Barry McNulty's home was found abandoned. She has not seen him since.

Father Ignatius believes that he may have fled the country. Having received us in the book-lined study of the abbey, he speaks frankly about the case. And Barry.

"She'll never be bothered by him again," he declares with confidence. "She's safe now, thank God."

We wonder about Barry's psychic gifts, if he can still call on them to help him work his mischief.

"Oh, he might have the Devil on his side," the priest says, "but Angela has God on her side now, and he's no match for God."

Was it coincidence then, his running into Angela after all that time, in Galway, in the same city?

"I don't hold with coincidence. Barry had a purpose in mind when he bumped into Angela as if out of the blue. He knew what he was doing; I'm sure of that. Someone in the grip of demonic control feels compelled to act, to do the most objectionable things to others in order to somehow save themselves. There's a hierarchy of evil spirits. The minor ones, the foot soldiers, do the dirty work, to prepare the way for the generals. Their job is to enslave. Barry was attempting to enslave Angela, make her suffer so much fear that she'd have to turn to him to take the 'thing' away. If she hadn't sought out God's help, heaven knows how she might have ended up."

"I pray for Angela," he says later. "I pray for Barry as well. Now *there's* a man who's in sore need of prayer! I hope and pray that wherever he is, he'll receive the help he needs."

We ask him his opinion of Barry's TC, the transference of consciousness. He shrugs.

"I'm not saying it's not possible. Of course it is. If you read up on a number of saints, you'll come across that kind of thing. Except in Angela's case it wasn't what she thought it was. Barry probably started out innocently enough, then got deeper and deeper into it until he'd gone too far. We know so little about ourselves, how our minds work, that we can be easily fooled. And Satan and his minions are out there, just waiting for a chance to fool us. That's how it's always been, ever since Eve was tempted with the apple."

He chuckles.

"We aren't half as advanced as we think we are," he concludes. "We know so little. When you reach my age, that's the time you'll come to realize how little you really know."

DEVILRY ON THE DINGLE PENINSULA

❖

Erin Ferguson knew at once she had taken the bend too sharply, but knew too late. She had made no allowance for the fresh fall of rain. Her car was skidding toward the white van, and there was nothing she could do to prevent it. She braced for the impact.

She must have blacked out. She came to, after what seemed like hours but could surely have only been seconds, brought around by an urgent rapping on her window. The face she saw through the glass startled her. It was a man's face—a man with eyes so dark and penetrating that her immediate impulse was to reverse the car swiftly and flee the scene. She was a lone female on a remote road miles from nowhere; the stranger might be anybody, capable of anything.

He continued to stare in at Erin, saying nothing. Should he not, she thought, be asking if I'm all right? Should he not be showing some concern? She tentatively reached out a hand to lock the door, but he got there before her and yanked it open.

"Are you okay?" He had spoken at last.

"I think so."

It was a good way from the truth. Erin sat up in her seat, giving thanks that she had been wearing a seat belt. She had muscle pain, neck pain, a raging headache. But nothing seemed to be broken. She angled the mirror, and her eyes widened at the sight of the bruise above her left eye. It was going to be a nasty, ugly bump.

Erin climbed out. She did not like the way the stranger's dark eyes flicked to her skirt as she smoothed it down.

Surprisingly, the damage to the van was slight. Her car had grazed the rear mudguard and spun out of control, to collide with the mossy face of the crag that ran down to the road.

The owner of the van introduced himself as Ed O'Gribben. Erin apologized for the damage and offered to cover his repair costs without involving her insurance company—her premium was high enough as it was. He said very little, simply nodded when appropriate, and continued to stare at her in his unsettling way. They exchanged details; he would be in touch as soon as he had an estimate.

Ed O'Gribben helped her get her car back onto the road. There seemed to be very little wrong with it, and that was all to the good. Erin had no wish to remain on that isolated stretch of road a minute longer. More than the distress of the accident, the man with the too-dark eyes unnerved her. She departed with a sense of relief. As she drove away, she could not have imagined that a year later, in June 1996, she and Ed O'Gribben would be exchanging rings and vows at the altar.

They had met "by accident"; the elements had thrown them together. Perhaps that should have been a warning.

The first months of Erin's marriage were difficult. At Ed's insistence, she gave up her job as a legal secretary—in any case, commuting to and from work was becoming unsustainable. She was having to adjust to a whole new way of life. A city girl at heart, used to the bustle of Tralee, the Kerry capital, the twenty-six-year-old now found herself hopelessly isolated in the hinterlands of the Dingle Peninsula.

The house that "came with" her husband—as Erin joked in the beginning—was at least a century old. It was situated at the end of a long lane, and looked as lonely and forgotten as the landscape it stood in. Imposing though it was at a distance, when seen at close quarters, the gray stone, two-story building was downright shabby.

The moss-caked roof was dilapidated enough, but there was moss also on the paving that led to the front doorstep, and the window frames were peeling and decaying.

If the outside was disappointing, the interior was not much of an improvement. Erin was crestfallen when Ed showed her around; she just managed to hide her dismay. The rooms were large, yet frugally appointed with heavy oak furniture. The carpets were threadbare. The windows, hung with dusty drapes from another age, admitted very little light. She was reminded of the gloomy atmosphere of a funeral home.

"I tried to put a brave face on it," she tells us at our first meeting. "A lick of paint and some cheery wallpaper would soon put things right, I said to myself. It was also heartening to see that there were radiators in every room."

But the puzzling part was the cold. Why, she asked herself, was the house so cold when there was central heating? And why did every room reek of mildew?

Her husband was a successful building contractor. He had made a point of telling her as much when they started going out together; often he would proudly point out a school or development his company had built. Why, then, live in near squalor? Surely he could have carried out some improvements. Or, better still, tear the old house down and erect a new one. After all, the family land extended in all directions; the site was there already, so Ed could build with minimal outlay.

But he had very different views on the subject.

"My ancestors built this place," he declared one evening. He said it a little too gruffly for Erin's liking. They had just finished supper and he was preparing to look in on a client. (He seemed to be forever visiting some client or other.) "It doesn't do to tamper with the past."

"Ed, you're only thirty, for heaven's sake! You sound like an old man of eighty."

He did not respond, only stared at her in that unsettling way of his and left.

"And why do you need to go out so much?" she shouted after him, as the back door slammed shut. "Why am I always left alone with *her?*"

The "her" was Ed's seventy-nine-year-old mother, the woman Erin called the Matriarch—but only to herself, under her breath. Ed had referred to her in their dating days but always in an offhand way, as though his mother were no more than a minor part of his life.

The reality was otherwise, as Erin was to discover. Martha O'Gribben would command a principal role in the couple's marriage. Erin had made the old woman's acquaintance on her wedding day, when the bridal pair returned to the rambling old house on the Dingle Peninsula.

First, she discovered why Mrs. O'Gribben had been unable to attend her son's nuptials: she was very frail and confined to bed with arthritis. This was news to Erin. She had not bargained for the role of a geriatric nurse; worse, her husband seemed to take for granted that it was a natural extension of her duties as wife and housekeeper.

All might have been well had Martha been kindly and considerate, like Erin's own mother. But, frail though she was, the old lady nevertheless seemed intent on making her daughter-in-law's life as difficult as possible. She occupied a room on the ground floor, at the front of the house and, most disconcertingly, directly under the couple's bedroom.

Erin remained standing in the kitchen until the sound of Ed's jeep had died away. She sat down at the table again, buried her face in her hands, and wept. Her tears flowed freely; there was no mascara to run, for she had stopped wearing much make-up of any kind. Make-up seemed at odds with the drabness of the house—like wearing a ball gown to the office party. She desperately wanted to call her family for a heart-to-heart talk. Gemma would understand. But she was reluctant to disenchant her younger sister; Gemma had such idealistic notions of marriage. And as for her widowed mother, she could hardly go upsetting her, either. Her mother was so proud of the "wonderful match" her elder daughter had made. Ed was the perfect son-in-law: wealthy, courteous, and handsome.

"I should be happy," Erin sighed to herself. "By rights I should be happy." But, as she allowed her gaze to drift about the kitchen, lingering on the heavy cupboard with its display of decades-old crackle china, the distempered walls and ancient door, the overall dismalness of the place struck her. "How did I get here?"

She got up and began clearing the table. But no sooner had she finished than she heard an all-too-familiar sound. It was the frantic banging of a walking stick against the radiator in the front room. It made her feel even more depressed. Mrs. O'Gribben was demanding her attention.

"Yes, I'll be with you in a minute!"

She checked the clock. It was 9:15. Time for the bedtime ritual— time to metaphorically don her nurse's cap and do the necessary.

Erin recalls with dismaying clarity her first meeting with Martha O'Gribben. "I remember having the same uneasiness I felt on the day I literally ran into Ed on that winding road," she says. "To be fair to Ed, my first misgivings seemed cockeyed. He was a thorough gentleman. He was always so attentive and loving when we were going out together. He'd make a fuss of me. He was like that as well during the first months we were married."

To be sure, there were sides to him she neither liked nor understood, yet the good she saw in him outweighed the bad—or the mysterious. Perfection being impossible, Erin was willing to settle for less. As most women are wont to do, she had told herself.

But Mrs. O'Gribben was a different story. There was no discernible warmth in the woman. Her manner was as cool as the hand she offered in greeting. At first Erin felt sorry for her, interpreting the hostility in the old woman's eyes as (somehow understandable) resentment of her new daughter-in-law. That, coupled with the antipathy of the bedridden toward the able-bodied. Yet, as time wore on, she was to discover that the woman's hatred went deeper— deeper by far than anything she could have imagined.

Bang! The radiator was struck hard, its note reverberating through the house like a bell and sending Erin's nerves a-twitching. *Bang!* Again.

"I'm coming!"

The radiator had been struck twice more before the "nurse" could attend to the patient. She assisted Mrs. O'Gribben with her ablutions and gave her her medication and nightcap. These tasks had become so routine that Erin now performed them without a thought—and without a word. She had long given up on small talk and pleasantries, nor did she expect a word of gratitude for her trouble. Instead she awaited, as always, a complaint of some kind.

"This cocoa isn't hot enough!"

"Well, maybe if you drank it quicker, it wouldn't have time to go cold."

"Maybe if you left it longer on the boil, you mean."

The daughter-in-law made no reply. She knew the script too well. Acquiescing seemed the best way to keep the peace. She picked up the mug and headed for the door.

"I'll reheat it, then. Be back in a minute."

"And another thing: you're not allowed any callers to this house, d'you hear?" Mrs. O'Gribben tightened her crocheted bed jacket about her. "This is still *my* house, not yours. And as long as I'm here, you'll do as I say."

"I know," said Erin with exasperation. "You've been telling me that from the minute I got here."

It was a repetition of so many of her evenings. When she was single, working in the office in Tralee, Erin's life was relatively uneventful. Yet, compared to her new situation, it seemed almost exciting. Thinking back on those days, as she frequently did, she wondered if she had not made a blunder.

For marriage to Ed, far from the expected idyll, had become a mind-numbing routine. Her only outing was to the nearest town twice a week to do the shopping. Even then, her time was not her own, because old Mrs. O'Gribben could not be left unattended for long.

Gradually, the young Mrs. O'Gribben began to withdraw into this curiously caged world. Her friends stopped telephoning. No wonder; whenever she arranged to meet them, something would upset her plans, and Erin would have to cancel. That something usually involved her mother-in-law.

She rarely saw her husband. When he came home from work around five, somebody was sure to call, and he would be off again. Often she would fall asleep in the early hours while waiting for him and wake in the morning to find that he had already left.

The house received few visitors. No neighbors dropped by for a chat, as was the case with Erin's mother. From one end of the week to another she only saw her in-laws.

"If I'm honest with myself," she tells us, "I'd have to say I'd have preferred no visitors at all rather than that lot."

Ed's two younger brothers, Dan and Michael, were bachelors in their late twenties. They were plasterers by trade and worked in the family business. Their sister, Mary, the youngest sibling, worked in a daycare center. From the outset, all three made no secret of their dislike for Erin. Mary especially was highly critical of any changes she made in the home. Erin thought at first that her sister-in-law might be a sympathetic ally—she was, after all, the only girl in a family of boys—but Mary had other ideas. She seemed to resent the "intruder" who had the audacity to make a claim on her oldest brother's affections.

Dan and Michael were "odd"—Erin has no better word to describe them. They seemed incapable of holding a conversation and, when they tried to, could rarely maintain eye contact. For Erin, the effort to be friendly toward them was so taxing she gave up altogether. They were shy, she concluded; it was as simple as that. She got used to being ignored and was relieved to see them exit by the front door after they had visited their mother. Avoidance rather than embarrassment, she reasoned, was best all around.

Father Lyons, however, was quite another matter. He was the parish priest, the only other visitor to the O'Gribben home, and for

Erin a real enigma. A handsome man in his early forties, he did not fit the stereotype of the rural Irish priest. He seemed especially attentive to Mrs. O'Gribben's needs, and called several mornings each week while on his rounds of the sick.

What disconcerted Erin most was the freedom with which the priest came and went. He never bothered knocking but would materialize in the kitchen at any hour he pleased, grunt a greeting, and disappear into the patient's room. Often he startled Erin by emerging from the mother's bedroom when she had no inkling he was even in the house.

The situation reached absurd heights one morning. Ed had left for work and Erin was dressing in the bedroom. She was intrigued to hear the upstairs toilet flush; it was at the end of the corridor. She peered out her door and was in time to see Father Lyons steal down the stairs. It was eight o'clock. What on earth, she wondered, was going on?

"That made me *so* indignant," she says, and it is plain to see that it still rankles almost a decade later. "After all, I was Ed's wife, the 'mistress of the house,' even if ol' Martha had other ideas. I thought it was a bit rich of Father Lyons, treating the house as his own. It just wasn't on."

But he was a priest, and Erin's upbringing dissuaded her from challenging him then and there. She was determined to do just that in the event it should happen again. It did, a day or two later. Father Lyons's response astonished her.

"Oh, but I have my own key," he said cheerily, as if that explained everything.

"Your own key. I don't understand."

"It's very simple," he said, as if speaking to a child. "Ed had one made for me. Martha wanted me to have one." He was no longer smiling, and his voice had taken on a patronizing tone. "After all, this is Mrs. O'Gribben's home. If you don't want me to have a key, perhaps you should discuss it with her."

Erin was flabbergasted. "Oh no, that's all right," she heard herself say. "Do as you please, Father."

"Good. As long as we know where we stand." He rubbed his palms together and grinned. "Now, a cup of tea would be lovely. Bring it down to the room, would you. Time to look in on the patient."

He left Erin fuming. It was all she was going to take. She vowed that before the week was out she would tackle her husband about the intolerable situation.

"I knew I was as much to blame," she says. "I stood meekly by and allowed a bedridden old harridan to dictate my life, aided and abetted by a priest who showed no respect for another person's privacy. So, right there and then, I swore I was going to have it out with Ed. I'd had enough—of him, his mother, and that stuck-up priest."

But the confrontation was postponed. Two days following Erin's exchange with Father Lyons, the unexpected happened. Martha O'Gribben suffered a severe stroke and slipped into a coma. She was removed without delay to the county hospital.

For the first time in seven months, Erin found herself quite alone in the old house. Ed and his siblings maintained a rotating bedside vigil, and the priest had no reason to visit. The young housewife was not unhappy being left by herself. She was taking a correspondence course in the hospitality trade and was working on completing the first module of the two-year program. Now she could study undisturbed and undistracted.

All the same, the house was having an unsettling effect on her. She put it down to the isolation; she could not help comparing it to Wuthering Heights or some other bleak old ancestral home of fiction. And she knew full well that West Kerry had lost some of the innocent charm she remembered from childhood. Crime had affected the locality just as much as elsewhere; out-of-the-way dwellings had become easy pickings for burglars. Before going to bed each night, she made certain that all windows and doors were secured. She even locked her bedroom door.

She slept well on those first two nights of solitude. Not so the third. That night she was to have her first brush with the paranormal.

At about two in the morning Erin was awakened by a frightful pounding on her bedroom door. It was terrifyingly loud; it was as though somebody was pounding fists against it.

She switched on the light, thinking it was Ed angered that his own bedroom door was bolted against him. Was he drunk? Trembling, Erin slipped out of bed.

"Wait now, Ed! I'm coming."

Fumbling, she unlocked the door and yanked it open.

There was no one. The landing was disconcertingly deserted.

"Ed," she called out hesitantly, "is that you?"

No answer came. My God, she thought, what is going on? There was plainly someone in the house. The pounding on the door had sounded while she slept but continued after it roused her. It was no dream. Every fear she had entertained while alone in the house was lining up to assail her. She thought of burglars, thieves, rapists, murderers. . . .

She was standing on the landing wondering whether she should brave it down the stairs when she noticed something odd. The door to old Mrs. O'Gribben's room was slightly ajar, and the light was on. It had not been on in days, not since they had taken her to the hospital.

"Hello, who's there?" she called out. She was endeavoring to keep the fear out of her voice. "You'd better come out right now or I'm calling the police!"

She waited. There was no response.

The bedroom seemed the safest place at that moment. She dashed back in and slammed the door shut. She fumbled with the key; her fingers were trembling. She sat down on the bed and tried to reason things out.

"I'd been in ol' Martha's room only the day before," she recalls. "And I distinctly remembered locking it. There'd been no one in the house since then—no one. I was frantic; I got down on my knees and started to pray to try and calm myself. It helped."

Eventually, Erin climbed back under the covers and switched off the light. The house was silent, reassuringly so. She drifted off.

Shortly after six she was awakened by the telephone on the nightstand. It was Ed, always the early riser. Yes, he had been at his mother's bedside all night. Why?

"Just wondered, Ed. Thought maybe you'd come back for something and didn't want to wake me."

"No," he said, half-stifling a yawn.

Erin decided to keep her unsettling experience to herself.

"How is she? Any change?"

"No, not really. But we lost her for a bit."

"What?"

"Around two. Only for a few minutes, thank God." She thought she heard Father Lyons's voice in the background. "Look, got to go. See you at lunchtime."

The following night proved even more disturbing.

Ed had left her on her own again. She slept fitfully and awoke in the early hours. She had had a very vivid and distressing dream: old Mrs. O'Gribben had appeared in the corner of the room, screaming at her over and over. "Get out of here!" she had ordered. "You're not wanted in this house!"

The dream seemed so real, almost as though Mrs. O'Gribben had been there in the flesh; it had none of the vagueness and disjointedness one associates with ordinary dreams.

"It upset me no end," Erin says. "I kept thinking something must be wrong. It was like one of those premonitions people say they have. So I called the hospital and got Ed on the line."

His mother had passed away a few minutes earlier.

Sitting in the kitchen drinking cup after cup of tea, not daring to return to bed and perchance to dream again, Erin was knitting together strands of evidence and drawing a disquieting conclusion. Her "Wuthering Heights" was haunted.

"I didn't want to admit it to myself before then," she says, "mainly because I always thought ghost stories were rubbish. Now I wasn't so sure. All those weird things that were happening—they were like something out of a ghost story."

There was, however, a glaring inconsistency in Erin's theory. Ghost stories involve ghosts, phantoms of the dead. Ed's mother, though terminally ill, was still alive when the alarming disturbances began. She wondered how it was possible for a *living* person to haunt her.

But Mrs. O'Gribben was certainly dead now. Erin could not bring herself to mourn her passing. Nevertheless, she did her duty and attended the funeral service; it would have been the scandal of the parish had she not. Predictably, Father Lyons conducted the service, and equally predictably eulogized at length about the kind, generous, and pious lady the deceased had been. One thing puzzled Erin: she was not the only person present who showed no grief. Neither Ed nor his siblings shed a tear. All seemed somehow relieved at their mother's passing.

She was missing something. She felt almost like an actor called upon at the last minute to stand in for a role—and nobody had given her the script to read.

On January 18, 1997, one month after Mrs. O'Gribben's death, Erin discovered she was pregnant. She was overjoyed. All the difficulties that had been plaguing her seemed to melt away. With her mother-in-law gone and having the house to herself at last, she felt freer and happier than she had ever been.

Her difficult in-laws no longer had reason to visit, and she saw less of Father Lyons. The priest did not altogether stop coming around, though. Twice a week he would collect Ed on "parish business." Both were members of the local Gaelic football *cumann,* or club. Every Tuesday and Thursday evening, Ed gave up his free time to coach the boys' under-twelve team.

As her pregnancy progressed, Erin became used to being left alone for most of the day and evening. The old house seemed somehow less intimidating; she felt that it was becoming *hers.* It no longer made her nervous. The two frightening episodes she had had concerning her mother-in-law—the pounding on the bedroom door and the nightmare—she put down to stress. It was a new year, she had made her resolutions, and a baby was coming. The new mistress of the house felt better about everything.

Surveying *her* home early one morning, she made a decision: a clean sweep was called for. And the best place to start was the bedroom vacated by the scarcely lamented Martha O'Gribben. She would clear it out, perhaps turn it into a sitting room or study.

There was something about the room that made her uneasy, even *sans* patient. It was not just the cold—that particular room had always been colder than the rest of the house, but she had got used to that. There was something else. An odor: "a dirty rotten odor, as though a toilet had never been cleaned in ages." This noisome stench persisted even after everything—Mrs. O'Gribben's effects, bed and bedding, the trappings of home nursing—had been disposed of.

"The strange thing about it," Erin says, "is that it didn't seem to fade, as smells normally do. I could stand in the hallway with the door to that room open and I wouldn't smell anything at all. But once I put my head in, it was overpowering."

After that, it began to follow her.

"There was something really unnatural about it, because it would come and go at random all over the house, as if it was being switched on and off, almost like a light."

At first Ed claimed he smelled nothing but eventually gave in. "It's probably a blockage in the sewerage system," he said.

Erin had her doubts. There were only two bathrooms, one upstairs, one down, both at the rear of the house. The smell had begun—and was still at its most pungent—in the mother's room. It had no adjoining bathroom; none of the bedrooms had.

It seemed to Erin that something was determined to thwart her attempts to set her own stamp upon the house. The smell was only the beginning. One evening, while in the kitchen writing up an essay, she felt certain she heard her name being called, but there was no one. On another occasion, she distinctly heard someone knocking on the back door and was surprised to find no visitor on the step. Sometimes she would awaken in the middle of the night with a jolt, believing she had heard old Mrs. O'Gribben's summons—the walking stick being dragged across the radiator in the room below.

Again, Ed was not prepared to share her concerns. "Maybe it's my mother wanting you out," he said dismissively.

And Erin had the crazy notion that he meant it, too.

In October 1997, Mrs. Erin O'Gribben gave birth to a healthy baby boy. Quentin was all a mother could wish for: a beautiful, brown-eyed little bundle, who rarely cried and rarely disturbed his parents' sleep.

Ed turned out to be an attentive enough father, but as Quentin's first birthday drew near, he made a rather strange announcement. "We'll not be having a birthday party for him," he said.

"What do you mean?"

"There'll be no parties in this house."

"Why not?" She was puzzled. It seemed an odd thing to say. What was wrong with a birthday party?

"We've never had them. My father didn't like them, and neither did *his* father."

"Are you telling me you never had a birthday party? None of you? Not even when you were kids?"

"That's right."

"So it's a family tradition, then." Erin knew she sounded scathing but did not care. It was ridiculous.

But Ed simply glared at her, saying nothing. She hated it when he behaved that way. It made her feel as if *she* were being the unreasonable one.

"Okay, we'll go out to a restaurant," she said, annoyed. "Is that allowed?"

"Fine," he said after a time. "Yes, fine. You go ahead. I'll be working anyway."

Father Lyons's car pulled into the yard then, and presently Ed took his leave. Erin was left once again holding the baby. It was a situation she had come to accept as normal.

Looking back now, she admits that there was a good deal wrong with her marriage. "All the signs were there," she says, "but I chose to ignore them. You know how it is. I was young, idealistic. I thought I could change him and that things would work out. But I know now that you can't change anyone. Not really."

But there were other, ominous signs that there was something not altogether right about the house. Erin could not help but conclude that the signs had multiplied around Quentin's birth and in the months that followed. Nor was it her imagination; they were physical, concrete signs.

The bedroom on the ground floor—the old sickroom—seemed to be the focus. She had succeeded in clearing it out but never actually got around to redecorating it. Time after time, the coldness and foul smell put her off. She let the room be, promising herself to tackle it "at some stage." Quentin's approaching birthday seemed to be the incentive she needed. She unlocked the door—and was greeted by a very odd sight.

The windowsill and the floor below it were covered with dead black flies. This was puzzling. After all, it was wintertime and the window was perpetually shut. On closer examination, Erin saw that some of the flies were incomplete. It was as if they had been chopped in two or—more worryingly—bitten in two. A shiver ran through her. She remembered seeing the same phenomenon some years before in a movie—*The Amityville Horror.*

"I go cold thinking about it," Erin says, "and not just because of the chill in the room. It was only later that I remembered more about that film, about the awful smells and the flies. A long time later. If I'd remembered then, I'd have been out of there immediately and taking Quentin with me. The slaughter of a whole family was responsible for the evil in Amityville, and I suppose I realize now that murder doesn't always have to be physical; killing a person's spirit is just as evil—maybe worse."

"I don't know what was going through my head half the time," she confesses. "I was beginning to think all kinds of things about the O'Gribbens. They were definitely dysfunctional; there was no love lost between them, that's for sure. I had the idea that they all really hated each other. I just didn't dare think about what might have gone on in their past. From what Ed told me, his father sounded like a right header. And as for the grandfather... I'd seen enough of the mother and the others to convince me they were all a bit loopy. Not dangerous, you understand—just loopy."

She hurriedly vacuumed up the flies, made the room a little more presentable, and left. It made her uneasy.

But the following week curiosity got the better of her, and she went to check the room again. This time, the smell was worse—and the flies had returned. There were more of them, too: little black corpses on the sill, and more forming a semicircle below the window, as though somebody had spilled a jar of black peppercorns. Erin was repelled by the sight; she cleaned up quickly again and left.

"It went on for weeks," she says. "I'd hardly got rid of them but they'd appear again. I couldn't understand it; there was no rational explanation I could think of. I thought about spiders. But there weren't any, not in the winter. There shouldn't have been flies either—but there they were. They made me sick just to look at them. Horrible things!"

When finally the flies stopped appearing, their absence was compensated for by something equally bizarre.

Like most new parents, eager to capture each precious, never-to-be-repeated moment of their child's development, the O'Gribbens had taken countless photographs of their son. The sitting room especially had become a showcase, with framed pictures everywhere. Erin's particular favorite showed Quentin in a local park on his birthday. She loved it so much that she had had several copies made.

One medium-sized print held central position in a silver frame on the mantelshelf. A second, larger version hung on the wall.

Erin suspected nothing when, two days after the disappearance of the flies in the sickroom, she found the photo on the mantelpiece lying face down. She righted it without giving it much thought. Perhaps Ed had been looking at it, she told herself, and had not replaced it properly.

But inexplicably, the circumstances repeated themselves on four more occasions.

"I asked him about it," Erin tells us, "but he said that he hardly ever went near the room—which was true—and I'd had no reason to doubt him. There was a TV in the sitting room, but we rarely watched it. That would have been Ed's only reason for going in there. The room was for 'visitors'; it was just the same in my mother's house."

Both pictures became targets. Each time she entered the room, she found the one on the mantelpiece lying face down, and the bigger one turned to face the wall. And each time she righted them, the following day she would find them disturbed again.

It was almost as if somebody was targeting her little son.

In October 2003, on the eve of Quentin's sixth birthday, Erin drove away from the old house on the Dingle Peninsula for the last time. She left behind the man who had masqueraded as her husband, who had vowed to love and cherish her, but whose vows had been a sham.

She shut the door on the priest who had proved to be a travesty of a priest: Father Lyons. And finally she bade adieu to her in-laws, asking God to forgive them all and praying that she would never set eyes on any one of them again. She had lived for seven years in the grip of depravity; she was determined to put as many miles as possible between herself and the evil that was threatening her and her young son. So she chose County Donegal, 250 miles distant.

She settled in a picturesque locality on the northwestern coast. Her smart semidetached bungalow is a world away from the decrepit farmhouse that was her home for too long. The sun is streaming through the patio doors of the living room where we sit as she relates her story. The peach-and-white color scheme is bright and uplifting. There is no whiff of mildew here, and it is hard to imagine the paranormal intruding on Erin's "hideaway."

She escaped, then—left it all behind her.

"That's what you would think," she says with a shrug, "but my story is far from over. When I stumbled on the horrific truth of what I had married into, all those weird happenings, the coldness, the foul smells, the flies, the strange noises in the house, my child's photo being upset, suddenly everything made an appalling kind of sense. You know there were times when I thought I was going mad. Little did I realize that I was the only sane one among a whole network of mad, evil people."

It took Erin six years to come to terms with the full extent of that evil. In that time, the manifestations came and went, each one making way for a new one. In hindsight she sees that all were related, that each fresh outbreak of the paranormal should have been a warning to her.

To be sure, she had her suspicions almost from the beginning. In the five months preceding her departure, all were confirmed.

"Having Quentin and raising him almost single-handedly made me more conscious of a mother's role," she says. "I wanted to protect him at all costs, and it got to the point where I was not prepared to stand idly by and stay in my pretend marriage just for appearances' sake. I had a responsibility to get at the truth for my son's sake. When I began to face up to things, my world fell apart. It was just too bizarre to take in."

Her husband's behavior and habits ought to have alerted her, and they did, to some extent. Yet Erin made the mistake so many women do when they marry into a set of circumstances that are insufferable: she came to accept them and grew to look upon them as normal.

It started with those evenings spent at the football club.

There were the children—always the children. Whenever Ed called Erin from the club, she would hear children in the background. Not playing football, as one would expect, but screaming and wailing. If she asked what was going on, he would say that someone had fallen down and hurt himself. The explanation did not ring true somehow; Erin had no recollection of Gaelic games inducing so many injuries.

Then there was her own child. She had indeed brought him up single-handedly. Ed took virtually no interest in Quentin; he seemed content to have merely produced an heir. He showed no tenderness toward the boy. He did not behave as Erin, in her naiveté, had expected a father to behave. She had grown to accept this as normal.

Likewise, Ed's brothers—Dan and Michael—seemed strangely reluctant to show affection for their little nephew. They brought no candy, never spoke to him, complained when he cried. She had put this down to a lack of experience with children. This, too, she came to regard as normal rural bachelor behavior.

But one day, when Quentin was four, Erin came downstairs to hear voices coming from the "sickroom," Mrs. O'Gribben's old room. No one but herself ever went in there. She opened the door—and got the shock of her life. Quentin was sitting on the windowsill, and Dan was removing the boy's shirt.

"What the hell are you doing? Jesus Christ, what do you think you're doing?"

"Nothing." He could not meet her eye. He stood up to leave and tried to brush past her. Quentin seemed not to be perturbed.

"I swear to God, Dan O'Gribben, if you ever so much as lay a hand on that boy again I'll report you to the police!"

A ghastly picture was taking shape. And Father Lyons seemed always to be part of that picture, whether in the foreground or behind the scenes. Right from the start, he had made Erin feel uneasy. There were times when she felt that he truly resented her. She would catch him looking at her in a disconcerting way. Not sexually—more antagonistically. From time to time, he would ask her questions that she felt no priest had a right to ask. They were intrusive and made her uncomfortable.

"Everything all right on the family side of things now, Erin?" he inquired one evening in the summer of 2003. He was having a cup of tea in the kitchen, waiting while Ed was upstairs changing. The two were off to yet another "parish meeting."

"The family, Father? Oh, they're all grand, I'd say. Mary calls now and again, but I haven't seen Michael lately. I think him and—"

"I didn't mean that, Erin. I meant the physical side of things. Between Ed and yourself."

She was caught off guard. She reddened, unsure of what to say. She caught him looking at her queerly again.

"You know I run marriage guidance courses, so I'm well acquainted with the physical side of things," he said, without a trace of irony. "You can always confide in me."

Confiding in this man, who had consistently remained aloof from her, was the last thing Erin wished to do. But Ed saved the day, and her blushes, by appearing in the doorway. What happened next, however, unsettled her even further.

It was as if the men had rehearsed a scene together, she thought, or that Ed had overheard the priest discussing him. In any event, he entered the kitchen and beamed at Father Lyons, ignoring her. The priest went immediately to him and clapped an arm around his shoulder. Erin half-expected them to embrace.

"You wouldn't want this good man running off with someone else now, Erin, would you?" the priest said with a grin.

"I think that was the clincher for me," she tells us. "It's hard to put into words, but I think you know when a relationship is *wrong*. That night I really felt there was something very unhealthy about Ed and the priest. It was the way they looked at each other. It wasn't the sort of thing fellas who've known each other for years have. I knew by the way Father Lyons kept his arm around Ed's shoulder as they left. It was altogether too intimate for my taste."

Erin believes it was at that moment that she put two and two together. "All those nights they spent at the football club and at parish meetings—how did I know if they were for real? My mind was racing that night. I went to bed and couldn't sleep. I couldn't get certain thoughts out of my head. I kept thinking of Ed, the priest, and those children. I was determined to get to the bottom of things."

She was still awake hours later when she heard the priest's car coming around the back of the house. He was dropping Ed off, as he had done on a thousand occasions. Erin, driven mad by then with her suspicions, got up and went down the hall to Quentin's room. It overlooked the backyard. He was sleeping peacefully, as expected. Carefully, she went and drew aside the curtain.

The moon was high, gibbous, its light bathing the yard. The paintwork of Father Lyons's black Mercedes gleamed. She saw the two men step out of car. The next thing she knew, they were locked in a passionate embrace.

Erin reeled back from the window in horror. She almost woke Quentin with her sobbing. She hurried back to the bedroom and bolted the door. In a few heartbreaking seconds her marriage had ended.

"What was that all about last night?" Ed demanded of the wronged wife the next morning. "Locking the door like that?"

"What, *you're* asking *me?*" She was furious. Lack of sleep seemed to have given her a courage she rarely had. She loathed confrontation with Ed. "You're asking me about bolting the door? What were you doing with Lyons in the yard? I *saw* you."

"Oh, that." He said it with a shrug. His nonchalance astonished her. "I thought you knew. Me and Frank have been lovers for years. And what of it?"

She could not believe what she was hearing.

"Sure, wasn't it Frank who persuaded me to get married? Just to be on the safe side and to stop the gossip."

So all those evening trips to the football club were just a sham. Erin tried to take it all in. She was weary. She felt on the verge of a nervous breakdown. But she pressed on; there were still some matters that needed clearing up. She was still thinking of the football club—and drawing frightening conclusions.

"My God, Ed, what have you been doing? The children …?"

"What children?"

"I heard them in the background. Crying. When I phoned you at the club. What were you doing? Ed, what was going on there?"

He turned his back to her and crossed to the window. She waited. There was a part of her that wanted to run from the nightmare. But she knew that what she was experiencing was not a nightmare; it was real and it was happening to her. The only way to end it was to learn the truth.

"The truth, Ed—no matter how terrible. I have to know. You owe me and our son that at least."

He turned back from the window, calmly took her by the arm, and led her down the hallway to what was once his mother's bedroom. The foul smell had lessened over time, but the coldness was as bone chilling as ever. It was a dismal place.

"This is where it all started," he said evenly. "This is where I cried and screamed—just like the little brats that you heard on the phone."

There was so much fury in his eyes, Erin feared for her own safety. "Go on," she managed to say. "I'll try to understand."

But he seemed not to want her understanding. Her patience and her attempt at empathy seemed to make him even angrier.

"Oh, you will, will you?" he roared, his face gone crimson. "Well, here's the thing. My father raped me in here." He pointed toward the mildewed baseboard. "He raped me there on his dirty old bed, nearly every night from as far back as I can remember. Then, when Dan and Mick and Mary came along, I got a break and he did the same to them. Then we started doing it with each other, because he liked to watch. And then—"

"Enough!" Erin screamed. "Oh, Jesus Christ, *enough!*"

He laughed in her face. He adopted a mock female voice. "'The truth, Ed,'" he mimicked. "'The truth, no matter how terrible.'

Well, now you're getting the truth and you're going to hear every nasty, horrible, dirty little bit of it."

She stood back against the wall, using it for support, as the monster that had taken the place of her husband continued his horrific confession—a confession that seemed to her to be more of a boast.

"God, I was so happy when the old bastard died," he said. "But I might have known it wouldn't last long. Then *she* started."

He kicked the wall where his mother's bed had been.

"'Gentlemen friends,' she called them. They came at all hours, and 'had' all of us. Right here in this f***ing room. She used to wake us up and say, 'Now go and be good to Mister so-an'-so. We need the money, now that Daddy's not here.' So what do you expect me to do, now that I'm supposed to be a man? I take revenge, that's what I do. Because that's what men did to *me*. Those little brats you heard deserve it. As long as I'm alive I'll mess up every little bawling brat I see. I'll take—"

"Stop it, *stop it!*"

She ran from the room, to emerge into the hallway. She heard him pull the door shut behind him.

"His anger was like this living thing that took hold of him," Erin says. "I could feel all the hate, going back years, all pouring out of him that day. Quentin was in the yard playing with one of his friends. They were on their summer holidays. Well, the last thing I wanted was for him to come in and see his daddy like that."

Erin had to know about Quentin. In her mind's eye, she was back in the sickroom, when the child was four, and his uncle Dan had brought him in there. She could still see his rough hands with their permanently dirty fingernails undoing the buttons on Quentin's shirt. She tried to form the question that she could not bring herself to ask. But Ed got there before her.

"No, I haven't touched Quentin, all right? Now, I've got things to do."

He strode from the house, slamming the front door behind him. Through the glass in the side panel she saw Quentin following his father's departure with curiosity.

"I think my heart was breaking at that moment," she says.

Ed's confession gave Erin little relief. He had lied to her about everything, from the day they met. But at that moment, she accepted what he said; her sanity depended on it.

Nonetheless, her marriage was over. The following day, she and Quentin moved out of the godforsaken old farmhouse and returned to her mother's home in Tralee. Only after a couple of months did Quentin feel confident enough to confide in his mother; his new surroundings and his caring grandmother dispelled his fear. Erin learned what she had feared the most. She becomes terribly upset when recalling this.

"You have no idea how horrible it was," she says. "I'd begun to guess the truth, but it turns out it was worse than I'd dreamed of. They were all at it: every single one of those sick people. Ed had abused him, but so had his filthy brothers, Dan and Michael. And of course Father Lyons. I don't know how they managed it, right under my very nose! But I suppose people like that are clever. They're up to all the dirty tricks in the book."

With her mother's help, she arranged counseling for the boy in Tralee. She could not send him back to school, not in Dingle. Instead, she decided she would keep him at home for a year, "to have him under my wing; I didn't want to let him out of my sight." She arranged for private tuition in September.

Meanwhile, she was determined that the O'Gribbens and their degenerate priest be brought to justice. She set about having them prosecuted. That proved unexpectedly difficult.

"I tried to get something done and alerted the powers that be, but I was thwarted at every turn. My letters would go missing or not get answered. I got tired of not being believed and of people thinking I was crazy."

Then the calls started.

"They were anonymous at first, but pretty soon they began to turn nasty. They threatened that if I persisted with a prosecution I'd 'be dealt with.' God, even my own mother thought I was inventing things. I suppose it was inevitable that I would have a nervous breakdown. Thankfully, I wasn't so bad that I had to go into hospital. I needed to be there for Quentin, so I had to keep going. I'd a good friend living here in Donegal. Linda and me met on holiday in the mid-eighties and we'd always kept in touch. Her phone calls kept me sane throughout it, and when me and Quentin came to stay with her for a while I fell in love with the place. That's when I decided to buy this house and make a clean break. I just wanted to get as far away from Kerry as was humanly possible without actually leaving the country."

In June 2004, Erin moved into her new home. She put the past behind her as best she could. She distracted herself with interior decorating and getting Quentin settled. He seemed to be happy and even had made a friend: little Connor from next door was a regular visitor. Linda was of tremendous help and a great boost to her self-confidence. She is an educational psychologist, a very necessary shoulder to lean on. She also introduced Erin to a whole new network of friends.

Her life was returning to normal. Quentin had never known a truly normal life and was consequently enjoying its pleasures for the first time. Anxiously, Erin watched the boy as he got through his day, quietly registering every little quirk of personality, every little deviation from "acceptable" behavior, every word or gesture that might signal a reaction to the abuse he had suffered. Linda told her what to look out for.

At the end of August, out of the blue, Erin got a phone call. At first, it seemed relatively innocuous: it was her attorney in Tralee. He was working with Ed's lawyer negotiating her divorce settlement, and was keeping her abreast of progress. But he had news as well. A month earlier, Father Francis Lyons had died in a car crash.

Such a shame, the attorney said, and so young—just forty-six. Erin feigned what she felt was the expected response.

"I remember feeling sick and angry at the same time when I put down the phone. And I remember saying over and over to myself: 'God, the monster got away with it, the monster got away with it!' But, as I soon learned," she says with a sigh, "you might get away with things in this life, but not in the next."

The day after the upsetting phone call, a change took place.

It was as if, with the news of the priest's death, something dark and malefic was loosed. Erin's lovely home, her retreat from the bleak past, was to become the focus of an evil presence. And it would announce itself in an all-too-familiar way.

"It started with the smell again," she says. "When I came down the stairs the next morning to get breakfast, the strange smell from the old Dingle house was in the kitchen. It was faint, but it was there. I checked the bin, checked everywhere, but there was no telling where it was coming from. I knew it wasn't blocked drains, because these are new houses."

Although mild at first, the stench seemed to grow stronger as each day passed. This was the first disquieting sign that something was not quite right. Linda suggested that it was perhaps a symptom of stress brought on by news of the priest's death. But when visitors to the house started to comment on it, she knew something was seriously wrong. Erin called in a plumber, but he found nothing.

Soon she began to discern another odor, different from the first. "It was like what you would get in a church. Not unpleasant—like the smell of incense and candle wax, not lighted candles but ones that have been extinguished. The funny thing was, I would only get it in Quentin's room and my own bedroom, and only at nighttime."

Erin might have left Dingle, but Dingle seemed bent on coming to her. A third manifestation arrived: the coldness. The chilling coldness that had plagued the house in Kerry started to creep into her new bungalow. It was September and still very mild outside, but inside the house it was near freezing. Sometimes she kept the radiators on all day, but to no effect. At night she piled both beds with extra blankets. It was the only way they could get to sleep.

She was reluctant to confide in anyone except Linda, not least because none of her new friends was aware of her past. She had mentioned Ed and Father Lyons and their gay relationship, but kept the unsavory details concerning the incest and pedophilia to herself. She was careful of what she said lest they think she was deranged. After all, if her own family found her story simply too hard to believe, what might her new acquaintances think?

She could not run; she could not hide. She had fled and it had found her again. She felt helpless in the face of encroaching evil. Erin resolved that she would make a stand in Donegal. She was going to draw on the power of prayer.

"I knew the local priest here to see," she says, "but obviously I'd gone off the Catholic Church and all it represented. I hoped that prayer would work, and I made a point of praying with Quentin before he went to sleep."

It worked. As the days passed and her prayers became more fervent, the stench and the bitter coldness began to abate. She was so relieved that she vowed to keep up her prayers. It was a matter of necessity.

The haunting of Erin, her son, and her home was to progress as a sequence of discrete manifestations. First came the olfactory: the foul or intrusive smells. Next, the auditory: unaccountable sounds and disturbances. There followed prophetic dreams and daytime visions, before the haunting culminated—most frighteningly—in a combined assault on all the senses.

The manifestations could occur at any time, without warning. She remembers one particular afternoon. It was a Saturday. Quentin had a day off from school. He was in the backyard, playing with little Connor from next door. Erin could keep an eye on him, or at least be assured of his whereabouts.

She had a mild headache, brought on by four loads of laundry and spin drying. She settled herself on the loveseat in the living room, thinking that watching an episode of *Murder She Wrote* might help her relax. Ten minutes into the show, she lost interest, lowered the sound, curled up on the sofa, and closed her eyes.

After some minutes, she could feel the headache easing; the rest was helping. She resolved to keep her eyes shut, even when she heard Quentin come in. Drowsy, she heard him slide back the glass connecting door to the living room. He followed his usual pattern and crossed to the sofa. Instinctively, Erin pulled up her legs to make room for him.

"That you, sweetie?" she asked, not bothering to look. "Mommy's tired." She stifled a yawn.

She felt the cushion yield as he sat down. The characters on television argued over the details of an L.A. murder as Erin tried to sleep.

After about ten minutes, she heard Quentin get up and leave, go down to his room, and shut the door. Unusual, she thought. Quentin never closed doors behind him—or drawers for that matter. Erin sensed that something was not as it should be. She went out into the corridor. His door was indeed shut. She thought he might not be feeling well. She knocked gently. There was no response.

"Quentin?"

It was most unlike him. She opened the door. The room was empty.

Erin was perplexed. She decided she must indeed have nodded off. She went out to the back garden. He was nowhere to be seen.

"Quentin!" she called out loudly. "Where are you, Quentin?"

There was no sign of him. She called again.

"He's in here with Connor, Erin." Connor's mother was hanging out her washing. "They're in the front room playing. Did you want him home?"

"Thank God for that. How long's he been with you, Liz?"

"An hour, maybe more."

Erin was stunned. It made no sense at all. At that moment Quentin appeared, excited.

"Mommy, come and see! Me and Connor built a castle."

"Not now, sweetie. You need your dinner."

She waited until she got him indoors.

"Quentin, answer me truthfully now, okay? Did you come in here a few minutes ago when I was lying down? And go to your room?"

"No, Mommy." He shook his head solemnly.

"Are you sure, sweetie? Mommy won't be at all cross if you did." Erin's heart was beating very fast and her mouth was dry.

Quentin was quiet for a time. Then he said: "It might've been the little boy, maybe, Mommy."

"What little boy?"

"I see him sometimes in the garden. But Connor can't see him. Then sometimes he's in the house and he's crying." Quentin became earnest. "And when I ask him why he's sad he goes away."

"Does he run away?" Erin tried to smile to hide her mounting panic.

"No, he just goes into the wall. But he goes all blurry first."

Erin could barely speak. She sat down heavily on the sofa and took Quentin on her knee.

"D'you know who he is, sweetie? I'll tell you who he is. He's a little angel that God sent. Now, the next time you see him, you must—"

"No, Mommy, he's not a little angel!" Quentin was adamant. "He's got no wings."

Erin smiled. "That's because they're hidden under his shirt, sweetheart."

Quentin's little face puckered with annoyance. "No, Mommy," he protested, "he doesn't have any clothes on."

Erin felt the color drain from her face. She could not speak. She was barely aware of Quentin squirming out of her embrace and leaving her lap. He went to the shelf under the TV and took out his favorite wooden jigsaw. All angels—and devils—were instantly forgotten.

"I'll make dinner now," she heard herself saying, and went to the kitchen, much troubled.

That day saw the beginning in earnest of the renewed extra-physical assault on Erin. The new phase assured the return of many sleepless nights.

She began to experience unusually vivid dreams. Many were of a sexual nature; others—of diverse content—proved to be unerringly prophetic, and were all the more disturbing for that.

She dreamed of a wedding that, in the fluid way of dreams, turned into a funeral. Three weeks later, her cousin's wedding echoed the dream in chilling detail: halfway through the wedding breakfast the groom's father suffered a fatal heart attack. Erin kept the dream, and its tragic mirroring in reality, to herself.

One of her more curious dreams involved a frail old priest on a beach. It resembled the beaches close to her new home, but a larger town was visible in the background. The priest was standing behind a red line he had just drawn in the sand. He carried a stick—or it might have been an old-fashioned cane, such as those wielded by teachers of another era to punish recalcitrant pupils. Repeatedly, the priest pointed at the sand with his cane.

"Don't cross the line!" he said, over and over.

Liz, Erin's next-door neighbor, appeared later on in the same dream.

It disturbed Erin. Priests rarely figured in her dreams. She had the nagging feeling that the old priest carried some hidden meaning, and that he was somehow linked to the recurrence of the manifestations. She could not keep it to herself. She decided to confide in Liz.

"Can you remember what he looked like?"

Erin described the priest as best she could. And the beach. She surprised herself with the amount of detail she had retained.

"It sounds like my uncle," Liz laughed.

"How can that be? I've never met the man. How would I know what he looked like?"

"Beats me. But I'll show you a photo."

She brought an album. Erin gasped, hardly able to believe her eyes. The old priest in the snapshot was the same man she had seen in her dream. Not only that—the picture had been taken on a beach.

"Father John Scully," Liz said. "I believe it was taken in Bundoran. He spent his last days in a retirement home there, run by the Augustinians. God, now let me see...he must be dead about fifteen years at least."

Erin did not know what to think. This was the stuff of ghost stories. Until that day, she had never set eyes on Liz's family album. It seemed inconceivable, then, that an image from that album should come to vivid life in her dreams. Something was invading her senses and her subconscious mind. The implications were both profound and alarming. Liz saw her distress.

"Wouldn't pay much heed to it, Erin," she said. "If it makes you feel any better, I'm not surprised he was giving out to you about not crossing a line or whatever. He was a teacher in his day, and a holy terror from what I heard. Beat the life out of every child who sat in front of him. God forgive me, but I sometimes wonder how these people can call themselves men of God."

"I know." She wanted to say, "Liz, you don't know the half of it," but all at once the image of Father Scully reared up in her mind and she heard him reiterate his ominous words. "Don't cross the line."

Later, in her own home, she would mull over the possible significance of those words—and the fact that a priest had uttered them. Try as she might, she could not see how she was crossing any line. She had aborted her attempt to bring Father Lyons to justice, and his death certainly put an end to any prosecution. Nonetheless, the dream must be important and have a bearing on her present circumstances; why else did it include an uncle of her next-door neighbor? It was all very puzzling.

Sleep became impossible for Erin. Like the teenagers of Elm Street, she feared the dreams that might come and their consequences.

"I was dreading nighttime," she says. "I would put off going to bed for as long as I could. I knew it was stupid. I'd have to sleep eventually, and then I'd dream. I kept asking myself what I'd do if I dreamed about my own death. Or worse still, Quentin's. I was at my wit's end. Linda said I should go to see the doctor, so I did."

She told him about the nightmares but did not elaborate. He prescribed a short course of sleeping pills. The pills, he explained, would relax her but not prevent her dreaming. He recommended instead that she refrain from watching stimulating or violent television shows before bedtime and avoid alcohol late at night. Lastly, he suggested that she listen to soothing music while drifting off to sleep.

The doctor also advised a course of antidepressants. Erin declined.

"I couldn't tell him this but I knew it wasn't my mind that was being attacked," she says. "It was my 'spiritual integrity.' That's what I picked up later on. Linda called it that: my spiritual integrity. So medication wasn't going to help; I knew that. If I was really and truly honest with myself, I knew that the only thing that was going to help was an exorcism. But how do you find an exorcist in Donegal? Where do you even begin to look?"

Seeking an exorcism was no precipitate decision on Erin's part. She had been considering it for many weeks; in fact, she had thought long and hard on exorcism at the time of the more traumatic paranormal episodes in Dingle. But she knew very little about it beyond its lurid Hollywood portrayal. She did not even know if it was still being practiced. This time, she resolved to find out.

Common sense told her to seek out the parish priest and ask his advice. But she was still nervous around priests; she had not yet set foot inside her local church. Events took a hand, however. The presence she calls her "intruder" was to make up Erin's mind for her and send her hurrying to the priest. It happened less than a week after her visit to the doctor.

At about 4 a.m. she awoke to find herself pinned to the bed. Erin had always suffered from mild claustrophobia. Her worst nightmare was finding herself a victim of an earthquake—awakening to discover that a ceiling, or an entire building, had collapsed on top of her, and the slow, agonizing death that would ensue. She could not believe that her nightmare had become real. She was being crushed by a paralyzing weight.

"God, it was awful," she recalls with a grimace. "I thought I was going to die. I couldn't move. And the cold was back—much worse than before. It was *so* cold in the room. I couldn't decide if it was the weight or the cold that was paralyzing me. The only part of me I could move was my head."

There was a smell too: the same pungent odor she had experienced before. More than ever it resembled burned candle wax.

She tried not to panic. It occurred to her that her intruder was immobilizing her for a reason, that she was being held against her will to prevent her accomplishing some action or other. She could not begin to guess what that action might be. Then she heard a child crying out, and that was explanation enough.

"It's Quentin, I thought. I was frantic. My whole body was numb. I couldn't budge. I remember screaming and calling his name over and over. And then I called out for God to help me."

In that instant, all changed. Time for Erin seemed suddenly to telescope; the normal laws of space and motion no longer applied. In the next instant, she was out in the corridor and running toward her son's room. To this day, she cannot fill the gap in her memory between being trapped on the bed and finding herself out in the corridor. There is no logical joining up; it remains a mystery for her.

But she found Quentin deep in sleep. There was nothing to suggest that his sleep had been disturbed.

Then she heard the sound again: a child crying. It was coming from *elsewhere* in the house. She stood still, trying not to breathe too loudly, trying to place its exact whereabouts.

The pieces of the puzzle were snapping into place. She remembered the night in Dingle when she heard someone call her name. It was the voice of a little boy. She remembered the little boy Quentin claimed to have seen. It was all starting to make sense—of a kind. She remembered the wailing of children heard down the phone line....

All of a sudden, the crying stopped. She returned to her own room but remained uneasy. She was telling herself that she could not leave her son on his own. What if something were to happen to him? What if the "intruder" were to turn his attention on Quentin? She would never forgive herself.

Erin went out into the corridor again. She was pulled up short. The sobbing had resumed. It was most definitely coming from some other part of the house, not from her son's room. The sobs of the phantom child were heart-wrenching: continuous, inconsolable, un-utterably sad. As a mother, she felt moved to act, to rescue the child who was in such torment. But it was impossible to determine where the cries were coming from. One moment they would sound behind her, the next to her right or left. She would go in one direction and find that the sobbing had shifted. A line or two of a poem learned in childhood went through her head: *Little one! Oh, little one! I am searching everywhere.*

She gave it up. Her rational mind told her that she was chasing after ghosts. She went into Quentin's room, locked the door, and eased herself into bed beside him. He slept on, oblivious to the danger that Erin felt convinced was threatening him.

Through the locked bedroom door she continued to hear the heartrending sobbing of the ghost child. Erin clasped Quentin to her and began to pray. Gradually, the weeping faded away, then ceased altogether.

At 8:30 a.m., having dropped off Quentin at school, she made an appointment to see the parish priest.

While walking the short distance to the parochial house, Erin was uneasy, for she was going against many years of unbelief. She could no longer recall when it was that doubt about God had set in, but she thought it must have been soon after she left school and began to make her "way in the world," as her late father put it. Her attendance at Mass stopped being a weekly duty and settled down to become the Christmas and special-occasion observance of the lapsed Catholic—again to quote her father, "hatchings, matchings, and dispatchings." Erin usually smiled at that, but not now.

As for Quentin, she had not gone out of her way to bring him up in "the faith." She had always considered it to be slightly hypocritical to instill Christianity in the child when her own faith was weak, to say the least. Ed, however, had made a point of having Quentin accompany him to Mass each and every Sunday, with Father Lyons as the celebrant. They shared a pew with Ed's siblings; Quentin had assured her that he derived little from the Masses. In hindsight, this came as no surprise to Erin. Like her, Quentin had not seen the inside of a church since they fled the Dingle Peninsula.

She did not know what to expect from Father Maurice Higgins. A part of her told her that she was doing the right thing, but in her heart she had little faith in the enlisting of a priest. Faith was the key, she decided. She had lost whatever faith she had a long time before. As she looked into the well-kept gardens along the route she was taking, she wondered how many of her neighbors shared her lack of faith. She wondered how many of them paid lip service to religious worship. God was a different matter, she thought. Erin had never lost her faith in God, her belief that the righteous would prevail, as they used to say. She asked herself how the priest would receive her.

He turned out to be a wiry man in his late sixties. He wore the tired, rheumy look of someone who had seen it all, done it all, and was not overly interested in seeing or doing much more of it. But he listened patiently, punctuating Erin's words from time to time with "dearie, dear," tut-tutting and raising his eyes to heaven with a "merciful God!" or a "Lord save us!"

She could not tell him all; that much she had decided on, even before she reached the parochial house. She had asked herself what a fellow priest would make of her husband's homosexual affair with

Father Lyons. It was 2004, and the wounds to the Church inflicted by the disclosure of clerical sex abuse were still very raw. On meeting the elderly priest, she decided that he was not ready for yet another scandal. It might turn him against her, and she desperately needed him on her side.

When she finished, he sat back in his armchair and said, "Now, to be honest with you, Mrs.... ah ...?"

"Ferguson."

"Mrs. Ferguson, to be honest with you, I'm not used to this kind of thing at all. All that exorcism business isn't done these days anyway. But what I could do is come and say a Mass with you and the boy, and anybody else you'd like to be there—"

"Oh no, Father—just me and Quentin. I don't want anyone to know."

"I understand. That's all right. But I think a Mass should do it." He got up and fetched a diary from a writing desk. "The day after tomorrow, around eight in the evening?" He stood with his pen poised above the page.

"That would be very good, Father. I'm very grateful. Thank you so much."

"That's all right, Mrs. Ferguson. We'll do what we can and trust that it works. And if it doesn't, then we'll try another way."

Trust that it works? Erin had expected somewhat more from the priest. She knew very little about exorcism but had understood that it was the Church's most effective weapon against the paranormal. She also had been encouraged to place her trust in the extraordinary spiritual power of the Mass. The priest's words did not inspire confidence.

It seemed to her that Father Higgins was preparing her for failure.

He was as good as his word. He arrived at the appointed hour and celebrated a Mass in the living room.

Erin was acutely aware of the effect he had on Quentin. The boy was nervous; he could not meet the priest's eye.

"I sensed what was going through his head," she tells us. "I'd prepared him as best I could for Father Higgins. 'He's a nice old

man,' I told him. 'He's coming to say prayers for us.' I thought he'd
be okay with all of it, but he wasn't. I know it was the collar that
did it. As soon as he saw that, he went all nervous. I was hoping
he wouldn't. It wasn't fair that Frank Lyons turned Quentin off all
priests. But who could blame him?"

Father Higgins, for his part, did not seem to notice or, if he did,
paid no mind. Erin had the impression that he tolerated children
but had no great affinity for them. After some minutes, however, the
priest had, to some extent, won Quentin's confidence. It was enough
for the ceremony.

It was not the first time that Erin had participated in a Mass
celebrated in the home. The Station Mass, a survival from Penal
times, was an important ritual in her native Kerry. She and her family had often been invited to attend such an event. It was regarded
as a great privilege that the priest should grace one's home with the
sacrament. Candles would be bought and the best linen brought
out. The altar would be set up in the parlor with great solemnity,
chairs arranged in the room. The priest would make a great show of
bringing out the sacred vessels and disposing the holy water and oil.
The parlor would be thronged with the devout of the parish.

But on this occasion, Erin made no such elaborate preparation,
nor did she invite anybody else to participate. Father Higgins had
asked her not to "go to any trouble." He came alone; she would
assist, reading the responses from a printed sheet. The altar was
simple: she used the drop-leaf table in the dining room, draping the
middle section in white linen.

The Mass progressed smoothly. At its close, Father Higgins
blessed mother and son. Quentin seemed to have overcome his initial aversion to anything priestly; he had followed the ritual with
great interest.

Lastly, the priest blessed the house, sprinkling holy water in
each room while employing suitable prayers. Erin saw him frown
when all was completed. Something was troubling him.

"I see you have no holy pictures in the house."

"No," said Erin, taken aback. She had never gone in much for the iconography of Catholicism, believing that her religion was a personal thing, not something to be validated through a display of imitation art.

"Oh, it's very important to have a picture or two of the Sacred Heart or the Blessed Mother herself," Father Higgins assured her. He was stowing his consecrated objects in a small case. "She's our protector from all harm, you know, the Virgin. He could never get near her."

Erin did not much care for the sound of that "he"; she did not have to ask whom the priest was referring to.

"Call in to the house and I'll give you a picture," he said, as he made ready to leave. "Anytime. I'll leave them with Tricia. That's my housekeeper, don't you know; so if you don't see my car outside, don't be put off."

"I'll remember that, Father. Thank you very much. A cup of tea, perhaps?"

"I'd love to, Mrs. Ferguson, but I've another visit to do, so I'd just as soon get on. Thank you all the same."

And he was gone. Erin hesitated for a long time at the door. She freely admits that she expected a miracle that day, that her bungalow would be transformed and it would feel different. In fact, it did.

"Call it imagination; I don't know," she says. "But there was a special feel to the place when I went back inside. Quentin seemed to feel it too, because he wasn't a bit nervous, like he was when the priest came. There was such a sort of *glow* of peace about the place."

Best of all, the coldness that had plagued the house had retreated. That night, Erin slept better than she had in a long time. She awoke the next morning feeling refreshed and, in a sense, liberated.

The days passed. The glow of peace remained in Erin's home. Life returned to normal. Quentin seemed calmer, too. Often she would watch him at play with the other children, and there was nothing about his behavior that set him apart. On the contrary, the other boys accepted him readily. They might tease him about his "funny" accent, but that was all. Linda looked in on them and complimented Erin on how well both were faring.

Then the cracks began appearing in the newfound quietude. The first incident occurred ten days following the Station Mass. It was afternoon. Quentin had just come in and gone to his room to change out of his school uniform. Erin, as usual, prepared a snack for him in the kitchen. He was taking longer then usual. She went to see what was keeping him and found him struggling with his jumper, one arm in, one arm out.

"Here, let me," she said, stooping to help him.

Quentin sat on the bed as Erin adjusted his jumper. But as she straightened, she found him looking over her shoulder and wearing an expression she could not read.

"Mommy, who's that man behind you?" he asked. "The man in black."

Erin dared not look around. She could feel her scalp crawling, as if bugs were moving over it. Quentin seemed unperturbed; she was beside herself with fright. There *was* someone behind her. The sense that alerts us to the presence of another in close proximity was telling her there was a third person in the room. Somebody was breathing on the back of her neck. She could feel her hair being gently disturbed with each gust of breath.

"Nonsense," she managed to say, despite her disquiet, "there's no one here but you and me, sweetheart."

It was true. As she spoke, she could feel the presence behind her departing, almost as though somebody had gone out the door without making a sound. She could see Quentin following something with his eyes, and it horrified her. She could barely contain a scream. Her impulse was to bundle the child into her arms and get as far away from the house as possible. Instead, she tousled his hair and took his hand.

"Here, come. Your tea's getting cold."

In those few minutes, Erin's home had subtly changed. It was as though Father Higgins had never been there and no Mass had been said. She thought of the "holy pictures" given to her by the priest's housekeeper, some of which she had placed in Quentin's room. She

asked herself why they were not doing the job the priest had promised they would. She wondered if her own lukewarm faith was not
lessening their efficacy.

"I got really scared that day," Erin confesses, "but I prayed that
it would be a one-off. Even though I had felt some kind of presence, I was willing to believe that it could just as easily have been
my imagination. Children can have very colorful imaginations too,
so I managed to convince myself that Father Higgins's Mass had
worked, and I tried to get on with things as normal."

But normality did not wish to come to Erin. That same evening,
the electricity started going haywire. Lights dimmed and bright-
ened again for no apparent reason; the refrigerator went off ten or
twelve times a day; the electric shower turned icy without warning.
Often the television set and Quentin's PlayStation switched themselves off, much to the boy's annoyance.

The erratic surges and power outages became so frequent that
Erin learned to anticipate them; she knew instinctively when the
lights would fail and would go in search of candles and matches.
She called an electrician in to inspect the wiring. He gave the house
a clean bill of health. The wiring was new, he said; there should, by
rights, be no disruptions. He muttered something about the "local grid" and "surge impedance," and left without charging her any
more than his call-out fee.

The electricity was not the most ominous sign that the attacker
had returned to the house in Donegal. Quentin reported seeing the
strange, unclothed boy again.

"It made me go cold," Erin says. "I know kids sometimes have
invisible friends, but this wasn't like that. For me, the naked boy and
the sobbing I heard that night were connected. Quentin told me
he was playing with Connor in the back garden and he saw the boy
come in the back door. He followed him and found him in his room.
He was kneeling beside the bed and praying. How was I going to
explain to Quentin that him seeing this strange boy was somehow
'normal' behavior—that all children saw spirit children?"

A catalog of events followed the apparition in quick succession. They left Erin in little doubt that she was dealing with the preternatural, as opposed to benign or even neutral forces. The foul odor and the freezing cold returned. The sobbing of the phantom child could be heard not only in the middle of the night but during the day as well. Often she would feel a presence behind her in the kitchen. And, in a ghastly echo of her experience in the old house in Dingle, something would pound loudly on her bedroom door.

She had lost faith in Father Higgins's Eucharist but still clung to the hope that prayers and holy pictures would keep the darkness away. That hope was to disappear when a final and terrifying manifestation intruded into her home.

"I'd just come back from shopping and unlocked the front door when I saw it. There, in front of my eyes, was a black thing. It wasn't real; it wasn't a human being. It was half shadow, half creature. It was moving at great speed down the hallway. I nearly collapsed."

She could not remain alone in the house yet had to be there for Quentin. She called Linda and had her come over. She vowed to say nothing about the apparition; she was convinced that her friend would not believe her. As it turned out, explanations were superfluous. The moment she opened the door, Linda recoiled in fright. She grasped Erin's arm and pulled her outside.

"Close that door quick!" she cried. She seemed near hysteria.

"What is it? What's the matter?"

Linda could hardly speak coherently. She retreated down the path.

"Oh my God, Erin, *you* tell *me*. I just saw the most awful-looking black thing on your stairs! What the hell is going on?"

In the stillness of a monastery in a neighboring county, the venerable Father Ignatius McCarthy listened to Erin's story without interruption. She told him everything: about the car accident that had brought her into Ed O'Gribben's life; about his rapist of a father and the despicable mother who prostituted her own children; about Ed's incestuous siblings; about his gay lover, Father Lyons, and the pedophiliac crimes the pair engaged in. She told him of the paranormal events that had persecuted her in Dingle and followed her to Donegal. Lastly, she told him about the most frightening thing of all: the black entity that appeared to be no more substantial than a shadow.

For the first time in a long while, Erin experienced the relief that came of unburdening herself, of confiding her distress to this kindly stranger in that silent, sanctified place, without fear of censure or of not being taken at her word.

"I think that it's old Mrs. O'Gribben, Father," she said. "She resented me from the beginning. And when she died...well, it was then that all those strange things started happening."

"In the Dingle house, yes. But not now. I believe it's Father Lyons who's haunting you."

"A priest?"

"Yes. But it wouldn't be the priest himself, you understand. It's whatever it was that got into him while he was alive. It still has him in its clutches, you see. And there's only one thing that will make it let go. Father Lyons needs your prayers and forgiveness, Erin. He won't leave until he gets them."

It was the last thing she had expected. If she understood correctly, Father Ignatius was placing the burden of the manifestation on *her*. As though she had brought it all on herself. She felt anger well up inside her.

"Can you forgive him?" the priest asked.

"No, I can't. Not after all he did. To Quentin, and me."

Father Ignatius patted her arm. "Erin, forgiveness is a crucial part of healing. Forgiveness frees us from all those emotions Satan uses to keep us bound: hatred, unkindness, revenge, depression—all the unloving ways of being. Father Lyons did wrong; we both know that. But what he needs more than anything is the forgiveness of those he did most harm to. In this instance, he needs *your* forgiveness."

Erin found it difficult to return his steady, kindly gaze.

"I...I'll ..." She was lost and did not know what to think or say.

"That's why he's come back, my dear. You must pray for his soul. Can you do that?"

"I'll do anything, Father." Erin was weeping. "I'll do anything you suggest—whatever it takes—to be free of this. Truly!"

"I'm glad." Father Ignatius laid hands upon her head and prayed silently over her.

"I'll come tomorrow," he promised, "to offer a Mass and bless the house."

It took Father Ignatius McCarthy more than three hours to perform his "blessing" of Erin's home. It was a considerably more elaborate ritual than he had given her to believe and differed greatly from that enacted by the other priest.

After offering Mass in Latin and English in the parlor, he went through the house, spending a considerable time praying in each room and blessing it with holy water and incense. He requested that he be left alone in each of the rooms and that all doors remain shut.

Erin has vivid memories of the sacrament. It evidently made a tremendous impression on her.

"It was an unusual Mass," she recalls. "After Father Ignatius had taken the Communion host and sipped the wine, he raised his eyes heavenward and started praying in Latin—at least I think it was Latin. It sounded a bit strange at first, but as he went on I realized he was 'talking to God' and that I was being given the privilege of witnessing something special."

The sacrament being ended, the priest bade Erin and her son to remain where they were. He asked them to kneel for his blessing. He was going to anoint them, he said.

"It's oil, sweetheart," Erin told Quentin. "Father Ignatius is going to rub a little bit of oil on your forehead."

"But I don't want to get dirty."

The priest chuckled. "It's not that kind of oil," he told the child. "It's sweet oil. It's like a sort of perfume."

As is the case with holy water, holy oil—or chrism, a mixture of oil and balsam—is important to all Christian rites of exorcism. Oil, when used by the faithful, is believed to negate the power of demons, their attacks, and the preternatural forces they invoke.

Father Ignatius moistened a thumb and went to Erin first. He paused and frowned.

"I saw him looking past me," she says. "He was looking the same way Quentin did that day when I was helping him with his jumper. I had the distinct impression that Father Ignatius might be seeing something in the room behind me. But he never let on. I'm sure he didn't want to frighten Quentin. Or me, for that matter."

It was growing dark when the last room in the house was puri-fied to the satisfaction of the priest. If Erin expected a dramatic change in her home, she was disappointed. She could not help feeling that, far from helping, the Mass and the blessings had made matters worse. There was an eerie sense of foreboding about the place. Quentin must have felt it too; not in a long time had she seen him so morose.

Father Ignatius took her aside. He seemed to sense what she was feeling.

"You mustn't think that everything will be as right as rain now," he said. "These things take time. But be assured that from now on, those things that were afflicting you will lessen considerably. In time, they'll disappear altogether."

"Remember what you said in the monastery, Father: that you thought it might be Father Lyons."

"Yes, and I'm still of that opinion. That's why, when I get back to the monastery, I intend to storm heaven for the release of his soul."

Erin would not know how many long hours of prayer lay behind that statement, and Father Ignatius, being a humble man, did not confide this to her.

"Don't forget, now," he said, as his taxicab arrived, "that prayer can work wonders. Pray for him, Erin. He needs your forgiveness and he needs the grace of God."

"He was right about everything," she recalls. "When he left, there wasn't really what you'd call a great change in the atmosphere. But every day it would get better. I just knew everything would be all right. I had complete faith in Father Ignatius's power, and over the days he was proved right.

"The coldness, the foul smell, the crying—it all started to lessen. We had no more blackouts, no messing around with the electricity. Two weeks later we were totally free of all that, and our lives were back to normal."

Father Ignatius McCarthy believes that Erin's case is a classic example of generational evil. He believes that, at some point in the family's past, an unholy thing entered the O'Gribben line and persisted down the generations, tainting and corrupting all those born into that benighted house. It was Erin's great misfortune to unwittingly marry into such an ill-starred family.

The foul smell and the coldness had coincided with the onset of her pregnancy. The house had not known a child's presence for many years, and the prospect of a child in the house again—in a place that had been the focus of so much incest in the past—was perhaps a cause for "celebration" in the darkest realms imaginable. The old house had been the seat of repeated generational perversion. The fact that all the O'Gribben siblings of the present generation acquiesced in and perpetuated that perversion meant that evil was allowed to flourish.

But, we wonder, is it not so that innocent little children have no choice in the matter?

Initially no, the priest concedes. But, by the age of seven, if not before, a child knows the difference between right and wrong. Furthermore, when a child is coerced by his abuser to keep silent about the abuse or deny it, he is being asked to lie, and the wickedness of the deed is thereby compounded. It is imperative that the child tell somebody about the abuse: his mother, a teacher, a neighbor, a grown-up he can trust.

"It would appear that in this unfortunate case, the mother—Martha—had chosen to accept the lie as well," Father Ignatius says. "I'm sure that in the beginning she was as appalled as any sane person could be, but then at some point she decided, for the sake of security and family 'unity,' to keep quiet about it."

"The Father of Lies!" he exclaims, uncharacteristically raising his voice. "It is no accident how he came to be called such. The Devil seeks to oppose truth at every turn and is no respecter of innocence. It is what he seeks endlessly to corrupt. Children are a prime target. The sexual abuse of children: can there be a more evil or effective way to poison humanity and destroy lives? The abused child grows up full of hate, not only for his abuser but for himself as well. In other words, he has allowed evil to enter him, and so perpetuates the whole dreadful cycle again. Ed O'Gribben is a good example."

The priest's analysis of the O'Gribbens is hard to fault. But what of Erin? When she finally freed herself of that degenerate family, how is it that the evil pursued her and her son?

"Father Lyons died very suddenly," the priest says. "He'd no opportunity to repent and to mend his wicked ways. So he was still very much earthbound and attached to his earthly lusts. His soul could not be at rest, so he followed the little boy Quentin. That was all he knew. By persecuting the innocent he knew he could find some relief. Oh, he needed a great deal of prayer, a great deal."

We are curious about the Mass, and especially if he saw anything when anointing Erin and her boy. He sidesteps the issue.

"Such things are dreadful," he says. "Whenever I hear of black shapes or shadows and suchlike invading a home, I'm on the alert at once, because it can only mean one thing: evil spirits are at work. I don't know what Erin or young Quentin saw before that day, but when such things make themselves visible it's a very bad sign. Let's say that, after offering the Mass, I had a clearer idea of the kind of danger Father Lyons was in."

We wonder if the Kerry priest is at rest now.

"I expect he is," Father Ignatius McCarthy says wistfully, then adds: "Yes, we should always pray for the dead, especially when we believe that their immortal souls may be in danger. But even when we're convinced that a man has died in the state of grace, we should still remember him in our prayers. Every little helps."

The bell for compline tolls and he gets up to go. There are important duties to attend to.

"Yes, every little helps," he says again, "and we should always pray for the dead."

As this holy and humble man takes his leave, we understand that he is going to the chapel to do just that.

EXORCISM AND HISTORY

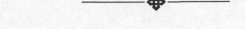

> I interpret this hypothetical fall of man to be the groping
> of newly conscious men to narratize what has happened to
> them, the loss of divine voices and assurances.
>
> —JULIAN JAYNES,
> *The Origin of Consciousness in the
> Breakdown of the Bicameral Mind, 1976*

In all likelihood the rites of exorcism are as old as civilization it-self—and perhaps predate the first human settlements.

The earliest recorded instance is in Sanskrit, contained in one of the thousands of vedas, or teachings, that are fundamental to Hindu-ism. This is the Atharvaveda, a collection of some six thousand verses written down by the sage Atharvan, at some time between 1,500 and 2,200 years before the birth of Christ. It is possible that the words were not those of Atharvan, but that he was the chief celebrant of these ceremonies. He was said to be the son of Lord Brahma, the chief Hindu god. The Atharvaveda is the oldest Indic text alluding to healing, and is part of a much earlier tradition, which was trans-mitted orally for several centuries before being written down.

From the vedas one learns that two classes of priests were custo-dians of the "sacred fire." Of the two, the followers of Atharvan were largely the soothsayers of this fire-cult and performed propitiatory rites, while another class—the Angiras—were tasked with sorcery and exorcism. No details of those exorcisms have come down to us; we have only the assurance that "evil spirits" were expelled, thereby protecting the community from harm.

We do, however, have examples of the words used. The rituals—or "charms"—were employed for all manner of purposes, from encouraging the growth of hair to curing leprosy. One such charm was used by the exorcist to drive out the classes of demon known as Rakshas and Pisâkas:

1. Do ye well offer within the fire this oblation with ghee, that destroys the phantom! Do thou, o Agni, burn from afar against the Rakshas, [but] our houses thou shalt not consume!

2. Rudra has broken your necks, ye Pisâkas: may he also break your ribs, ye phantoms! The plant whose power is everywhere has united you with Yama [death].

3. Exempt from danger, o Mitra and Varuna, may we here be; drive back with your flames the Atrin [devouring demons]! Neither helper nor support do they find; smiting one another, they go to death.

In neighboring Tibet, in later centuries, arcane rites were carried out in the chapel of Mahakala—literally, "the protector"—at Samye, the oldest monastery in the country. The chapel was kept locked for most of the year and only the chosen were allowed to enter. What occurred there at night was a mystery, but it was said that the monks would battle demons within its precincts. Most nights, screams could be heard emanating from within the walls, even though the place was uninhabited. Once a year, the chapel's guardian would ceremoniously replace a crescent-shaped chopper and wooden chopping board, which had—very mysteriously—become worn from use.

Even today, the chopper or cleaver is still essential to Buddhist ceremony. It has the symbolic use of slicing through ignorance or superstition—rather as Alexander the Great cut through the Gordian knot. In many ways, the chopper serves the same purpose as the *dorje* or the *phurba*, both being ritual daggers. It is employed in rituals of exorcism by priests and shamans. Many Buddhist exorcists also rely on a wooden staff embedded with metal rings. When the staff is shaken, the rings create a great cacophony designed to frighten away evil entities.

But Buddhist exorcism relies also to a great extent on humor. An evil spirit is quite simply laughed at, held up to ridicule and so made to depart in shame. This is achieved by friends or relatives of the afflicted person dressing up as demons, donning hideous masks, and acting out the demonic affliction.

Down the centuries, the mask has been a feature of both Chinese and Japanese cultures, the latter greatly influenced by Buddhism. For thousands of years, the Japanese have held processions and ceremonies during which fearsome masks were worn, each type of mask representing a certain class of demon. Such ritual was, and is, a prime example of imitative magic: by aping the demon, a human being can appease it.

MESOPOTAMIA AND THE HOLY LAND

In the Middle East, the Babylonians of Mesopotamia were the principal practitioners of exorcism. During the period 1900–500 BC, magic was practiced by a priestly sect called the Asipu. Their activities ran the gamut from hypnosis to magic, and included the casting out of troublesome spirits.

Christian demonology had its basis here, but it was another people, the Assyrians, who gave definition to belief in the preternatural. There was the "official" religion of the priests, which coexisted comfortably with the demotic faith, the more primitive religion of the people. This "underground" religion was the forerunner of European sorcery and magic. It was also the template for Satan: the Assyrians believed in a principal demon, or devil, who ruled over a vast hierarchy of lesser evil entities.

At about the same time in nearby Israel and Judea, another Semitic race of people, the Israelites, gave rise to prophets who had the ability to perform miracles, prefiguring the coming of Jesus. Angels and devils were everywhere. We learn from the Book of Tobit of an incident involving an entity named Azarias. He instructs Tobias in the roasting of a huge fish for the purpose of exorcism:

> And the angel, answering, said to him: If thou put a little piece of its heart upon coals, the smoke thereof driveth away all kind of devils, either from man or from woman, so that they come no more to them.

But it is to the Talmud we must look for prime examples of Jewish exorcism. Noteworthy among the scourges of demons was Simon ben Yochai, a second-century rabbi "learned in miracles," who is reputed to have performed feats of exorcism. One such involved banishing a female demon.

According to one source, Rabbi Simon was vexed that God had sent five angels to Hagar of Egypt, Abraham's maidservant, and not a single one to him. He saw his chance to summon an angel of his own when the king issued a decree that contravened Jewish religious practices. Simon set off to the palace to have it abrogated.

On the way, he encountered a female spirit, or angel, who was perched atop the mast of a ship. She informed him that she had been sent so that he might perform a miracle. She would enter the stomach of the king's daughter, who would scream out in her agony: "Bring me Rabbi Simon!" The rabbi would then whisper in the daughter's ear, causing the spirit to leave.

All went according to plan. The girl was possessed by the spirit and duly requested that Rabbi Simon exorcise her. He whispered as instructed and the spirit departed, shattering every glass vessel in the palace at her parting. So impressed was the king that he at once tore up his decree.

It is a curious tale and in all likelihood apocryphal. Yet it seems to show an ambivalent attitude toward spirits in ancient Palestine. There is confusion as to what constitutes an angel. At no time is Rabbi Simon's angel considered to be evil; she is, after all, sent by God. She arranges her own demonic infestation so that Simon must exorcise her and thus impress the king. Such symbiosis between the divine and the preternatural has echoes in Christian theology: for instance, God's plan must of necessity include Satan to bring about the "Fall," which in turn is reversed by Christ, who was betrayed by Judas Iscariot, thereby completing the circle.

There are many more allusions in the Talmud, the Torah, and the Old Testament to demons and how to combat them, yet it is not until the writing of the New Testament that exorcism is treated in any great detail. Scripture makes it clear that with the coming of Christ, Satan's days as ruler of the earth are numbered. Matthew also points out that Jesus could differentiate between the mentally ill and the demoniac.

> And his fame went throughout all Syria: and they brought unto him all sick people that were taken with divers diseases and torments, and those which were possessed with devils, and those which were lunatick, and those that had the palsy; and he healed them. (4:24)

"MY NAME IS LEGION"

The Jews had long been accustomed to prophets and magi in possession of ancient wisdom and the power to expel evil entities, but this new miracle worker seemed to them to have infinitely more power than those who had gone before him. News of truly remarkable supernatural feats began to filter back to the Pharisees. Mark (5:1–20) gives an elaborate account of the notorious incident of the "Gadarene swine" and the demon who told Jesus that his name was "Legion." Luke (8:26–33) offers a slightly more succinct version.

There was the celebrated episode involving the woman whom the church fathers in a later century would—erroneously—brand a harlot: "And certain women, which had been healed of evil spirits and infirmities, Mary called Magdalene, out of whom went seven devils" (Luke 8:2).

Wherever he went, Jesus performed the twin rituals of healing the sick and casting out demons. The two ministries seemed almost to go hand in hand: "And in that same hour he cured many of their infirmities and plagues, and of evil spirits" (Luke 7:21).

Scripture leaves us in no doubt that Jesus wished his disciples to continue the work of exorcism. Mark relates how the Lord trained the twelve apostles: "And he called unto him the twelve, and began to send them forth by two and two; and gave them power over unclean spirits" (Mark 6:7). Further on: "And they cast out many devils, and anointed with oil many that were sick, and healed them" (Mark 6:13).

In the Acts, we learn that the apostles carried on a successful ministry after Jesus had left them. Paul's work is the best documented.

As we have seen, neither Jesus nor the apostles were enacting truly exceptional rituals in the eyes of the people—or their priests. Exorcism was an accepted therapeutic practice in the ancient world, from India to Mesopotamia, to Palestine, to Greece and Rome.

The ancients believed that all maladies were caused by wicked spirits invading the body; it followed that the removal of the spirits would effect a cure. Thus, medicine and ancient folk wisdom recognized exorcism not necessarily as a magic operation but as a matter of therapy, a cure for sickness both spiritual and physical.

By the middle of the third century, the Christian Church had established the formal office of exorcist as a minor order. The office is mentioned in a letter written to the bishop of Antioch by Pope Cornelius in AD 253, which coincidentally was the year of the pontiff's death; it is believed that he died in exile, having been banished to the port city of Cittavecchio by the Roman emperor Decius.

The exile was complaining about the man who had taken his place as head of the Church, Novatian, the "antipope": "He knew that there were in this Church forty-six priests, seven deacons, seven subdeacons, forty-two acolytes, and fifty-two exorcists, lectors, and porters."

It is worth remembering that at the time—when Christianity had been little more than two centuries in existence—there could not have been over 30,000 believers in Rome. To have more than a score of exorcists serving this one community seems excessive.

ST. PATRICK AND OTHER EXORCISTS

The year was AD 441. Attila the Hun was galloping into the Balkans with his brother Bleda at his side, to capture the city that would become Belgrade. The Saxon Revolt had left towns and cities throughout Britain aflame, their pro-Roman citizens fleeing before the German invasion. On a tall, conical mountain overlooking Clew Bay in Connacht, St. Patrick was deep in prayer.

He had spent forty days and forty nights on the bleak summit. It was known to the Celts of Ireland as Eagle Mountain, the home of the pagan deity Lugh. In time it would become Croagh Patrick.

The future patron saint was engaged in his second mission to convert this heathen nation to Christianity. He had succeeded well; already half the tribes had come over to the foreign God of Palestine, turning their backs on the ancient divinities of their forefathers. Patrick needed but one more small push to evangelize the Irish, and it was to this end that he had chosen the high mountain for his forty days of prayer and penance. Like Moses in the Sinai desert, he believed that the peak of a great mountain would bring him closer to God.

But Patrick was about to do battle with terrible entities ranged against him. The dark pagan gods were not about to yield this green land without a fight. They converged on the mountain and attempted to thwart Patrick in his mission.

First, they used temptation, as they had done with St. Anthony on his mountaintop in the Egyptian desert. A procession of voluptuous Celtic women appeared, dancing nude about the holy man, offering him their bodies and all the carnal delights he had vowed to forgo. He remained steadfast in his prayers.

Next, they tried belligerence. They gathered about the mountain as vast flocks of black birds: ravens, rooks, and crows. So many were they in number that they dimmed the light of the sun. They came, too, as dragons and, lastly, as snakes—if the oral tradition is to be believed. To no purpose. Patrick fought the snakes and won. He banished them, driving them into a cavern in the mountain known as Lugh na Deamhain, or "Hollow of the Demons."

In our enlightened times, we know with certainty that snakes were never actually native to Ireland. At the close of the last Ice Age—about ten thousand years ago—the northeast of the country was still joined to Scotland by a land bridge, and Britain to continental Europe by the great plain that would become the North Sea. The slow migration of wildlife from the south was beginning. Some two thousand years later, three species of snake had settled in England—but, by that time, the land bridge between Scotland and Ireland was no more. The reptiles would remain unknown in the island.

So what was it that St. Patrick drove from Ireland in AD 441? Some commentators suggest that the snake represented the old gods that Patrick's new religion supplanted. They advance the argument that the snake was commonly associated with Satan—*an Diabhal*—and that the Celtic gods were somewhat demonic in character.

But this is to ignore the fact that far and away the majority of Celtic deities were quite benign when compared to, say, the bloodthirsty gods of ancient Rome. Most Celtic gods were worshiped as protectors of home and hearth, and bringers of health, wealth, and happiness. Crom Dubh, a fertility god, was regarded as a friend, a force to call upon in one's hour of need. Lugh was among the most benign of all. When Patrick ascended the mountain sacred to that divinity, Lughnassadh ("Lugh's Feast"), observed on the first day of August, was approaching. It was a time of celebration, a harvest feast.

There is, however, a consensus among church scholars that Patrick did drive out something of importance that day on Eagle Mountain, and the evidence seems to point to evil spirits. This was only the first skirmish of his long war against the powers of evil. Patrick was Ireland's first Christian exorcist, and his legacy has endured for over fifteen hundred years.

IRELAND AFTER PATRICK

Patrick and the saints who came after him were always going to have a difficult struggle against the Celtic spirit world. This "otherworld" was never far beneath the surface in pre-Christian Ireland. The gods were everywhere, not only in the forests, where they might take the forms of living creatures, but in the home as well. Communication with the otherworld was therefore relatively easy.

Even the Irish board games seem to have had a dual nature, further facilitating communion with the dark side. The games of Branfad and Brandubh were associated with the raven or crow, a bird sacred to the warrior goddess Morrigan. More sinister, however, was the board game known as Fidchell. It could be played in much the same way as chess or checkers, but its original and more important function was to communicate with noncorporeal entities. It was therefore a forerunner of the Ouija board.

The task of the early Christian missionaries was to supplant the indigenous beliefs with a monotheistic religion, whose very setting—the Holy Land—would have seemed impossibly alien to the people. For this reason, they found it expedient to graft Christianity onto an existing credo rather than try to entirely eradicate the old beliefs. And so it was that pagan sites became associated with saints, whether real or imagined. The first churches and monasteries even incorporated pagan symbols and art. The Celtic belief system endured far into the first centuries of Christianity, in particular the notion that human consciousness occupied a position between two worlds: the material and the spiritual. At any time, the spiritual might intrude; it could also be summoned at will, demons and all.

The Patrick mythology would have us believe that Christianity triumphed in heathen Ireland without a struggle beyond the saint's skirmishes with court sorcerers. In fact, for close to two hundred years there was a battle for hegemony, engaged in fiercely by both sides. The pagan demons were not prepared to go quietly.

There were heroes in those days. Or so the surviving manuscripts would suggest. One such demon battler was St. Fursey. The year of his birth is not recorded, but we do know that he died in France circa AD 650.

Born the son of Fintan, a prince of south Munster, he received his baptism in a monastery on the island of Inisquin in the west of Ireland. He eventually joined the community there, going on to found his own monastery on the lake shore.

On a journey to his father's princedom in Munster, Fursey was stricken with a serious illness, which laid him low and put him into a coma. While in this state, he received the first of the extraordinary visions that would characterize his ministry. Fursey saw angels who battled demons for possession of his soul. Good triumphed, but not before the saint had a vision of the fires of hell. On his return to consciousness, his fellow monks observed that he had developed actual burn marks over much of his body—scars that remained with him for the rest of his days.

The saint set out on a mission through Ireland, exorcising demons wherever he found them. He was to preach and exorcise in Wales and East Anglia before settling in northern France in 648. He became bishop of Lagny, near Paris. On his death, his body lay unburied for thirty days and was visited by thousands of pilgrims, many of whom claimed that the corpse showed no decay. A litany attributed to him is in the Trinity College Dublin collection of manuscripts.

Yet, for all the old saints Ireland is said to have produced, and for all their wondrous deeds, there is but meager evidence that they physically engaged, much less overcame, the forces of evil. For historical evidence of exorcism in Ireland we must turn our attention to later centuries. In doing so, we must also briefly examine the traditional alliance between the Devil and witchcraft.

WITCHCRAFT AND EXORCISM

Practitioners of Wicca, or witchcraft, are adamant that their religion is a benign one, that it is no more than a nature religion. Its gods are those of the earth, sea, sky, and forest. They argue that, of all the thousands of adherents in Ireland and other parts of the world, the percentage who use their powers for evil is negligible—no more, they contend, than the percentage of Christians who subvert the message of Jesus for improper ends.

This is unquestionably true. Yet for centuries witches were pursued mercilessly for no better reason than suspicion of diabolic collusion. This was due in part to witches' devotion to the so-called horned god of the forest, a deity who unfortunately bore more than a passing resemblance to the Devil of Christendom. There was more. Witches were said to worship Satan himself during their infamous sabbats, gatherings at which the Devil was sometimes present in person. He was known to "brand" a new recruit with a mark concealed on a part of the body not usually visible.

There is no doubt that witches, or "wise women," played an important role in ancient societies. Where medical doctors were scarce, they provided cures for a variety of common ailments. In many parts of the developing world they still do.

But in doing so, such women were exposing themselves to danger. By openly demonstrating their powers, they were leaving themselves vulnerable to accusations of maleficence in the event an inexplicable malady suddenly beset the community. If God had not poisoned the wells, sickened the livestock, or sent pestilence, then surely the Adversary was responsible. At such times, the local witch, known for her occult arts, became an easy target. In a patriarchal society it was deemed inappropriate that a woman should wield as much influence as did the witch.

THE IRISH WITCHES

The witch trials that raged throughout Europe from about the fourteenth century on were somewhat more subdued in Ireland and England. In fact, only in the late sixteenth century did English law make it an offense to practice witchcraft. In Scotland it was otherwise.

Scottish witches bore the brunt of much of the frenzy. There was wholesale torture, hanging, and burning alive, though not on the same, almost industrial, scale as was witnessed in France and Germany. It is difficult to see in hindsight what the Devil had to do with all this, but as time went on and the madness grew, wild accusations came to be leveled, chief among which was that of a witch having made a pact with Satan. How else but through diabolic abetment could a mere woman exercise power?

The first Irish witch trial took place in 1324: that of Dame Alice Kyteler of Kilkenny, a member of a prominent Anglo-Norman family. It was rumored that she had already dispatched three husbands by poison when, at the urging of the bishop of Ossory, she and her band of reputed sorcerers were arrested. The litany of accusations was lengthy and imaginative. Dame Alice and her cohorts were, it was alleged, guilty of every vice from denying Christ to seeking "by their sorcery advice and responses from demons."

They had, it was reported, sacrificed animals to the Devil; they had wrought spells using mixtures containing "certain horrible worms, various unspecified herbs, dead men's nails, the hair, brains, and shreds of the cerements of boys who had been buried unbaptized, with other abominations, all of which they cooked, with various incantations, over a fire of oak-logs in a vessel made out of the skull of a decapitated thief." Most damning of all, Dame Alice had her very own "familiar" spirit:

The said dame had a certain demon, an incubus, named Son of Art, or Robin son of Art, who had carnal knowledge of her, and from whom she admitted that she had received all her wealth. This incubus made its appearance under various forms, sometimes as a cat, or as a hairy black dog, or in the likeness of a negro (Æthiops), accompanied by two others who were larger and taller than he, and of whom one carried an iron rod.

But Dame Alice escaped punishment; she was well connected. In her stead, her accomplices were pursued and punished. One such victim, Petronilla of Meath, was repeatedly flogged and tortured into confessing her guilt. Her "crimes" included acting as a medium between Alice and a number of demons. At the behest of the bishop, Petronilla was burned alive in Kilkenny on November 3, 1324. This is the first recorded witch burning in Ireland.

THE WITCH OF YOUGHAL

From that time on, the country produced a small number of witch trials, noteworthy among which was that of Florence Newton, the "Witch of Youghal," in County Cork. She was accused in 1661 of casting a spell on a servant girl and causing the death of a boy. Apparently she felt no pain when, during her "examination," an awl was plunged several times into her hand. When called to testify, a witness reported that Florence, like Dame Alice, had demonic "familiars resorting to her in sundry shapes."

A curious aspect of the testimony concerned the Lord's Prayer. It seems that Florence was incapable of reciting it. When asked to do so, "she excused herself by the decay of Memory through old Age."

The fate of the Youghal Witch is not known. It is likely that she was put to death; she was, after all, accused of murder. In total, there are nine recorded witchcraft trials in seventeenth-century Ireland, only two of which resulted in the death of the accused. Later centuries would see even fewer trials.

Similarly, reports of exorcism in Ireland are concentrated in the seventeenth century. A notable case involved what was believed to be a fragment of the True Cross. The relic was preserved in the suitably named Holy Cross Abbey, near Thurles, and attracted a constant stream of pilgrims, for it was reputed to possess miraculous powers of healing. In 1609 a woman named Anastasia Sobechan, a native of County Kilkenny, came to the abbey and told the monks that she was the victim of magic spells.

The abbot, Reverend Bernard Foulow, had someone fetch a belt that had touched the relic of the True Cross, and placed it about Anastasia's waist. As soon as the belt touched her, she began to vomit up pieces of cloth, wood, sheep's wool, and a variety of other foreign objects. This evacuation continued for a month, and there was no doubt in the abbot's mind that the power of the cross had exorcised the evil.

A PRESBYTERIAN EXORCIST

Reverend Robert Blair, a Presbyterian minister, enjoyed a reputation as an exorcist from the time of his arrival in 1623 in the coastal town of Bangor, County Down. Blair recounts one instance where a wealthy parishioner, a Scot, called at his door and requested that they speak in the church. He was trembling. He told the minister that the Devil had appeared to him on a number of occasions, the first time offering him a purse of silver. The Scotsman made the sign of the cross, causing the Devil to vanish at once.

But Satan returned again and again, urging him "to kill and slay" at random. The parishioner refused and fled to Ireland. After the confession to Reverend Blair, the Devil appeared again. He admonished the Scot for seeking the minister's help and promised him that, unless he murdered soon, the Devil would kill him on Halloween.

The night arrived. The Scot went in desperation to the minister, and Blair agreed to hold a vigil with him. They prayed together in the church the night long. The Devil failed to show, and the Scot, in gratitude, devoted the rest of his life to prayer, temperance, and good works.

It was not an exorcism in the fullest sense, but it enhanced Reverend Blair's reputation in the district. Soon after, he encountered many cases of religious hysteria. He described parishioners who suffered bouts of weeping and convulsions. He knew who was behind it: it was, he said, demons "playing the ape, and counterfeiting the works of the Lord."

At worship one particular Sunday, a member of the congregation went berserk. The woman, "one of my charge, being a dull and ignorant person, made a noise and stretching of her body. Incontinent I was assisted to rebuke that lying spirit that disturbed the worship of God, charging the same not to disturb the congregation; and through God's mercy we met with no more of that work."

News of the exorcism reached Archbishop James Ussher, the man responsible for dating Creation to the year 4004 BC. At his next meeting with the minister, he congratulated Blair on a job well done.

These incidents, which Reverend Blair recorded in his autobiography, suggest that exorcism was still a haphazard affair until recent times, and could be carried out at a priest's own discretion without prior consultation with his bishop.

This was to change in 1641. In that year, the solemn rite of exorcism, the Rituale Romanum, or Roman Rite, became standardized in the Catholic Church. It would remain unchanged for over three centuries. In 1971, following the Second Vatican Council, Pope John XXIII overhauled the minor rites of ordination, which included exorcism. Then, in 1999, the Vatican again revised the ritual, shortening it and translating the Latin words into the vernacular.

ROME'S EXORCIST SPEAKS OUT

Those decisions were not well received. Father Gabriele Amorth, Rome's chief exorcist and author of *An Exorcist Tells His Story*, publicly expressed his disdain for the new rite and the Vatican Curia that implemented the changes. "They approved a new ritual which, for the exorcist, is a disaster," he said. "I continue to use the Rituale Romanum, which is still valid. If it were not, I would have to resign."

The 1641 ritual had been drawn up in a time that had witnessed an outbreak of witchcraft across Europe, one that spared few countries. As we have seen, Irish witches were only rarely executed. Elsewhere, a conviction of witchcraft almost always carried the death penalty. In the few instances where clemency was shown, a priest might perform a ceremony of exorcism to drive out the demon that was supposed to have taken possession of the witch. Or the priest might seek to nullify any "pact" the accused had made with Satan.

Although the notion of pacts with the Devil vanished almost entirely in later centuries, pockets of belief and superstition persisted, especially in remote rural areas. In Germany, such superstition, or *Aberglaube*, relied on "names of power" by which a demon might be brought to heel or warded off. As late as the last century, farmers would nail pieces of cardboard above doors and stables before dawn on January 6, Three Kings' Day. The letters CMB were written on the cards, a reference to the magi: Caspar, Melchior, and Balthazar. The ritual was intended to keep Satan—and his minions—away.

THE EXORCISM OF MARY X

One of the most notorious cases of alleged possession had its roots in the closing decade of the nineteenth century. The victim was a girl of fourteen called Mary who was born and raised in an undisclosed location in the American Midwest. She began hearing voices that made obscene suggestions and developed a distaste for anything religious. She could speak in languages she had never learned and manifested many other signs that could indicate demonic possession.

Strangely enough, however, it was not until 1928, when Mary was forty years of age, that she finally agreed to an exorcism—we do not know what happened in the intervening twenty-six years. She was taken to a convent in Earling, Iowa, there to await the arrival of an exorcist.

The man appointed to the task was a German-American priest named Theophilus Riesinger, a member of the Capuchin order. He enjoyed a reputation as a successful banisher of unclean entities. Yet Mary would prove to be the greatest challenge of his career.

Begun on the first day of December, the exorcism was to last for a grueling twenty-three days. Father Riesinger was assisted by his friend and fellow monk Father Joseph Steiger. The two were to experience terrible resistance from a number of demons who appeared to have taken control of the woman, chief among whom was one who identified himself as Beelzebub.

As the days wore on, certain details about Mary's past emerged. The priests discovered that her father, Jacob, had attempted an incestuous relationship with her. We do not know for certain if he succeeded. It also came to light that Mary's mother had killed four of her own infants. It seems that for these crimes the parents, on their deaths, were damned. Among their infernal "tasks" was to demonize their daughter and to curse her.

A fearsome array of demons presented themselves; among them was one called Mina, who, it seems, in life was Jacob's mistress. The demons used many stratagems to thwart the exorcism: Father Steiger had a freak auto accident but survived, and the entities unsuccessfully attempted to drive a wedge between the priests.

Again and again, the Rituale Romanum was enacted, without any outward sign that the victim was responding. Demons continued to speak out of Mary's mouth, at times divulging information that she could not have known. At times the voices could be heard even when Mary's mouth was shut.

But the entities left in the end, two days before Christmas. At their leaving, the priests heard a piercing scream, followed by a raucous cacophony of voices filling the room where the victim lay. Evidently they were those of the demons, including her father and his mistress. Their parting words were, "Beelzebub, Judas, Jacob, Mina—hell, hell, hell!"

The curses had been lifted. Mary regained her own consciousness. Her first words were in praise of Jesus.

SATANISM AND THE BEAST

In England in 1929, a flamboyant braggart named Aleister Crowley (1875–1947) published his *Confessions*, in which he all but admitted "going over" to the Devil. His enemies—and he had made a great number—needed no such admission. Throughout his long career as a magician, scandal followed Crowley wherever he went, and he was accused of all manner of perversion, from satanism to human sacrifice. A newspaper famously called him "the wickedest man in the world"; he himself rejoiced in the title of The Beast—the name by which his own mother knew him.

When he died in a boardinghouse in Hastings, a hopeless drug addict, he bequeathed to posterity a system of magic (or "magick" as he preferred to call it) that was at the very least ambiguous in its dealings with the preternatural, the demonic.

But generally speaking, demonic possession, its prevention and cure, did not figure largely in the early and middle decades of the twentieth century. There were isolated cases, most of which merited little more than a footnote in a news report.

That was to change. "This is the dawning of the Age of Aquarius," sang the chorus of the rock musical *Hair* in 1968, and we were invited to believe that we were entering a period of

Harmony and understanding,
Sympathy and trust abounding;
No more falsehoods or derisions,
Golden living, dreams of visions.

It was a charming but dangerous naiveté. The reality would prove very different indeed.

DEMONS IN A TIME OF SCIENCE AND WONDERS

With the turn of the century—and the millennium—a paradox like no other in history arose. In the face of encroaching secularism and a flowering of science and technology, exorcism was more prominent than it had been for hundreds of years.

Even the pope was engaging in it. In September 2000, John Paul II cast a demon out of a nineteen-year-old Italian woman. She had attended a public audience with the pontiff in St. Peter's Square.

She was brought to Father Gabriele Amorth, who tried twice to rid her of the evil that had taken control. He failed. It was a measure of Amorth's confidence in the pope that he allowed the woman to be brought before him. John Paul prayed over her for more than half an hour, and succeeded in banishing the demon—though only temporarily. At one point, the young woman, in a loud, masculine voice, was heard to bellow: "Not even the head of your Church can send me away!"

Catholics everywhere greeted the news with bemusement tinged with awe; when it became known that it was the *third* exorcism performed by that particular pope while in office, eyebrows were raised even more. Pontiffs are not supposed to soil their hands with the "dirtier work" of the Church; they are expected to fulfill a more symbolic role.

The Holy Father's intervention served also to endorse a growing development within the twenty-first-century Christian Church: the recognition that Satan was at work with a vengeance, and battle had been joined.

Few could have imagined, half a century ago, that the third millennium of Christendom would be ushered in by the pope of Rome battling Christ's greatest adversary. The notion is unsettling for Christian and unbeliever alike. Satan ought not to have a place in our modern world.

Yet there are those who do not doubt that responsibility for many of the world's woes can be laid at the Devil's door. They argue that our species could not possibly visit so much evil on its fellow creatures alone and unaided. It is not part of our make-up, they contend; when men commit the most unspeakable crimes, they are going against human nature.

The debate—an important part of it, in any case—is whether evil is innate or demonic forces are at work in the world, forces that can turn ostensibly normal, rational individuals into monsters. British author and former crime reporter Brian McConnell chooses to believe the latter.

> The twenty-first century is...here, and more and more people are asking whether demonic possession exists. Who else but the demonically possessed could become cult leaders with one solution to life—mass murder and mass suicide; or serial killers; or Satanists; or sectarians slaughtering people in Northern Ireland because they belong to another religion; or religious people ethnically cleansing their fellow human beings in the former Yugoslavia; or tribal rivals committing genocide in holy places in Rwanda?

PRAYER TO ARCHANGEL MICHAEL

The name Michael means in Hebrew "he who is like God." The Archangel Michael is traditionally seen as the archfoe of Satan, since it was he who fought Lucifer and his angels when they challenged God. The Revelation of St. John the Divine (12:7–9) recounts how "there was war in heaven."

> Michael and his angels fought against the dragon; and the dragon fought and his angels, and prevailed not; neither was their place found any more in heaven. And the great dragon was cast out, that old serpent, called the Devil, and Satan, which deceiveth the whole world: he was cast out into the earth, and his angels were cast out with him.

Pope Leo XIII had a curious experience in 1884, toward the end of his reign. In conclave with his cardinals, he suddenly fainted. They feared him dead, but he recovered consciousness with the words: "I have had a terrible vision." He told of the legions of the Devil overrunning the world, yet repulsed in the end by Michael and his forces. The pontiff took the vision to be a sign that the importance of the archangel should be acknowledged, and to this end composed a prayer to be included at the close of all "low" Masses. It is a bone of contention for many Catholics, both clerics and laity, that this prayer—a powerful petition in the fight against evil—was dropped in 1970, during the reign of Pope Paul VI.

Two translations from the original Latin follow. The first is the full prayer, complete with responses, as written by Leo XIII. The second is the shorter version.

PRAYER TO ARCHANGEL MICHAEL
FULL VERSION

Most glorious Prince of the Heavenly Armies, Saint Michael the Arch-angel, defend us in "our battle against principalities and powers, against the rulers of this world of darkness, against the spirits of wickedness in high places" (Ephesians 6:12). Come to the assistance of men whom God has created to His likeness and whom He has redeemed at a great price from the tyranny of the Devil. Holy Church venerates thee as her guardian and protector; to thee, the Lord has entrusted the souls of the redeemed to be led into heaven. Pray, therefore, the God of Peace to crush Satan beneath our feet, that he may no longer retain men captive and do injury to the Church. Offer our prayers to the Most High, that without delay they may draw His mercy down upon us; take hold of the dragon, "the old serpent, which is the Devil and Satan"; bind him and cast him into the bottomless pit, "so that he may no longer seduce the nations" (Revelation 20:3).

In the Name of Jesus Christ, our God and Lord, strengthened by the intercession of the Immaculate Virgin Mary, Mother of God, of Blessed Michael the Archangel, of the Blessed Apostles Peter and Paul and all the Saints, we confidently undertake to repulse the attacks and deceits of the Devil.

"Let God arise, let His enemies be scattered; let those who hate Him flee before Him. As smoke is driven away, so drive them away; as wax melts before the fire, so the wicked perish at the presence of God" (Psalm 68).

V. *Behold the Cross of the Lord, flee bands of enemies.*

R. *He has conquered, the Lion of the tribe of Juda, the offspring of David.*

V. *May Thy mercy, Lord, descend upon us.*

R. *As great as our hope in Thee.*

(At the ✠ make the Sign of the Cross.)

We drive you from us, whoever you may be, every unclean spirit, all satanic powers, all infernal invaders, all wicked legions, assemblies and sects; in the Name and by the power of Our Lord Jesus Christ, ✠ may you be snatched away and driven from the Church of God and from the souls made to the image and likeness of God and redeemed by the Precious Blood of the Divine Lamb. ✠ Most cunning serpent, you shall no more dare to deceive the human race, persecute the Church, torment God's elect and sift them as wheat. ✠ The Most High God commands you. ✠ He with whom, in your great insolence, you still claim to be equal, "He who wants all men to be saved and to come to the knowledge of the truth" (1 Timothy 2:4). God the Father commands you. ✠ God the Son commands you. ✠ God the Holy Ghost commands you. ✠ Christ, God's Word made flesh, commands you. ✠ He who to save our race outdone through your envy, "humbled Himself, becoming obedient even unto death" (Philippians 2:8); He who has built His Church on the firm rock and declared that the gates of hell shall not prevail against Her, because He will dwell with Her "all days, even to the end of the world" (Matthew 28:20). The sacred Sign of the Cross commands you, ✠ as does also the power of the mysteries of the Christian faith. ✠ The glorious Mother of God, the Virgin Mary, commands you. ✠ She who by her humility and from the first moment of her Immaculate Conception, crushed your proud head. The faith of the Holy Apostles Peter and Paul and of the other Apostles commands you. ✠ The blood of the Martyrs and the pious intercession of all the Saints command you. ✠

Thus, cursed dragon, and you, diabolical legions, we adjure you by the living God, ✠ by the true God, ✠ by the holy God, ✠ by the God "who so loved the world that He gave up His only Son, that every soul believing in Him might not perish but have life everlasting" (John 3:16); stop deceiving human creatures and pouring out to them the poison of eternal damnation; stop harming the Church and hindering her liberty. Begone, Satan, inventor and master of all deceit, enemy of man's salvation. Give place to Christ in whom you have found none of your works; give place to the One, Holy, Catholic and Apostolic Church acquired by Christ at the price of His Blood. Stoop beneath the all-powerful Hand of God; tremble and flee when we invoke the Holy and terrible Name of Jesus, this Name which causes hell to tremble, this Name to which the Virtues, Powers and Dominations of Heaven are humbly submissive, this Name which the Cherubim and Seraphim praise unceasingly repeating: Holy, Holy, Holy is the Lord, the God of Armies.

V. O Lord, hear my prayer.

R. And let my cry come unto Thee.

V. May the Lord be with thee.

R. And with thy spirit.

Let us pray.

God of Heaven, God of Earth, God of Angels, God of Archangels, God of Patriarchs, God of Prophets, God of Apostles, God of Martyrs, God of Confessors, God of Virgins, God who has power to give life after death and rest after work, because there is no other God than Thee and there can be no other, for Thou art the Creator of all things, visible and invisible, of whose reign there shall be no end, we humbly prostrate ourselves before Thy glorious Majesty and we beseech Thee to deliver us by Thy power from all the tyranny of the infernal spirits, from their snares, their lies and their furious wickedness; deign, o Lord, to grant us Thy powerful protection and to keep us safe and sound. We beseech Thee through Jesus Christ Our Lord. Amen.

From the snares of the Devil, deliver us, o Lord.

That Thy Church may serve Thee in peace and liberty, we beseech Thee to hear us.

That Thou may crush down all enemies of Thy Church, we beseech Thee to hear us.

Holy water is sprinkled in the place where we may be.

PRAYER TO ARCHANGEL MICHAEL
SHORT VERSION

St. Michael, Archangel, defend us in battle. Be our protection against the wickedness and snares of the Devil. May God rebuke him, we humbly pray; and do thou, O Prince of the Heavenly Host, by the Divine Power, thrust into hell Satan and all the other evil spirits who prowl about the world, seeking the ruin of souls. Amen.

ST. PATRICK'S BREASTPLATE

OR

THE LORICA OF ST. PATRICK

❖

Much of what we know of Ireland's patron saint derives from his *Confessio,* a document comprising a little over ten thousand words and written in Latin—probably his first language. It is part memoir, part meditation.

In later life he wrote in Irish, his adopted language. The "Lúireach Phadraig" may or may not be from his hand, and there are a number of variations in existence. Though commonly known as "St. Patrick's Breastplate," "Lorica of St. Patrick" is perhaps a better translation, since the lorica was segmented Roman upper armor offering protection on *all* sides. This would be in keeping with the spirit of this beautiful prayer, of which a new translation is given here.

I armor myself today
With the power of the Trinity.
I believe in the Trinity,
In the Oneness of God,
Creator of the universe.

I armor myself today
With the grace of the Nativity,
With the Baptism of Christ,
His Crucifixion and Entombment,
His Resurrection and Ascension,
His glorious Second Coming
Upon the Judgment Day.

I armor myself today
With the grace of the seraphim,
The submissiveness of angels,
The attendance of archangels,
The prospect of resurrection,
And everlasting life.
The prayers of patriarchs,
The predictions of prophets,
The preaching of apostles,
The faith of confessors,
The purity of the Virgin,
The deeds of righteous men.

I armor myself today
With the majesty of heaven,
The splendor of the sun,
The brightness of the moon,
The radiance of fire,
The flashing of lightning,

The swiftness of the wind,
The deepness of the ocean,
The vastness of the earth,
The solidity of rocks.

I armor myself today with:
God's power to direct me,
God's might to sustain me,
God's wisdom to instruct me,
God's eye to watch over me,
God's ear to hearken to me,
God's word to give me speech,
God's hand to direct me,
God's way to lie before me,
God's shield to protect me,
God's army to defend me,
Against the snares of demons,
Against the lure of vices,
Against the lusts of nature,
Against all who plot to harm me,
Be they far, or near at hand,
Be they few or be they many.

I invoke today all these virtues
Against every hostile, merciless power
Which may assail my body and my soul,
Against the incantations of false prophets,
Against the black laws of heathenism,
Against the false laws of heresy,
Against the deceits of idolatry,
Against every art and spell that binds
The soul of man and woman.

Christ, guard me today
Against poison,
Against burning,
Against drowning,
Against fatal wounding,
That just reward be mine.
Christ be with me,
Christ be before me,
Christ be behind me,
Christ be within me,
Christ be beside me,
Christ to win me.
Christ to comfort and restore me.
Christ be beneath me,
Christ be above me,
Christ be at my right,
Christ be at my left,
Christ guard me in the home,
Christ be my transport,
By land and by sea,
Christ be in quietude,
Christ be where danger threatens,
Christ be in the hearts
of all who love me,
Christ be in the mouth
of friend and stranger,
Christ be in every eye that sees me,
Christ be in every ear that hears me.

I armor myself today
With the power of the Trinity.
I believe in the Trinity,
In the Oneness of God,
Creator of the universe.

The Lord is salvation,
The Lord is salvation,
Christ is salvation,
May your salvation, O Lord,
be ever with us.

TRANSLATED FROM THE IRISH
BY DAVID M. KIELY

PRAYERS OF EXORCISM

❖

PRAYER AGAINST MALEFICE
(FROM THE GREEK ORTHODOX RITUAL)

God, our Lord, King of Ages, All-powerful and Almighty, you who made everything and who transformed everything simply by your will. You who in Babylon changed into dew the flames of the "seven-times hotter" furnace and protected and saved the three holy children. You are the doctor and the physician of our soul. You are the salvation of those who turn to you.

We beseech you to make powerless, banish, and drive out every diabolical power, presence, and machination; every evil influence, malefice, or evil eye and all evil actions aimed against your servant [name here]. Where there is envy and malice, give us an abundance of goodness, endurance, victory, and charity.

O Lord, you who love mankind, we beg you to reach out your powerful hands and your most high and mighty arms and come to our aid. Help us, who are made in your image; send the angel of peace over us, to protect us body and soul. May he keep at bay and vanquish every evil power, every poison or malice invoked against us by corrupt and envious people. Then under the protection of your authority may we sing, in gratitude: The Lord is my salvation; whom should I fear? I will not fear evil because you are with me, my God, my strength, my powerful Lord, Lord of Peace, Father of All Ages.

Yes, Lord our God, be merciful to us, your image, and save your servant, [name here], from every threat or harm from the Evil One, and protect him by raising him above all evil.

We ask you this through the intercession of our Most Blessed, Glorious Lady, Mary ever Virgin, Mother of God, of the most splendid archangels and all your saints. Amen.

PRAYER AGAINST EVERY EVIL

Spirit of our God, Father, Son and Holy Spirit, Most Holy Trinity, Immaculate Virgin Mary, angels, archangels, and saints of Heaven, descend upon me.

Please purify me, Lord, mold me, fill me with yourself, use me. Banish all forces of evil from me, destroy them, vanquish them, so that I can be healthy and do good deeds.

Banish from me all spells, witchcraft, black magic, malefice, ties, maledictions, and the evil eye; diabolical infestations, oppressions, possessions; all that is evil and sinful, jealousy, perfidy, envy; physical, psychological, moral, spiritual, diabolical ailments.

Burn all these evils in hell, that they may never again touch me or any other creature in the entire world.

I command and bid all the powers who molest me—by the power of God All Powerful, in the name of Jesus Christ our Savior, through the intercession of the Immaculate Virgin Mary—to leave me for ever, and to be consigned into everlasting hell, where they will be bound by St. Michael the Archangel, St. Gabriel, St. Raphael, our guardian angels, and where they will be crushed under the heel of the Immaculate Virgin Mary. Amen.

SELECT BIBLIOGRAPHY

Alexander, William Menzies. *Demonic Possession in the New Testament: Its Historical, Medical and Theological Aspects.* Eugene, OR: Wipf and Stock Publishers, 2001.

Allen, Thomas B. *Possessed: The True Story of the Most Famous Exorcism of Modern Time.* New York: Doubleday, 1993.

Amorth, Gabriele. *An Exorcist: More Stories.* San Francisco: Ignatius Press, 2002.

———. *An Exorcist Tells His Story.* San Francisco: Ignatius Press, 1999.

Clark, Stuart. *Thinking with Demons: The Idea of Witchcraft in Early Modern Europe.* New York: Oxford University Press, 1997.

Cornwell, John. *Powers of Darkness, Powers of Light: Travels in Search of the Miraculous and the Demonic.* London: Penguin, 1991.

Crabtree, Adam. *Multiple Man: Exploration in Possession and Multiple Personality.* London: Grafton Books, 1988.

Cuneo, Michael. *American Exorcism: Expelling Demons in the Land of Plenty.* New York: Doubleday, 2001.

Curran, Robert. *The Haunted: One Family's Nightmare.* New York: St. Martin's Press, 1988.

De Certeau, Michel. *The Possession at Loudun.* Chicago: University of Chicago Press, 2000.

Ebon, Martin (ed.). *Exorcism: Fact Not Fiction.* New York: Signet, 1974.

Ferber, Sarah. *Demonic Possession and Exorcism in Early Modern France.* London: Routledge, 2004.

Finlay, Anthony. *Demons! The Devil, Possession and Exorcism.* London: Cassell Illustrated, 1999.

Klass, Morton. *Mind over Mind: The Anthropology and Psychology of Spirit Possession.* Lanham, MD: Rowman & Littlefield, 2003.

Lendrum, Canon Revd. W. H. *Confronting the Paranormal: A Christian Perspective.* Belfast: Self-published, 2002.

Lewis, I. M. *Ecstatic Religion: Anthropological Study of Spirit Possession and Shamanism.* London: Penguin, 1971.

Lutzer, Erwin W. *Serpent of Paradise: The Incredible Story of How Satan's Rebellion Serves God's Purposes.* Chicago: Moody, 2001.

———. *Seven Snares of the Enemy: Breaking Free from the Devil's Grip.* Chicago: Moody, 2001.

Martin, Malachi. *Hostage to the Devil: The Possession and Exorcism of Five Contemporary Americans.* San Francisco: HarperSanFrancisco, 1992.

McAll, Kenneth. *Healing the Family Tree.* London: Sheldon Press, 1982.

McConnell, Brian. *The Possessed: True Tales of Demonic Possession.* London: Headline, 1995.

McNutt, Francis. *Deliverance from Evil Spirits: A Practical Manual.* Grand Rapids: Baker, 1995.

Oughourlian, Jean-Michel. *The Puppet of Desire: Psychology of Hysteria, Possession and Hypnosis.* Stanford, CA: Stanford University Press, 1991.

Peck, M. Scott. *Glimpses of the Devil: A Psychiatrist's Personal Accounts of Possession, Exorcism, and Redemption.* New York: Simon & Schuster, 2005.

———. *People of the Lie: The Hope for Healing Human Evil.* New York: Simon & Schuster, 1983.

Pelton, Robert W. *Confrontations with the Devil: Arts of Exorcism.* New York: Yoseloff, 1980.

Pocs, Eva, and Gabor Klaniczay (eds.). *Communicating with the Spirits: Christian Demonology and Popular Mythology: Demons, Spirits and Witches.* Vol. 1. Budapest and New York: Central European University Press, 2005.

Richards, John. *But Deliver Us from Evil: An introduction to the Demonic Dimension in Pastoral Care.* London: Darton, Longman & Todd, 1974.

Seymour, St. John D. *Irish Witchcraft and Demonology* (1913). New York: Causeway, 1973.

Van der Toorn, Karel, et al. (eds.). *Dictionary of Deities and Demons in the Bible.* Leiden & Grand Rapids: Brill, 1999.

READER'S NOTES

❖

Page numbers reference topics that appear in the various chapters and are linked to text found on those pages.

INTRODUCTION: EXORCISM IN OUR TIME

XVI BURNING LAKES AND CAVERNS: The Christian conception of hell has an intriguing history. The notion of a flaming pit dates from biblical times, when the inhabitants of Jerusalem burned their rubbish in the Valley of Hinnom, to the south of the city. In Hebrew the name was rendered as Ge Hinnom, which came to be corrupted to Gehenna. Fires burned day and night in Gehenna, as the city disposed of its detritus—which included, rather brutally, the corpses of those who had been executed, i.e., those condemned to death.

The metaphorical step from "the condemned" to "the damned" was an easy one for the ancients to take, particularly because the Valley of Hinnom was also the site of an old temple to Moloch, the malevolent solar (or fire) deity of the Canaanites. Moloch's enormous bronze statue was hollow, and a fire burned perpetually within. The Israelites sacrificed their firstborn to him. Evidently, they were confusing the entity with Yahweh, whom they sought to propitiate. The victims, after being ritually killed, were placed in the idol's hands and raised to the mouth by a system of pulleys, thereby simulating their devouring by the fire-god. The practice continued into the sixth century BC.

XVI VAST HOSTS OF DEMON ARMIES: Milton was relying for the most part on *Pseudo-monarchia Daemonum,* a catalogue of demons compiled in 1583 by the German necromancer Johann Weyer (1515–88). Derived from earlier works of magic, it lists 7,405,926 demons, all under the command of sixty-nine Princes of Hell, each of whom commands legions of lesser demons. The Englishman Reginald Scot published a translation the following year in *The Discoverie of Witchcraft.* In 1904 S. L. McGregor Mathers, who cofounded the Hermetic Order of the Golden Dawn, a magical society based in London, published a new translation of *The Goetia: The Lesser Key of Solomon the King*, with the addition of a further three chief demons, bringing the total to seventy-two.

XVI ADMONISHMENTS OF THE BESTIARY: Bestiaries were medieval books illustrating mythical creatures such as the unicorn and the manticore. Each drawing was accompanied by a morality lesson. The earliest form dates from second-century Greece, and they were extremely popular in twelfth-century France and England. The bestiary often served as a legitimate zoological guide, but toward the close of the seventeenth century its influence waned as science overtook myth and superstition.

XIX TIMOTHY LEARY: The son of an Irish-American dentist, Timothy Francis Leary (1920–96) was educated by the Jesuits in Massachusetts. He completed degrees in psychology in Alabama and California, becoming a lecturer at Harvard. Having taken magic mushrooms in Mexico, he went on to explore the therapeutic benefits of hallucinogens, such as psilocybin and lysergic acid diethylamide (LSD). He was dismissed from Harvard for allowing his students to experiment with the latter. Leary protested that his work had importance in the treatment of alcoholism and in criminal reform, but he is remembered chiefly for his advocacy of "mind-expanding" drug use, as encapsulated in his catch-phrase: "Turn on, tune in, drop out."

XIX THE MOMENT THE MOVIE WAS SHOWN: *The Exorcist* was never banned in Ireland, but was screened with some of the more lurid scenes and those containing blasphemy deleted. The uncut version was re-released for Irish cinemas in 1998. In 1995, twenty-five years after the film's debut, it was finally allowed on video and DVD in the UK. The delay was caused by a number of allegations, such as claims that its showing had led to the suicides of young people and the "satanic" child-abuse scandals of 1989.

Criticism in Europe and elsewhere was mixed. The Tunisian authorities banned it outright, claiming it was "propaganda" for Christianity. At the same time, the film reviewer in *The Times* of London commented that "*The Exorcist* lacks any kind of resonance and shows little sense of the way in which good and evil might be seen to function in our society." All the same, a video release was banned in both Britain and Finland, as well as in other countries. The ban was lifted only recently. In 2001, the state of Victoria, Australia, refused to allow a television network to screen the movie on Good Friday—which happened to fall on the thirteenth of the month.

XXIII PSYCHIATRIST DR. KENNETH MCALL: Robert Kenneth McAll (1910–2001) was born in China and worked as a doctor in a mission hospital when the country was under Japanese occupation. When the United States entered WWII, he and his family were interned and suffered great hardship. After the war the McAlls moved to Britain, and Kenneth went on to qualify as a psychiatrist, eventually progressing to private practice. A devout Christian, he came to perceive the spiritual dimension in many cases of mental illness. His first book, *Healing the Family Tree* (1984), advanced the revolutionary—and hotly disputed—proposition that the deeds of one's ancestors can have a bearing on contemporary mental problems.

Dr. McAll relates the case of a patient whom he calls Margaret. After her mother died, the seventy-three-year-old began having outbursts of aggression, which took the form of unprovoked attacks on Violet, her younger sister. Margaret would go wild, breaking things and being uncharacteristically abusive. Afterward, she would be genuinely remorseful but unable to explain her behavior. The doctor learned that her mother had behaved in much the same way throughout her life.

With the help of Violet, Dr. McAll drew up a family tree covering six generations. They found that in 1750 a murder had been committed in the family and that subsequently the eldest daughter died from alcoholism, but not before she had destroyed much of the family property.

From that time on, the eldest female in each generation presented similar disturbing behavior. This continued on down to Margaret, who was born in 1904.

Moreover, Margaret's thirty-two-year-old niece, Rhonda, the eldest daughter of her youngest sister, was undergoing psychiatric treatment for a similar malady. Her husband had threatened divorce when, on returning home on several occasions, he found the house trashed—an eerie echo of the ancestor's destructive bouts.

Dr. McAll, together with two clergymen and Violet, offered a Eucharist for Margaret and Rhonda, and for the eldest females of the previous six generations. The service was held in private and without the knowledge of Margaret and Rhonda. The doctor records that, with the conclusion of the service, neither woman required any further psychiatric care. Rhonda's husband dropped his threat of divorce, and Margaret became the loving, quiet sister that Violet had always known.

XXVI THE CURÉ D'ARS: Jean-Baptiste-Marie Vianney (1786–1859) is perhaps France's most celebrated saint. He was born in Dardilly, near Lyons, of poor farming stock. He started school at the age of twenty and proved to be a below-average student. It took him ten years to struggle through his exams (he failed Latin twice) and so realize his ambition of becoming a priest.

In 1815 he was given his first parish. The parishioners were not impressed, believing him too stupid for the task, and they circulated a petition to have him removed. When the petition reached Jean he agreed that he was indeed inadequate and duly signed it too. On reading the list of signatories, the bishop was amused but took Jean's side.

In 1818 he was sent to Ars to be parish priest, or curé. Soon word spread about the holy man's ability to "see into people's souls" and his extraordinary healing ability. By 1855, thousands were flocking to him for healing.

He would fast for days, hear confessions for eighteen hours a day, and get by on only one or two hours' sleep. For thirty-five years Satan is said to have attacked him, trying constantly to break his will. The abuse took the form of severe beatings and strident noises—singing in a deafening voice and shouting, "Vianney! Vianney! Potato Eater!" This last was a reference to what the Curé d'Ars would eat after days of near starvation.

The Devil allegedly told him, in frustration, that if there were just three men on earth like him, Satan's kingdom would be at an end.

xxx A "SUITABLE" EXORCIST: In *Hostage to the Devil*, the former Jesuit Malachi Martin offers a more elaborate definition of what constitutes the ideal exorcist.

> Usually he is engaged in the active ministry of parishes. Rarely is he a scholarly type engaged in teaching or research. Rarely is he a recently ordained priest. If there is any median age for exorcists, it is probably between the ages of fifty and sixty-five. Sound and robust physical health is not a characteristic of exorcists, nor is proven intellectual brilliance, postgraduate degrees, even in psychology or philosophy, or a very sophisticated personal culture…. Though, of course, there are many exceptions, the usual reasons for a priest's being chosen are his qualities of moral judgment, personal behavior and religious beliefs—qualities that are not sophisticated or laboriously acquired, but that somehow seem always to have been an easy and natural part of such a man. Speaking religiously, these are qualities associated with special grace.

xxxi THE FAITH MOVEMENT: Michael Cuneo is bringing together the various strands of evangelism operating in America today. They are the successors to preachers of earlier decades like Oral Roberts and A. A. Allen. Their leaders include charismatic individuals such as Benny Hinn, the team of Robert Tilton and Marilyn Hickey, Kenneth E. Hagin, Kenneth Copeland, and Paul Crouch and his wife, Jan, whose Trinity Broadcasting Network has assets exceeding $600 million.

THE HOUSEWIFE AND THE DEMON DUBOIS

39 CASES OF DEMONIC ATTACK: Possession or infestation is usually defined as the appropriation of a person's psyche by a preternatural entity. Most com-

mentators are of the opinion that such an entity can only gain access when the person chooses to allow it. Julie, in contrast, fought against the entity, and it was never able to possess her to any extent. It goes without saying that it is far more difficult to banish an entity that has gained full or partial control of its victim.

47 ONE WHO LIES UPON: *Incubus* has the same root as *incubation*, originally the process by which a bird hatches her eggs, i.e., by sitting on them. With the naming of the hospital incubator, the device that assists a premature infant, the idea of lying or sitting upon was lost. It is perhaps significant that the Latin *incubito* means "to defile."

The word *nightmare* has curious origins. In fact, it has nothing at all to do with horses. We can trace the root of *mare* to the Anglo-Saxon verb *merran* or *myrran*, meaning "to obstruct" or "to impede," which is related to Old Icelandic *merja* (pronounced "mer-ya"), meaning "to bruise" or "to crush." According to Nordic folklore, the *mare* or *mara* was an evil spirit known to visit women at night and paralyze them. Often there was a sexual dimension to the haunting but certainly not in all cases. It was believed that other demons actually had sexual intercourse with humans while they slept; the entity that attacked women was known as the incubus, while the succubus molested sleeping men.

53 IN THE NAME OF JESUS CHRIST: It will be seen that the uttering of the Lord's name is a common feature of the cases covered in this book. From earliest Christian times it was held that the name of Jesus contained great power and could be used for the subjugation of demons. In Acts of the Apostles 16:18 we read: "But Paul, being grieved, turned and said to the spirit, I command thee in the name of Jesus Christ to come out of her. And he came out the same hour." See also Appendix 2, p. 361.

THE BOY WHO COMMUNES WITH DEMONS

73 A MILD FORM OF EPILEPSY: There are a number of misconceptions surrounding epilepsy, not least being the belief that it is a mental illness. In fact, it is a type of physical dysfunction that takes the form of a seizure, which can occur (and recur) at any time. Epilepsy is caused by abnormal electrical activity in the brain and can be treated with medication or surgery, although not all sufferers respond equally well. It is more common than many people imagine. Dr. John Wilkinson, author of "The Bible and Healing: A Medical and Theological Commentary" in *Review of Biblical Literature* (2000), is among those who have researched the historical incidence of epilepsy and a possible link to possession. "If demon possession is a fact, there seems no reason why it could not be the cause of some cases of epilepsy," he argues. "We do not know enough about the spirit world to disprove demon possession nor enough about epilepsy to deny that it may be caused by such possession."

73 COMMONLY CALLED A SEIZURE: In brief, a seizure is a sudden and erratic firing of neurons that effects a change in behavior. The so-called myoclonic seizure would be the first suspect in Gary Lyttle's attack, as it results in muscle spasms on both sides of the body. It is, however, of short duration, in contrast to Gary's attacks or "spells."

Epileptic seizures were undoubtedly one cause of the persecution of Europe's witches in earlier centuries, since frequently the seizures suffered by epileptics were identified as the mark of a witch.

In 1494, two German monks, at the behest of the Vatican, produced the definitive handbook on witch hunting, *Malleus Maleficarum* (the Hammer of Witches), which linked seizures and diabolic control. Apart from Hitler's *Mein Kampf* and the *Thoughts of Chairman Mao*, there can hardly have been a more incendiary book in the history of mass murder. The *Malleus* was largely responsible for the deaths of hundreds of thousands of innocent people, mainly women. We have no way of knowing how many of its victims were actually epileptics.

THE UNQUIET SPIRIT OF CHILD SARAH

105 EVIDENCE OF "PSYCHOKINETIC" ENERGY: It is also known as telekinetic energy. The most celebrated pioneer in the field of parapsychology and related research was Joseph Banks Rhine (1895–1980). In 1966, he and a number of colleagues, including J. Gaither Pratt and Charles E. Stuart, published the definitive work on PK: *Extra-sensory Perception After Sixty Years: A Critical Appraisal of the Research in Extra-Sensory Perception.* This was based on results first published in 1940.

Recent research into the PK phenomenon itself—as purportedly demonstrated by groups of people who lift heavy objects with the power of the mind alone—was led by British psychologist Kenneth J. Batcheldor, who believes that "unconscious muscular action" is the basis for telekinesis, which relies to a great extent on the faith of the participants. He holds that fear is the key: that it is the fear of the power itself that inhibits the successful application of PK.

LITTLE LUCY AND THE PHANTOM FAMILY

150 "RESIDUAL" OR "MENTAL IMPRINT" HAUNTING: Peter Underwood, Britain's foremost researcher into the paranormal and author of *The Autobiography of a Ghost-Hunter* (1983), broadly categorizes ghosts thus:

1. Elemental (or primitive or racial-memory) manifestations. They are mainly seen in rural areas and in particular sites. They are rare and appear to be malevolent.

2. Poltergeists, which include death-bed visions and manifestations triggered by crises or traumas.

3. Traditional or historical ghosts. They usually dress in period clothing and follow old floor plans of houses and other buildings, thereby appearing to "walk" several inches above the floor. They neither speak nor interact with the observer. Often it is found that they are the ghosts of those who suffered trauma during their lifetimes.

4. Mental imprints. They are some kind of imprint upon the atmosphere and resemble holographic images. Often they must be viewed from a specific angle and at a given time. The manifestation they produce never alters, as though a film sequence is being played back over and over.

5. Time distortion and cyclic ghosts. They seem to be replays of past events, often the reenactment of famous battles.

6. Ghosts of the living, which may be part of the phenomenon known as bilocation, or the result of clairvoyance and telepathy. Observers claim that the apparition is all but indistinguishable from the real person.

All the ghosts seen by Lucy Gillespie seem to fall into more than one of these categories, in particular the third and fourth.

THE PIT BENEATH THE HEARTHSTONE

173 THE MYTH OF THE BANSHEE: It is difficult to say whether the belief was common to all Celtic peoples or if it was brought to other parts of Great Britain by visitors from Ireland. Certainly the Scottish variant bears more than a passing resemblance to her Irish counterpart, as does the Gwrach-y-rhybin, the Welsh equivalent. According to legend, this "night-hag" has much in common with the banshee, attaching herself to ancient families, in other words, nobility. She is ugly, with long black hair and garments. In some versions of the legend she has black wings, too, and often flies low over the landscape. When lamenting an imminent death, she imitates the voice of the soon-to-be-bereaved. For instance, she will cry something like, "Oh, my poor husband!" if a woman is to be widowed.

The banshee and her Celtic cousins may be a throwback to pagan worship of the Dark Goddess or Crone, who was an aspect of the Goddess, the others being the Maiden and the Mother.

183 LAY BENEATH THE HEARTHSTONE: There can be no underestimating the importance of the hearth and hearthstone in rural Irish life in past centuries, and still today in certain outlying communities. There were plantations in the sixteenth century, and wholesale confiscation of lands in Munster and Ulster in the mid-seventeenth century. The "rebel" chieftains and their tribes were driven "to the fern." Those evictions left an indelible hurt on the Irish psyche,

and led to an exaggerated importance being placed on the home hearth. There is even a notable Irish maxim that says, *Níl aon tinteán mar do thinteán fhéin:* "There's no hearth like your own hearth."

It should be remembered, too, that those dispossessed by foreign planters were of families who had occupied the same land for hundreds, if not thousands, of years.

The poet Lauchlan MacLean Watt (1867–1957) summarized the Irish obsession with the hearthstone:

> A man who loves his own hearthstone, and all it stands for, always carries into every conflict a principle of more sacred steadfastness than the homeless, nameless, characterless and hopeless outcast who has no anchorage for his soul.... When I was young we learned at our fireside the native names of our towns, rivers, clan and family names—our genealogy, the story of our people and the ideals which ought to be ours.

In ancient times, the hearthstone was bound up with a variety of rituals. One example was the chieftain's practice of burying one or two of his enemies under the hearthstone of a new dwelling or fort. This was believed to bring luck.

A less gruesome use was found for the stone by a mother-to-be. To avoid having her child stolen by the fairies and a so-called changeling substituted, she would crush a new potato on the hearthstone.

MR. GANT AND THE NEIGHBOR FROM HELL

200 THERE'S NO GOD HERE: This is strikingly similar to the utterance of the demented nun in the case entitled "The Temptation of Father Fintan." In one, the site of the manifestation was Lourdes; in the other, Luxor, ancient Thebes of the Egyptians. Both are or were sacred sites. The two instances seem to give the lie to the common supposition that such sacred places are out of bounds to demonic influences.

205 THE SMURL FAMILY IN PENNSYLVANIA: The case is the subject of *The Haunted: One Family's Nightmare* by Robert Curran (1988). It details the extraordinary manifestations that terrorized the Smurls—infestations that could be banished only after four exorcisms. Ed and Lorraine Warren—who collaborated in the writing of the book—conducted the most extensive investigations into the phenomena and were themselves apparently the target of demonic attack. Ed Warren has the distinction of being the world's only lay demonologist trained by the Vatican.

208 MY NAME IS LEGION: Some believe that the notorious New York serial killer who called himself Son of Sam was demonically possessed. Sam Berkowitz, who embarked on a horrific murder spree in the 1970s, was asked his name

when arrested. He replied: "My name is Legion, for we are many," the precise words contained in Mark's Gospel (5:9). It remains a puzzle as to why Berkowitz, an orthodox Jew, should have quoted the New Testament, a collection of books normally read only by Christians. As with the demoniac of Scripture, cemeteries held a curious fascination for Berkowitz; he liked to spend time among the tombstones, especially those of the women he murdered.

Interestingly, Peter Sutcliffe, England's "Yorkshire Ripper," also worked in a cemetery. He claimed it was while he was digging a grave there that a voice spoke to him from the grave of a Polish man. The voice told him that his mission in life was to rid the streets of prostitutes. Between 1975 and 1981, Sutcliffe attacked twenty women, not all of whom were prostitutes. Only seven survived his savage assaults.

Sutcliffe underwent several exorcisms conducted by a Catholic priest while awaiting trial in Armley jail, Leeds.

217 St. Benedict medal: The saint was born in Nursia, near Rome, ca. 480, and went on to found the monastic order that bears his name. This particular medal features a cross with the letters CSPB, signifying *Crux Sancti Patris Benedicti*, the cross of Father Benedict. The cross was a favorite Benedictine emblem. Inscribed also are the initial letters of a Latin prayer, which translates as "May the holy cross be my light. May the dragon never be my guide." Just why this saint came to be associated with exorcism is not clear. Many miracles were attributed to him, some of Christlike proportions, such as enabling a follower to walk on water. Such miracles would have identified Benedict in the minds of the faithful as one possessing power over Satan.

THE HESSIAN WHO RETURNED TO HAUNT

238 The spirit of a Hessian: The notoriety of the Hessians may be unearned. They were, it is true, mercenary soldiers, although not in the same sense by which we understand mercenaries today. They were a private army recruited in the main by Count Frederick II of Hesse-Kassel, a principality in northern Hesse, Germany. They owed allegiance to their aristocratic masters but were not well paid; in fact, many drew only the cost of food and lodgings in return for their fighting skills.

They first made their appearance on the international stage during the American War of Independence, when some thirty thousand of them fought on the side of King George III, who was monarch to a great many of them. The Hessians distinguished themselves in a number of engagements.

In Ireland, the position was somewhat different. Coming, as it did, two decades after the War of Independence, the Rising of 1798 was fought by a different body of Hessians. Many accounts from that time depict an undisciplined and savage band of mercenaries, many of whom were drawn from prisons or were impressed into service, and whose conduct led to their being held in loathing by the Irish people. Whereas the name of Hessian carries with it few negative connotations in American history, in Ireland it is reviled.

THE WOMAN WHO LEFT HER BODY AT WILL

245 TUESDAY LOBSANG RAMPA: Cyril Henry Hoskins (1911–81) made a spectacular literary debut in 1956 with *The Third Eye: The Autobiography of a Tibetan Lama,* in which he claimed to be a Buddhist master. Millions of copies were sold around the world. The writer was actually a plumber's son from Devon, a fact uncovered by a private detective hired by a group of academics who grew more than a little suspicious of "Dr." Rampa's teaching, and by extension his bona fides. By way of explanation, Hoskins revealed that the real Lobsang Rampa had taken over his body as a means of continuing his teaching. Hoskins went on to publish many more books, sustained by a gullible public. Eventually, however, mounting allegations of fraud forced him to flee to Canada, where he died in obscurity.

255 CLAIRVOYANCE, REMOTE VIEWING: The two terms are cognate, though the latter has come to be associated with, among others, the U.S. military, which sought to develop this "gift" in groups of volunteers. The research went by different titles, beginning in the 1970s as a response to reports of Soviet investigation into so-called "PsyOps"; the final phase was Project Star Gate, which was abandoned in 1999. Although more than $20 million was spent, it is not known if any success was achieved, and skeptics cast doubt on the claims made by the participants. Clairvoyance should not be confused with astral projection, which appears to be an altogether different phenomenon, related to the near-death experience reported by many.

256 MEMBERS OF THE GOLDEN DAWN: This was the Hermetic Order of the Golden Dawn, a magical society founded along Rosicrucian lines in London in 1887 by three Freemasons. Aside from W. B. Yeats, its membership included the notorious Aleister Crowley. Several of its rituals were based on ancient documents translated by S. L. MacGregor Mathers, one of the founders, including the fearsome *Goetia, the Lesser Key of Solomon the King* and *The Book of the Sacred Magic of Abra-Melin the Mage.* The Golden Dawn drew on the philosophies of ancient Egypt and Greece, combined with threads of gnosticism and the Jewish Qabalah. It inspired many of the magical lodges found throughout the world today.

262 DAVID KORESH AND JIM JONES: James Warren Jones (1931–78) set the precedent for the charismatic cult leader who induces mass suicide in his followers. Jones was born in Indiana to a father who was a member of the Ku Klux Klan, and from an early age seemed determined to make reparations. On becoming a minister, he actively sought to embrace black America and

promote racial equality. He founded the Peoples Temple in Indianapolis, but in 1977 moved it to Guyana, South America, when he was accused of tax evasion. Most of his one thousand followers joined him, where they established a commune in the jungle.

Jones was becoming increasingly delusional, claiming to be an incarnation of Jesus Christ, the Buddha, and others, and to be capable of performing miracles. He ruled his "people" with an iron fist, demanding total obedience. When U.S. authorities moved to arrest him, his men fatally ambushed the party, including a senator. Jones then induced his remaining 914 disciples—including 276 children—to commit suicide by consuming a soft drink laced with cyanide.

David Koresh (1959–93) was born Vernon Wayne Howell in Houston, Texas. He never knew his father and was sexually abused by his stepfather. He went to California to become a rock guitarist but failed. He returned to Texas and joined a breakaway sect of Seventh-Day Adventists calling itself the Branch Davidians. Soon after, Koresh proclaimed himself leader. There were growing reports of brainwashing and child abuse at the Davidian ranch near Waco, as well as accusations that Koresh demanded sex from any female member he chose. In 1993, the FBI raided the farm. The fifty-one-day siege resulted in the deaths of four agents and seventy-six sect members, including Koresh. It was found that several adults had killed their own children before shooting themselves.

266 THE COLLECTIVE UNCONSCIOUS: Carl Gustav Jung (1875–1961) was born and spent most of his life in Switzerland. As a pioneering psychiatrist, he collaborated with Sigmund Freud for many years until they had a notorious falling-out after WWI, owing to Freud's fixation on sexuality as the root of numerous psychological problems. Jung became immersed in spirituality and the symbolism of dreams. He developed many theories on the subconscious mind, including the notion of the collective unconscious (which he later referred to as the objective psyche) and the archetypes: symbols common to all human beings and arising in that part of the psyche "shared" by all.

The New England Transcendentalists, a group of writers led by Ralph Waldo Emerson, perceived a similarity between Jung's collective unconscious and the concept of the oversoul. They believed that both ideas referred to a force pervading the universe upon which all individual human souls may draw, thus enabling one to communicate with God. It transcends the individual soul or consciousness.

DEVILRY ON THE DINGLE PENINSULA

306 DEAD BLACK FLIES: Flies seem to figure in an inordinate number of hauntings that have unpleasant overtones. In this regard it is intriguing to

note that the archdemon Beelzebub is sometimes known as Lord of the Flies. Indeed, this appears to be a Hebrew-Aramaic translation of the name itself, in earlier texts rendered as Baalzebûb. It is also cognate with the Philistine god Ba'al, who may or may not have been a malevolent entity.

332 DEALING WITH THE PRETERNATURAL: It is often thought that the terms *preternatural* and *supernatural* are interchangeable. In fact, *supernatural* should be used only in reference to God and that which is of God. A preternatural entity, such as an evil spirit, is considered to be superior in power to a human being but inferior to the divine.

334 HOLY WATER AND INCENSE: The use of incense predates Christianity by many centuries, if not millennia. There are countless references to it in the Old Testament, for example: "And Aaron shall burn thereon sweet incense every morning...a perpetual incense before the Lord throughout your generations" (Exodus 30:7–8). The New Testament also mentions it, for instance, in Revelation 8:3–4: "And another angel came and stood at the altar, having a golden censer; and there was given unto him much incense, that he should offer it with the prayers of all saints upon the golden altar which was before the throne. And the smoke of the incense, which came with the prayers of the saints, ascended up before God out of the angel's hand." However, there is no record of its Christian use until the fifth century. The symbolism of incensation is threefold: the burning zeal of the faithful, the fragrance of virtue, and the ascent of prayer on high. The cloud it produces may also symbolize the incorporeal nature of the divine.

APPENDIX 1: EXORCISM AND HISTORY

339 SANSKRIT: One of the oldest Indo-European languages, written Sanskrit is some 3,500 years old. Today it occupies a position similar to that of Latin in the Christian Churches, being the liturgical language of Hinduism, Buddhism, and Jainism. There have been recent attempts to revive it as a vernacular.

342 BOOK OF TOBIT: From 6:8. Protestantism regards this biblical book as apocryphal. In older Catholic Bibles it is known as the Book of Tobias, Tobias being the son of Tobit, a Jew who was exiled in Nineveh, Mesopotamia.

344 POPE CORNELIUS: The emperor Caius Messius Quintus Decius reigned in Rome from AD 249 until his death in 251. This was a time of great persecution of Christians, enthusiastically continued by his successor, Caius Gallus, who, it seems, died in the same year as the exiled pontiff. Although Cornelius was declared a martyr, there is no evidence that he suffered a violent death. Novatian, the theologian who took his place in 251, thereby creating a schism, was also exiled and was said to have died a martyr.

345 EAGLE MOUNTAIN: The god Lugh, father of Cúchulainn, had his place in all the Celtic pantheons. The Welsh knew him as Llew Llaw Gyffes, "Lew of the Versatile Arm." To the Gauls he was Lugos. In ancient Ireland he was known as Lugh Lámhfada, or "Lugh of the Long Arm." He was a solar deity possessed of many skills, including medicine and brewing. He was also a shape-shifter, his favored animal being a raven, sometimes an eagle. This last might account for the old name of Croagh Patrick.

345 MOSES IN THE SINAI: "Now Moses kept the flock of Jethro his father in law, the priest of Midian: and he led the flock to the backside of the desert, and came to the mountain of God, even to Horeb" (Exodus 3:1). The biblical Horeb, where Moses communed with God, was renamed Mount Sinai by Greek Orthodox monks in the fourth century AD. There is some confusion today when identifying it; Gebel Mûsa (Moses's Mountain) is taken to be the original Horeb, although the nearby (and smaller) Mount Serabit seems a better contender, being the site of an ancient Egyptian temple to Hathor.

The temple site was excavated in 1904 by Sir William Matthew Flinders Petrie. Mount Serabit (Serabît el-Khâdim) lies some twenty miles east of the Gulf of Suez and nearly one hundred miles from the border with Israel.

346 ST. ANTHONY ON HIS MOUNTAINTOP: Sometimes known as St. Anthony the Great, he was born in upper Egypt in AD 251 to wealthy parents, became a hermit, and wandered in a mountainous desert region some sixty miles west of Alexandria. His hagiographer, Athanasius, recorded that Anthony was subjected to a bewildering gamut of dreams, hallucinations, and temptations. These last have had an enduring influence on Christendom, becoming the inspiration of several painters, from Hieronymus Bosch to Dali.

In 1874 the French philosopher Gustave Flaubert published his masterpiece *The Temptation of St. Anthony*. It is a drama that features a bewildering cast of players, from ancient kings to the Devil, all of whom try to tempt the hermit away from the spiritual path. The dream aspect of the work influenced the young Sigmund Freud.

Flaubert's translator, Lafcadio Hearn, summarized the more lascivious temptations: "His thoughts wander...he dreams of Amonaria, his sister's playmate.... He beholds the orgies, the luxuries, the abominations...and the Queen of Sheba descends to tempt the Saint with the deadliest of all temptations. Her beauty is enhanced by oriental splendor of adornment; her converse is a song of witchcraft."

346 LUGH NA DEAMHAIN: It is unfortunate that the name of the Celtic deity Lugh is so close to the old Irish word *lug*, which means "hollow" or "valley." The word has survived unaltered in other Irish place names that have undergone a crude anglicization, e.g., Lugnaquilla or Lug na Coille, "The Wooded

Hollow." The addition of the aspirative *h* may well have been an attempt by the early Church to demonize Lugh. Interestingly, his name is also a cognate of the Latin *luceo*, "to be bright," from which the name Lucifer, or "Shining One," is derived. Lugh was the Celtic solar god, the bringer of light and, as such, an important heathen deity. It would have been natural for the early churchmen, in their efforts to supplant the "false" gods, to identify him with an evil entity.

346   AN DIABHAL: The Devil has a fascinating etymology. Linguists trace the word's origin to the Sanskrit *deva*, meaning "god" or "giver of light." (Intriguingly, it is also close to *diva*, the leading light of the opera.) Via the Greek verb *diabalein*, meaning "to oppose," the word entered Latin as *diabolus*, Italian as *diabolo*, French as *diable*, and English as *diabolic*. German and Dutch rendered the consonantal sounds as *Teufel* and *duivel*, the latter becoming "devil" upon reaching Britain. It is possibly no more than coincidence that the Irish version, *diabhal*, contains within it *dia*, "god." This is derived from the Latin *deus* and has another root entirely. The word *god* seems to be largely a late European innovation. It appears in German, Dutch, Danish, and Swedish as, respectively *Gott*, *god*, *gud*, and *gud*. There have been attempts to trace the root back to the Sanskrit *hu*, "to invoke." It seems a weak argument. That root has indeed come down to us, though in a different context: the "hue" of "hue and cry."

350   FIRST IRISH WITCH TRIAL: One would expect that Ireland, given its reputation as the "natural" home of all things paranormal, had more than its fair share of witches and sorcerers. Not so, according to St. John D. Seymour, who, in 1913, published *Witchcraft and Demonology in Ireland*, an exhaustive work that examined the phenomena from 1324 to 1808. He concluded that witchcraft was far less prevalent there than in England and Scotland and offered a curious explanation. He noted that fairy lore was largely confined to the "Celtic" section of the community, whereas the "English" in Ireland—the descendants of the Anglo-Norman colonists—were more likely to practice witchcraft. In short, witchcraft and sorcery were principally Protestant phenomena. He wrote:

> In England after the Reformation we seldom find members of the Roman Catholic Church taking any prominent part in witch cases, and this is equally true of Ireland from the same date. Witchcraft seems to have been confined in the Protestant party, as far as we can judge from the material at our disposal, while it is probable that the existence of the penal laws (active or quiescent) would deter the Roman Catholics from coming into any prominence in a matter which would be likely to attract public attention to itself in such a marked degree.

352 MADE THE SIGN OF THE CROSS: The symbolism of this minor ritual has a colorful history. Obviously, it represents the cross upon which Christ was crucified, which came to symbolize the Christian Church. It is used by Roman Catholics, Anglicans, Eastern Rite Catholic Churches, and the Orthodox Churches.

Reverend Kenneth W. Collins notes a curious interpretation of the Western style. He believes that the movement from left to right represents Jesus's descent into hell, or Hades (the left side), and his ascension into heaven (the right side). This is consistent with the tradition that holds that all matters demonic, including black magic and Satanism, belong to the "left-hand path."

The sign of the cross was not exclusively Christian. In the ancient world, Indian Buddhists as well as members of Hindu sects used it when anointing the forehead.

353 ARCHBISHOP JAMES USSHER: Also written Usher (1581–1656). He was born in Dublin and was Anglican archbishop of Armagh from 1625 to 1656. His scholarship was legendary, as was his fervent anti-Catholicism, despite his mother being Catholic. He is best remembered for having dated the Creation, a date still recognized by many Christians as being the true one. Ussher was able to narrow it down not only to the year but to the very time of day: dusk on October 22, 4004 BC.

357 HOLY FATHER'S INTERVENTION: Pope John Paul II, during a 1987 visit to the Temple of Saint Michael in Perugia, Italy, spoke of "the battle against the Devil, which is the principal task of St. Michael the Archangel." He reminded the faithful that it is "still being fought today, because the Devil is still alive and active in the world." He spoke of evil in the modern world and its causes. "The disorders that plague our society," he declared, "man's inconsistency and damaged state, are not only the results of original sin, but also the result of Satan's pervasive and dark action."

ACKNOWLEDGMENTS

This book would not have been possible without the contributions made by a great many people, on two sides of the Atlantic Ocean.

On the Irish side, our thanks go to Fergal Tobin of Gill and Macmillan, Dublin, who encouraged us to undertake the project; to Reverend W. H. Lendrum and Father Ignatius McCarthy, who provided their spiritual guidance and generosity; to many other religious, who gave of their time and wisdom; to the men and women who related their experiences out of the goodness of their hearts.

On the American side, our thanks go to the publishers: Roger Freet, our editor, who recognized the importance of the book, and whose enthusiasm infected and inspired so many; including Kris Ashley, whose dedication to quality never flagged; Terri Leonard and Lisa Zuniga, our production team at HarperOne, whose professionalism proved invaluable when preparing the work for printing; and, finally, Beck Stvan and Kris Tobiassen, whose cover design and page layout truly brought our work to life.

—DAVID M. KIELY AND CHRISTINA McKENNA

INDEX